Anti-politics in Contemporary Italy

This book explores the discourses, attitudes and behaviours of professional politicians and ordinary citizens alike characterized by hostility towards the political sphere, political parties and, above all, professional politicians. It furnishes a clear, consistent depiction of the anti-politics phenomenon in general using Italy as a "laboratory" where anti-politics is widespread. After an original reconstruction of the concept of anti-politics, the author charts the rise of Silvio Berlusconi, the success of Umberto Bossi's Northern League, the resounding electoral victories of the Five Star Movement and the League (La Lega), all rooted in the anti-political rhetoric of Italy's leaders and the anti-political sentiment of its population. The author also traces the socio-political profile of the anti-political citizens of the main European democracies. This broad, consistent view of anti-politics will attract academics, journalists and policy makers interested in anti-politics in Italy and elsewhere. Students and scholars of party politics, party leaders, democracy and political participation will also find the volume of great interest.

Vittorio Mete is an Associate Professor of Political Sociology at Florence University (Italy), where he teaches courses in *The Sociology of Leadership, Criminal Networks* and *Society and Democracy*. His research interests include anti-politics, political leadership; local politics; political careerism and the political class; political parties; voting behaviour and political participation; organised crime; anti-mafia policies and anti-mafia movements. His recent publications include *The trader perspective: researching extortion in Palermo*, in Modern Italy (2018); (together with Anna Carola Freschi), *The electoral personalization of Italian mayors. A study of 25 years of direct election*, in the Italian Political Science Review (2020); *Antipolitica. Protagonisti e forme di un'ostilità diffusa*, (il Mulino, 2022).

Routledge Studies in Democratic Crisis

Series Editors: Matt Wood, University of Sheffield, Sadiya Akram Manchester Metropolitan University, UK and John Boswell University of Southampton, UK.

We live in an age in which popular disaffection threatens to undermine the very foundations of democratic rule. From the rise of radical right-wing populism through to public cynicism towards politicians, institutions and processes of government are being buffeted by unprecedented change that raises questions about the viability of seemingly foundational practices. At the same time, the boundaries of the political as it relates to the social are shifting, leading to more demands for better democratic practices, and creating new opportunities for different groups to resist and change traditional institutions.

This book series provides a forum for the discussion of topics and themes related to democratic crisis in a wide range of substantive areas of research, which not only address political arenas but also overlap with, or extend to, the social. We seek works that push forward debate and challenge taken-for-granted orthodoxies and privilege ambitious proposals that ask big questions and engage with a range of materials. Reflecting this, the series is intentionally pluralistic in its geographic, methodological and disciplinary scope. Empirical and comparative contributions are especially welcome.

Political Meritocracy and Populism
Cure or Curse?
Mark Chou, Benjamin Moffitt, and Octavia Bryant

Liberal Disorder, States of Exceptions, and Populist Politics
Edited by Valur Ingimundarson and Sveinn M. Jóhannesson

The Politics of Populism in Hungary
Robert Csehi

Anti-politics in Contemporary Italy
Vittorio Mete

For a full list of available titles, please visit https://www.routledge.com/ Routledge-Studies-in-Democratic-Crisis/book-series/RSDC

Anti-politics in Contemporary Italy

Vittorio Mete

Routledge
Taylor & Francis Group

LONDON AND NEW YORK

First published 2023
by Routledge
4 Park Square, Milton Park, Abingdon, Oxon OX14 4RN

and by Routledge
605 Third Avenue, New York, NY 10158

*Routledge is an imprint of the Taylor & Francis Group, an informa
business*

© 2023 Vittorio Mete

British Library Cataloguing-in-Publication Data
A catalogue record for this book is available from the British Library

Library of Congress Cataloging-in-Publication Data
A catalog record has been requested for this book

ISBN: 978-0-367-62399-9 (hbk)
ISBN: 978-0-367-62401-9 (pbk)
ISBN: 978-1-003-10927-3 (ebk)

DOI: 10.4324/9781003109273

Typeset in Times New Roman
by KnowledgeWorks Global Ltd.

To Anna Carola.
And to our son Giovanni who for ten years now
has lit up our lives.

Contents

Figures

Tables

Acknowledgements

Writing a book is a solitary endeavour, word after word, day after day, quote after quote. As you write, the time you thought it would take simply doubles as the manuscript bloats. But you have made a start and you know you will get there in the end. To have a book published is not simply an "academic necessity". Writing one, particularly about something like anti-politics, is also a way of bringing together a multitude of experiences: not only the things learnt by reading other people's works, and attending academic seminars and conferences, of course, but also random thoughts, the ideas that come to mind as you run in the park, anger over the disheartening political situation, the disappointment with the policies adopted by the party you voted for, and the profound sense of injustice you feel when you see what is going on in the world. A book is an attempt to bring all of this together and is so much more than just a distillate of its own bibliography. It is also a somewhat ambitious attempt to contribute to public debate, in the belief that what one writes can positively impact reality.

In any case, the journey I undertook one year ago has almost reached its end, and now that I have arrived I would like to thank my friends and colleagues who have accompanied me along the way.

First of all, I would like to thank Paolo Turi, my mentor and friend, with whom I began to discuss "anti-politics" some 20 years ago as a young postgraduate student.

Thanks also go to Luciano Brancaccio, Anna Carola Freschi, Alfio Mastropaolo and Dario Tuorto for kindly having carefully read previous drafts of the book. I have not always been able to follow their suggestions as I should have (and would have wished to), but I am sure that they will understand. Therefore any error or imprecision is attributable to my own limits and not to any lack of zeal on their part.

Discussing the book with Dario Tuorto and Daniele Vignoli also proved invaluable to the development of the secondary analysis presented in Chapter 6. The empirical analysis would certainly have been inadequate had I not been able to count on the information provided by the Italian National

Election Studies (ITANES) research team, whom I would thank in the person of its chair, Mauro Barisione.

A great many small, yet invaluable, suggestions and practical contributions concerning their own fields of research were received from a number of friends and colleagues, including Luca Barra, Ferruccio Biolcati Rinaldi, Enrico Borghetto, Carlo Cosentino, Rossella Ghigi, Sheyla Moroni, Giulia Sandri, Attilio Scaglione and Alberto Vannucci. I would like to thank them all for their help.

Writing a book, as I said, entails solitude. Many people both near and far have made this solitary endeavour that much more bearable. So my final, and most important, thanks go to my family, friends and colleagues whose paths I have crossed – in Calabria, Tuscany and elsewhere – over the years.

Introduction

Anti-politics and democracy

This volume explores the various forms and meanings of anti-politics, together with its significant presence in contemporary Italian society and politics. Anti-politics is a clearly visible, extremely common feature of advanced democracies. Nevertheless, due precisely to its extent and pervasiveness, scholars often find it difficult to define this phenomenon conceptually and to analyse it empirically. In fact, anti-politics overlaps, and is often confused with, a number of other expressions of political discontent that generate disaffection and hostility towards politics, politicians, political parties and representative institutions. Expressions such as "critical citizen" (Norris 1999a), "political distrust" (Bertsou 2019a, 2019b), "political disenchantment" (Stoker 2010, Eder et al. 2015), "political disaffection" (Torcal and Montero 2006a), "anti-establishment" (Schedler 1996, Hartleb 2015), "anti-partyism" (Ignazi 1996a, Poguntke 1996, Scarrow 1996), "anti-politicians" (Corbett 2016), "political cynicism" (Agger et al. 1961, Pattyn et al. 2012, Rooduijn et al. 2017) and others refer, at least in part, to the same phenomena denoted by the term "anti-politics". Furthermore, the term "anti-politics" is often used to indicate a cause or symptom of the poor functioning of democracy. Several expressions have been coined in this regard, including: "demopathy" and "democratic malaise" (Geissel and Newton 2012, Di Gregorio 2021), "democratic deficit" (Norris 2011) and "disaffected democracies" (Pharr and Putnam 2000). Of course, anti-politics is often associated – albeit not always in a clear manner – with the equally elusive concept of "populism" (Abedi 2004) which has been studied extensively in recent years.

The growing interest in these diverse forms of dissatisfaction with the workings of politics, of democracy and of its representative institutions and principal actors is understandable. The proliferation of such terms and of studies dedicated to the analysis thereof can be seen as a reflection of the profound changes that modern democracies, and relations between citizens and the political sphere, are currently undergoing. Such changes include: an increase in electoral abstention; the success of populist leaders and parties;

DOI: 10.4324/9781003109273-1

the convergence of party programmes, which reduces the options available to voters; the gradual withdrawal of citizens from militant action and party involvement; the electorate's profound mistrust of democratic institutions and politicians; the oligarchical, collusive transformation of political parties. Indeed, certain observers have argued in favour of the beneficial effects of ignoring politics altogether (Freiman 2021). These and other changes may in fact lead one to conclude that perhaps politics as such is a lost cause (Mastropaolo 2012), and to wonder if there remains any kind of connection between politicians and voters, or whether democracy has become an empty space governed by a succession of self-referential parties and politicians (Mair 2013). The changes to democracy and to people's relationship with politics have even led to a series of reflections on how democracies die (Levitsky and Ziblatt 2018, Runciman 2018).

This vast, complex debate on the present and future of the world's democracies has increasingly focused on the question of anti-politics. This term is not a new one since it goes back at least to the time of the French Revolution, and there are equivalent words in all of the major European languages. As we shall see in Chapter 1, from the 1980s onwards, this term was employed increasingly just about everywhere and is frequently found in academic literature, in parliamentary speeches, in everyday language, in newspapers and other mass media. Given this extensive use of the term, and the importance of the phenomena associated with it, some have called the present era the "the age of anti-politics" (Clarke *et al.* 2018, p. 2).

The increasing use of the term "anti-politics" both within and outside of academia, together with the partial semantic overlapping of "anti-politics" and the other items mentioned above, makes it difficult to define it precisely. In fact, as is often the case in the social and political sciences, the term is used with various different meanings. In the present volume, "anti-politics" shall basically be used to refer to the aversion to, hostility towards, and contempt and even hatred for the principal contemporary symbols of democratic politics, as expressed not only by citizens but also by certain political leaders and other political representatives. These symbols include professional politicians, political parties and representative institutions such as parliament and other representative assemblies. These are the actual items that people have in mind when considering politics. The same "items" are referred to by politicians, newspapers and other mass media when they speak of "politics". In an important work on anti-politics, Nick Clarke and colleagues had the following to say: "politicians deserve (…) a central place in research on anti-politics because when citizens think of more abstract objects (…) they often think of the politicians who make up those institutions. They use politicians as a heuristic to judge the activities and institutions of formal politics in general" (ibid., p. 7).

This preliminary brief definition may be expanded on by distinguishing, for purely analytical purposes, between two principal forms of anti-politics: anti-politics from below (or bottom-up) and anti-politics from above (or top-down) (Mete 2010). Bottom-up anti-politics comprises citizens' negative attitudes and behaviour in regard to politics. It includes the following: harbouring feelings of aversion towards the principal symbols of politics; deciding not to vote as a form of political protest; voting for, or actively supporting, anti-party and anti-political parties and/or leaders; voting at referenda in favour of clearly anti-political issues, such as the referendum for the reduction in the number of parliamentarians or the abolition of public funding for political parties; deeming all career politicians to be untrustworthy, incapable, morally unworthy and corrupt; expressing a lack of trust in parties and politicians. Top-down anti-politics, on the other hand, is that expressed by political leaders and other political representatives or members of other society élites. This form of anti-politics includes: speeches and political discourse that take aim at professional politicians, political parties, representative assemblies or indeed politics as such, considering them worthless or damaging; attitudes and behaviour detracting from or denigrating the role that politicians traditionally play in the public sphere (by using foul language in their public speeches, showing up or being photographed wearing eccentric clothing, such as bathing attire, or appearing bare-chested on the beach; foregoing part of their salary or the public funding of their party etc.); proposing (or adopting, when in government) measures of an anti-political nature, such as a referendum to abolish certain "privileges" enjoyed by politicians, or a reform limiting the public funding of political parties. Finally, it should be noted that anti-politics is not a prerogative of those outside of the political arena or of outsider leaders and parties, or of those among the opposition ranks. In fact, the anti-political cause may also be embraced by experienced politicians in power (Campus 2010). Of course, as we shall clearly see in the case of Italy, the anti-politics expressed by the opposition and the anti-politics of those in government have rather different roots and aims.

The root causes and political utilisation of anti-politics

Studies of anti-politics have investigated the social causes of the phenomenon in the past and today. The explanations advanced for the emergence and diffusion of anti-politics are somewhat similar to those given for the rise of the other phenomena usually associated with it and previously mentioned. Generally speaking, two main categories of reason for the emergence of anti-politics can be distinguished: there are those concerning the demand side of political representation and those concerning the supply side (Hay 2007). No scholar would be naïve enough to deny the connection between the two. Nevertheless, some give precedence to the social, economic and cultural changes affecting citizens' identity and political values (the demand side), while others place greater importance on the changes in recent decades that have impacted political parties, leadership styles and the way in which politicians go about their business (the supply side). The former scholars mention, among other things: the process of individualisation that has seen citizens moving further away from political organisations and the major ideologies of the 20th century (Beck 1986); increased cognitive mobilisation which has narrowed the status gap between citizens and politicians (Dalton 1984); the general reduction in civic and associative participation, which is also reflected in citizens' declining participation in political life (Putnam 2000); the post-materialist, anti-hierarchical, anti-authoritarian transformation of citizens' values, with citizens now being less deferential to, and demanding more from, politicians (Inglehart 1977). As regards the supply side, the factors driving anti-politics generally include: the transformation of political parties which no longer perform those functions that concern society (such as the social and political integration of citizens) (Bartolini and Mair 2002) but tend to withdraw within the confines of the institutions and to collude, rather than compete, with one another (Katz and Mair 1995); the further professionalisation of politics and political careers (Borchert and Zeiss 2003); the advancement of processes of de-politicization and globalization, which lessen the powers of national politicians and transfer decision-making processes to other arenas, thus rendering traditional forms of political participation worthless and ineffective (Habermas 1998, Giddens 1999, Burnham 2001). In addition to these phenomena, one might also add the mediatisation of politics, which has significantly affected the relationship between citizens and the political sphere (Mazzoleni and Schulz 1999), in particular by personalising and popularising the public's image of politicians (Van Zoonen 2005, Garzia 2011, Stanyer 2013, Caprara and Vecchione 2016), and changing their ways of behaving. More specifically, the popularisation of politics resulting from mediatisation symbolically narrows the distance between voters and politicians, thus undermining political representatives' authority. As General De Gaulle declared, authority is based on prestige, and there can be no prestige without distance (quoted in: Campus 2016, p. 44).

In addition to these macro-factors which, as mentioned, account for the spread of anti-politics and of the majority of associated phenomena such as populism, certain other more specific and distinctive factors need to be taken into account. Once again, for presentation purposes we may wish to make a general, analytical distinction here. On the one hand, there are social and political dynamics resulting in politicians being criticised and denigrated, thus generating anti-political feelings. In this case, the political class "is subjected to" the anti-politics of the people. On the other hand, it can be argued that there are social and political dynamics whereby it is the politicians who have recourse to anti-politics for their own political purposes, and in doing so, they exacerbate what we have termed "anti-politics from below".

In order to at least partly account for the anti-politics that politicians are subjected to, we may wish to recall the observations made by Matthew Flinders (2012a) with regard to the gap between citizens' expectations of politicians and the actual capacity of those politicians to impact reality. According to Flinders, citizens develop expectations and ideas regarding politics and democracy that necessarily lead to generalised, bitter disappointment.[1] Increased expectations and the frustration inevitably resulting from such are hardly a new phenomenon; indeed, it underlies one of the earliest sociological approaches to the study of collective movements and even of violent action (Gurr 1970). What Flinders managed to do, however, was to effectively identify and describe three specific gaps undermining the relationship between citizens and politicians, which thus generate anti-political feelings among those citizens. The first of these is the "perception gap": citizens construct an abstract idea of political questions and actors, which does not always correspond to their real experience of the political world. In other words, citizens share a generalised disdain for parliament as such, while perhaps holding in considerable esteem their own mayor, or even their MP who they know personally or who in any case they perceive as being close and similar to themselves. Their opinion of public policy may also be characterised by this perception gap: a person can have a very poor opinion of the workings of the health service in general, while still being satisfied with the most recent treatment received from that service. The second gap is the "demand gap": citizens demand that politicians take action in regard to a salient social problem (such as pollution, immigration policy, waste management policy) but then reject the proposed public policies designed to resolve such problems (policies such as a tax on polluting vehicles, the siting of an immigrant reception centre, the construction of a new waste dump). The third gap separating citizens and politicians is the "social gap": citizens want politicians to be entrusted with super powers to resolve the problems of an increasingly complex, hard-to-govern society, but at the same time, they want those politicians to be "ordinary citizens" who dress, speak, eat and earn "just like us" (Wood *et al.* 2016). Finally, in a heated climate of anti-political feelings, in the introduction to his "defence of politics", Flinders rather provocatively writes as follows: "Let me stand up and argue against the current anti-political sentiment and state in no uncertain terms that the vast majority of politicians are over-worked and under-paid, that public servants generally do a fantastic job in the face of huge pressures, and that, most broadly, democratic politics delivers far more than most people acknowledge or understand" (Flinders 2012a, p. vii).

Anti-politics is not, however, something that politicians merely suffer the effects of. They may also have recourse to anti-politics themselves, as we shall shortly see, not only to get other politicians removed from office, or to gain power within their own party, or to obtain the consensus needed to have the reforms they desire approved; but they may also pursue less evident and obvious aims than these, but one that are equally as important nevertheless. It is true that, as Mastropaolo suggests, the spread of anti-politics from below is also facilitated by the disappearance of any critiques of society and the economy, which were frequent during the period of great ideological polarisation (Mastropaolo 2012, p. 170). Nevertheless, using politics and politicians as scapegoats – as politicians themselves often do in the knowledge that they can count on the complicity of the mass media – and accusing such of being responsible for all of the things that create dissatisfaction among the populace (ibid., p. 167) hides the structural causes of people's discontent. By doing so, the problems afflicting society are not correlated to social inequality, unsustainable models of growth, or the exploitation of workers and the environment. On the contrary, all of society's ills are imputed to corrupt, incapable politicians. This representation of reality has anesthetised social conflict, and in practice, has hindered the development of any critique of prevailing economic and cultural models. The demonisation of politics and politicians (Flinders 2012b) has thus overshadowed the real causes of those social and economic problems causing discontent, and it renders invisible those responsible for such discontent who often lie beyond the political sphere altogether. Without putting too finer point on it, this is a case of anti-politics being deliberately used for political ends.

Another political use of anti-politics is to a degree related to the latter. It consists in branding the critical views and discontent of the nation's citizens as "anti-political" (or populist). By doing so, many forms of protest are stigmatised or ignored, and legitimate demands are dealt with in a contemptuous manner, which if taken seriously, on the other hand, would require a far more serious response from the governing classes (Mastropaolo 2005, p. 68, Streeck 2014, p. 160). Likewise, as a way of depoliticising their own decisions and shifting responsibility for the consequences of such, the politicians in power can blame voters for the failure of their own policy decisions (Dowding 2020). Of course, strategies like this are not always successful and do not always manage to weaken or thwart popular protest: the emergence and growth of anti-austerity parties is proof of this (Kriesi and Pappas 2015, della Porta *et al.* 2017). In many cases, these parties avoid falling into the de-legitimation and stigmatisation trap by claiming to be of an anti-political, anti-establishment, populist nature. In other cases, labelling different phenomena as anti-political (or populist) serves to play down and conceal attitudes which instead ought to be defined as racist, discriminatory, nationalistic, anti-Semitic and so on (Mastropaolo 2012, p. 183). This approach contributes towards the gradual normalisation of extreme right-wing discourse (Wodak 2021). Finally, representing politics and politicians as dirty, corrupt and ineffective can pave the way for technocratic government (Bertsou and Caramani 2020a).

Ultimately, the story of anti-politics fostered by politicians, which academics themselves often encourage (Mastropaolo 2005, pp. 101–2, Hay 2007, p. 4, Flinders 2012a, pp. 47–50),[2] risks weakening democracy and emptying it of meaning, by de-politicizing it and disparaging anyone who tries to challenge the existing power arrangements. As we shall shortly see, it would seem that democracy can be cured by administering more democracy to the democratic system; that is, by introducing democratic innovations strengthening participation and getting citizens more interested in political life. Nevertheless, the possible paradoxical results of such treatment should not be underestimated, as in the medium term, they can lead to a further weakening and de-legitimisation of politics and political parties (Rosenbluth and Shapiro 2018). In other words, treating the apparent failings of democracy by introducing more democracy may undermine the pillars of contemporary democracies (even if of a uncertain, sometimes shaky, nature). The unscrupulous, political utilisation of anti-politics by politicians not only can transform democracy into a sham, that is, a "democracy without the people (*demos*)" (Mair 2013, p. 10) but also may even go further to forge a "democracy against the people" (Mastropaolo 2005, ch. 12).

With this in mind, it is important to explore in detail the dynamics of contemporary anti-politics in an effort to understand who is responsible for stoking the fires of anti-politics, and why they are doing so. It is also important to reflect on the various different meanings and aims of anti-politics when proclaimed by those in opposition (or those lying outside of the institutional sphere), and how this changes when the persons in question are elected to government. Finally, it is interesting to consider the possible consequences of the massive use of anti-politics by political leaders and parties. In this regard, a distinction should be made between the consequences affecting the leaders and parties, those affecting citizens and their political beliefs, and those that impact the political system, the institutions and, more generally, the quality of democracy as such. The analysis of the Italian case conducted in this volume aims to provide some answers to these research questions.

Overview of the book

This volume aims to offer a contribution to our understanding of the origins, nature and conceptual confines of anti-politics, and of the way in which anti-politics manifests itself. It also hopes to shine some light on the methodological approach to the empirical analysis of anti-politics, of its political use and of the relationship between anti-politics and democracy. The book has been subdivided into six chapters. The first chapter regards the terminological, conceptual and methodological aspects of anti-politics. Chapters 2–5 are specifically concerned with the manifestation of anti-politics in Italy. As we shall see, due to the considerable diffusion and political importance of anti-politics, Italy constitutes a particularly significant and productive case study. The Italian case helps us establish the causes, dynamics and effects of anti-politics. The final chapter offers an empirical and methodological analysis consisting in a spatial and diachronic exploration of the anti-politics of Italians. This same chapter also outlines the socio-demographic characteristics and values of those Italians driven by anti-political feelings and attitudes.

More specifically, Chapter 1 offers a detailed lexical analysis of the term "anti-politics", of its meanings in the major European languages (English, French, Italian, German and Spanish), and of its diffusion over the course of time in the aforesaid languages. The overview of the meanings of the term shown in the principal dictionaries, and the broad recognition of its uses in the fields of the social and political sciences, reveal the problems of homonymy (when the same term has a variety of meanings and indicates diverse empirical referents) and of synonymy (when several terms have the same meaning and indicate the same empirical referents) with regard to the term "anti-politics". In order to overcome this linguistic confusion and to establish a clearer formulation of the concept of anti-politics that distinguishes it from other associated concepts, it was decided to follow the recommendations of Giovanni Sartori in his classical study of the analysis of concepts (Sartori 1984). The concept was thus reconstructed in order to obtain a consistent semantic nucleus surrounded by other, less important, more eccentric meanings that are nevertheless presently in use. This initial achievement bridges a gap in the literature on this subject and represents an important guide for those intending to study the phenomenon of anti-politics.

This theoretical and conceptual reflection is followed by an empirical analysis. To this end, the final section of the first chapter discusses the ways of studying anti-politics. In the literature, in fact, one finds several authors who study anti-politics also from the empirical viewpoint. However, this interest is not accompanied by any specific analysis of the chosen methods, the available sources, the social research techniques or the appropriate indicators of anti-politics. Therefore, at the end of the terminological and conceptual analysis presented in Chapter 1, I have included a discussion of the methods of studying anti-politics. Three levels (of analysis) have been identified at which anti-politics is manifested and can be empirically observed, namely: the individual level of the citizen/voter; the level of politicians and political leaders; the level of the political system as a whole. The final section of Chapter 1 identifies a number of possible indexes of anti-politics relating to each of these three levels understood as representing potential units of analysis for the study of anti-politics.

Having explained, insofar as is possible, the background and semantics of anti-politics, Chapter 2 marks the beginning of a lengthy examination of the Italian case. There are a number of reasons why Italy was the place chosen for the purpose of studying the anti-politics phenomenon. As the terminological analysis in the previous chapter indicates, the origins of the term "anti-politics" in Italy go back a long way in time, and the term is more commonly used in Italy than in other comparable nations. Furthermore, as we shall see in Chapter 6, Italian people appear to be those who harbour the strongest anti-political feelings, on average, from among the citizens of western democracies. This inevitably implies the presence of strong, long-lasting, battle-hardened anti-political parties and leaders, who are analysed in some detail in the three subsequent chapters. Moreover, Italy was the first major country to elect a proudly anti-political government (from 2018 to 2019), comprising a coalition of the League and the Five Star Movement (5SM). The electoral weight reached in 2019 by Italian parties considered populist is not by chance the highest among all European countries (Zulianello and Larsen 2021, p. 5).

In Italy, manifestations of anti-politics go back much further in time. Chapter 2 examines the principal expressions of anti-politics in Italy, from the foundation of the Republic (in 1946) to the political rift resulting from the Tangentopoli bribes scandal in the early 1990s, which marked the symbolic transition from a first to a second Republic. Citing certain pioneering, albeit rather fragmented, social and political studies conducted in Italy in the 1950s and 1960s, Chapter 2 starts by challenging the idea of a golden age of relations between the country's citizens and the world of politics. In keeping with the findings of Clarke and colleagues with regard to the British case (Clarke *et al.* 2018), during those years, Italy also witnessed the low esteem in which politicians were held and often patent hostility towards those politicians. However, the widespread anti-political attitudes of the immediate post-war years were accompanied by the considerable political mobilisation of the nation's citizens and by the existence of mass parties deeply rooted in Italian society.

The first organised, politically important expression of anti-politics following Fascism was the Common Man Movement inspired and led by the playwright Guglielmo Giannini. The movement, together with the political party that derived from that movement, despite their short-lived character, significantly contributed to the emergence of anti-politics in the public imagination. Unsurprisingly, many anti-political actors and parties emerging thereafter were compared, sometimes inappropriately, to Giannini and his Common Man Movement. A second criticism of the self-referential nature of politicians and of the parties' excessive powers, which in fact would have emptied Italian democracy of all meaning in the 1950s and 1960s when it was still in its infancy, was that formulated by Giuseppe Maranini. Maranini was a jurist, an opinion-maker and for a long time Dean of Florence University's Political Science Faculty. The third section "Against partitocracy" of Chapter 2 focuses on the figure of Maranini and his critique of "partitocracy", a term which entered common usage thanks to Maranini and which resurfaced over the course of the years thereafter.

In virtue of their importance for the political history of Italy and for their capacity to clearly show the anti-political dynamics we are concerned with in this volume, the events of the early 1990s shall be the focus of the remaining two sections of Chapter 2. There were two principal figures involved in these events: on the one hand, civil society, which offered itself as an alternative to the political class and the political parties under investigation for alleged bribery during that period; and on the other hand, Silvio Berlusconi, a successful businessman who at the beginning of 1994 unexpectedly decided to set up his own personal political party – Forza Italia – which from that moment on was to have a significant impact on Italian political life. The second part of the chapter illustrates how the widespread anti-political attitudes of the population, which had grown markedly following the aforesaid political scandals, served as an important resource for political entrepreneurs who wished to capitalise on the political ruins left by the scandals and the judicial investigations. The anti-political rhetoric of civil society exalting the latter's purity compared to the ills of politics was to consolidate those linguistic and cultural themes taken up by other political actors, such as the 5SM, in the following decades. For his part, Berlusconi instilled beliefs, attitudes and behaviour of an explicitly anti-political variety into the Italian political system and, even more so, into the political culture of the Italian people. More than the political heritage he bequeathed on the Italian people, it was this cultural heritage that was to characterise Italian political life for a long time thereafter.

Chapter 3 focuses on the Northern League (now the League) and its two most important leaders: firstly, Umberto Bossi, its founder, followed by Matteo Salvini, its current leader. The League, which is commonly seen as a populist party, first entered the political arena back in the 1980s. However, it was not until the political system's crisis during the early 1990s that the party had the opportunity to become a key player in that arena. The League mixes anti-political rhetoric and behaviour with the adoption of regionalist, anti-state positions, and even encourages acts of tax resistance. With a sprinkling of racist, xenophobic attitudes and behaviour, the League's political and cultural actions first targeted southern Italians, then immigrants together with the European Union. The League's success is clearly not entirely ascribable to the party's anti-politics. Nevertheless, the anti-political discourses and rhetoric of Umberto Bossi undoubtedly helped him to emerge and consolidate his position in the political sphere. The window of opportunity that enabled the League to grow from being a marginal, almost folkloristic entity in the 1980s, to become a party of government in the 1990s (and in the years thereafter), consisted in the de-structuring of the existing political system in the early 1990s. During that period, the League stood out as a hard-line, intransigent critic of the "old politics", and its MPs even went as far as displaying a hangman's noose, during one parliamentary sitting, for the "corrupt politicians" present in parliament.

The history of the League shows, however, that focusing all one's energies on anti-politics can be a double-edged sword. In fact, campaigning for the moralisation of politics requires the conduct of the moralisers to be beyond reproach, which in the world of politics is not an easy thing, particularly when governing for an extended period. So it was that the League itself fell short of its own purported standards, when it was caught up in a scandal concerning the management of party funds. This scandal was to mark the end of the leadership of Umberto Bossi, who in the meantime had also fallen seriously ill. Faced with such a patent betrayal of the party by its leadership, the League's members and voters began to abandon ship, and the very survival of the party was at risk at that point. In an attempt to avoid its disgraceful demise, the League sought to repair the significant damage to its reputation by handing over the reins of the party to one of its young leaders, Matteo Salvini, a self-professed anti-political outsider at the time. The final section of Chapter 3 offers a portrayal of the party's new secretary and analyses how he managed to conceal the fact that he himself was a member of the political élite, and how his anti-political attitudes and behaviour were employed to re-establish and re-launch the League on a different basis than before. The strategy adopted by the party's new secretary proved successful, and the League gradually managed to recover following the internal scandals that had rocked its very foundations a few years earlier. Under Salvini's uninhibited leadership, the League quickly became Italy's most voted party. By introducing itself into existing local power networks, often of a patronage nature, the League became the most voted party even in many provinces of Southern Italy where, up until a few years earlier, not only has been totally absent but had also been heavily criticised for its patent anti-southern stance.

The League and its leadership's expressions of anti-politics are of a clear and explicit variety. However, in Italy's recent political history, there are numerous other less evident forms of anti-politics, involving other actors. These are no less important and laden with consequences, and consist of subtler, more sophisticated varieties of criticism of professional politicians, parties and representative assemblies advanced by certain centre-left parties, the most important of which being the Democratic Party (PD). Chapter 4 examines this specific issue. From the early 2000s on, these parties followed the lead of the global justice movement. On the instigation of the local authorities they governed, these centre-left parties introduced a series of democratic innovations designed to encourage bottom-up participation. A few years later, these participatory practices were broadened to include the holding of "primary elections". These open primaries were adopted wholesale by the PD, at both national and local level (including those called for the direct election of the party's national secretary). The subtle anti-political message that this sent out was that the party's apparatus was not capable of adequately performing all of its assigned functions, including that of political recruitment. By offering the opportunity to "ordinary citizens" not organised in stable groups, who preferably have no prior political experience or beliefs, to take decisions regarding leadership candidates or choice of policy, was seen as the way forward in the endeavour to remedy the failings of representative democracy.

Among other things, the introduction of these primaries changed the internal balances and operating mechanisms of the parties concerned. It sped up the marginalisation of party activists and militants, a process that has been emphasised by the literature on the transformation of political parties (Mair 1994). The role of the primaries has been strengthened by the involvement of party members and supporters who, however, as atomised individuals only involved when the party leadership demands it, are not able to impact the party's political direction or the selection of its more important leaders. For politicians, on the other hand, the primaries have offered opportunities to those hoping to see their political careers fast-tracked. This was precisely what Matteo Renzi managed to do. First of all, he won the party's primaries for the position of mayor of Florence; then he won those held for the post of party general secretary, and he was to become the youngest ever Prime Minister of the Italian Republic. Renzi could not count on significant support from within his own party and so had to find a way of standing out from the rest in order to win such elections. He chose an unconventional, provocative leadership style. Anti-political attitudes and behaviour were to be essential ingredients in what was an innovative style of leadership for a centre-left party. Suffice it to say that Renzi's catchphrase, which helped him become successful both within the PD and among the nation's voters, was "scrapping" the old political guard (particularly those within his own party). Thus, it was that the anti-political attitudes and rhetoric traditionally associated with right-wing leaders and parties were repeatedly copied by the principal party of the centre-left, thus legitimising patently anti-political attitudes among that party's voters as well.

The purest, most explicit form of anti-politics witnessed to date in modern Italy is that embodied by the 5SM, a movement-party analysed in detail in Chapter 5. The central figure in the incredible story of the 5SM's rise to power, which has transformed Italian politics over the last decade, is that of Beppe Grillo, a famous Italian comedian well-known for his campaigns in favour of the environment, consumers and small shareholders. In the mid-2000s, Grillo created a blog that immediately achieved a huge following, and which in 2009 was to lead to the foundation of the 5SM. Grillo's rhetoric and preaching was of a very coarse, fiercely anti-political nature. His favourite targets included professional politicians, each of whom was given a disparaging nickname by Grillo. He adopted a political-satirical approach, complete with offensive and sometimes violent language, in his blog, his theatre performances and his mass rallies (which were pointedly entitled "fuck-off days"). This anti-political strategy proved highly successful, and when the 5SM stood for election for the first time – at the 2013 general election – the party obtained 25% of the vote. It performed even better at the 2018 election, when it won 32% of the vote, thus becoming the largest party in parliament, at which point it entered government for the first time.

The 5SM did not only use these more immediately recognisable forms of anti-politics, which had traditionally been the preserve of Italy's right-wing and populist parties. By embracing and fostering citizens' hopes of participating in the political process, which were also aided by the democratic innovations introduced just a few years earlier by Italy's centre-left parties, the 5SM created and implemented various forms of direct democracy. Criticisms of the political "caste" were thus accompanied by a different idea of democracy, whereby parliamentary representatives act merely as spokespersons for the collective will expressed via the Internet. From this point of view, the 5SM reformulated a number of organisational and representational practices that had already been employed by the parties of the new left, in particular the green parties, during the 1980s. As the history of these latter parties shows, the promises made by a new party are invariably hard to keep, particularly when the party's institutionalisation takes a leap forward as a result of the party entering the nation's institutions and government (Frankland *et al.* 2008). Anti-politics thus remains a tactic designed to convince voters and supporters that the original battles fought by the movement have not been betrayed or side-lined. The most important "proof" of anti-political consistency and intransigence that the governing 5SM offers to an electorate witnessing the gradual normalisation of the party and its leadership is the constitutional reform providing for a reduction in the number of parliamentarians, from 945 to 600, which was approved in September 2000. This reduction in the number of seats held by privileged, idle politicians (as they are perceived by those harbouring such anti-political views) has always been a distinctive aim of the country's anti-political parties.

Having recounted and analysed the principal events pointing to the significant presence and political usage of anti-politics in current-day Italy, the final chapter portrays the values and socio-demographics of those Italians holding strong anti-political feelings. This operation is based on a secondary analysis of certain national and international surveys conducted in the period from the mid-1980s to 2020. The first question that the chapter attempts to answer is whether or not anti-politics is more widespread in Italy than elsewhere. The analysis of two different recent surveys would seem to indicate that this is the case. In fact, Italy leads the rankings of those countries where citizens are more hostile towards and angry with politics and its main symbols. In these rankings, Italy finds itself in a similar position to certain "democratically-challenged" countries such as Greece, a nation under incredible strain as a result of the economic crisis; and to countries led by populist leaders, such as Brazil and Hungary. At the bottom of the anti-politics rankings, on the other hand, lie the North European democracies where, it should be added, social inequalities are less pronounced than in the aforementioned countries.

As well as viewing Italy from a comparative perspective, the secondary analysis conducted in the final chapter of the volume serves to outline the social, demographic and political characteristics and values of anti-political citizens. A diachronic viewpoint is adopted to show that the aforesaid socio-demographics and values change over time, and that overall the anti-political attitudes of Italians have intensified in recent decades. Finally, the chapter specifically focuses on the relationship between anti-political feelings and attitudes towards democracy. Those scholars who have concerned themselves with anti-politics theoretically distinguish between the two phenomena, and it is clearly a good idea to keep them separate at the analytical level. However, in order to contribute towards the debate on democracy's future, it is necessary to determine whether, to what degree and under what conditions anti-politics is correlated to the limited achievement of democracy, or indeed to support for openly anti-democratic solutions. As Sartori wrote shortly after the enormous political corruption scandal that broke out in Italy in the early 1990s: "the broom of anti-politics is a most necessary broom (...). Yet, as the dirty water of corruption is thrown overboard the baby must be saved. The distaste of parties and the disrepute of politicians inevitably reflect themselves on the institutions in which they are housed. And if representative institutions themselves are generally perceived as inadequate instruments of democracy, then the saving of the baby becomes quite a task" (Sartori 1994, p. 147).

Vittorio Mete
Firenze and Campogialli, October 2021

Notes

1 A similar interpretation of the origins of anti-political feelings among citizens is given by Stephen Medvic in his work entitled "In defence of politicians" (Medvic 2013). He argued that the increased expectations, which politicians cannot realistically meet, lead them into an "expectations trap". Cécile Hatier, on the other hand, argues that the poor opinion of politicians, and consequently of the entire political sphere, derives from people's adoption of "moral double standards". She believes that people are more demanding of politicians than they are of other individuals who behave in the same way, but who play different roles in society (Hatier 2012).
2 In this regard, Wolfgang Streeck rather pointedly notes the following: "Professionalized political science tends to underestimate the impact of moral outrage. With its penchant for studied indifference, which it regards as value-free science, it strives to develop theories in which there can be nothing new under the sun, and has nothing but elitist contempt for what it calls 'populism', sharing this with the power elites to which it would like to be close" (Streeck 2014, p. 163).

1   The concept of anti-politics

Anti-politics – a successful term

Since the post-Second World War years, the world of democracy has continuously expanded, with various waves of this form of political governance sweeping across an increasingly large part of the globe (Markoff and Burridge 2019). At the same time, however, democracy itself has become impoverished within, and the debate regarding the crisis of democracy – be it true or purported, present or future – continues to animate the work of scholars in the field (Merkel and Kneip 2018). While it is true that the majority of people judge democracy positively and acknowledge its value and importance, those same people display considerable dissatisfaction with the way democracy operates (Klingemann 2014). Furthermore, certain small groups with authoritarian views remain in the world's advanced democracies (Norris and Inglehart 2019, Mauk 2020). Socio-political scientific literature has generated a whole range of terms to describe and grasp this growing sense of dissatisfaction with democracy: "critical citizen" is one of the best-known, most commonly used such terms (Norris 1999a, 2011), while various authors have also made reference to "democratic malaise", "democratic deficit", "political distrust", "political disenchantment", "dissatisfied democrats" to describe the phenomenon in question. Although these terms are all different, each possessing its own particular meaning, they all portray contemporary democracies as "disaffected democracies" (Pharr and Putnam 2000, Torcal and Montero 2006a).

Of all such terms, the one that has become best established and most widely used in a variety of different academic fields is "anti-politics" (or "antipolitics"). This is not a new term,[1] and the simplicity of it gives it considerable evocative weight, together with a capacity to express those feelings of hostility expressed towards politics, political actors and political rituals and practices, at one and the same time. Its simplicity constitutes not only a strength but also a weakness given that the term is often used in a confused, spontaneous manner. The main reasons for this terminological confusion are probably ascribable to the rapidity with which the term has spread, and to its generalised employment both in academic

DOI: 10.4324/9781003109273-2

literature and in political and journalistic discourse. Moreover, as with other terms, there is a certain degree of linguistic contamination between academic language and everyday language. Anti-politics thus seems to suffer from what has been referred to as "terminological chaos", that is, it finds itself in a

> situation in which interpersonal communication and in our case the debate between students of humanity and society is made precarious, superficial and misleading by the fact that a substantial number of authors use a substantial number of related terms in senses which are significantly a) different from those which were previously shared, b) different among themselves (author X gives a different meaning to author Y), and c) different within works, and even individual passages, by the same author.
>
> (Marradi 1987, p. 136)

This terminological chaos is clearly a common problem within the social sciences, and one that regards a great many different terms and concepts. As we shall see shortly, however, the semantic confusion regarding the term "anti-politics" is particularly marked. Therefore, it is important to establish a clear picture of its principal meanings before attempting to deal with those phenomena that the term refers to. As Peter Mair has pointed out:

> Concepts are sometimes difficult to define and to specify, and there may be different dimensions that are difficult to untangle, but the research effort can be badly undermined if any attempt at definition and specification is written off from the beginning. Indeed, complex phenomena and so-called umbrella or multidimensional concepts are those that are especially in need of clear definitions, since it is often these concepts in particular that are the source of the greatest scholarly confusion.
>
> (Mair 2008, p. 185)

In order to try and clarify the term's uses and meanings, and understand exactly what form the concept of anti-politics takes, it is thus a good idea to follow the golden rule established by Giovanni Sartori in his classical work *Guidelines for concept analysis* (1984). Sartori suggests that a three-step approach be adopted: "in reconstructing a concept, first collect a representative set of definitions; second, extract their characteristics; and third, construct matrixes that organize such characteristics meaningfully" (ibid., p. 41). More specifically, Sartori states that definitions may in turn be collected in three separate stages, that is: "1) establishing the etymology; 2) following the *Geistesgeschichte* of the word; and 3) a text analysis of key authors or sources" (ibid.). The following two sections are given over to this recognition and processing of meanings.

Dictionary meanings

A useful starting point when analysing the meanings of "anti-politics" is an overview of the meanings given to the term in the main European languages. The present work deals principally with the Italian case, and thus we shall start with the Italian language. In the *Grande dizionario italiano dell'uso* [The Complete Italian Dictionary of Usage], the adjective "*antipolitico*" is defined as follows: "opposed or indifferent to politics: anti-political conduct that achieves effects contrary to the set objectives: anti-political measure or programme". This dictionary thus offers at least three separate definitions of the term "anti-political": an aversion to politics; an indifference/ extraneousness in regard to politics; the undesirable effects of a specific form of political conduct.

The consultation of diverse dictionaries and encyclopaedias, written in languages other than Italian, offers further information which may be of use for the purposes of a semantic analysis of the term "anti-politics". Works in French (the language the term was first coined in) are a particular wealth of such information. For example, one historical dictionary of French (*Tresor de la langue francaise: Dictionnaire de la langue du XIXe et du XXe siecle (1789–1960)*) contains four different meanings of the term "*antipolitique*": "*Contraire aux intérêts de l'État, de la société politiquement organisée*"; "*Contraire à la politique considérée comme saine*"; "*Opposé à l'esprit de la politique de l' État*"; "*Opposé à la politique considérée comme saine*". The French word "*antipolitique*" may thus be used to refer to both individual and collective phenomena; what is common to all the definitions is the very same aversion to "sound politics", and to the political "spirit" and "interests" conveyed and pursued by the State. The French definition appears to lack one of the two aspects of the Italian definition. French "*antipolitique*", in fact, indicates a clearly active stance against politics, but it does not include the indifference/extraneousness which, as mentioned, is the second definition of the term "anti-politics" to be found in dictionaries of Italian.

Moving on to English, the term "anti-political" is given the following definition in the *Oxford English Dictionary*: "opposed to sound political principles", to which a second definition is added: "impolitic". Thus, the people labelled as promoters/supporters of "anti-politics" are those who challenge society's most widely shared political principles, or in the second definition, are those who, as in one of the Italian definitions of the term, are indifferent to politics and keep well away from it.

The Spanish equivalent term is "*antipolitica*", written the same as in Italian. Despite its appearance in journalistic language and in social science texts, the term itself does not appear in Spanish dictionaries. It is present, on the other hand, in the Catalan language. The *Gran Larousse Català* published in 1987 gives the following definition of the term "*Antipolitic/ Antipolítica*": "*contrari al sentit polític*". Essentially, the Catalan definition of the term reinforces the adversarial character present in dictionaries of

Italian, French and English. However, no reference is made to other meanings implying indifference/extraneousness, or to unforeseen outcomes of political conduct.

In German, the word *"antipolitik"*, although frequently to be found in both academic and non-academic works, is not mentioned in the most authoritative dictionaries, or in social science encyclopaedias (such as the *Enzyklopaedie der Sozialwissenschaft*). In fact, the German language expresses an aversion to politics by using the word *"politikverdrossenheit"*. This is a modern term, voted "word of the year" by the Society for the German Language in 1992 (E. Dietze cited in Scarrow 1996, p. 309), and was taken from the scientific field and adopted by journalism and politics. It comprises a broad range of citizens' states of mind in regard to the political system and to those phenomena pertaining to that system: discontentment, criticism and delusion. The term underlines in particular the cognitive and affective gap that has gradually developed between citizens and the political sphere. The result of this ever-widening gap is, in fact, a *"verdrossenheit"*, literally "discontent", the direct consequence of which is indifference to politics rather than any criticism thereof or membership of extremist parties.

After discussing the various meanings of the term "anti-politics" to be found in a number of dictionaries of the principal European languages, a number of general observations may now be made summarising the information gathered. The one outstanding feature of the semantic field covered by the term "anti-politics" is an *aversion* to politics. This active aversion differs from passive extraneousness or indifference which, nevertheless, is present in certain definitions. In addition to its aversive character, the adjective "anti-political" can be used both to describe individuals or groups and to define the nature of abstract or collective phenomena such as political decisions and protest movements.

The overview of the dictionaries of the principal European languages has made it possible to take a step forward in analysing the term. As mentioned, the term's meanings not only resemble one another to a degree in the various European languages but also differ in certain ways. Apart from the obvious fact that two terms from two different languages never completely overlap semantically, the aforesaid differences are ascribable above all to the fact that the respective historical and social contexts also differ. One important aspect, which nevertheless unites the terms that refer to anti-politics in the various languages in question, is their recent diffusion, which in certain cases has been both rapid and enormous. Figure 1.1 shows the estimated (albeit approximate) diffusion of the terms used in the various different languages considered up to this point.

Although for various reasons it cannot be said to faithfully reflect reality, Figure 1.1 offers at least two interesting points for further reflection regarding the use of the term in the different contexts in question. The first point is that the overall use of the term has grown, in particular from the late 1980s

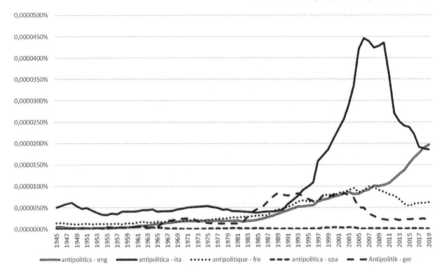

Figure 1.1 Trend over time of the diffusion of the term "anti-politics" in the principal European languages[2]

Source: The author's processing of the data from the Google Books database.

onwards. The second point concerns the differences between the different languages. There are various similarities and differences among these languages regarding the diffusion of the term "anti-politics". It has been little used in Spanish, while in English the term "anti-politics" was uncommon in both American and British publications until the late 1970s, after which its use gradually increased and has expanded very quickly in the last decade. The German term *"Antipolitik"* was little used until the early 1980s but has since become quite widely employed. In France, employment of the word *"Antipolitique"* began to slowly increase in the mid-1960s, reaching its peak in the mid-2000s. Finally, in the case of Italy, three peculiarities were noted: the term is relatively common throughout the period considered here; *"antipolitica"* is by far the most frequently used of the terms denoting a similar concept in the languages in question (but has been overtaken by "anti-politics" over the last two years); its usage grew considerably from the early 1990s onwards, during the period of crisis of the Italian political system. This latter consideration leads us to believe that although not stringent or linear, there is a link between the diffusion of the term and the phenomena to which it refers.

Having illustrated the meanings given in the dictionaries, it is now time to examine the meanings given to the term by the social sciences. As we shall see in the next section, the heterogeneity of the meanings attributed to "anti-politics" is no less than that encountered in the aforementioned dictionaries.

Meanings attributed to the term by the social sciences

As we have seen, the use of the term "anti-politics" goes back a long way in history; however, it has increased significantly in recent times.[3] Both of these aspects, while tending to complicate any conceptual clarification of anti-politics, also render it even more necessary. One further facet of the question that should be taken into consideration when reconstructing and organising its various meanings regards the various fields in which the term is employed. In fact, anti-politics has been the focus of scholars from different fields, each with its own lexical system and with different cognitive objectives. Therefore, as Sartori has pointed out, "our inability to find any order [in the meanings of a term] may also depend on the fact that a concept adapts itself to, or is changed by 1) the disciplines (political science, sociology, anthropology, economics, psychology, etc.) within which it is developed, and/or 2) the theoretical context, frameworks, and approaches (e.g. cybernetics, decision making, functionalism, structuralism) that employ it" (Sartori 1984, p. 49).[4] Building on this wise cautionary remark, it would seem a good idea to circumscribe our conceptual clarification to those scholars working in the fields of political sociology and political science, whilst leaving aside those articles of a purely theoretical, speculative nature. In fact, this limiting the scope of our survey of the meanings given to the term "anti-politics" does not result in a weakening of our analysis, since, as Sartori points out, "homonyms hardly create ambiguity when they fall into different disciplinary fields" (ibid., p. 35).

In the light of these observations, and following Sartori's recommendations, I shall therefore set out certain definitions of "anti-politics" that I believe may illustrate the meanings generally given to the term in the sociological and political science literature. This overview of definitions is not meant to be exhaustive but aims to offer a targeted, rational selection of those scholars (together with their works) who have specifically focused on the phenomenon of anti-politics, in order to reveal any similarities and differences, and to develop the conceptual analysis in question.

A terminological overview

One very weighty, complex, albeit extremely clear, definition is to be found in the opening pages of the work by Nick Clarke *et al.* (2018), specifically dedicated to a diachronic comparison of anti-politics in the United Kingdom. The authors state as follows:

> We define anti-politics as citizens' negative sentiment towards the activities and institutions of formal politics (politicians, parties, elections, councils, parliaments, governments). Anti-politics, we argue, should not be confused with healthy scepticism towards formal politics, which most theories see as an essential component of democracy (...). Anti-politics goes beyond healthy scepticism to the point of unhealthy

cynicism. Nor should it be confused with apathy, where citizens are less disaffected with and more just indifferent to formal politics. Nor should anti-politics be confused with a changing party system. Many citizens around the world are currently shifting their allegiances from older, larger, established parties to newer, smaller, challenger parties. But many others are disengaging completely, having decided that all parties and politicians are just as bad as each other. Finally, anti-politics should not be confused with a crisis of democracy.

(Clarke et al. 2108, p. 3)

Also Paul Fawcett *et al.* in the introduction to a collected volume on the link among anti-politics, de-politicization and governance explicitly define anti-politics. The authors first argue that "both 'de-politicization' and 'anti-politics' remain essentially contested concepts" (Fawcett *et al.* 2017, p. 5), before stating that "for the purposes of this book, anti-politics is defined in a relatively narrow way: as public disillusionment and disengagement, associated with declining turnout at elections, declining membership of parties and political movements, and public opposition to a paradigmatic policy agenda" (ibid, p. 6).

Both of these definitions refer to the mass-level aspects of anti-politics constituted by attitudes, behaviour and actions characterised by a mix of disillusionment with, and hostility towards, official political actors and institutions. Clearly, the aversion of citizens to the world of politics is not without consequences for the targets of such criticisms, be they political leaders, parties or key institutions in democratic systems. In order to further develop this overview of the meanings of "anti-politics", however, it is a good idea to treat the forms of anti-politics expressed by subjects other than citizens, in a specific manner. In this regard, I previously proposed (Mete 2010) that a distinction be made, purely for analytical purposes, between the anti-politics of the élites and the political class, and the anti-politics of the people. The former may be referred to as "anti-politics from above", and the latter as "anti-politics from below".

The aforesaid anti-politics from above may be subdivided into "external" and "internal" anti-politics. Internal anti-politics concerns the speeches and symbolic actions of, and the messages expressed by, representatives of the political class aimed at certain important aspects of contemporary politics, namely: political parties, the political class, political professionalism, political careers and political institutions such as government and parliament. In many ways, this category of anti-politics comprises the rhetoric animating populist leaders and the heads of anti-political establishment parties (Abedi 2004). External anti-politics, on the other hand, is the form expressed by non-institutional élites criticising the contemporary nature of politics, or the idea that politics is an independent sphere of power. This kind of anti-politics is expressed by, among others, those who exalt the technocracy, those who propose the theocratic governance of public life and those who argue that society can be self-regulating, based on market rules without the need for politics.

Anti-politics from below, that is, the form regarding ordinary citizens may be subdivided into "active" and "passive" anti-politics. The feature shared by these two forms of anti-politics is an aversion to the principal symbols, actors and practices of contemporary politics: ranging from political parties to the political professionalism and the political class. While aversive attitudes are shared by both categories, what distinguishes active supporters of anti-politics from their passive counterparts is their political behaviour. Thus, the former category is constituted by citizens who are interested in political affairs and who take an active part in political life, by discussing politics, voting in elections, and even joining a political party or taking part in public demonstrations of a political nature; while the latter category consists of those who feel political outsiders and who hardly participate in politics, if at all.[5]

Alfio Mastropaolo, the author who has dedicated the most time and thought to the analysis of anti-politics within Italy (Mastropaolo 2000, 2005, 2012), also defines the term on two levels:

> Today, politicians and journalists polemically call antipolitics any manifestation of democratic malaise (...). Not voting, electoral volatility, the protest vote or the vote for populist parties are all considered disturbing and disqualified by calling them antipolitics. We will define this sort of antipolitics as "antipolitics from below", but there is also a second, equally thriving version of antipolitics, made up of the immense repertoire of polemical discourses, gestures and actions regarding politics that fill public debate and electoral competition. (...) this can be defined as "antipolitics from above" [and] it is reasonable to suppose that it contributes abundantly to exciting protest and 'antipolitics from below'.
>
> (Mastropaolo 2012, p. 170)

Other uses of the term

In addition to the aforementioned definitions of the term "anti-politics", the literature also features a number of completely different ones. An initial, full classification within an essentially theoretical sphere is proposed by the aforementioned Andreas Schedler. After having stated that "we do not even quite know what antipolitics actually is" (Schedler 1997a, p. 1), Schedler identifies the two principal forms taken by anti-political thinking: "[the] pretension to dethrone and banish politics as opposed to [the] pretension to conquer and colonize politics" (ibid, p. 2). In the first form, the political sphere is weakened, loses relevance and becomes impotent. The space normally taken up by politics could thus remain vacant. Alternatively, it may be occupied by other spheres: the economic sphere and the sphere of technical and scientific knowledge are the two best candidates to replace the political sphere. In the second form of anti-political reflection, politics continues to be of relevance and to exercise its social functions, but the people who legitimately exercise political power are deprived of their prerogatives. In other words, the political sphere stops functioning on the basis of its own rules and adopts other, external rules (for example, rules taken from the economic or religious sphere). Each of these two forms embraces a series of specific theoretical positions that the author critically presents in his essay, and that are discussed further in the other chapters of the book edited by him (Schedler 1997b).

Another fairly common use of the term "anti-politics" can be found in the literature on opposition movements in authoritarian regimes. The most famous example of this is probably the work by György Konrád (1987) on Hungary's communist regime. In the view of the Hungarian sociologist and novelist, during the years of the Cold War and the threat of nuclear conflict in which he was writing, anti-politics was capable of constituting a moral force opposed to the totalitarian politics of the time. Konrád emphasised the political energy of anti-politics and distinguished between the terms "anti-political" and "apolitical", the latter being reserved for forms of conduct implying the giving up of any active involvement in society. Anti-politics, on the contrary, counters the omnipotence of politics, its self-referential status, and the threat that the degeneration of politics represents for a nation's citizens. Anti-politics necessarily implies the cogent criticism of established political power; however, it refuses to take part in power games and rejects its own direct involvement in the political conflict. In this regard, Konrád points out that: "Anti-politics is the political activity of those who don't want to be politicians and who refuse to share in power"; and then a little further on he argues that "Anti-politics and government work in two different dimensions, two different spheres. Anti-politics neither supports nor opposes governments; it is something different (...). Anti-politics is the rejection of the power monopoly of the political class. The relationship between politics and anti-politics is like the relationship between two mountains: neither tries to usurp the other's place; neither one can eliminate or replace the other" (ibid, p. 207). Anti-politics is a necessary response to the excessive power of politics; in fact, Konrád affirms that it first emerged "the year that Hitler took power, the month in which he burnt the books" (ibid, p. 224).[6]

Similar observations could be made with regard to another nation formerly part of the Soviet Union, that is, Czechoslovakia, the last president of which was Václav Havel, an historical critic of the communist regime had the following to say: "I favor 'anti-political politics,' that is, politics not as the technology of power and manipulation, of cybernetic rule over humans or as the art of the utilitarian, but politics as one of the ways of seeking and achieving meaningful lives, of protecting them and serving them" (quoted in: Renwick 2006, p. 289). Again in regard to the case of Czechoslovakia, Vaclav Belohradsky observes that "the expression 'anti-political politics' is well-rooted both in Central-European political culture and in Czech political culture, goes back a long way, and is closely linked to the political traditions of the Risorgimento and to the experience of 'dissent', that is, to the necessarily 'apolitical' forms of cultural resistance to Nazi and Communist totalitarianism" (Belohradsky 1999, p. 73). Anti-politics in authoritarian regimes is thus an alternative politics in contrast to the official forms of politics expressed by the State.[7] From this point of view, there is no shortage of similar experiences in democratic contexts as well, such as those of European countries, which have also been labelled as expressions of anti-politics (Berger 1979). Following on from Konrád's perception of anti-politics as the rejection of institutional politics and as the governance of power by younger generations, Ulrick Beck offers a persuasive, interesting take on the question, in which he also adopts the term "subpolitics". The "children of freedom" as he calls them, in an effort to emphasise the one aspect that he believed best characterised young people in the 1990s,

> hate the formalism of organisations and their model of commitment built on the imperative of the sacrifice of the individuality of each, which they see as bizarre and hypocritical, and they react simply by staying away from politics (...). Whosoever wants to campaign, turns to Greenpeace (...). Since politics, at least in the way it is implemented and represented, is perceived as the mortal enemy of enjoyment, initially it would appear that young people are "un-political", and consider themselves as such. However, there is something very political about being un-political: the children of freedom come together in, and identify with, a multi-coloured rebellion against monotony and against the duties they have to perform for no apparent reason, and thus without involvement. There is thus a hidden link between the desire to enjoy oneself and basic opposition (...) which constitutes the true core of what may be termed «the politics of youth anti-politics». Those who for whatever reason (...) are not involved in institutional politics (parties, associations, etc.) but let themselves get playfully involved, for example, in the temptations of advertising, are acting, knowingly or unknowingly, in an eminently political manner, insofar as they take away interest and participation in, and support for, politics (...). Presence at meetings is not the only way of positing the question of power; it is raised in a much more convincing and effective manner, the more young people silently but firmly decide to remain outside of politics.
>
> (Beck 2000, pp. 7–8)

A further meaning of the term "anti-politics" can be found in the anthropological literature on local development processes, which is fairly close to the definition of de-politicization mentioned above. Those scholars, who have dealt with the question, use the expression "anti-political machine" to indicate those international cooperative undertakings involved in local development projects. The anti-political aspect of their operations lies in their negation of the structural and political nature of the problems to be dealt with, which they see as of a purely technical character. Such dynamics have been highlighted by the work of James Ferguson (1990), who investigated local development processes in Lesotho.[8]

Homonymy and synonymy

The survey of the various uses of the term "anti-politics" could continue with the addition of several further meanings.[9] However, it already appears clear from the observations made so far that the term suffers from a problem of homonymy, that is, the situation where the very same word has a number of different meanings (Sartori 1984, p. 35). In order to map out the various meanings of the term, therefore, it is a good idea to distinguish among words, referents and meanings, as Sartori suggests when re-proposing an idea originally put forward in Charles Ogden and Ivor Richards' classical study (1923). On the basis of the discussion up to the present point, Figure 1.2 represents the aforesaid three-way distinction in graphical form.

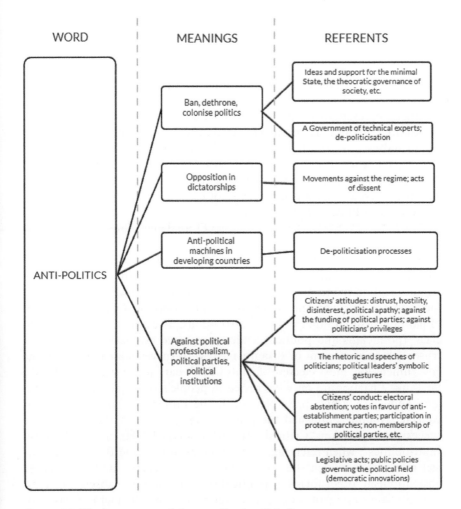

Figure 1.2 The homonymy of the term "anti-politics"

The term "anti-politics", however, does not only suffer from the problem of homonymy, that is, the same word having a number of different meanings, but also of synonymy, that is, when several terms have the same meaning and indicate the same empirical referents. If we take the most common meaning given to the term "anti-politics" – namely, an aversion to professional politics, political parties and elected representatives – it is fairly easy to find several other terms having the same meaning, either in part or in full. Among the best-known examples of this, in his work W*hy we hate politics*, Colin Hay (2007) only uses the adjective "anti-political" twice when referring to hostility towards, and distrust of, politicians; when referring to the decline in political and electoral participation, he prefers to use other terms, such as "political disenchantment" and "political disaffection".

The question of "political disaffection" is also focused on by other authors who have dealt with the question of citizens' hostility towards various aspects of politics. Such authors define it as:

> a certain estrangement or detachment from politics and the public sphere, as well as a critical evaluation of their core political institutions, their representatives, and the democratic political process. This attitudinal attribute is characterized by a number of specific symptoms, including a sense of personal inefficacy, cynicism and distrust, lack of confidence in representative institutions and/or the representatives elected, the belief that political elites do not care about the welfare of their citizens, and a general sense of estrangement from both politics and the political processes.
>
> (Torcal and Montero 2006b, p. 5)

Furthermore, *Disaffected democracies* is the title of a collected volume edited by Susan Pharr and Robert Putnam (2000). Although the authors do not mention the term "anti-politics", the empirical indicators that they focus on are: "attachment to and judgments of political parties; approval of parliaments and other political institutions; assessment of the 'political class' (politicians and political leaders); assorted evaluations of political trust such as agreement or disagreement with survey statements like 'the government [or 'most elected officials'] don't care much what people like me think', 'parties are only interested in people's votes, not in their opinions' and so on" (ibid., p. 8). Neither do the authors of another influential collected volume published the previous year, in which they coined the successful expression "Critical citizens" (Norris 1999a), utilise the term "anti-politics": when referring to the same meanings and the same empirical referents to which the term "anti-politics" usually applies (such as abstentionism, other forms of political participation, the absence of trust in politicians and institutions), they prefer the term "democratic crisis" or

"democratic malaise". The editor of said volume, Pippa Norris, returning to the argument ten years later (Norris 2011), by which time the term
"anti-politics" had entered common parlance and was frequently used by
academics, never mentions "anti-politics" but prefers to use other expressions such as "democratic deficit".

Without examining the question any further – given that there are a great
many other examples and works that could be mentioned here – we are
going to conclude this brief, non-exhaustive overview of the synonyms of
the term "anti-politics", by examining other terms often used to indicate,
at least in part, certain meanings and/or referents of the concept of anti-
politics. These terms include: "anti-establishment", "anti-party", "anti-system"
and "challenger party". They are terminological labels which in turn suffer
from similar problems of definition, including the indeterminate nature of
their semantic scope and of their empirical referents.[10] However, the term
"populism" is the one that is frequently used to indicate certain phenomena
characterising anti-politics. The term "populism" is known for its lengthy,
troubled history, which is something that we cannot really go into here.
Nevertheless, in order to draw a demarcation line between the two terms
and the corresponding phenomena, it can be argued that anti-politics is
a typical aspect of populism, whereas not all anti-politics is of a populist
character. Thus, populist leaders usually resort to using anti-political rhetoric (Mastropaolo 2008, p. 34, 2012, ch. 8). The parties labelled as being
"populist" are in many cases also called "Anti-Political Establishment
Parties" (Abedi 2004). The electors of populist parties, albeit extremely varied (Rooduijn 2018), are often just as animated by anti-political feelings.
However, voters, who act or behave in an anti-political manner, do not necessarily express sympathy for populist parties and leaders.

In summing up the foregoing, Figure 1.3 offers a breakdown of the synonyms of the term "anti-politics".

Reconstructing the concept

The concept of anti-politics may thus be portrayed as a semantic field that
incorporates, or partially overlaps, other semantic fields. The meanings that
this concept refers to, which are partly shared with other concepts, are: hostility towards the political profession, political parties, representative institutions etc. The empirical referents of such meanings are, among others:
feelings of hostility towards political parties and politicians expressed by
citizens; the forms of conduct that reveal such hostility (such as abstentionism, supporting anti-party parties and anti-political politicians, or protest-
ing against mainstream politics); and the symbolic gestures and discourse of
political leaders as they distance themselves from traditional forms of politics. As seen above, an overview of the literature also reveals other concepts,
once again denoted by the term "anti-politics", which however indicate a

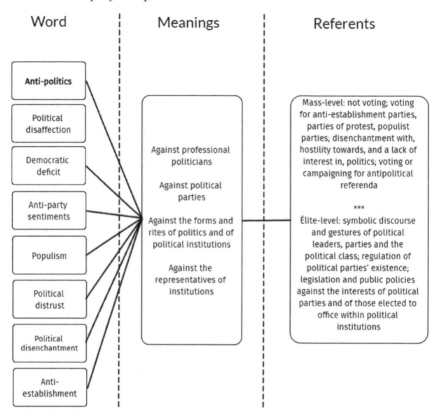

Figure 1.3 The synonymy of the term "anti-politics"

series of completely different meanings and empirical referents, such as political opposition to authoritarian regimes or "anti-political machines" in developing countries. Figure 1.4 offers a simple graphical breakdown of the concept of anti-politics and of other concepts closely linked to it.

Among the various possible configurations of a concept presented by Sartori (1984, p. 47), the concept of anti-politics appears to be the most problematic, given that the corresponding term is characterised by synonyms, homonyms and uncertain semantic overlapping. Even in such circumstances, Sartori invites the reader not to give in to the reigning chaos, and to try to clarify the concept in question. This is possible if one "filters" the meanings of the concept by taking account of both the disciplinary field in which it is used, and the observational or analytical unit to which it refers (ibid., pp. 49–50). By not strictly following the complex process of formation of the concept (the outcome of which, in our case, would probably also be uncertain) recommended by Sartori, it may suffice to perform another operation suggested by the same author, namely that of "disambiguation". This procedure, most of which has already been followed in the preceding pages,

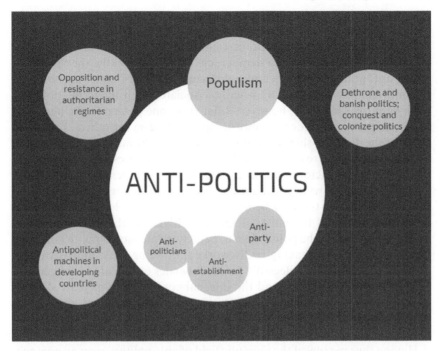

Figure 1.4 The concept of anti-politics

is designed to distinguish the diverse meanings of the term by linking them to context. In Sartori's view:

> To be sure, in a natural language almost no word is univocal (i.e., endowed with only one meaning): All words are polysemes. Therefore the defect is not in the multiplicity of the meanings of each word per se (out of context) but resides in their entanglement, in the fact that it is unclear (in context) which meaning is intended. In short, the problem is confusion of meanings. The activity that we have to come to call disambiguation does not purport, then, to attain univocity – a one-to-one correspondence between meaning and word – but clarity (of meaning). Thus, univocal meanings are, eventually, an ideal objective. The concrete problem that we confront is reducing ambiguity and dispelling equivocation.
>
> (ibid., p. 26)

For the purposes of this study of the anti-political stances and feelings expressed by citizens and political representatives in modern-day Italy, it is sufficient to "filter" selected meanings of the term presented previously. By restricting the analysis to political science and political sociology, the meaning of "anti-politics" used in the present study can be better circumscribed.

By "anti-politics" we do not mean any sentiment against politics as such, as certain definitions of the term have suggested (for example, Schedler 1997b), but rather, sentiments against certain contemporary forms of politics characterising representative democracy. More specifically, the "politics", which anti-political citizens and politicians willingly berate, is composed of empirical referents that are usually associated with the term "politics". Such empirical referents, however, differ from one person to the next, and what one person considers "political" may not be so for others. Empirical study of the question shows that the differences in the meaning attributed to the term "politics" are not random but depend on a series of social, political and institutional factors.[11] In order to overcome this semantic complexity and uncertainty, a widely recognised hard core of targets for anti-political individuals and parties may be identified. This acknowledged hard core is composed, first and foremost, of the most highly visible individuals and symbols populating the political field, namely: professional politicians (who are accused of never having really worked, of being liars, untrustworthy, corrupt, useless and privileged)[12]; political parties (which are no longer considered useful in any way, and the internal conflicts of which are deemed to be incomprehensible); representative and governmental institutions (deemed cumbersome, slow, inconclusive and generators of unjustified privileges for their members).

Having thus narrowed the semantic field of anti-politics, we may now proceed to reflect on the concept's various empirical indicators and on the ways in which it is usually studied.

Studying anti-politics

The terminological chaos involving the anti-politics phenomenon is also due to the heterogeneity of the term's empirical referents. As explained in the preceding section, the "anti-political" label is given not only to the speeches of populist leaders but also to citizens' aversion to professional politicians. At political system level, an increase in electoral abstentionism or the success of populist parties are also interpreted, at least in part, as the result of the diffusion of anti-politics. Despite the fact that these phenomena are all undoubtedly interrelated and interdependent, for analytical purposes they should be distinguished and treated separately. In order to clarify matters, therefore, we suggest that manifestations of the anti-political phenomenon be observed, by taking into consideration different units of analysis. More specifically, and simplifying matters somewhat, I believe it is a good idea to organise this analysis at three different levels, in regard, that is, to: citizens/voters; leaders (or in any case, representatives of the political class); the political system as a whole. Distinguishing the three levels at which diverse manifestations of anti-politics may be observed and also helps us to develop a methodological reflection that is virtually absent in this field. The empirical investigation of anti-political phenomena is based, in fact, on a multitude of research methods, and on the adoption (implicit more often than not) of concept indicators.[13] To try and establish some order in the discourse and analyses regarding anti-politics, I believe we need to consider the three units of analysis in question together with the diverse methods by which the phenomenon of anti-politics has been studied or could be studied.

Citizens' anti-politics

One initial, very important distinction to be made in regard to the anti-politics of citizens and voters, is that between attitudes and behaviour. Here again, it is clear that this distinction is beneficial in heuristic terms, and that in practice the two aspects are inextricably interwoven. As previously mentioned, the literature on anti-politics has focused on people's disenchantment with, and hostility towards, politicians, political parties and representative institutions. Thus, possible indicators of the concept of anti-politics in this regard include: the sentiment of trust in politicians, political parties and institutions; the subjective feeling of political efficacy; the idea of politics as a dirty, corrupt thing to be avoided; being against the funding of political parties, and in favour of a reduction in MPs' numbers and salaries; the belief that politics, parties, political institutions and politicians are all worthless, if not harmful; the subjective feeling of satisfaction with the workings of democracy; the intention not to vote as a form of political protest; the belief that politicians look after their own interests rather than those of citizens and so on. As a rule, such anti-political attitudes are investigated in the literature by means of surveys of representative national samples, and at times using cross-national comparisons.[14] In certain cases, those who are not interested in politics are also considered anti-political. While it is true that in practice this feeling of distance from the world of politics is often associated with negative feelings towards that world, it is also true that the two things do not necessarily go together. Thus, for analytical purposes, it is a good idea to distinguish hostile feelings and behaviour, which we may call "anti-political", from feelings of detachment from, and indifference towards, politics, which would be better labelled as "apolitical".[15] The psychological distance from political themes and actors is also often the subject of surveys containing sets of questions.[16]

Anti-political behaviour as well is generally analysed by means of surveys; often the same ones used to establish the sentiments of citizens/voters. The indicators of anti-politics constituted by forms of behaviour include: abstention from voting, returning a blank or spoilt ballot paper; taking part in referenda of an anti-political nature (for example, in favour of the abolition of the public funding of political parties); vote on, sign up for and participate in, the activities promoted by a populist party or a protest party; follow and forward anti-political messages posted by political representatives.[17]

While surveys remain the most commonly used means of analysing anti-politics from below, they are not the only source of information regarding what citizens think of politics and how they act politically. Another, less commonly used approach, but one that is extremely useful for an understanding of the phenomenon, is in fact constituted by qualitative and ethnographic studies.[18]

One of the rare attempts made to investigate anti-politics using different research methods and sources is the study of the British case conducted by Nick Clarke and colleagues (Clarke *et al.* 2018). Their research approach enabled them to compare survey results with the information contained in the Mass Observation Archive. This invaluable dataset established in 1937 – the same year that the British Institute of Public Opinion began systematically collecting survey date – contains information that is extremely useful for an historical analysis of the United Kingdom's social, cultural and political life. The diaries kept, with certain continuity, by a panel of volunteers, are particularly useful when trying to understand how the public's opinions and social representation have changed over the years. A close analysis of the mass of information contained in these diaries reveals that anti-political feelings are extremely widespread, going back well into history, and have grown in intensity over the course of time. Furthermore, the social base of those fostering anti-political ideas and feelings has gradually changed and grown, as has the range of charges and accusations aimed at politicians.

Thus, the phenomenon of anti-politics, as previously mentioned, is not a new one. Despite the fact that there has never been a period in history when citizens/voters have looked on politics in a broadly favourable light, there can be no doubt, as Clarke and colleagues have argued in regard to the British case, that diffidence and hostility towards politicians and politics have grown in recent years. Numerous scholars have set out what they believe to be the underlying reasons for this growth in citizens' anti-political sentiments and conduct. Some of these scholars have also conducted specific empirical studies, both quantitative and qualitative, of this very question, some of which have just been mentioned here. Other scholars, on the other hand, although not relying on empirical analyses, have offered reflections on the matter that ought to be taken into account in order to provide a broader picture of the origins and underlying causes of citizens' anti-political sentiments.

Following the reasoning of Colin Hay (2007), the explanations for the contemporary diffusion of anti-politics may be subdivided into two large categories: those that place the emphasis on the transformation of political demands and those that on the contrary focus in particular on political supply. Despite acknowledging the various forms of interdependence and feedback between the two aforesaid factors,[19] the explanations given based on demand tend to focus on the social, economic and cultural changes affecting the citizens of the advanced democracies, which are perceived as having an impact on those citizens' relationship with politics. On the contrary, those scholars focusing more on the supply side of politics make more frequent mention of the changes affecting parties, institutions, the political class and political careers. Since the debate about anti-politics (whether it be called this or not) is a very broad one,[20] the explanations centring on political demand can include the traditional one of the decline in social participation and civic culture (Putnam 2000). The growing criticism of politics, seen from a different point of view, is the result of the increasing expectations that today's citizens – better educated and less subservient than in the past – have of politicians and of the political sphere as a whole (Dalton 1984). As far as concerns the explanations given in terms of political supply, the contemporary changes deemed to have led to an increase in widespread anti-political sentiments among citizens, regard the following phenomena among others: the collusive, oligopolistic development of political parties (Katz and Mair 1995), the tendency towards the professionalization of politicians (Borchert and Zeiss 2003) and the depoliticisation process (Burnham 2001, Hay 2007).

The anti-politics of political leaders

A second unit of analysis that should be taken into consideration when studying anti-politics, after that of ordinary citizens, is constituted by the representatives of the political class, in particular political leaders. While citizens and voters express "anti-politics" through their behaviour and attitudes, in the case of the country's political élite, "antipolitics [could be] understood as a feature of the language used by leaders, parties, and movements who oppose the political establishment and denounce its incapacity or bad faith in governing the country and managing the bureaucracy" (Campus 2010, p. 1). In addition to the strictly linguistic and discursive aspects focused on by Donatella Campus in the aforementioned work, political leaders can generate anti-political messages by means of other symbolic acts: the way that they dress, the places they frequent, the people they choose to be seen with in public and so on. When they sit in public institutions, they may express their anti-political positions by means of bills, administrative or legislative acts, even those of a constitutional nature (such as the abolition of political parties' public funding, or the reduction in MP's salaries or numbers). When anti-political leaders are heads of political parties, they may even change the rules governing the functioning of their respective parties, adopting measures that extol members' direct participation in decisional processes (or indeed the participation in such of non-members, as in the case of open primaries), in the name of the revitalisation of the party and against "old", criticisable forms of politics. This is an example of the introduction of measures of democratic innovation designed to counter – at least on paper – declining political participation (and thus the reduced legitimisation of the leadership). Furthermore, the creation of new participatory spaces can be seen as a countermeasure in relation to the anti-political criticism of party leaders. As we shall see later in this volume in regard to the Italian case (Chapter 4), such democratic changes risk resulting in anti-political outcomes. This may hold true in the case of traditional parties that wish to re-invent themselves. In the case where the parties in question are new parties, on the other hand, then anti-political principles, rhetoric and practices may constitute an important aspect of the identity of the parties themselves and of their political leaders.

The main thing encouraging a political leader to adopt anti-political actions and words is, of course, the desire to dislodge the criticised holders of power. Thus, anti-politics can be seen as an arm used by emerging anti-system or opposition politicians and parties. However, as Mastropaolo has pointed out (2005, p. 138), and as the aforementioned work by Campus clearly shows, anti-politics may also be used as a weapon by leaders already firmly in power and supported by solid majorities, as populist leaders increasingly are (Albertazzi and McDonnell 2015, Dieckhoff *et al.* 2019, Zulianello 2019b, Taggart and Pirro 2021). In this case, the recourse to anti-politics plays a slightly different role. Firstly, it may be part of a going-public strategy (Kernell 1986), and as such serves to put pressure on the leaders' own parliamentary groups in order to facilitate the passing of the leaders' own bills. Furthermore, the leaders' criticism of political professionalism, of the delays and rituals of politics, of party bureaucracy and so on are an attempt to delegitimize and thus weaken politics' intermediate bodies. In this way, leaders circumvent parliamentary groups and parties' apparatus and institute a direct link with the base of the party and the electorate; and in doing so, they increase their own power to the detriment of the other traditional political actors. By focusing their criticisms on parties and professional politicians, these political leaders shift the public's attention away from social conflict, the failures of public policy implemented by the political decision-makers, and the economic and social problems that they, as the governing parties, should be dealing with. Given that at elections, voters punish the politicians in office even when the problems that voters complain about are clearly beyond the powers of the governing classes (Achen and Bartels 2016, ch. 5), it is plausible that politicians try to shift the attention away from their own failings and from the limited nature of the government's actions, and towards the (real or alleged) ills and faults of politics. Thus, politics becomes the scapegoat for everything that does not work in society (Mastropaolo 2012, p. 167), with the result that politicians are constantly discredited and demonised, paradoxically by the politicians themselves (Dogan 2005, Flinders 2012b).

Since the anti-politics of political leaders is strictly linked to populism, it may be investigated, at least in part, by using the analytical instruments characteristically employed when studying the phenomenon of populism.[21] First of all, therefore, one method that can may be adopted is an analysis of the political language, discourse and messages of political leaders, and in particular of populist leaders (Aalberg *et al.* 2016, Hidalgo Tenorio *et al.* 2019, Reinemann *et al.* 2019). Biographical analyses and political biographies are also useful tools and sources of information when investigating the origins and development of the anti-political aspects of political leadership. Likewise, it may be useful to analyse the various aspects of a political leader's leadership style, using a different technique for each such aspect (Campus 2016). This may include a comparison of the psychological traits of political leaders with those of a sample of citizens (Caprara and Vecchione 2016). In other words, various aspects may be investigated and diverse methods utilised also with regard to the anti-politics of political leaders. As with the preceding unit of analysis – the individual citizen – indicators of anti-politics may also be identified in regard to this second unit of analysis. Such indicators clearly depend on the chosen research method. Such indicators may include: the frequency of anti-political speeches and appearances, both in public and in the media; symbolic acts against parties, professional politicians, political privileges; bills, political decisions, the regulation of parties' workings and public policy of an anti-political bent.

The anti-politics of the political system

A third unit of analysis with which anti-politics may be observed and studied – in addition to the previously mentioned two units, consisting of citizens and political leaders respectively – is the political system itself. What is analysed here are certain characteristics of the political system, with the aim of establishing to what degree that system is permeated with anti-politics, or from a comparative perspective, of establishing whether the chosen system is affected by anti-politics to a greater or lesser degree than other political systems. It goes without saying that the empirical referents, on which such an analysis is based, are no different from those of the two analytical levels considered previously, that is, the level of citizens and the level of political leaders. However, the research methods and indicators employed are different. Thus, while at the individual level, knowing whether a citizen abstains from voting (and possibly why that person abstains) may be considered an anti-politics indicator, at the political system level an indicator of the concept of anti-politics could be the level of electoral participation, perhaps seen from a diachronic perspective. Likewise, indicators of anti-politics at the systemic level may include: the presence and percentage of votes cast for anti-system or anti-establishment parties, new challengers, or explicitly anti-political parties; the existence, frequency and results of referendums of an anti-political nature; the level of approval for anti-political leaders measured by means of surveys; the anti-political content of political parties' electoral programmes; electoral volatility and so on.

The research methods are largely similar to those employed (or employable) in studies of anti-politics at the individual level, namely opinion polls revealing the beliefs, behaviour and actions of the interviewees, but in this case considered at aggregate level. Other methods include the processing of information taken from official sources, in particular information of an electoral nature (such as that provided by the International Institute for

Democracy and Electoral Assistance (IDEA), or from political parties or political and representative institutions. Generally speaking, those methods, usually employed to study public opinion, the political class, political parties, elections and populism, are also valid in this case.

Summing up then, the reflections set out in this chapter point to the multifaceted, changeable nature of anti-politics, a phenomenon that has diverse effects on the political life and political actors of the community in which it manifests itself. Furthermore, anti-politics may be considered and empirically observed at different levels: at the level of individual citizens, at that of political leaders (or the political class) and at that of the political system as a whole. Account shall be taken of these diverse aspects in the chapters to follow, where the focus will be on the various different expressions and implications of anti-politics in the political and social life of contemporary Italy.

Notes

1 In the *Enciclopedia del pensiero politico*, Loretta Monti reconstructed the various stages of the term's divulgation in the major European nations. De Balzac, who introduced the term in the year 1650 in France, was followed by the Englishman Thomas Paine some 150 years later, in his work *The Rights of Man*. In Italy, the word "anti-politics" appeared for the first time in 1849, on the pages of the first copy of the Turin newspaper "L'istruttore del popolo" (Monti 2000). In his *Grande Dizionario Italiano dell'uso*, Tullio De Mauro relates that the term first appeared in Italy in 1794, in a work by P. Zanguri entitled: "*Carteggi casanoviani*".

2 The graph is based on the querying of the Google Books database using the app Ngram Viewer (https://books.google.com/ngrams), and it shows the percentage presence of the term among all of the terms contained in the same text corpus. For further details, see also Michel *et al.* (2011). In the case of English, two text corpora of books were consulted: those published mainly in the USA and those published mainly in the United Kingdom. The occurrences of the terms "anti-politics" (more frequently found in British English) and "antipolitics" were summed together. In the case of French, the term "*antipolitique*" was used, while for Italian the chosen term was "*antipolitica*"; for Spanish it was "*antipolitica*" and for German it was "*antipolitik*". The use of Google's Ngram to study the diffusion of terms and phrases over time has been widely criticised for various reasons: due to the limited accuracy of the system of OCR text recognition; due to the excessive weight given to scientific literature in the composition of the corpora; due to its inability to consider the diffusion of the volumes in question (a volume that has sold a million copies is given the same importance as one that has sold 100 copies) and so on. For an overview of such criticisms, see Pechenick *et al.* (2015). In our case, Nrram is not used to develop a solid, accurate linguistic analysis of the term "anti-politics", but merely to obtain further information on its presence in the various languages considered here, and subject to the limitations mentioned above, to get a better understanding of the diffusion of the term in the various languages over the course of time.

3 Perhaps it would be no exaggeration to say that the term – at least in the Italian context, to judge by its considerable and rapid diffusion – is affected by what Sartori calls "the frenzy of novitism", described as follows: "Until quite

recently scholars usually did not perceive themselves as having to be 'new' and original at whatever cost: they understood their main task to consist of transmitting knowledge. Clearly, this is less the case. However, it is not easy to be 'original' and perhaps the easiest way of appearing to innovate is to play musical chairs with words. One can indeed appear both powerfully destructive of others and mightily innovative, simply by rearranging a string of words with the help of a handful of stipulative definitions" (Sartori 1975, p. 9).

4 In addition to the two factors identified by Sartori, a third may also be taken into consideration which often renders the terminology of the social sciences imprecise and confusing, namely: the geographical/territorial area within which the term is used. In regard to anti-politics and other associated terms, in fact, Robert Barr states that: "Although some populist literature does cross regional boundaries, the conceptual boundaries between terms like populism, anti-politics and outsiders remain largely closed (exceptions include Kenney, 1998). This is a problem, because too often different terms describe the same phenomenon, and the same terms describe different phenomena" (Barr 2009, p. 30).

5 This idea of subdividing anti-politics into four types – two from above and two from below – was subsequently also taken up by Flinders *et al.* (2019).

6 A similar definition of anti-politics, in the sense of a form of resistance to absolutist politics in the Communist States, was used by David Ost (1990) in regard to the case of Poland. Dick Howard (2016) has presented a philosophical discussion of anti-politics as a force challenging authoritarian politics.

7 For a more in-depth discussion of the meaning of anti-politics in the Communist Bloc countries, see the work by Alan Renwick (2006), which distinguishes between eight different forms of dissidence in regard to the established power. See also the essay by Knud Erik Jørgensen who, once again in regard to the pre-1989 Central European context, identifies five different dimensions of anti-politics (Jørgensen 1992, p. 42).

8 For a survey of other studies of an anthropological nature conducted along the lines of this seminal study by Ferguson, see the work by William Fisher (1997).

9 A simple examination of bibliographical references throws up "Gandhian (or theological) anti-politics" (Mohan and Dwivedi 2019), anti-politics comprising unconventional public and political activity in Imperial Germany (Repp 2000); anti-politics as a topic of discussion in the debate regarding early British socialism (Claeys 1989); and even certain anti-political aspects to the works of Shakespeare (Gil 2013). Bernard Crick also dedicates a section in his influential volume (1962) to "The anti-political socialist". In reconstructing the various meanings of "anti-politics" and applying such to Italian political affairs, Giuseppe Gangemi found traces of anti-politics in the writings of classical scholars like Machiavelli and Vico (Gangemi 2008). In a recent work, Matteo Truffelli and Lorenzo Zambernardi offer an interesting take on the intellectual roots of anti-politics, which they believe lie in the development of political modernity. Anti-politics can be considered shadowing that development, as a kind of "dark side of politics" (Truffelli and Zambernardi 2021, p. 103). In another recent article, Matthew Wood identifies four types of anti-politics – technocratic, elitist, populist and participatory – each of which he links to the ideas of an important political thinker: "Joseph Schumpeter (elitist), Friedrich Hayek (technocratic), Ernesto Laclau (populist) and Carole Pateman (participatory)" (Wood 2021, p. 2).

10 A careful survey of the numerous "anti" terms, including those previously mentioned here, has been conducted by Mattia Zulianello (2019a, ch. 2).

11 For a summing up of the question, together with a specific overview of the literature, see Fitzgerald (2013).

12 For a more detailed discussion of the criticisms that citizens made and make of politicians, see Clarke *et al.* (2018). These authors argue that "politicians deserve such a centrale place in research on anti-politics because when citizens think of more abstract objects (...) they often think of the politicians who make up those institutions. They use politicians as a heuristic to judge the activities and institutions of formal politics in general" (ibid, p. 7). Another study conducted in France on the basis of qualitative methods reached similar conclusions: "Politics is thus perceived from various different viewpoints. As currently defined, the most commonly found understanding of the term, 'politics' is associated with political parties, politicians, elections, speeches, electoral programmes and promises, arguments, the struggle for power, political office and benefits, ambition and manipulation" (Gaxie 2001a, p. 84).

13 In Sartori's view, an indicator is "a variable that stands for another factor in order to facilitate its measurement. Indicators help operationalization" (Sartori 1984, p. 78).

14 The best known research programmes containing questions that are often used by researchers to explore political disaffection and disenchantment, and other aspects related to the meanings of anti-politics examined up to this point, include the World Values Survey, the European Social Survey, the Comparative Study of Electoral Systems; and the Eurobarometer surveys promoted by the European Union. In addition to these sources, there are national-level electoral studies programmes such as the Italian National Electoral Studies (ITANES) for Italy. The information gathered through these research programmes constitute the main empirical basis for many studies into the question of political disenchantment and anti-politics, including, for example: Norris (1999a, 2011), Pharr and Putnam (2000), Torcal and Montero (2006a), Hay (2007), Stoker (2017). For an overview of the studies conducted in regard to Italy, see, at the very least, Maraffi (2007) and Bellucci and Segatti (2010).

15 In a comparative study of Italy and Argentina coordinated by the methodologist Alberto Marradi (2020), the questionnaire used to collect data contained a question on the interviewees' self-assessment of their own political position, the possible answers to which included the category "apolitical". Given that this was the category in which the highest percentage of interviewees saw themselves (28.5%), one can deduce that offering this option to interviewees is a very good idea. It should encourage researchers preparing such questionnaires to specifically offer interviewees the opportunity to express their disenchantment with, and hostility towards, politics. For a methodological reflection of the difficulties of giving an opinion on political aspects with which one is not familiar, such as the one in question, see Gaxie (1990).

16 The classical questions posed to interviewees in many surveys of public opinion consist of statements like the following (to which interviewees are to respond by indicating their degree of agreement/disagreement with such statements): "All candidates sound good in their speeches but you can never tell what they will do after they are elected"; "People like me don't have any say over what the government does"; "I don't think the government cares much about what people like me think"; "Those in power, always pursue their personal interests". For a survey of the questions on this theme used in questionnaires submitted within the context of Italy, see Segatti (2006).

17 A study based on a survey, and specifically focusing on the questions of political disenchantment and anti-politics, which also offers some insight into methodology, was conducted by Jennings *et al.* (2016). As we shall see in Chapter 6,

in a survey of nine European countries, Eri Bertsou and Daniele Caramani (2020b) employ a specific index of anti-politics based on four questions.

18 Daniel Gaxie used qualitative methods to explore the theme of political disenchantment among citizens and electors in a thorough, original manner. Among his numerous writings, this theme is specifically dealt with in Gaxie (2001b, 2001c, 2003, 2007, 2008). With regard to the same argument, and specifically in regard to the works and intellectual standing of Gaxie, see the collective volume by Barrault-Stella *et al.* (2019), and specifically the afterword written by Gaxie himself. An interesting study of the meaning that French electors attribute to voting is that of the *Collectif Sociologie politique des élections*, whose promoters include Gaxie. The main findings of the study have been published in a sizeable collective volume (SPEL – Collectif Sociologie politique des élections 2016). These findings reveal the beliefs and debate regarding French citizens' hostility to the world of politics. Another French writer who has examined the question of citizens' views of politics, using methods other surveys, is Philippe Aldrin. In one of his most recent works (but see also Aldrin 2003, Aldrin and de Lassalle 2016), Aldrin finds that electors feel that they are like small-scale shareholders in the French political system, and that they "perceive voting (votes, blank votes, abstention) and their political preferences (vote for the left, the right, the centre, the extremists) as a way of expressing their support for, their discontent with, or their rejection of, the 'system'" (...). The world of professional politicians, which is always judged severely by those with varying degrees of knowledge of such, depending on where the observer stands in society, is frequently seen as a world of 'the privileged', 'removed from reality', who are seen as not very effective or even 'worthless' (2020, pp. 51–2). A grand historical portrait of informal politics in France, extending to the present day and written from a multidisciplinary point of view, is contained in the volume edited by Laurent Le Gall, Michel Offerlé and François Ploux (2012). Still about France, a qualitative study on citizens' expectations of the political system was carried out by Camille Bedock (2020). There are also numerous qualitative studies of the North American situation with regard to the relationship between citizens and politics, and in particular people's aversion to politicians and political parties. The most well-known such studies are probably those conducted by Nina Eliasoph (1998) and by John Hibbing and Elizabeth Theiss-Morse (2002), partially replicated also in the French political context (Gourgues *et al.* 2021). These two studies reach the same conclusion, albeit interpreted differently, namely that citizens prefer to avoid politics if they can. In other words, they prefer a system in which there is a "stealth democracy" that operates without their involvement and contribution. A further two studies, conducted in deepest America, examine citizens' political alienation and anti-establishmentarianism. These studies, which adopt a specific ethnographic approach that Katherine Cramer has called "a method of listening", aim at understanding not so much what people think, as how they formed their opinions (Cramer 2016, Banack 2021). An overview of the ways in which citizens around the world talk of politics (and also of anti-politics) is contained in a recent work by Clare Saunders and Bert Klandermans (2020). A study of the same questions, conducted in Australia and based on interviews and focus groups, is that by Paul Fawcett and Jack Corbett (2018). Eri Bertsou, having offered his thoughts on the concept of political distrust (Bertsou 2019a), carried out a comparative study of Italy, Greece and the United Kingdom based on 48 narrative interviews and concluded that "the structure of political distrust as it is expressed by citizens [is] similar across the three countries" (Bertsou 2019b, p. 15). A combination

of surveys and focus groups forms the basis of the study, conducted by Gerry Stoker and Colin Hay (2017), of the anti-political behaviour of British citizens. For Italy, see the analysis by Alfio Mastropaolo in his work on the future of democracy (2012, pp. 235–41). A detailed methodological proposal for the study of certain aspects of the anti-politics phenomenon, using ethnographical techniques, has been put forward by Boswell *et al.* (2019).

19 For a critical discussion of, and a proposal for going beyond, the supply and demand dichotomy, see the work by *E*mma Vines and David Marsh (2018).

20 A survey of the reasons for the emergence of the "critical citizen", which distinguishes between social, political, institutional and cultural factors, is presented by Pippa Norris (1999b, pp. 21–5). Gerry Stoker proposes and discusses 12 causes of political disenchantment, ranging from changed values to the transformation of the mass media system with "the emergence of intense 24-hour media coverage of politics" and the impotence of the political class in the face of epoch-making challenges of the modern world (2017, ch. 3). More in general, there is a broad discussion of the factors underlying political disenchantment in the works by Nye *et al.* (1997), Pharr and Putnam (2000), and Torcal and Montero (2006a). The distinction between supply side factors and demand side factors as the causes of anti-politics, featuring a specific focus on the processes of politicians' professionalization, is presented by Paul Fawcett and Jack Corbett (2018).

21 Growing interest in populism has also led to an increased focus on the appropriate methods by which this phenomenon may be measured and studied. For a survey, see Pauwels (2017). For an empirical comparison of seven populist attitudes scales, see Castanho Silva *et al.* (2020).

2 Anti-politics prior to anti-politics

Citizens and politics in Italy after the Second World War

A golden age?

After the lengthy interlude of Fascism (1922–43), which had put an end to the on-going process of extending political and citizenship rights within the nation, at the end of the Second World War, Italy was finally able to embark on a period of democratic government. The first real test of the new Italian democracy, following the ravages of the Fascist dictatorship and the war itself (which towards the end had turned into a civil war in northern and central Italy), was the institutional referendum held on 2 June 1946. On that day, Italians were called upon to choose between the rule of Monarchy and a Republican government. Furthermore, they were asked to elect a Constituent Assembly tasked with drafting an Italian Constitution, which subsequently came into force on 1 January 1948. This historical electoral event had been preceded, and was accompanied, by a climate of uncertainty. In fact, the elections marked the advent of universal male and female suffrage in Italy, and there were significant fears regarding the actual participation of a culturally and socially backward population seriously affected by 20 years of one-party rule. This atmosphere of uncertainty also concerned the Italians' positions regarding the Monarchy, many of whom held to be jointly responsible for the political and social debacle that the country had suffered, and its members' political position regarding those parties emerging from the Resistance movement, or those that had survived years of clandestineness under Fascism.

Despite these fears, the Italian people passed the first real test of democracy with flying colours, given that 89% of those entitled to vote did so. While the electorate answered the call to vote en masse, the election resulted in the country being deeply divided between supporters of the Monarchy and those who voted for a Republican form of government, and in terms of the parties for whom they cast their votes. A total of 54.3% voted in favour of the Republic, compared to 45.7% who voted for the Monarchy. The country was also divided geographically between pro-Republican and pro-Monarchy voters. In the centre and north of Italy, the pro-Republican vote clearly prevailed, whereas votes for the Monarchy prevailed in the South.

DOI: 10.4324/9781003109273-3

Votes were split also into political terms. The Christian Democrats (DC) obtained 35.2% of the total votes cast, while the two left-wing parties – the Socialist Party Partito Socialista Italiano di Unità Proletaria (PSIUP) and the Communist Party Partito Comunista Italiano (PCI) – obtained 20.7% and 18.9%, respectively. These elections were to establish the characteristic traits of the Italian political system, which were to persist up until the crisis of that system in the early 1990s. These traits were summed up in a series of three expressions coined by a similar number of eminent Italian experts in the field of Italian politics. The first such expression was the "Republic of parties" (Scoppola 1997), with which the scholar in question wished to underscore the considerable importance played by the country's mass parties in the political, social, cultural and economic affairs of Republican Italy. These parties, which were ideologically divided, gave rise to a "polarised pluralism" according to the political scientist Giovanni Sartori (1982). Sartori used this expression to indicate the fragmentation of the Italian party system compared with that of other Western democracies, and the ideological gap separating the country's parties. This ideological gap principally concerned the communist/anti-communist divide underlying Italy's "imperfect bipartism" (Galli 1966, Galli and Prandi 1970), which for many years dominated Italian politics. The presumed imperfect nature of said system lay in the absence of any natural alternation of the two dominant political blocks, unlike what happened in the post-war years in other Western democracies, where this alternation was very much in evidence. In Italy, on the contrary, the strength of the PCI, the largest communist party in any Western democracy, prevented the development of a social-democratic party capable of challenging Christian Democrat rule. Furthermore, Italy's internationally strategic position made it an invaluable pawn for the North Atlantic powers in the game being played against the USSR and its satellite countries. This is why the moderate wing of the DC remained constantly in power, and why the PCI was permanently relegated to the role of opposition party, except during the brief period of the so-called historic compromise in the second half of the 1970s.

The co-existence of political partisanship and anti-partyism

These parties, which were firmly opposed to one another and miles apart ideologically, together generated a fierce political rivalry that was fed by, and also produced, the vast mobilisation of Italy's populace. The period stretching from 1946 to the 1992–4 crisis is commonly considered to be the golden age of political participation among Italy's citizens. This may be represented summarily by a series of indicators. The first and most important such indicator is voter turnout. For the entire second half of the 20th century, Italy remained the Western democracy with the highest percentage of those eligible to vote actually casting their votes at the country's elections (Dalton 2020, p. 44). This primacy was the result of a combination of strong, well-organised, ideologically polarised parties, a proportional electoral system and the status of voting as a "civic duty". However, things changed rapidly, and indeed for the worst, from the 1990s onwards. The crisis in the early 1990s and the "never-ending transition" that has characterised Italy up to the present day have led to a dramatic reduction in voting figures since then. Indeed, Italy has seen the largest fall in voter turnout (−26%) among all major democracies (ibid.).

The previous high turnout levels can be accounted for, and were accompanied by, the preeminent role of the country's parties in Italy's political system from the Second World War onwards. In fact, a very high percentage of Italian electors identified with one political party. A survey conducted in 1956 established that 76% of the sample of Italian electors identified with a given political party (Morlino 2001, p. 115). A similar degree of identification with a chosen party (77.8%) was also found by researchers in 1968, when more systematic, specific surveys began to be conducted into the political views and behaviour of Italians. The findings emerging from said surveys reveal that such levels of identification held up fairly well in subsequent years (64.5% in 1972 and 56.8% in 1975), before falling dramatically prior to the political transformation witnessed in the early 1990s, when only 25.8% of those interviewed stated that they felt fairly or very close to a given political party (Biorcio 2010, p. 193). This was in line, nevertheless, with what was happening in other Western democracies at that time (Schmitt 2009, p. 82).[1]

The high degree of party identification, together with the key role played by political parties in Italian society, in turn meant high levels of turnout and party membership among Italy's citizens. If we compare the ratio of party members to those citizens entitled to vote, what we see is that Italy displayed much higher degrees of party membership than the other major Western European democracies.[2] This was due to the exceptional performance of the PCI, which had over 2 million members in 1946, and the members accounted for 47.5% of all those people who voted for the PCI at the time. In 1987, just before the party disappeared altogether, it still had a million and a half members. In the case of the other mass party in Italy – the DC – while in 1946 its membership was not as large as that of the PCI, standing at about 600,000, this figure was to rise to 1.8 million by 1972. Membership subsequently declined markedly, returning to its post-war levels by 1987. The membership of the Italian Socialist Party (PSI) was smaller than that of the PCI and the DC but was nonetheless significant: in 1946, the party had 860,000 members, and subsequently this level varied, reaching a minimum low of 470,000 in 1979 (Morlino 2001, p. 111).

Strong, deeply rooted parties, a significant portion of the population that identified with one party or another, high rates of voter turnout at elections, strong ideological differences, the persistence of the aforementioned "imperfect bipartism", the combination of these factors accounts for low electoral volatility in Italy from the immediate post-war years up to the break-up of the traditional party system in the early 1990s. Between 1946 and 1948, said volatility reached 16.3%, although this figure was quickly to drop to 5.3% by

1958, and then further to 3.7% by 1969, before rising once more to 15.7% in 1992, and then shooting up to 39.3% at the 1994 elections, the highest figure in the history of the Italian Republic (Chiaramonte and Paparo 2019, p. 266).

The picture to this point is one of considerable political mobilisation on the part of the Italian electorate during the period between the advent of the Republic and the crisis of the party system in the early 1990s. However, on closer examination, what one finds is considerable variety among Italian regions. In fact, parties are stronger and voter turnout is higher in northern and central Italy, particularly in the so-called red belt, that is, in those central Italian regions where socialist and communist traditions are stronger (Tuscany, Umbria and Emilia-Romagna). Party organisation, militancy and electoral participation are weaker in Italy's southern regions, on the other hand. The idea of a golden age of party politics and electoral participation is more complex than it may seem however and tends to conceal the existence of other, opposed phenomena, that is, of an aversion to political parties, the political class and representative organisations. In other words, the "golden age" concept tends to obscure those empirical indicators referred to in Chapter 1, which point to the existence of what we have termed "anti-politics". On closer inspection, said indicators would lead us to agree with what Clarke *et al.* argue in reference to the case of the United Kingdom: "we argue that no golden age of political support existed. Even in the immediate post-war period, substantial proportions of the population disapproved of governments and prime ministers" (2018, p. 8).[3]

Politicians and political parties' bad names, together with the low esteem in which they are held according to the aforesaid study, are accompanied in the United Kingdom by the presence of well-organised parties and high voter turnout. Despite not having complete, reliable data for the Italian case which could reveal the nature of the relationship between the nation's citizens and the political sphere in the immediate post-war years, it could plausibly be argued that the mass political mobilisation of the population was accompanied by hostility towards politics and its symbols on the part of a certain section of the population nevertheless. In fact, hostility towards the world of politics is not something that emerged for the first time in the post-war years. On the contrary, as Piero Ignazi pointed out in his book, significantly entitled "Uneven road to party legitimacy" (2017), over the course of history and during the development of democracy, there has always been a certain diffidence and hostility shown towards political parties. The reason for this is that the political party (from the Latin "*partire*", that is, "divide") underlies division and struggle rather than unity and harmony. In Italy in particular, according to David Ragazzoni, "Antipartyism, rather than the appreciation of parties, is what gives cohesiveness to the history of Italy's party democracy" (2020, p. 86). In fact, politicians and parties were already being criticised during the advent of *trasformismo* (1882–3) (Sabbatucci 2005, p. 15), and the terms and rhetoric established at that time were to re-emerge in the years thereafter. Even during Fascism, which was based on the mobilisation of the masses and the central importance of the one party, as the Italian historian Salvatore Lupo has noted: "the hyper-party was always accompanied by the anti-party" (2013, p. 209).

Despite the rather fragmented, incomplete nature of the information available, certain signs of this co-existence of hyper-politics and anti-politics seemed to survive beyond the end of the Fascist regime and have characterised the Italian people's relationship with politics since the foundation of the Republic. As Nadia Urbinati has pointed out: "The Italian case is an eloquent example of the fact that political practice in the age of democracy has generated, and continues to generate, party-ism and anti-partyism ceaselessly. It proved that this dynamic seems to be in effect the 'spirit' of representative democracy (rather than its pathology) and a government that is based on election, and produces both partisan affiliations and parties and also a reaction against them" (Urbinati 2020, p. 69). This hostility towards politics, parties and politicians was to be expressed by a considerable number of people, in particular those of right-wing tendencies, some of whom were to become key players in the political life of the new Republic (Mastropaolo 2000, Tarchi 2015).

Pioneering studies of the Italians' political opinions

Despite the absence of systematic studies and research into the political behaviour of Italians during the parties' golden age, certain sources of information can be used to draw up a brief picture of that behaviour. One invaluable source of information regarding Italians' political opinions after the end of the Second World War is constituted by the DOXA studies subsequently collected in one volume (Luzzatto-Fegiz 1956). These initial surveys, conducted on representative samples of the Italian population, revealed among other things that in April 1946, just weeks before the institutional referendum of 2 June, 54% of interviewees believed that "the people" should be the ones to elect any future President of the Republic, whereas only 15% thought that this was the duty of parliament (ibid., p. 418). While a certain degree of caution is called for here, given the high levels of illiteracy and Italy's limited political expertise at the time, this first finding could be seen as a somewhat damming assessment of Italy's parliamentarians and political parties. Even when asked who should choose the electoral candidates, the interviewees appeared reluctant to assign this role to the political parties. When in 1953, a sample of 1,138 people were asked the question "As you know, the lists of political candidates are drawn up by the governing body (or secretariat) of each political party. Are you in favour or against this system?", only 33% stated that they were in favour of such system, while 19% were against it (the remaining 48% either did not express an opinion or did not understand the question) (ibid., p. 501). Those who were against lists of candidates being drawn up by the parties observed, in particular, that the lists "should be proposed by the people", that they should be chosen "on the basis of the votes of all party members, through internal elections", thus circumventing the party leadership through the holding of primaries, and that the candidates "should be competent, honest people" (ibid., p. 503).

Another study conducted by DOXA reveals that in March 1948, one month prior to the elections held to choose Italy's first Republican parliament, a "total disinterest in politics" was the main reason for abstaining from voting.[4] Despite having no statistical validity, nor the systematic character of the diaries completed by the members of the British BIPO panel (Clarke *et al.* 2018), DOXA's researchers gathered a number of the "characteristic comments" spontaneously made by the interviewees with regard to their intentions to vote or to abstain. These included comments of a clearly anti-political nature: "I want to go and vote once more this time; but then if I see that [those elected] are just the same as all the others, that's it, I'm not voting again" (pensioner, Communist Party); "I disapprove of the battle between the parties, and I hope that the 18 April election is Italy's last" (farmer, MSI – a neo-Fascist party); "I'm going to vote, even though I know they [the parties] are all the same" (housewife, no political preferences); "us working-class women shouldn't be voting, because we're not properly educated and we don't have a clear idea of things" (tram conductor, Communist Party); "I don't concern myself with politics, and I don't care who wins the election" (barber, no political preferences); "as far as I'm concerned they're all OK, just as long as we live well" (housewife, no political preferences); "perhaps I'll vote, although I'm sure that my life won't change at all regardless of who wins. I'll remain poor just like before. I've lost all faith" (a very poor housewife, no political presences); "I'm not that bothered about voting, I don't believe in any of the parties" (rural housewife, no political preferences); "I don't understand politics, and I'd rather not vote – I'd leave it up those who know what they're doing to go and vote" (housewife, no political preferences); "they made a mistake giving us women the vote, since most of us don't understand anything about politics" (housewife, no political preferences) (Luzzatto-Fegiz 1956, p. 481).

With regard once again to women's relationship with politics, a survey of almost 1,500 women conducted in 1951 revealed the considerable distance separating women from the world of politics. When asked "Do you believe that women should hold specific political views, and should join a political party?", 52% of respondents stated that "women shouldn't get mixed up in politics", while only 11% thought that women "should hold political views and join a political party". As expected, such views are significantly influenced by the interviewees' level of education: the better educated among them were more in favour of women's political involvement (ibid., p. 339). A few years later in 1964, only 11% of the women interviewed (compared to 29% of the men) were capable of naming the parties sustaining the government majority, while 35% of both men and women failed to name the Prime Minister and the key government ministers (ibid., pp. 488–9).

In the mid-1960s, Italians were thus mobilised in electoral and political party terms but were not very knowledgeable about, or interested in, political affairs, as shown by the fact that 53% of those interviewed declared that they "never" discussed politics (ibid., p. 508). They were poorly informed and generally disinterested but were nevertheless highly critical of politicians. A 1965 survey concerning Members of Parliament's salaries, in fact, reveals considerable hostility towards a possible increase in those salaries, and this hostility remains a cornerstone of the public's criticism of the "privileges" enjoyed by professional politicians. A total of 66% of those interviewed deemed that 500,000 lire (the equivalent of around 5,000 euro in 2022) was an excessively high monthly salary (while 12% did not respond or did not understand the question). Only 3% thought that an increase of 250,000 lire was justified, on the other hand (ibid., p. 518). Despite this clear hostility displayed by Italian citizens, including those of a left-wing persuasion, with regard to the proposed measure, the salary increase was nonetheless approved by the Italian Parliament with a large majority of MPs voting in favour. This represented a clear sign of a rift between the electorate and MPs, which also concerned the related question of party funding eventually regulated in 1974 (Monina 2012). In addition to the politicians themselves, Italy's political parties also came under fire in the late 1950s. In fact, a large majority of citizens (68%) wanted a reduction in the number of political parties (Luzzatto-Fegiz 1956, p. 604).

Another work that throws some light on the opinions held by Italians during the early years of the Republic is the volume by Giovanna Guidorossi (1984), in which the author brings together a number of different sources of information in order to build historical data series. Of particular interest from our point of view is the assessment given of the "worthiness and honesty" and the "capacity and competence" of "the men of government". In the 1960s, just over 30% of interviewees declared that they were fairly or very happy with these aspects of the political class. These values then fell dramatically to around 5% by the mid-1970s, and only the level of satisfaction with the "capacity and competence" of politicians rose again to around 15% in 1980, whereas people's satisfaction with their "worthiness and honesty" remained at the previous levels (ibid., p. 58). The public's feelings of mistrust, scepticism and hostility are also revealed by another study carried out in 1976, according to which around 60% of those interviewed agreed with the statement that "whoever gets to power always tries to further their own personal interests". Moreover, around one half of the sample believed that "in all parties there a few at the top who command, while all the others have no say in matters", while 40% agreed with the idea that "regardless of who wins the election, things will remain just as before" (ibid., p. 71).

From the early 1970s on, large-scale international research programmes have made it possible to regularly monitor Italians' faith in the country's political system and compare it to that of the citizens of other countries, particularly in Europe.[5] In the ranking of citizens' satisfaction with the way democracy works in their respective countries, and of their faith in parliament, government and political parties, Italy has always found itself in the lower positions, together with various East European countries (Martini and Quaranta 2020, p. 92). Finally, in addition to the aforesaid international studies, the Italian National Election Studies (ITANES) research team's subsequent studies have also permitted a more accurate portrayal of Italians' opinions of politics. The findings from such studies confirm Italians' considerable sense of disaffection and political inefficacy. This was already substantial in the late 1950s and has only grown further in the decades thereafter (Segatti 2006, p. 247).

In concluding this brief overview of the political opinions and behaviour of the Italians over the course of the Republic's history, a note should also be made of the fact that, contrary to the stereotypical idea of a golden age of relations between citizens and the world of politics, the degree of interest in politics has risen over the years (Guidorossi 1984, p. 139, Segatti 2007, p. 62), also as a result of the generalised improvements in the population's schooling, which has produced the increased awareness of political affairs that the literature has pointed to (Dalton 1984).

The picture that emerges from the aforementioned data would seem to negate the existence of any such golden age prior to the substantial rift seen in the early 1990s. People's hostility towards, and lack of trust in, professional politicians, political parties and the representative institutions, on the contrary, constitutes a continuous presence in Italian political culture (Donolo 2000, p. 84). This has been further encouraged by the considerable degree of ideological polarisation witnessed in Italy, whereby political adversaries are seen as enemies. This continuous presence has taken a number of different forms. These range from Guglielmo Giannini's coarse, popular critique of politics, and his "Common Man" movement, to the more refined, academic criticisms advanced by intellectuals such as the jurist Giuseppe Maranini, who employed the term "partitocracy" when criticising the politicians and parties of the time. These are two cogent examples of the anti-political positions advanced in Italy during the post-war years, and we shall be examining them more closely in the following two sections. Together with other phenomena, which for reasons of space we cannot examine in detail here, they helped shape a cultural repertoire which Italy's political entrepreneurs were to delve into during the 1990s and 2000s. Such entrepreneurs included, of course, Silvio Berlusconi whose case we shall be examining in the final section of this chapter, together with the other key politicians who shall be dealt with in Chapters 3–5. Anti-political rhetoric and arguments also found fertile terrain among certain sections of Italy's electorate. The final chapter of this book will examine these electors of an anti-political character.

The advent of anti-politics: the Common Man

Post-war Italy was a country in physical, social and political ruin. Italians were exhausted following years of Fascist dictatorship and a war that they had first fought alongside, and then against, Nazi Germany. The country was also geographically divided, with the north and centre having experienced the harrowing experience of an insidious civil war and armed resistance against the Fascist government, while the South had been bombed and occupied early on by the British-American armed forces, and where living conditions remained dramatic and insecure. The winds of storm blew across the country: there was the "northern wind" as the Socialist Party leader Pietro Nenni called it, as well as the "southern wind". In the North, where the end of the war led to the break-up of the old social and political hierarchies, the wind brought progressive change to the State, politics and society. In the South, on the other hand, although there were still large-scale protests, such as those concerning the distribution of land to peasant farmers, the positions taken were more moderate and, in some cases, somewhat reactionary, and the left's promises of a break with the past were looked on with certain diffidence. The clearest, most tangible sign of this geographical, cultural and political divide was the different way people voted in the South compared with the Centre-North, at the institutional referendum held on 2 June 1946. As mentioned in the preceding section, votes in favour of the Monarchy prevailed in the South, whereas in the Centre-North, the majority voted for a Republic.

For the entire period of this complicated political and institutional transition, which was only concluded with the general election held in April 1948, Italians had great expectations for the future. However, these expectations were mixed with a generalised discontent in regard to the political sphere, and in particular to the political parties themselves.[6] This discontent was much stronger in the South than elsewhere. However, it also varied from one part of the South to another, where different cultural and political currents held sway. These included the "Common Man" (*Uomo Qualunque*) movement during the early years of the Italian Republic, which is of particular interest for the purposes of the present study of anti-politics. This movement represented "a combination of myths, ideas, images, prejudices and feelings that express, often symbolically, alienation, diffidence, hostility, contempt, mistrust and disenchantment in regard to the world of politics, and in particular to political parties and government" (Imbriani 1996, pp. 10–1).[7]

The beginnings, the successful years and the period of decline

The Common Man movement (*Qualunquismo*, in Italian) originated and developed from this cultural and idealistic disaffection, and it is thus no surprise to discover that it was particularly strong in the South. In this part of Italy, the movement consisted of an intense form of political and social mobilisation, in which individuals associated with the previous Fascist regime looked for (and sometimes found) refuge as well. The most celebrated actor in this brief, but striking political project, was Guglielmo Giannini, a Neapolitan playwright, journalist and man of theatre. His story is a well-known one, and this is not the right place for a detailed reconstruction of the Common Man movement's meteoric rise to fame.[8] What concerns us here is how these anti-political sentiments, rooted in the interests of a southern Italian conservative petit bourgeoisie, came to gel around the figure of a political entrepreneur, and what actual form they took. Giannini, in fact, reinterpreted and renewed anti-political beliefs, attitudes and behaviour, before re-launching them into the political and cultural world of post-war Republican Italy.[9] As we shall see in the following chapters, this Common Man movement, which certain observers believe to have been the "prototype of contemporary European populism" (Tarchi 2002, p. 121), was to be evoked every time that anti-politics burst onto the Italian political scene.

The creation of the Common Man movement can be dated to December 1944, when the first copy of the weekly *L'Uomo qualunque* was published. The first edition of this weekly sold 80,000 copies, but less than a year later, it was selling some 850,000 copies, thus becoming the best-selling weekly in Italy (Setta 2005, p. 136). This newspaper, the cover of which bore the symbol of a press moved by invisible hands and squeezing a poor man with coins spilling out of his pockets, wanted to denounce the growing power of political parties and of the anti-Fascist block, the privileges of politicians who are only apparently divided, but who are instead collectively intent on harassing Italians who simply wish to be left in peace. The colourful language and the polemical, unconventional arguments of the newspaper and its editor soon made it a benchmark for that southern middle class that "was insensitive, indeed at times hostile, to the values of anti-Fascism and the Resistance movement; it continued to be considerably influenced by the ideas of order and anti-Socialism, within a psychological context full of disdain for politics and politicians. This disdain is an ever-present feature of our national character, but one that emerged strongly after the fall of Fascism, as a result of the serious mistakes made by the anti-Fascist political class" (Setta 2005, pp. XI–XII). The great success that the weekly enjoyed encouraged Giannini to set up a daily paper as well, followed by other periodicals, often of a local nature.

This publishing project reflected and resonated with the wave of popular opinion, which Giannini decided to build a party around. Thus, it was that in August 1945, a few months prior to the elections held on 2 June 1946 to form a Constituent Assembly and choose between the Monarchy and a Republic, the Common Man's Front (*Fronte dell'Uomo qualunque* – FUQ) saw the light of day. After a disappointing showing at the local elections held in the spring of 1946, the FUQ obtained a far from negligible 5.3% of the votes cast at the 2 June election, and in doing so, it won 30 of the 556 seats available in the Constituent Assembly. The votes cast for the FUQ, in reflecting the moderation and conservatism of the southern middle classes, were distributed very unevenly across the nation. In fact, the party gained nearly 10% of votes in the South, while its MPs were almost all of southern, bourgeois origin (ibid., p. 309). At the local elections held in the autumn of that same year, the FUQ further increased its share of votes, becoming the leading party in many areas of southern Italy, and performing well in many towns and cities in the Centre and North as well. However, in the 1948 general election, the FUQ performed much worse, winning only 6 out of a possible 811 seats (in the Chamber of Deputies and the Senate), and this result was effectively to put an end to the adventures of Giannini and his FUQ. This electoral disaster can mainly be accounted for by two factors. The first factor, an internal one, concerned the rifts and in-fighting within the movement that were already apparent following its electoral success in 1946. The second, external factor was the end of the National Liberation Committee, and the formation of a government led by the Christian Democrats and without the support of the left-wing parties, who had been confined to the opposition benches. This government reassured the middle classes, who saw the DC as a new, more solid bulwark against the advance of socialism. Towards the end of 1946 furthermore, the neo-Fascist Italian Social Movement (*Movimento Sociale Italiano* – MSI) was set up, which competed with the FUQ for the right-wing electorate's sympathies. The combination of these two factors thus led to a substantial weakening of the FUQ's electoral potential.

The anti-politics of the Common Man movement

Having briefly examined the social, political and cultural roots of the Common Man movement in Italy, and its fleeting success, we shall now analyse the anti-political nature of its rhetoric and actions, meaning its critical stance vis-à-vis politicians, parties and parliament. Giannini's harshest criticism was of those he termed "upp" – an acronym of the Italian expression "*uomini politici di professione*" meaning "professional political men". According to Giannini, the political class was full of careerists possessing no political qualities or convictions whatsoever, but simply driven by the hunger for power and the desire to enjoy the privileges accompanying parliamentary or governmental office. This privileged class of professional politicians was completely different from "The Crowd",[10] who Giannini argued, in true populist style, were genuinely wise and just but were made to suffer as a result of politicians. He explained this point very clearly in his editorial to the first number of the weekly publication "*L'Uomo qualunque*": "we are witness to the disgraceful spectacle of brazen careerism, of craven ambition, of a ferocious fight for the positions of power enabling such men to do as they like and feather their own nests. This fight, 'Uomo Qualunque' is not going to get involved in, takes place between professionals politicians, people who make a living from politics, who are incapable of doing anything else, and who, for economic reasons, have transformed politics into a career. Career politicians number but a few thousand individuals who hold Italy in their grip, fighting over five hundred seats in the Chamber of Deputies, a similar number of seats in the Senate, around a thousand [other seats]. As a result of the war between these ten thousand men, Italy knows no peace:

millions of Italians have died (...) due to the fact that some of those professionals politicians could become ministers or more. The disproportion
is excessive. On the one hand, there are 45 million human beings. On the
other, 10,000 gossips, pen-pushers, exploiters, bearers of bad luck" (quoted
in: Setta 2005, p. 5).

This profound disdain for, total mistrust of, and explicit hostility towards
professional politicians (whom Giannini either gives nicknames to, or
whose real names he constantly mispronounces) underlie the belief that
they are not fit for office. In fact, the Common Man movement believed
that politics as such were unnecessary, since things would be fine through
administration alone. As the aforesaid editorial states: "We only need to be
administered, and thus what we need are administrators rather than politicians (...). A good accountant would suffice (...) who would take up office on
January 1 and leave on December 31, and would not be re-electable for any
reason". Given that the people are equally wise, and that the administration
of public affairs requires no specific skills, a "good accountant" could be
chosen by lot.[11] If a group of politicians is really necessary, these politicians
should simply control those who actually administer public affairs: "they
shall be chosen by lot and shall always hold office for a limited term, and
given that their power will not offer them the disproportionate advantages
they previously enjoyed, politicians by profession will disappear, together
with the misfortunes of The Crowd; the community's administrators shall
be controlled honest men who return to a form of politics that is no longer a
struggle for power" (ibid., p. 48).

This clear, and at times ferocious, hostility towards politicians inevitably
resulted in an equal aversion to the "places" they frequented. Once they had
been elected as members of the Constituent Assembly, Giannini and his MPs
sought to ridicule the forms and rituals of parliamentary politics. For example, he threatened to sing a popular Neapolitan ballad in parliament if the
left-wing benches tried to sing "The Internationale" (ibid., p. 229). However,
the FUQ not only targeted the representative assembly, and indeed perhaps
its most damning criticism was reserved for the political parties themselves,
which it considered worthless, expensive organisational machines, as well
as the artificial ideological container that allowed politicians to prosper.
This deliberate anti-party stance also resulted in Giannini's extremely pragmatic, anti-ideological character. As far as he was concerned, there was no
left or right. Nor was there any appreciable difference between Fascism and
anti-Fascism, both of which he considered his enemies (ibid., p. 59). This
led him to performing a series of political contortions, from moderate and
reactionary positions centred on his virulent anti-communism to a kind of
"superficial liberalism" (Zanone 2002, p. 33), and even to a dialogue with
the PCI and its leader Togliatti. Giannini rather naively believed that this
dialogue with Togliatti represented the key to gaining governmental positions, whereas Togliatti thought that this opening up by a self-declared
anti-communist force could help the PCI get out of the corner it was stuck in

following the end of the phase of national unity. However, this blatant political U-turn led to rifts appearing within the FUQ itself, and to its founder, Giannini, being openly contested from within the party.

The political differences within the FUQ were not the only problems that Giannini had to deal with. In fact, he "was increasingly forced to admit the incredible naivety of his faith in the total lack of vested interests of the FUQ's political amateurs: rivalries and personal ambition, together with careerism and the consequent struggle for power within the party, were constantly on the increase, both at central level and locally, in many cases exacerbated by the very limited human qualities of men sharing their substantial disengagement from ideological values (…). It was not long before the leader of a movement whose leitmotif had been its battle against political professionalism, had to bitterly confess that 'the most serious risk is within, and not outside of ourselves, [and it is] political professionalism'" (Setta 2005, p. 165). In order to avoid the disintegration of his political creation, he thus tried to gain control over it, "through the top-down supervision of local nominations and developments, by sending out inspectors, and by referring any members disobeying 'higher orders' to disciplinary boards. At the same time, the Front reorganised its own offices, increasing the number of powers thereof, and introduced a full membership system, and as a result of this it had over 100 office staff in Rome alone" (ibid.), that is, party officials who only a short time before the leader of the party had considered a mere window dressing, and the cause of all ills.

The confused political position of the party, its internal rifts, the very same conflicts that characterised all other parties, and as mentioned, the changing political scenario in which the DC had become the real, solid bulwark against the socialist and communist threat was to destroy the political experience of the FUQ, now destined for political and cultural irrelevance. Thus, within the space of a couple of years, the clear genetic paradox of the FUQ had led to the day of reckoning for its founder. The anti-party party hc had created was a party just like the others, and he himself, from being a fierce opponent of political careerism, had become a professional politician himself, and like all career politicians, Giannini had to take account of the fragility of his own position. The Common Man project came to an end shortly thereafter. As early as 1948, nearly all of its 30 members of the Constituent Assembly had left politics (ibid., p. 309). After a number of clumsy, humiliating attempts to preserve his political presence, Giannini was forced to abandon politics altogether.

Against partitocracy

During the early years of the Italian Republic, criticism of political parties and "professional political men" was not only expressed in the colourful, rough forms described in the previous section with regard to Giannini and his Common Man movement. In fact, there were many critics of the new regime and the dominance of the political parties that, following the fall of Fascism, monopolised the political scene within the new democracy (Imbriani 1996, Capozzi 2009). The reasons for the political dominance of the parties were of a political and institutional nature. During that period in history, in fact, Italy was busy creating and building a new form of State following the demise of the Monarchy and of the Fascist, one-party regime. Nevertheless, the central role of the parties also had deep social and psychological historical roots in the Italians' collective experience during the 20 years of Fascist rule, when the one (Fascist) party overlapped the State, and membership of that party was a necessary requisite for inclusion in the social and working life of the country. In other words, during the immediate post-war years, the experience of the one-party system had bequeathed a certain image of the political party's role in society, and as has been pointed out, "people had become accustomed to the idea that a political party should play a role that went beyond the purely political debate of ideas, and instead extend to more mundane aspects of day-to-day life, essentially working as a subsidiary to the state" (Cotta 2015, p. 45). In the view of many critics, party pluralism was a mere facade concealing the basic continuity with the excessive power exercised by the Fascist regime's one-party system (Capozzi 2009, p. 45).

One of the most authoritative critics of the pervasive role of political parties and the professional politicians leading those parties was Giuseppe Maranini, Dean of Florence University's Political Science Faculty from 1949 to 1968. His criticism can be summed up by the term "partitocracy"[12] used in the title of his opening address at the start of the academic year 1949–50. In order to fully understand Maranini's place in the debate on-going at that time, account should be taken of the two roles he played: on the one hand, he was a constitutional expert and political scientist heading a Political Science Faculty, while on the other he worked as a columnist for several popular dailies. In his role as an academic, Maranini returned to certain criticisms of political parties previously made by Carl Schmitt and offered an analysis of partitocracy, which he described as a regime in which political parties, and in particular their leaders, divest the State of its sovereignty. He saw the power of the parties – which colonise the institutions and increasingly control society and the economy – as a genuine threat to the State's democracy and the proper operation of the nation's institutions, thus nullifying, for example, the constitutional principle banning imperative mandates. "Our constitution" – Maranini wrote in 1952 – "for bids any form of imperative mandate binding the elected representative to the electors' wishes; however, at the same time, the constitution and electoral law create the strict premises of a much more fearful imperative mandate subordinating the elected representatives to their true principals, who are no longer the electors but are now the parties' leaders" (Maranini 1958, p. 204). If we now move on from the formal to the substantive level, the partitocracy that Maranini criticizes also does away with that key underlying principle of any democracy constituted by the separation of powers. "Parliament controls the government, but the parties' leaders control parliament, and through parliament, the government itself. Consequently, if the party leadership and the leadership of the government are one and the same, the controlled party becomes the controller, resulting in the subversion of any parliamentary government" (ibid. p. 205).

Foreseeing some of the questions that were to be dealt with in the criticism of the "degenerated consociationalism" *(consociativismo)*,[13] characteristic of Italian democracy (Bogaards 2005), and which are also to be found in the analysis of the cartelisation of the party system (Katz and Mair 1995), Maranini criticised the collusive practice of sharing out positions of power and government among parties *(lottizzazione)*. He argued that the underlying causes of partitocracy's development included, first and foremost, the proportional representation law, which he claimed to render elected representatives dominated by their respective parties: "the proportional system is the ideal way of establishing the tyranny of the party apparatus, and of lowering the intellectual, moral and political standards of representation" (Maranini 1963, p. 89). Furthermore: "Proportional representation makes it very difficult, indeed impossible as a rule, for the electorate to form and express its will in the only democratic manner, that is, as the will of the majority. It only offers the electorate the opportunity to issue carte blanche to uncontrolled and uncontrollable political clans" (Maranini 1958, p. 425). A second target of criticism is the lack of internal regulation within parties (ibid., pp. 250–3). This is why Maranini was to insist, both as an academic and as a newspaper columnist, on the need for certain reforms. The first such reform was the introduction of an electoral law establishing a majoritarian system accompanied by constituency primaries, along American lines, in an attempt to strengthen the direct relationship between the electorate and the elected and reduce the intermediary powers of the parties. The second key reform he proposed concerned the parties themselves, which were regulated in a very elusive, unclear manner by the 1948 Constitution, and which Maranini believed needed to be governed in a similar way to that provided for by Germany's Basic Law.

The excessive power of the parties denounced and described by Maranini was not however something exclusive to Italy. In fact, political and social life was monopolised by parties in a number of other European democracies, and the term "partitocracy" became commonly used in other nations and languages (Caciagli 2004, p. 244).[14] As well as spreading through the European political sphere, the term continued to be employed in Italy for many years afterwards, although its significance gradually changed from that originally given to the term by Maranini. In addition to being one of the watchwords of Italy's Radical Party, which employed the term in pushing through a series of referenda, such as those for the abolishment of the public funding of political parties (1978 and 1993) (Capozzi 2020, p. 16), the word "partitocracy" was to accompany the process of political

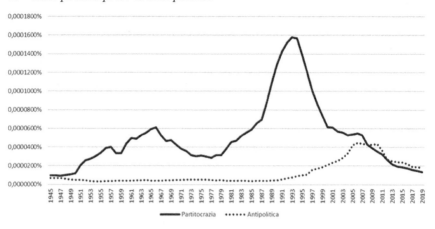

Figure 2.1 Diffusion of the terms "partitocracy" and "anti-politics"

Source: The author's processing of data using Google Books.

transition in the 1990s. In truth, as Figure 2.1 shows, the term began to be used in the 1980s, when criticism of the parties' taking over of the State intensified and became more explicit. However, it was during the three-year period from 1992 to 1994 that witnessed the fragmentation of the existing Italian party system, that the use of the term in public debate reached its peak.

While the term itself has remained unaltered, its meaning has changed considerably from Maranini's time. "Partitocracy" no longer has any analytical value but merely indicates the political class' malpractices, the parties' degeneration, profiteering and widespread corruption. Political parties and professional politicians are portrayed as a cancer on democracy, and this cancer must be eliminated through a new political undertaking on the part of civil society, and by using the constitutional device of the popular referendum, to curb the power of those politicians at the head of the nation's political parties. As we shall see in the following section, the "anti-party" or "anti-partitocracy" referenda held in 1993 put an end to the proportional electoral system, which was replaced by a mainly majoritarian system based on single-member constituencies. In doing so, they in fact adopted the idea already proposed by Maranini at the end of the 1940s. These same referenda also eliminated public funding of political parties, succeeding this time round where the 1978 referendum had failed. The "great avalanche" (Cafagna 1993) witnessed in the early 1990s was not, therefore, a totally unforeseeable event, insofar as it reflected a series of institutional issues, instruments and solutions that had already emerged in previous decades. As one scholar has pointed out, "when anti-partyism vigorously erupted in the late 1980s, it was as if it had been smouldering under the ashes for decades" (Ragazzoni 2020, p. 100).

The new bipolar nature of the Italian political system, established in 1996, characterised by an exacerbated centre-left/centre-right divide, resulted in the mitigation of criticism of partitocracy seen as an alliance of political parties against the interests of the citizens they are supposed to represent. However, criticism of professional politicians, political parties and representative institutions persisted. This sentiment can be better described as "anti-politics", which, as Figure 2.1 shows, grew rapidly from the mid-1990s onwards and, some ten years later, was more widely employed than the term "partitocracy".

The anti-politics of civil society

The hostility towards political parties and professional politicians, which had characterised Italian political life in a rather insidious, creeping manner at least as far back as the foundation of the Republic, exploded in the early 1990s. As is widely acknowledged, Italian politics was rocked by a judicial whirlwind at the beginning of 1992, which was to blow the lid off the widespread corrupt practices and illegal funding of political parties on-going at the time. The exposure of these bribery scandals became known as "Tangentopoli", and this marked the most significant turning point in the history of the Italian Republic. Indeed, it was seen as a moment of transition from a First to a Second Republic. It is for this very reason that the period from 1992 to 1994 is probably the one that has garnered the greatest interest from observers and scholars, both in Italy and abroad.[15] For the purposes of the present volume's analysis, nevertheless, we ought to briefly examine certain aspects of the socio-political crisis that struck Italy in the early 1990s, and the outcome of that exceptional period in terms of both political culture and anti-political practices.

The de-structuring of the Italian party system in the early 1990s can be accounted for by a series of different factors. The most important of these was the fall of the Berlin Wall, which resulted in the radical transformation of the main opposition party, the PCI. The end of ideological opposition also weakened the anti-communist leverage of the Christian Democrats and Italy's other moderate parties. Before the collapse of the Berlin Wall and the impact this had on the party system, Italy's political parties were already the subject of criticism for their occupation of the State and society as a whole. As Mastropaolo pointed out: "For almost a quarter of century, condemnation of politics' vices, and the appeal to popular sovereignty, constituted the leitmotiv of national political life (...). This resulted in a furious, anti-political atmosphere which was perhaps the principal driver of the earthquake that shook Italy's political system to the core between 1992 and 1994" (2005, p. 164). In fact, if we look at Figure 2.1 again, we see that use of the term "partitocracy" began to increase in early 1980; and it peaked in 1989, that is, prior to the unexpected fall of the Berlin Wall.

With regard to anti-politics from below, that is, the anti-political feelings of the nation's citizens, one interesting aspect of the whole Tangentopoli bribery scandal concerns the "sharing" of blame among the various social, economic and political actors involved in the investigations. As previously mentioned, the bribery system discovered by the courts involved not only politicians but also businessmen, freelance professionals, public officers, police chiefs, judges and others. Despite this, it was the politicians who paid the highest price for their involvement, also because, as Donatella della Porta and Alberto Vannucci pointed out in regard to Tangentopoli, "When a political scandal emerges, usually mass media and public opinion are ready to stigmatize corrupt politicians' behaviour, while the participation of entrepreneurs or other corrupters in the illegal transaction often remains within the shadows" (della Porta and Vannucci 1999, p. 179). Politics becomes the scapegoat (Tarchi 2015, p. 236) for this system of corruption, of which politicians are just one piece, albeit a very important one. During the Tangentopoli period, Italians became convinced that the responsibility for the country's problems lay first and foremost with the politicians, even when such problems were clearly beyond their scope (Achen and Bartels 2016, ch. 5).

The demonising of politicians (Flinders 2012b) and the belief that politicians were scapegoats for the country's problems were driven and rendered convincing by a rather new phenomenon within Italian society, namely the establishment of a TV that Umberto Eco had already labelled, in the early 1980s, as "neo-television".[16] Certain talk shows brought "ordinary people" into the TV studios, or interviewed them in the street, offering them the opportunity to voice their disdain for, and criticism of, politicians, who had been heavily accused during the bribery scandal. Politicians are regularly exposed to a TV public, denigrated by "ordinary people" interviewed on TV shows, humiliated live on TV when they mumble their replies in courtrooms. In short, they are subjected to "ritual degradation" (Giglioli 2001) which permanently changes their public image. One of the most successful programmes of that time – "*Il rosso e il nero*" (the Red and the Black) – conducted by Michele Santoro, has been described as follows: "A grand electronic square (...) becomes a large window on the corruption within a ghost nation, with politicians awkwardly defending themselves against accusations of misdoings (...). An electronic survey of 800 people representing the whole of Italy, hands down its ruling and smoothens out any differences" (Grasso 2019, p. 904). In short, this new way of providing news, together with the actions of the magistrates, opened the way, also in Italy, for a "monitory democracy" (Keane 2009) that Flinders sees as a threat to democracy, and one of the sources of anti-politics (Flinders 2012a, ch. 2). The mass media helped create a simplified, highly newsworthy opposition between honest magistrates and corrupt politicians: "the magistrates were portrayed as members and representatives of the people, as 'the true defenders of decent people' (...). Politicians, on the contrary, were represented as an arrogant caste, dishonest and incapable, isolated from and mistrusted by the people. The press pointed out that many of them had entered public life for the sole purpose of enriching themselves, that they considered themselves to be above the law and were trying in every way to evade responsibility for the offences they had committed. Gradually, in the press accounts, the responsibility for corruption shifted from individual politicians to the political class as a whole" (Giglioli 1996, pp. 388–9). Tangentopoli thus became the fault line that was to severely impact the extremely poor esteem in which Italians held their politicians and political parties.

This incessant criticism via the media had the effect of condemning everything associated with political parties, professional politicians, political representation and politicians' language, without any real right of rejoinder, and led to the exaltation of a new political actor: civil society itself.[17] The nomination of civil society as a key player in the country's political future embraced a number of questions that had already been at the heart of the Common Man movement's critique. These included the natural goodness of "the people", uncontaminated by politics and not corrupted by the struggle for power. Hence, the eulogising of political amateurism (Tarchi 2015, p. 281) overlaps to a degree with Giannini's criticism of professional politicians and his idea of the "good accountant" – chosen by lot and appointed on a temporary basis from outside of the political sphere – is to be entrusted with the administration of public affairs. This represents a new divide, separating the honest from the dishonest, which overshadows the classical political division between left and right. This is yet another feature that harks back to the Common Man movement: this celebration of the virtues of civil society, and hostility towards parties and politicians, ultimately led to Italy being governed by "technical" governments in 1992 and 1993, which guided the country towards the first election of the so-called Second Republic in March 1994. The first Prime Minister was Giuliano Amato, an intellectual and university professor from the ranks of the Socialist Party, with a long political career behind him but nevertheless considered one of the few presentable figures from the First Republic. Amato was subsequently replaced by Carlo Azeglio Ciampi, at the time Governor of the Bank of Italy (a considerable step up from the "good accountant"). Ciampi was to be the first non-parliamentary Prime Minister in the history of the Italian Republic, and he was subsequently elected Italy's President.

The anti-political referenda

So it is clear that during the 1990s, certain themes emerged that had already been present in political debate during the preceding decades. These themes were adapted to the new social and political context and then forcibly launched into the public arena. As we shall see in the chapters to follow, certain aspects of this anti-political narrative were embraced by other political actors who were to take advantage of the public malcontent in order to target political office, and then once in government to remain in power and to get their own political policies adopted more easily. In the short term, civil society's revolt against the world of politics, as it was portrayed during that period, produced a radical change in the political system and the institutional framework of the time. It did so through the massive, "creative" use of referenda. While the Italian Constitution provides for the use of the referendum exclusively as a means of abrogating existing legislation, and not for making legislative proposals, certain progressive, pro-civil society intellectuals, together with individual representatives of the old political class who had distanced themselves from their own parties, formulated referendum questions in such a way that the referenda ultimately proposed, rather than simply abrogating, legislation. In a climate of open hostility towards political parties and politicians charged by the courts with corruption, and given the profound crisis deriving from the Mafia massacres of 1992–3, the aforementioned coalition of actors managed to get the electorate to vote in referenda on a series of issues (Newell and Bull 1993) of a clearly "anti-partitocratic" nature (Barbera and Morrone 2003, p. 120).[18] In fact, as Lupo pointed out: "the term 'referendum', in Italian political language, means an appeal to the people against the parties" (2000, p. 25). The early 1990s referenda marked the beginning of a period that Giovanni Sartori has defined as one of "*direttismo*", that is, a series of practices designed to "bypass parties, circumventing their ineffective intermediation so as to impact public affairs directly" (Calise 2010, p. 30).[19]

There were two clearly anti-political, anti-party referenda in particular. The first of these regarded the abolition of the public funding of political parties. This time round, unlike at the first attempt in 1978, the electorate was not split between those for and those against; in fact, with massive popular support, the referendum abolished what was seen as an unjustifiable privilege enjoyed by political parties and politicians as a class.[20] The target of the second referendum was the existing proportional system for the election of MPs (for technical reasons, the question referred exclusively to the Upper House – the Senate – and not the Chamber of Deputies) (Corbetta and Parisi 1995). This system had already been considered in Maranini's days as one of the main causes of partitocracy and the degeneration of the political class. With its backs to the wall as a result of the outcome of the referendum, the political class made the best of a bad job and in August 1993 introduced a new, prevalently majoritarian, electoral law: 75% of all seats were to be assigned following elections in single-member constituencies, while the remaining 25% of seats were to be assigned on a proportional basis (Katz 2001). In trying to remedy matters, and under pressure from the wave of anti-political feelings, the political class had already introduced, in March of that same year prior to the series of referenda held in April, a reform of the electoral system for the direct election of mayors. This electoral reform was one of a "bundle of reforms" (Bedock 2017) introduced in 1993, which may be classified, according to the distinction made by Alan Renwick (2010), in the "elite–mass interaction" category rather than in the "elite majority imposed" category (Baldini 2011).[21] Furthermore, the electoral law governing municipal elections also embraced the majoritarian principle and renounced the proportional one, through the direct election of mayors and provincial presidents (Baldini 2002). In other words, this was now an electoral system which, in keeping with a trend spreading throughout Europe (Renwick and Pilet 2016), aimed to put citizens to the fore, encouraging the personalisation of local politics (Freschi and Mete 2020) while removing the despised parties from the scene.[22]

The two-year period 1992–3 ended with the disappearance from the political scene of the traditional parties embroiled in the Tangentopoli bribery scandal. The ensuing crisis offered a huge opportunity for the emergence of new parties and political figures untainted by any involvement in the system of corruption uncovered by Italy's magistrates. These new actors all chose to play the "anti-politics" hand, and consequently the political and cultural tradition of criticising political parties and professional politicians had in fact survived. However, anti-politics alone cannot suffice to guarantee success. Some of the leading players in this period of political reform, such as Mario Segni, wasted their political credit thereafter and quickly disappeared from the political scene altogether. Others, such as the anti-party "*La Rete*" (The Network), seemed destined for success but instead were short lived (Foot 1996). Others again, such as the famous businessman who turned his hand to politics, Silvio Berlusconi, and his "media-mediated personality party" Forza Italia, as well as the head of the Northern League, Umberto Bossi, managed to become the new leaders of the political scene in Italy.

Silvio Berlusconi, the anti-politics politician governs the country

The 1992–3 period, which was characterised by substantial scandals involving a large section of the political class, saw the break-up of the party system that had been in place in Italy since the end of the Second World War. This represented a wonderful opportunity for new political actors to emerge, and for the re-assessment of those figures and parties like the heirs of the neo-Fascist right, who up until then had been relegated to the margins of political life. This window of opportunity opened not only as a result of the judicial proceedings leading to the elimination of a political class accused of corruption but also because the expectation of radical change hovered over Italian society. Given the situation, only an outsider could step forward and offer himself as a credible leader, capable of guiding the nation out of the political crisis it found itself in, an outsider who was not only far removed from politics, but also, where possible, against politics. That is, a person capable of embracing and taking advantage of those anti-political feelings traditionally present in Italy's political culture, and which following Tangentopoli had come to dominate. That person, as we all know, was embodied by Silvio Berlusconi.

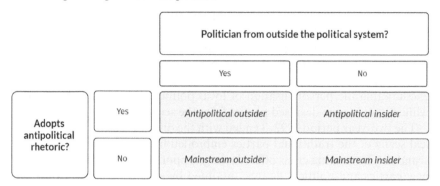

Figure 2.2 A typology of political actors based on their position as outsiders or
        insiders, and their use, or otherwise, of anti-political rhetoric

Source: The author's adaptation of Kenney (1998, p. 60).

Before analysing the events that he was a leading actor in, we should spec-
ify in what way Berlusconi can be considered a political outsider. Going
back to certain ideas and conceptual distinctions originally set out by
Charles Kenney (1998), and later discussed also by Robert Barr (2009), we
can formulate a typology (see Figure 2.2) of political actors on the basis of
their status as outsiders/insiders and their anti-political/mainstream rhetoric. The first dimension thus concerns their relationship with parties and the
party system, and it distinguishes those political success deriving from their
membership of an established party (the insiders), or from their belonging
to a sphere other than that of politics, to a little relevant party within the
party system (the outsiders). The second dimension concerns their use, or
otherwise, of anti-political and anti-establishment rhetoric. The proposed
typology thus produces four diverse types of politician. The first type, who
we may call the "anti-political outsider", is extraneous to the party system
and adopts attitudes and behaviour critical of the main symbols of politics, namely professional politicians, political parties and the institutions
of political representation. It goes without saying that Silvio Berlusconi is
this type of politician. The second type – the "anti-political insider" – on
the other hand is a combination of anti-political attitudes and behaviour
and membership of an established political party. Then there is the type of
politician who is from outside the party system but who does not employ
anti-political rhetoric – the "mainstream outsider". Then there is the fourth
type, who is referred to here as the "mainstream insider", as he/she comes
from the political sphere and from a political party but does not adopt
anti-political attitudes and behaviour.

Having perfected the analytical instrument, which will be useful when
examining other political leaders in the forthcoming chapters, let us now
see how Berlusconi, as an anti-political outsider, got into politics and the
use he made, and makes, of anti-political rhetoric. In January 1994, two and

a half months prior to the general election, Silvio Berlusconi, a successful businessman, the owner of three major TV channels and the chairman of one of Italy's most famous football clubs, announced that he was going into politics and intended to establish a new political party. Berlusconi's political rise and that of his new party, Forza Italia, is a well-known one.[23] What we would like to focus on here, on the other hand, is Berlusconi's role in revitalising certain anti-political themes that had already emerged in preceding decades, and in introducing other new such themes which, in turn, were to be embraced by other political actors. The interesting and innovative aspect of the figure of Berlusconi is that he employed anti-political rhetoric not only when among the opposition ranks, in order to gain political visibility, but also when in government, that is, when leader of the largest Italian political party of the time and the country's Prime Minister.

As several observers have noted, despite having succeeded in an unprecedented political undertaking, Berlusconi did not actually invent anything of a truly novel nature. He simply introduced into the Italian political system certain political marketing methods and strategies already employed elsewhere, particularly in the USA. Since the emergence of Berlusconi the politician, the personalisation and popularisation of politics,[24] together with the intensive use of opinion polls, have become permanent features of Italian politics. Hence, there has been no real invention, but simply a strong degree of political and cultural innovation. The most important aspect of this innovation has been the nature of Berlusconi's own political party, Forza Italia. Despite its embracing certain political figures and local groups associated with the old traditional parties, it did not come about either through the federation of existing local organisations, or as a result of a parliamentary split. If we follow Angelo Panebianco's classical analysis of the way in which political parties are formed, Forza Italia can be considered a party that was established and developed via territorial expansion, that is, as a result of a central impulse outwards towards the periphery. In this particular case, the party's external legitimisation was provided by Berlusconi's private undertakings; it was the result of a private initiative on the part of its founder and leader, whose destiny has been strictly correlated to that of his party, as is commonly the case with parties built around a charismatic leader (Panebianco 1988b, p. 67). This thus marked the emergence of the "personal party", of which Forza Italia is considered to be an "ideal type" (Calise 2015, p. 306). This phenomenon was part of a broader trend involving the strengthening of governments and their leaders (Poguntke and Webb 2005), which was to become a conspicuous part of Italian political life thereafter. The success of Berlusconi and his Forza Italia party, which partly followed the example set by Bossi and the Northern League, as we shall see in the following chapter, marked the transition from partitocracy to the dominance of personal parties (Venturino 2010).

While these were the forms of political innovation introduced by Berlusconi, let us now examine the changes witnessed in terms of anti-politics, considered by many to be "the trademark" of his leadership

(Campus 2010, p. 98). Once again, not all manifestations of Berlusconi's anti-politics are novel. Many of them can be considered a reworking of various forms already present and rooted in Italian politics, as mentioned in the preceding sections of this chapter. By treating politics as a marketplace, political leaders as entrepreneurs, parties as business undertakings and the electors as consumers, anti-politics can be considered a good in Berlusconi's view: a good that is in considerable demand, given the significant hostility towards politicians rekindled by the scandals of 1992–3. The surveys that Berlusconi commissioned one of his opinion poll companies to conduct prior to his entering the fray gave him to understand that "the keys to electoral success lay in novelty and in antipolitics" (Campus 2010, p. 95). Coming from the private corporate sphere enabled him to offer himself as a credible outsider leader (King 2002). In order to achieve success, he needed to add anti-political speeches, actions and attitudes, and these were to make him "the knight of anti-politics" (Pasquino 2007). He proved so successful in doing so that, for many years, he occupied the political space of the centre-right that had been left empty following the break-up of the Christian Democrats and the other moderate parties in the early 1990s.

Berlusconi's anti-politics are mixed with a series of other populist arguments and discursive elements already used by other anti-political political actors. One key term often used by Berlusconi, which can be seen as another good he offers the electoral market, is "freedom". "The Freedom Alliance" (*Polo della Libertà*) is the name that was given to the 1994 electoral alliance with the Northern League; "The People of Freedom", on the other hand, is the name given to the political party which saw Forza Italia allied with the National Alliance (*Alleanza Nazionale – AN*), a right-wing party heir to the former neo-Fascist Italian Social Movement (*Movimento Sociale Italiano – MSI*). In reproducing the line adopted by Giannini and the FUQ, who had been driven by their "total anti-statism" (Setta 2005, p. 99), Berlusconi also incorporated a number of arguments that had been characteristic of Thatcherism. These saw "freedom" as a form of intolerance towards the State, which in Berlusconi's view hinders economic enterprise, burdens workers with taxes, imposes absurd rules on citizens and generates a stifling bureaucracy. The clear aversion to the State and the public sector is combined with an insistence on the threat of communism. Despite the fact that Berlusconi entered politics four years after the fall of the Berlin Wall, anti-communism is another good that is widely appreciated and requested in the Italian electoral market, and Berlusconi, as a marketing expert, knew this well and thus took full advantage of the fact (Brusattin 2007). He believed that the threat to the freedom of the Italian people was represented by the "communists", that is, those left-wing politicians who had come through the Tangentopoli scandal unscathed. He mixed his anti-statism and anti-communism with a good dose of anti-politics as well, and these were the elements that enabled him to construct an internal enemy against whom Berlusconi could direct his arguments and actions.

Berlusconi's anti-politics consists of all three specific forms identified in Chapter 1: anti-partyism, anti-politicians and anti-establishment. His anti-partyism is already clear from the choice of name for his new party: "Forza Italia" is the cry of fans of the national football team, and certainly not an expression that brings to mind the world of politics. The local offices of Forza Italia are not the traditional branches of which Italy's historical parties are composed but take the form of "clubs". This same term is used both in the footballing world and in the sphere of associations such as the Rotary Club or the Lions Club. The elected representatives and leaders of Forza Italia are referred to as the "*azzurri*" (the blues), and the same name attributed to the players on the national football team, whose shirt is in fact blue. Those individuals who participate in the party's activities are not "members" or "militants", but "associates" like those in a joint-stock company or a sports association. While it may be true that the Northern League had already chosen a name with no reference to politics, it was not until the emergence of Forza Italia that this practice became the norm in Italian politics – with the significant exception of the Democratic Party, which was not set up until 2007 however. Furthermore, Berlusconi insisted on referring to Forza Italia as a "movement" rather than a "party".

In criticising parties, Berlusconi often employed the term "partitocracy" the use of which, as Figure 2.1 shows, peaked in the same 1990s. Its meaning in those years, however, was clearly disparaging and differed slightly from what Maranini's intended by the word. Berlusconi, in criticising an unspecified "establishment", chose to employ the expression "the petty theatre of politics". In his view, politicians, unlike those who actually work and help the country to grow, spend all their time in this "theatre", swapping roles and pretending to do something about the country's problems. Politics, according to Berlusconi, is not a job. He constantly criticised professional politicians for never having really worked all their lives (Campus 2010, p. 101), and who were thus not suited to governing the country or administering anything at all. Berlusconi's argument was that politics had to be a temporary undertaking; indeed, he continually referred to his involvement, even 20 years after he had gone into politics, as that of a businessman temporarily occupying himself with politics.[25] This idea that a person's involvement in politics had to be for a specific period of time only is not far removed from the term of office that Giannini had envisaged for the "good accountant", who was to be given the task, for one year only, of administering the country's affairs.

Berlusconi's anti-politics also targeted parliament and the traditional, liberal concept of political representation, consisting of a series of checks and balances, and of the majority-opposition dialectic. In fact, he argued for a plebiscitary democracy, whereby those elected by the people cannot be subjected to limitations on the part of other State powers that have not been similarly elected, in particular the judiciary.[26]

The rhetoric of anti-politics thus served Berlusconi, during the first phase of his political experience, to gain leadership of the country in the space of just two months, and to build the most voted Italian party starting literally from scratch. His blend of anti-politics, anticommunism and anti-establishment views convinced a great many voters, in 1994, to go to the polls and vote for his political creation. Once he got into power, furthermore, Berlusconi continued to play the outsider and ramp up his anti-political rhetoric, taking full advantage of the channels of communication available to him. While an anti-political stance when among the opposition ranks serves to gain political power, once in government that same anti-politics serves to keep people on board with your leadership and political actions, even when this runs contrary to the position of your own political party, your political allies and parliament in general. Once again, as Campus (2010) has pointed out, Berlusconi was not the inventor of this practice of "going public" (Kernell 1986), but he simply adopted it from other political leaders who had used it in other historical and political contexts. Anti-political and anti-establishment political communication, mainly through the use of TV (and more recently of social networks), is thus transformed from an "electoral arena to a governmental arena" (Campus 2010, p. 42).

Ultimately, with the appearance on the political scene of Silvio Berlusconi, politics took on what Alessandro Pizzorno has called a "consumeristic style of politics": "appearing as often as possible in public – not to communicate anything, but simply to be seen. And therefore: not communicating with the public in order to urge people to pursue certain political goals, but rather showing you are pursuing political aims in order to appear in public. Political power essentially manifests itself as the *power of appearance*. Because often, appearance is, for those in politics, the only method of recognition left" (Pizzorno 1993, p. 313 – the italics are from the Italian original). From this point of view, given the deeply rooted, persistent diffidence and hostility towards politics traditionally displayed by Italians, their criticism of parties and politicians is always a good opportunity to appear before the public and preserve one's dominance of media coverage and the political scene as a whole. This is one thing that Berlusconi is a master at, and as we shall see, his teachings were to find fertile ground, with a series of highly capable and highly motivated pupils following in his footsteps.

Notes

1 As in other democracies (Holmberg and Oscarsson 2020, p. 16), the level of party identification seems to have remained stable in Italy as well, or indeed has even risen slightly, in recent years.

2 In the 1950s, for every 1,000 electors, there were 139 party members, whereas this figure was 100 in the United Kingdom, 75 in France and only 29 in Germany. Italy maintained high levels of party membership right through the 1960s (127 per 1,000) and the 1970s (128 per 1,000): it only began to decline in the 1980s (97) and 1990s (91), before collapsing to 41 in 2000, and subsequently recovering slightly to 58 in 2008 (Scarrow 2015, p. 97). Luciano Bardi and Leonardo Morlino (1992, 1994) offer a highly detailed, well-documented

portrait of Italy's political parties and their respective organisation during the period between the end of the Second World War and the early 1990s.

3 Colin Hay comes to a similar conclusion in his influential work, when he states that: "The point is that in making such arguments we do not have to rely upon the nostalgic construction of a mythical past of near total participation and near perfect democratic political legitimacy. Such a world never existed, politics has always had its detractors, and there have been other times when disdain and cynicism for politics have proved dominant (...). Similarly, we would be wrong to assume that the predominantly negative associations and connotations of politics today are unprecedented historically. Politics has been seen as the problem rather than the solution at various historical junctures" (2007, pp. 6–7).

4 The question, submitted to a sample of 2,305 adult Italians, was formulated as follows: "in every election, a share of those entitled to vote decide not to vote. What do you think will be the main reasons people do not vote at the next election?". A total of 36% replied, in fact, that the main reason was their "complete lack of interest in politics"; 21% said it would be due to "their own illness or that of a family member"; 20% thought it would be for "fear (of violence, retaliation, etc.) and little trust in the secrecy of voting"; the remaining respondents gave a series of other reasons stopping people from voting. It is interesting to note that abstention due to disinterest is more common in the North (39%) and Centre (37%) than in the South (26%). This reason is also much more commonly cited in Sicily and Sardinia (45%) (Luzzatto-Fegiz 1956, pp. 474–5).

5 Philippe Aldrin (2010) offers an interesting, well-documented reconstruction of the advent of the Eurobarometer project, designed to monitor people's opinions in the member states of the European Economic Community (subsequently the European Union), and highlights the political significance of that project. Alfio Mastropaolo (2009), on the other hand, offers an account of the American studies of Italy conducted from the post-war period onwards and reflects on the impact such studies have had on the academic world and on public debate within Italy.

6 For an overview of the various actors concerned, and of the diverse forms of hostility displayed towards political parties following the fall of Fascism, see the works of Matteo Truffelli (2003, 2007).

7 The other three are "Southern Revendication", that is, strong opposition to the North of the nation; "popular legitimism" expressing support for the Monarchy; and "anti-communism", which expresses concern over, and hostility towards, the space gained by the left at that time in history (Imbriani 1996, p. 11).

8 There are quite a few historical analyses of the Common Man movement in Italian. These include the following studies: Sandro Setta (2005), Maurizio Cocco (2018a), and the political science work by Marco Tarchi (2015). Understandably, there are fewer such studies written in English. These include the following: Corduwener (2017), Cocco (2018b) and Gambarota (2019).

9 On this matter, Setta wrote: "This Common Man movement – the 'old anti-politics nonsense' as Salvatorelli came to call it – was certainly not invented by Giannini: being a man of theatre, he had noticed its increasing emergence as a state of mind throughout the country, and had tried to raise it to the status of political philosophy" (2005, p. 49). In addition to the deep-rootedness of the Common Man movement, another important factor was the influence on the thought and stance of Giannini exercised by wartime propaganda and English and American popular culture, including that conveyed through film and radio (Gambarota 2019).

10 "La Folla. Seimila anni di lotta contro la tirannide" (The Crowd. Six Thousand Years of Struggle Against Tyranny) is the title that Giannini had chosen for his book, written between September 1943 and June 1944, which summarised his view of the world and of politics. The book was not published until 1945, while an abridged version has recently been re-published (Giannini 2002).

11 The idea of a lottery as a guarantee of impartiality, and a means by which to prevent the existence of professional politicians, was of course not a new one. For a historical and theoretical overview, see the volume edited by Liliane Lopez-Rabatel and Yves Sintomer (2020). As we shall see later on, this idea has also been embraced more recently by the Five Star Movement (see the third section in Chapter 5) and the participatory practices aimed at greater citizen involvement in political matters (see the first section in Chapter 4).

12 The origin of the term is debatable. While it is true that other scholars had used it before he did, there can be no doubt that Maranini should be given credit for its success and divulgation during those years and in the decades thereafter. For a reconstruction of the origins and use of the term, see Griffo (2007). For an overview of the figure of Maranini, his academic and journalistic works, and his academic and intellectual career, and his success as a leader of political and public debate, see, among others, the volume edited by Sandro Rogari (2004). In ridding the term of its common anti-party connotations, Mauro Calise argues that partitocracy can be considered a form of political system in itself, different from parliamentary and presidential forms. Its three main features are claimed to be the "selection of the head of government is to a large extent an extra-electoral affair" and depends on negotiation among parties. Secondly, in a partitocratic system, there is a fusion of legislative and executive powers, and the "party is (...) the place where [that] fusion (...) takes places". Thirdly and finally, compared to the monocratic executive characteristic of presidential systems, and the collective decision-making process of parliamentary cabinet government, in a partitocratic system, there is a "straight collegial leadership" that prevents any one political actor from strictly dominating the political scene. For a more detailed discussion of the partitocratic system, and of its application in the Italian case, see the article by Calise from which the previous citations are taken (Calise 1994).

13 This term, not to be confused with Lijphart's "consociational democracy", refers to "unexpected consensual law-making in a polarized party environment" (Giuliani 1997, p. 67).

14 See, for example, the detailed analysis of the German case, which also contains several references to Italian affairs, by Klaus von Beyme (1993). Anti-partitocratic feelings were even more evident and explicitly expressed in the process that led up to the foundation of the French Fourth Republic, and in the country's Constitution (Debre 1957).

15 There are a great many socio-political studies of the early 1990s crisis and the subsequent transition. In English, see among others: Gilbert (1995) and Bull and Rhodes (1997). A detailed analysis of the roots of the profound crisis of 1992–3 is contained in Caciagli *et al.* (1994). There are a great many studies of the Tangentopoli bribery scandal as well: see, for example, Waters (1994), della Porta and Vannucci (1999) and Rhodes (2015). Alessandro Pizzorno (1992) has written a masterful study of the impact of corruption on the selection of political personnel and the transformation of political parties, while the volume edited by Rocco Sciarrone (2017) offers a substantial empirical portrayal of political corruption in Italy from the Tangentopoli scandal onwards.

16 For a discussion of TV as the driver of anti-political sentiments in the early 1990s, see, in particular, Mastropaolo (2000, pp. 99–105) and Tarchi (2015, p. 236). On the role played by the mass media in the political crisis of the early 1990s, see among others: Gundle and O'Sullivan (1996). On the history of Italian

talk shows and their impact on politics, see the work by Edoardo Novelli (2016). The same author has also written an article on political satire, which during those years contributed significantly towards the ridiculing and delegitimising an entire political class (Novelli 2012). As regards satire, a satirical weekly that proved highly successful in the early 1990s was *Cuore* (Lumley 2001). A film that came out in 1991, which appears almost a prophesy of the bribery scandal that was to emerge the following year, and which already embraced the feeling of strong aversion towards parties and career politicians, was *Il portaborse* (The Yes Man) by Daniele Luchetti (Jedlowski 2015, p. 302). In those years, television, and in particular its satirical programmes and light entertainment shows, invented and divulged anecdotes, jokes and other stories that all contributed towards constructing the public's image of politicians (Renard 2010).

17 Once again, as one can deduce from Google's Ngram database, this is not a new expression, but one that was already widely used in the 1960s, particularly after the mass movements of 1968. This expression was commonly used right through the 1980s and 1990s, and its employment peaked in 2003, in the very midst of Berlusconi's rule and opposition to that rule conducted, in fact, by what was to be termed "organised civil society" (Albertazzi *et al.* 2009).

18 The use of referenda was not a new feature of the Italian political system. There were two very important earlier referenda, namely the one concerning divorce (1974) and the one on abortion (1978). The 1993 referenda, however, marked a clear change in direction compared to previous ones, as they in fact were characterised by a clearly anti-political tone. One first sign of this people's battle against political parties and career politicians by means of a referendum was seen in 1978. The referendum in question, promoted by the small Radical Party which was fighting against the partitocracy, and was called the "party of the referendum" (Panebianco 1988a, p. 111), asked for the abolition of public funding of political parties, which had only been introduced some four years earlier following, in fact, the emergence of certain episodes of political corruption. As PierVincenzo Uleri has observed: "In 1978, the vote on party funding by the State was seen by many as 'a slap in the face' to the parties by the electorate. Although the alliance against abolition of the law providing funding enjoyed a potential consensus of more than 95 per cent, the NO vote got a mere 56.4 per cent" (2002, p. 882). The parties managed to save their public funding, although the 45% of whom voted for its abolition represented a serious warning to Italy's political parties. A subsequent referendum of a clearly anti-party flavour was held in 1991, for the abolition of the multiple preference votes provided for by the electoral system for the Chamber of Deputies, which was considered the cause of clientelism, nepotism and malpractices among parties and career politicians. On this occasion, just prior to the advent of the Tangentopoli bribery scandal, voters voted strongly in favour of the introduction of a single preference vote (62.5% participated, of whom 95.6% were in favour of the abolition of multiple preference votes) (McCarthy 1992). For an overview of the referenda held in Italy, see Uleri (1996, 2002). On the Radical Party and its referendum strategy, see Teodori *et al.* (1977), Gusso (1982) and Panebianco (1988a).

19 According to the same author, in addition to referenda, other anti-partitocratic forms of "*direttismo*" include individualised forms of participation together with the holding of primaries to choose candidates for monocratic office (mayors, regional presidents and the Prime Minister) (Calise 2010, p. 30). We shall examine both of these questions in the chapters to come.

20 Of the eight referenda held in April 1993, which saw a total turnout of almost 77%, the referendum on the public funding of parties saw the highest number of people voting "yes" (90.25%). Public funding of parties was abolished in April, while in December of that same year, the law governing the reimburse-

ment of electoral expenses was passed (Rhodes 1997, p. 75): many observers saw this latter measure as a trick with which to reintroduce the public funding that had only just been abolished. With regard to the question of the public funding of Italy's political parties and politics in general, see Newell (2000), Pizzimenti (2016), Tarli Barbieri and Biondi (2016) and Piccio (2018).

21 Another clearly anti-political reform that the political class had to take on board, as a result of the prevailing climate of dissent and of rejection of politicians' "privileges", regards the amendment of parliamentary immunity provided for by Article 68 of the Italian Constitution. In the autumn of 1993, in the middle of the political crisis resulting from the Tangentopoli bribery scandal, the Italian Parliament passed an amendment restricting the scope of this provision (Koff and Koff 2000, p. 114).

22 Annick Magnier observes in this regard: "At the beginning of the 1990s, the reform of the position of the mayor in Italy was regarded as a form of shock therapy, which would allow new individuals to lead the municipalities and introduce a 'modern' anti-party style of making decisions in the public sphere. Municipalities were considered a laboratory for the modernization of the whole political and administrative system, heavily paralysed by the influence of the political parties and the 'proportional' principle of decision-making" (Magnier 2004, p. 167).

23 There are several studies of Berlusconi, his role in the Italian political system and his cultural inheritance. For an overview of the question, see, for example, the following works: Ginsborg (2004), Orsina (2014) and Newell (2019). There have also been numerous studies of Berlusconi's creation, the political party Forza Italia. The most complete such study is the one by Emanuela Poli (2001). In English, see also the studies by Francesco Raniolo (2006) and Duncan McDonnell (2013).

24 At the time of the 2001 election, Berlusconi sent out a pamphlet to millions of Italians in which in true gossip magazine style, he recounted his life, showed photos of himself as a child, with his family and with his friends. According to certain observers, this moment marked "the start of Italian politics' popularisation and intimization" (Campus 2016, p. 72). This trait, as we shall see in the following chapters, was to become a permanent feature of Italian politics and was to be taken to the extreme by certain leaders such as Renzi and Salvini (see the third section in Chapters 3 and 4).

25 The temporariness and revocability of political involvement is a characteristic feature of outsider leaders and anti-political and anti-party political actors in general. In 2001, at the end of the electoral campaign, Berlusconi stipulated a "contract with the Italians" live on TV, whereat he promised he would retire from politics if he failed to achieve at least four of the five undertakings contained in the agreement (Ricolfi 2006). As we shall see in Chapter 4, Matteo Renzi also promised to leave politics if the Italians voted against the constitutional reforms he had pursued in the 2016 referendum. The Five Star Movement went one step further by setting a statutory limit of two terms of office for those elected from its lists.

26 As we shall see, this idea of a strong relationship between the elector and the elected, which removes the need for any other actors, rules and practices characteristic of representative democracy, was embraced, albeit in an inverted form – that is, with the movement aiming to monitor the elected representatives – by the Five Star Movement's "monitoring democracy" approach (Keane 2009).

3 The League
Anti-politics of struggle and anti-politics in government

The original anti-politics of the Northern League

The Northern League, which was founded in late 1989 following the unification of certain regional movements that had been active for over a decade in the principal regions of Central-Northern Italy,[1] can be considered the first manifestation of a broad, organised, durable form of anti-politics in Italy, after the fleering appearance of the Common Man Movement described in the preceding chapter. The Northern League's emergence preceded, and partly laid the ground for, the massive popular anti-political response to the Tangentopoli bribery scandal that swept aside an entire political party system, and left an indelible mark on Italy's political culture. The Northern League's rhetoric and political actions prepared the way for the rigorous growth of Berlusconi's creation Forza Italia from January 1994 onwards, which in turn yielded many other anti-political fruits (and seeds). In particular, the early 1990s saw the introduction of several reforms, the most important of which being those of an electoral nature. Such reforms altered the rules of the political game, in an attempt to curb the advance of the Northern League and its critique of Italy's political system (Donovan 1995).

Given the significant influence that the Northern League was to have on the political actors and affairs of the Second Republic, we shall now examine the type of anti-political tactics that the Northern League employed in its battle for power. An analysis of the League's affairs enables us to observe the various manifestations of anti-politics presented in Chapter 1: the anti-politics of citizens' attitudes and behaviour; the anti-politics of the political class, and in particular of the country's political leaders; the anti-politics which, through the League, gradually became a characteristic trait of the entire political system. An examination of the anti-politics of the League, which as things stand is the longest-lived parliamentary party in Italy, enables us to better understand the ways in which anti-politics can be employed and can be adapted to the contingent political situation. To put it very succinctly, the League's history shows that focusing on anti-politics can enable a party to overcome its own internal crises, as it guarantees the

DOI: 10.4324/9781003109273-4

new political legitimacy and credibility of those leaders who choose to have recourse to such a strategy.

To start with, the question we need to ask is the following: did the League merely update and revise anti-political themes and slogans that were already part of Italian political culture, having been introduced by some of the political actors discussed in the previous chapter, or did it actually introduce new anti-political themes and actions? First of all, it would seem that various themes, focused on by the Common Man Movement and others over previous decades, were reformulated and re-launched by the Northern League, thus transforming it into an "anti-political entrepreneur". In fact, it was thanks to the League that the widespread hostility and aversion to parties and politicians was channelled into electoral action (Cartocci 1991, p. 554). In presenting itself as a challenger party and playing the part of the political entrepreneur (De Vries and Hobolt 2020), the League encouraged what could be termed the "market of anti-politics",[2] in which various political leaders and parties compete, trying to get themselves recognised as the most credible and determined opponents of political parties and professional politicians. In other words, they try to appropriate the issue of public morality, and anti-politics is the best means by which to do so (Petrocik 1996). As we shall see, gaining a monopolistic – or at the very least an oligopolistic – position in the anti-politics market is one way of ensuring electoral support, a leading role, and room for manoeuvre, within the political sphere.

Anticentralism and the battle against partitocracy

The League, nevertheless, went beyond the mere re-proposal of existing anti-political arguments and issues, and linked the criticism of professional politicians and political parties to other political issues. Such issues included: the protest against taxation; the demand for local autonomy and freedom from the dictates of Rome, seen as the centre of the political system, and from the burden of the South, the poorest part of Italy. In this way, the League fostered a sort of frame alignment between anti-politics and federalist demands (Snow *et al.* 1986). In keeping with neo-liberal antistatism, and as happened in other areas of Europe (Dalle Mulle 2018), the League is an autonomist force that originated and developed in the wealthier parts of Italy. By embracing to an extent certain themes so dear to Margaret Thatcher, the League's main bones of contention have been excessive taxation, State inefficiency, Italy's excessive bureaucracy and the question of political centralism. According to the League, all of these problems derive from the arrogance of professional politicians and the self-referential nature of political parties, which limit individual and entrepreneurial liberty, and force the wealthy, modern, hard-working citizens of northern Italy to maintain the lazy, backward, poorer inhabitants of the South. Moreover, Italy has been historically characterised by its profound dualism, as summed up by the unresolved "southern question" (Davies 2015). In the face of this persistent historical scourge, the League "invented", and placed permanently on the political agenda, a "northern question" (Meridiana 1993, Chiarini 2004, Berta 2008).[3] With the rise of the Northern League, the latent anti-southern feelings of part of the northern Italian population came gushing out into the open and were now proudly touted and politically significant and fruitful.[4] From this point of view, "the LN thus constitutes a flagrant case of 'welfare chauvinism' (Kitschelt). Among the ethnoregionalist parties, the League is a precursor of the shift from identity politics to interest-oriented regional coalitions obviously supported by social coalitions" (Türsan 1998, p. 12).

Leaving aside this territorial reference, and taking account of the Thatcherite mood prevailing at the time of the League's emergence, the anti-bureaucratic rhetoric of Umberto Bossi and the other leaders of the party was not so different from that of Giannini 40 years earlier.[5] In the version of anti-politics championed by the Common Man Movement, which could not possibly have targeted southern Italians, since the movement was fundamentally rooted in the South, the citizen tormented by bureaucracy was an indistinct individual. The enemies were bureaucracy and professional politicians, with no geographical distinction. The League, on the contrary, mixed these two elements and saw the national political class as its number one enemy, which it deemed to be parasitic and corrupt, and whose actions benefited the inept southerners. As Mario Diani has observed in this regard: "Rather than taking an autonomous form, antisouthern sentiments were framed largely within the antipolitician perspective" (1996, p. 1060). Rome, the seat of the Italian Parliament and the government's ministries, became the symbol of a generic "South". As portrayed in a famous electoral poster, Rome stole the golden eggs laid by a northern hen (Tambini 2001, p. 108). Ultimately, "local areas became a political resource for anti-politics" (Diamanti 2003, p. 61); localism was the League's recipe for combating the nation's political parties and political class (Cartocci 1991).

As with the Common Man Movement, and as is also true of many other populist leaders and parties, the Northern League in its early days saw the division in society not as the one between left and right (Mannheimer 1991b, p. 135), but between the upper echelons of the political system (the politicians and the bureaucrats) and the lower levels thereof (powerless citizens). While in an ideologised context such as that of the 1940s Italy, the attempt to move away from the left-right dichotomy appeared rather faint-hearted, during the "pragmatic" 1980s, when the League re-launched the idea, it appeared a lot more convincing. Thus, the success of the League resulted not only in the politicisation of the centre/periphery cleavage, but also a decline in the significance of the owner/worker cleavage as it had been traditionally perceived, which in turn entailed the de-legitimation of those parties that had traditionally fed off said cleavage. In fact, the process of de-industrialisation and the profound economic transformation affecting northern Italy from the 1970s onwards, whereby production based on large-scale industry was gradually replaced by one centred on small and medium enterprises increasingly oriented towards the provision of services, changed the very economic and social character of this area of Italy (Berta 2008). In this new scenario, the League transformed the traditional owner/worker cleavage, by presenting itself as the spokes body for self-employed professionals and the entrepreneurial classes of the North, who had been increasingly unhappy with the State's fiscal policies and inefficiencies.

During the League's early days, that is, throughout the 1980s and up to the crisis of the political system in the early 1990s, the League grouped together all those parties wedded to traditional ideologies under the collective label of "partitocracy". In Umberto Bossi's crude language, the partitocracy is portrayed as an ill on the same level as the Mafia and represents the other side of the coin featuring that particular criminal organisation: "If Palazzo [government] equals partitocrazia and partitocrazia equals the Mafia, then the government equals the Mafia. Partitocrazia and the Mafia are thus two faces of the same coin" (quoted in: Leonardi and Kovacs 1993, p. 60). Use of the term "partitocracy", as we saw in Figure 2.1 from the previous chapter, peaked in Italian political debate between the mid-1980s and mid-1990s. That same period saw the League's initial success. At that time, the cultural climate seemed ripe for anti-party preaching. During the post-war years, Maranini and other critics of political party's action used the same term to underscore the false pluralism of the political system (*consociativismo*), and to denounce the parties' political stranglehold on society as a whole (*lottizzazione*) (whereby the parties share out key political positions while society splits along party lines). Almost half a century later, the League attacked the parties' cronyism and tacit toleration of corruption which, despite being historically rooted phenomena, could no longer be ignored in the 1980s (Pizzorno 1993). The replacement of a competitive logic with a collusive one (Katz and Mair 1995), and the regular agreement in Parliament on many legislative measures (Giuliani 1997, 2008) – which was not the sole preserve of Italy (Louwerse *et al.* 2017) and which continued during the Second Republic (De Giorgi and Marangoni 2015) – were judged, rightly or wrongly, to be the reasons for Italy's booming public debt and fiscal crisis.

Like Maranini earlier, and then Pannella and the Radical Party, the League identified the enemy as the old political parties and politicians. The historical opposition between the parties, and the communism/anticommunism cleavage that had characterised the Italian Republic since its very foundation after the Second World War, were dismissed as a game of mirrors designed to dazzle electors and prevent them from seeing the problems created by an inept political class. The early League did not want to be part of the privileged world of parties and politicians but wished to smash these mirrors and put a definitive end to the game being played. The instrument that Bossi and the League adopted to smash the "mirrors" of the First Republic was language. Unlike the incomprehensible language employed by the nation's old politicians, who expressed themselves in "political jargon" (*politichese*) (Croci 2001), the language of the League was characterised by "innovation" and "difference" (Diamanti 1993, p. 71). It was simple, common, at times vulgar, and always chauvinistic. To stress his anti-conformism and create his own style as a political outsider, Bossi sometimes gave speeches in the local dialect. This alternative, irreverent linguistic register was reinforced by Bossi's way of dressing and presenting himself in public. He continued to follow the more informal approach adopted in the 1980s by the Socialist Party leader Bettino Craxi, snubbing the jacket-and-tie "uniform" that politicians traditionally wore; indeed, Bossi was often seen in public wearing a simple singlet (Tarchi 2015, p. 251).[6]

Entering the Institutions

During the latter half of the 1980s, the League's outsider approach and its battle against political centralism and partitocracy began to bear fruit. At the 1987 general election,[7] the Lombard League (*Lega Lombarda*) won just 0.5% of the votes cast, although this was enough to get two of its candidates elected to parliament, one of whom was Bossi himself. This percentage rose to 1.8% at the 1989 European elections, when the League had two of its candidates elected as Euro MPs. However, it was at the regional elections held in 1990 that the League (which in the meantime had become the "Northern League") got people to sit up and take notice, after winning a healthy 5.4% of votes, enabling it to elect 24 regional counsellors, and making it the fourth most important party at national level. In the wealthy, densely populated Lombardy region, the Northern League indeed came second, with 18.9% of votes. Following this limited, yet resounding success, at a time when the Berlin Wall had already fallen but the Tangentopoli bribery scandal was still some way off, one of Italy's most famous journalists, Indro Montanelli, wrote: "those who voted for the Leagues, or at least the majority of such voters, did so as a sign of their opposition to the traditional parties rather than of their support for the Leagues" (Vimercati 1990, p. v). Another of Italy's leading journalists of the time, Eugenio Scalfari, agreed with Montanelli and stated that the League's electoral success "was the partitocrazia's 'last warning'" (quoted in Gilbert 1995, p. 54).

When news of the Tangentopoli scandal broke in February 1992, the League was already on an upward trajectory. Its status as a political outsider and its criticism of the traditional parties accused of involvement in the bribery scandal enabled the League to present itself to the electorate "as the political entrepreneur of the crisis that reiterates, and in turn produces, the feelings and resentment of broad sections of northern Italy's populace; and in doing so, it transforms the underlying causes and directions of the dissent building during the 1980s and '90s in this country, into electoral support" (Diamanti 1993, p. 85). The League was thus the right party, at the right time, to lend a voice to the aforementioned deep-rooted discontent among the North's professional classes and productive social categories.

The League was further encouraged by the votes it obtained at the April 1992 general election. The traditional parties still managed to paper over the cracks, albeit losing votes, but were subsequently swept aside by the political tsunami that struck Italy shortly afterwards. In the very midst of this transitional period, the League obtained over 8% of votes nationwide and became the leading party in a number of important northern Italian provinces. It now had 55 members of the chamber of deputies and 25 senators, and this represented a new phase in its development: it now had to deal with the fact that the party and its leading representatives, first and foremost Umberto Bossi, were now among the parties and politicians based in the capital of the political class – Rome – against whom it had only recently railed. During the Tangentopoli "storm", in an attempt to avoid ending up in the anti-political mincer and to continue, in fact, to take advantage of the political desperation of an entire nation, the League could hardly abandon its distinctive approach. In fact, Bossi's party was to use the Institutions as an arena in which it could flaunt its own "otherness" which distinguished it from the rituals and language of traditional politics. Indeed, in May 1993, its members even displayed a hangman's noose in Parliament, indicating how it thought corrupt politicians ought to have been dealt with (Tambini 2001, p. 67). As Antonio Di Pietro, the magistrate symbolising the Tangentopoli scandal[8] was to do, and as the Five Star Movement (5SM) was also to do subsequently (see Chapter 5), the League appropriated the question of honesty which, incidentally, had been one of the traits of the "good accountant" whom Giannini would have tasked with governing the nation. Trying to get the credit regarding the "valence issue" of honesty and the fight against corruption (Curini 2018), when the entire political class is accused of corrupt practices, is a politically successful strategy. However, as the League was to discover at its own expense (as was Di Pietro and the 5SM), focusing exclusively (or mainly) on the question of honesty, as we shall see, can be a risky, even counter-productive, strategy in the medium term.

Given that honesty and being outside of the traditional party system proved extremely remunerative during this phase of Italy's political development, the League was not the only force to appropriate said theme. In fact, as mentioned in the previous chapter, other actors in the anti-politics camp included the referendum movement as well as certain representatives of the traditional political parties who had left those parties prior to Tangentopoli. The anti-political front was not united, however. Apart from the shared rhetoric, each of those concerned tried to safeguard and further its own interests by adopting the anti-political approach. The League, for example, was initially against the abolition of multiple preference votes in elections to the Chamber of Deputies as envisaged by the "anti-partitocracy" referendum held in 1991. Bossi's position at the time was in-line with that of Craxi, the symbol of traditional politics. Just like Craxi, Bossi contemptuously invited Italians to "go to the seaside" rather than to the polling stations (Passarelli and Tuorto 2012, p. 39). However, he was to change his mind with regard to the 1993 referenda, not so much in order to support the movement which was critical of the old parties and politics, as he himself was, but because he realised that a majoritarian, uninominal electoral system would favour those political parties whose support was concentrated in territorial terms (Donovan 1995, p. 52).

The confrontation/clash between the League and the other parties, vying for the vast anti-political vote, was now taking placing in the electoral arena itself. In fact, in March 1993, in response to the criticism of the proportional system as one of the causes of bad politics, and in order to avoid a referendum being held a few months later regarding the same question, the Italian parliament introduced a new electoral system for municipal and provincial elections (Magnier 2004). This new system foresaw the direct election of mayors, and in the larger municipalities, a further ballot in the event that no one candidate obtained the majority of valid votes cast during the first round of voting. The first application of this new electoral system offered considerable opportunities to emerging political forces, and also to the nation's left-wing parties which had come through the Tangentopoli affair unscathed. For example, in Milan, the epicentre of the bribes scandal, the second ballot held in June 1993 pitted Marco Formentini, a senior figure in the League who had previously been a member of the Socialist Party, against Nando dalla Chiesa, son of a Carabinieri general murdered by the Mafia in 1982, and a leading figure in "The Network" (*La Rete*) and in that area of civil society which, as we saw in Chapter 2 was one of the leading anti-political and anti-party actors at the time. With the support of the city's entrepreneurs, also in virtue of his being part of Milan's establishment, Formentini won the second ballot and was elected Mayor of Milan. This strengthened not only the institutional status of the League but also its governmental position.

Between 1990 and 1993, also as a result of the crisis affecting Italy's parties following judicial investigations into their operations, the League shifted considerably closer to the centre of the political stage. In January 1994, however, Berlusconi's appearance on the political scene changed things radically. His advent meant the end not only of the left's political aspirations but also of those of the League. In fact, Berlusconi and Forza Italia operated in the increasingly crowded arena of anti-politics. The new system for election to the Chamber of Deputies and the Senate, which assigned 75% of seats on a majoritarian basis, and the remaining 25% on a proportional basis, led to a split in the League with regard to the party's identity. The majoritarian logic of the new electoral system forced Bossi's party to form an alliance with Berlusconi's Forza Italia in Italy's northern regions, and also, albeit indirectly, with the National Alliance, a right-wing party heir to the MSI), despite the opposing views of the two parties with regard to many aspects of policy, starting with regional political autonomy. The League, faced with the electoral test, was thus forced to compromise and to surrender some of its "purity". It sensationally forewent its "ideological neutrality" which had enabled it to claim that it was "neither of the right nor the left", and which had been one of its most attractive features in the eyes of those disgusted with politics in general and with the games played by the nation's political parties. The bitter pill it was forced to swallow bore substantial fruit, however. In fact, in 1994, it obtained almost 8.4% of votes at national level, a similar percentage to that of 1992, which meant that it was the fifth most voted party in the country. With the new electoral system, this modest achievement enabled it to increase the number of its MPs from 80 in 1992 to 177, making the League's parliamentary group the second largest of all, behind the left-wing "Progressives" alliance.

In and out of Government

The 1994 election resulting in the victory of the centre-right coalition meant that the process of transformation of the League from a party of struggle, and protest to a party in government, was now complete. This distancing itself from its historical roots needed to be offset by a symbolic appeal to anti-politics. Even more than before, the League needed to demonstrate that it was different from all the other parties; that its leaders and MPs were different from the much despised professional politicians; that the original spirit of a popular movement had not been affected by its coming to power. In addition to distinguishing itself from the "old politicians" through the language the League's leaders used, one of the ways that those leaders tried to show the party's militants and voters, and public opinion as a whole, that it had not been corrupted by politics and power, was to accentuate Bossi's plebiscitarian attitudes and behaviour. These manifested themselves, for example, in regard to the key question of whether or not to join the governmental coalition led by Berlusconi. When the League's leaders and militants came together two weeks after the election, at Pontida (in a huge meadow situated in the province of Bergamo) at the party's customary political rally, Bossi asked his people to "democratically" decide, by a show of hands, whether the League should be part of the Government coalition or not.[9] The staging of this process of direct democracy worked, and the League's leadership was given the go-ahead by the party's members to join the coalition. In obeying the "will" of the party's grassroots members, Bossi and the rest of the League's leadership finally managed to take over power from the politicians they had so harshly criticised beforehand. However, this meant that they had to regularly frequent the corridors of power in what they had always considered to be "thieving Rome".

The anti-political strategy was not deployed exclusively at Pontida, however. It was pursued with increasing conviction in those institutions that the League was now an integral part of. It is no coincidence that when the League was called on to nominate one of its MPs as Chair of the Chamber of Deputies, it chose Irene Pivetti, who at 31 was the youngest ever Chair of the Chamber, thus underscoring the League's status as a political outsider.

This anti-conformist approach was adopted by the party's other deputies and senators, who ignored parliamentary dress code, and by the League's members in governmental office. In this regard, Albertazzi and McDonnell have observed as follows: "In order to participate in national government without losing face, the League's ministers had to show that they had not been contaminated by the political behaviour of their allies, that is, of "the professionals politicians of the much despised 'Roman parties', spokespersons for territorial and social interests very different from its own. Consequently, the League's ministers and MPs did all they could, when in power, to show that they had not become like all the others, and this they did by using everyday language in their interviews, through their regular orchestrated, neo-futurist protests in Parliament, or by declaring that they did not care about office and did not intend to barter over appointments" (quoted in Tarchi 2015, pp. 265–6). This quote summarises the innovative use of anti-politics by the League within an institutional context, which was something that it bequeathed to the Italian political system. As we shall see in Chapter 5, the 5SM in particular was to place great value on this "inheritance".

Despite these strategies designed to distinguish the League from Italy's other political parties, it continued to run the risk of all parties presenting themselves as outsiders when they first get involved in government (Deschouwer 2008). As Giannini immediately realised when he founded the FUQ (Setta 2005, p. 65), the contradiction in having created and led to success an anti-party populated by professional politicians hostile to political careerism is clear. Bossi's joining forces with Berlusconi, and the League's move from the opposition benches to those of government, was too sudden a change for the electorate and for part of the League's political class. As with the Common Man Movement's entry into parliament, the League's transition to party of government threatened to be fatal. Differences and discontent emerged within the party's ranks, and these were brutally silenced through a systematic purge of the party's membership by its charismatic leader (Albertazzi *et al.* 2011, p. 477). The problems within the party, however, were not the only ones, nor indeed the most worrying ones, that its leadership had to face. In fact, the party continued to see its support decline in the polls conducted at the time (Diamanti 2003, p. 67). Moreover, at the European elections held in June 1994 the League lost votes, whereas Forza Italia, led by a more convincing anti-political outsider, obtained 30% of the total votes cast. In fact, Forza Italia and the League were competing for the votes of the same politically unsophisticated electorate (Brusattin 2007, p. 488). An analysis of the electoral flow at the 1994 elections show that 28% of those who voted for Forza Italia had voted for the League at the previous elections held in 1992 (Bull and Newell 1995, p. 88).

Following the substantial disappearance of the referendum movement, Berlusconi's natural monopolistic tendencies spread through the anti-political sphere as well. In order to avoid being crushed by the advancing Forza

Italia party, Bossi thus had no option but to try and distance himself and his party from Berlusconi and Forza Italia. He did so by heavily criticising the latter and by opposing the principal bills put forward by the Government (Cento Bull and Gilbert 2001, p. 36). The League thus launched a strategy that was to survive for some considerable time, appropriately termed the "struggle within government" (Passarelli and Tuorto 2018a, p. 27). However, not even this strategy could placate the electorate's discontent or that of one section of the League's leadership. The only way out of this impasse that could avoid the party's losing all of the political credibility it had built up over the years was to return to the opposition benches. Thus, it was that in December 1994, only seven months after its inception, the first Berlusconi government came to an end, and with it, for the time being, the deadlock in the League's relationship with the other parties of the centre-right coalition.

For the purposes of the present study, this affair shows that once the political leadership has invested so much in anti-politics as a means of gaining electoral support, by getting through to that vast anti-political public, anti-politics from below is wedded to anti-politics from above. The attempt to break this close relationship by entering Government can lead to tensions and disappointment within the League both as a party in public office and in central office (characterised by the challenges and purges we have mentioned), and as a party on the ground, that is, among its supporters (leading to a decline in support in the polls and at the ballot box).

The historical nemesis: the scandals and the crisis

Having withdrawn from government and having vociferously broken its pact with Berlusconi and the other centre-right parties, the League found itself isolated and, moreover, once again among the opposition ranks. At the 1996 elections, the decision to stand on its own proved highly successful however, as the League obtained more than 10% of votes nationwide. Nevertheless, the divisions among the centre-right parties, in a prevalently majoritarian electoral system, resulted in the victory of the centre-left, which was to remain in power, subject to various vicissitudes, until 2001. During those years, the League was able to more convincingly play the part of the party of protest, focusing in the main on two questions that marked it out from the other parties. The first was its discrimination of southern Italians and of the South of Italy in general, together with its opposition to the centralist State, which it had been forced to curb whilst in government given the national character of the coalition it was part of. The second question was that of anti-politics which, as an opposition party once again, could now be expressed in more caustic, credible, explicit tones.

The radicalisation of the League's criticism of central government came about through the transformation of its demands for federal autonomy, to calls for the North's secession from the rest of Italy. The separatist strategy was seen as a clear, albeit somewhat comical, attempt to invent tradition

(Hobsbawm and Ranger 1983), where the tradition in question concerned the existence of a *Padania* – the purported nation of the peoples of northern Italy (Albertazzi 2006). The League thus embarked on a series of initiatives – a combination of the folkloristic and the provocative – designed to emphasise its essential character as a battling movement operating outside of the political mainstream. Bossi and his fellow leaders went to the source of the River Po – the "Holy Po" – the river that crosses the vast Po Valley Plain, to collect a vial of its water which they then released into the Adriatic Sea. Bossi claimed that he was inspired by William Wallace, the Scottish national hero made famous at that time by the film "Braveheart". The League organised its own "Miss Padania" beauty contest as well as a "Padana" football team which was to play in international tournaments involving "stateless nations".

Anti-politics sat extremely well with the outsider approach that characterised this phase in the party's political development. The League renewed its criticism of the partitocracy and was highly critical of its former ally Berlusconi (who was openly and repeatedly accused of being a mafia-type politician). The political left and right were once again deemed to be the same thing. This was a mainstay of the League's early rhetoric, and all parties were denigrated in the slogan *"Roma-Polo e Roma-Ulivo"* ("Rome–the Pole of Liberties and Rome-The Olive Tree Coalition") (Tarchi 1998, p. 146).[10] The League used this slogan, the simplicity of which certainly caught people's attention, to underscore the collusion among all parties, who were also accused of concentrating power in the political centre, with little regard for the periphery. So once again there appeared to be a combination of anti-politics, anti-partyism and anti-centralism. One further important example of this wedding of anti-centralism with anti-politics was the referendum called in regard to the independence of Northern Italy, proclaimed and organised by the League in May 1997, the importance of which was mainly symbolic and was designed to demonstrate the League's capacity to mobilise the masses (Tambini 2001, pp. 132–3). Here again, this direct consultation with the electorate was designed to by-pass the corrupt, collusive political class and to re-establish the popular sovereignty that the political parties and politicians had taken away.

The return to Government and the emergence of the scandals

The spontaneous-movement approach that radicalised separatism and anti-politics turned out to be a blind alley, however. Not only was the League politically isolated as it could not form any coalition with the centre-right or the centre-left, but it also continued to see its share of the votes decline. At the 1999 European elections and the 2000 Regional elections, it failed to obtain even half of the votes it had previously received at the 1996 general election. Thus, the battling League gradually gave way once again to the League of government. After making up with Berlusconi, Bossi guided the League back into the governmental fold, that is, the centre-right coalition which was to govern the country from 2001 to 2006 (Albertazzi and McDonnell 2005). As in 1994, the alliance with other parties proved detrimental to the League, and at the 2001 general election, it got less than 4% of the votes cast. This was further proof of the fact that only strict opposition to all parties could get the League's electoral base to vote for it in substantial numbers.[11]

In the midst of this further period as a member of the governing coalition, however, the League was faced with something that risked plunging the party into further crisis. In 2004, its founder and leader, Umberto Bossi, had a stroke which forced him to retire from public life. He gradually returned to politics a year later but was visibly debilitated compared to the virile, battling figure of one year earlier. For a challenger party with a traditionally charismatic leader, it was very difficult and risky to continue as part of the governing coalition when that leader was clearly ill and/or absent. Notwithstanding this evident weakness, the party managed to soldier on, and as part of a centre-right coalition, it continued to govern the two most important northern Italian regions – Piedmont and Lombardy – which are also the richest regions in Italy. In doing so, it succeeded in furthering its institutional and governmental status. The original popular movement gradually gave way to a well-administered, efficient, politically trustworthy party.

Thus, the League gradually normalised, and from a political challenger, it became a dominant party (De Vries and Hobolt 2020) and was increasingly perceived as such. This process of normalisation, and the League's governmental presence at national level (from 2001 to 2006 and again from 2008 to 2011) and in important northern Italian cities and regions, did not seem to penalise the League from an electoral perspective (in the 2008 general election, it obtained 8.3% of votes), or inhibit its mid-level leaders or militants (Albertazzi and McDonnell 2015, p. 167). After the party leadership's lengthy presence in parliament and in governmental office, the League's electorate was no longer that of 1987 (the party's first time in parliament) or of 1994 (the year of its first involvement in government). The League's voters had become accustomed to voting for a party that was part of government either occasionally (at national level) or permanently (at local and regional levels). Thanks to its participation in government, the League succeeded in implementing its electoral programme in the form of public policy (ibid.). Furthermore, compared to the earlier days, the League's voters were now permanently part of the centre-right electorate, as they now fully adhered to the strict bipolar logic that characterised the Italian political system during that period. The successful defence of the North's interests, thanks to the League's participation in Government and its stubborn demands for "devolution", resulted in the nuancing of the leadership's anti-political attitudes. Thus, the League could be a little less a party of struggle and a little more one of government.

The prolonged exercise of power, however, resulted in the degeneration of part of the leadership, which got embroiled in a series of scandals concerning corruption and the personalised handling of public funds assigned to the party.[12] The consequent political scandal seriously impacted the party, since the cases in question often involved Bossi, his family and his closest aides.[13] The scandal assumed enormous importance for various reasons. The first is that it concerned the embezzlement of public moneys which, compared to other forms of political scandal, solicited a more negative reaction on the part of the public (Farrell *et al.* 1998, p. 88, Thompson 2000, ch. 6, Doherty *et al.* 2011, p. 751). The second reason is that the scandal revealed the hypocrisy and the incongruity of the actions of those committing them vis-à-vis their previously declared political positions; and this was one more reason why citizens were so quick to condemn the actions concerned (Bhatti *et al.* 2013, p. 419). In other words, the anti-politics that Bossi and the League had embraced and preached in order to gain power now came back to bite them. The person, who had harshly condemned the corrupt politicians of the early 1990s, was now a man weakened by illness who, in employing certain strategies to try and remedy the political scandals that had emerged (Benoit 1997, p. 179), whimpered and asked public forgiveness for the errors of his ways.

The caustic, unforgiving slogans it had aimed at an entire political class, designed to help construct the image of an intransigent party, were now being used, via a clever play on words, by the League's political adversaries and by those League supporters shocked and disillusioned with the corruption of the party and its leaders. For example, the slogan "masters in our hometown" (*padroni a casa nostra*), which had previously appeared on the walls of northern Italian cities, was now transformed into "thieves in our hometown" (*ladroni a casa nostra*); likewise, "Thieving Rome" (*Roma ladrona*) was changed to "Thieving League" (*Lega ladrona*). As Anna Cento Bull has pointed out:

> it would be difficult to underestimate the severity of the blow dealt to the League by this scandal. The very party that in 1992 had been at the forefront in the protest against systematic corrupt deals between business and politics, often involving criminal organizations, now found itself under investigation for corruption, misuse of public funds, fraud against the State, and money laundering, in connivance with Calabrian criminals. The League's image as a clean party of the periphery determined to clean up the Roman stables was now seriously – perhaps even irredeemably – damaged, and drastic measures were clearly required to attempt to restore at least part of its lost credibility
>
> (Cento Bull 2012, p. 98).

Anaesthetised by the fruits of the League's participation in government, the anti-politics of the League's electorate reawakened following the scandals involving the prophet and guarantor of a new, honest form of politics. As one can easily imagine, and as has happened in other situations (Farrell *et al.* 1998, p. 91), the negative effects of the political scandal threatened to spread to the party to whom the perpetrator of the alleged offences belonged; particularly given that he is the unchallenged leader of the party in question.

Changing in order to survive

With its historical leader ill and overwhelmed by scandals, there was a very good chance that the party would go into crisis and possibly disappear from the political scene altogether. After a heated internal dispute, the party's attempt at renewal and at repairing the damage to its reputation led to the replacement of the delegitimised leader Umberto Bossi, who resigned in April 2012, with the former Minister for the Interior Roberto Maroni. In other words, the party aimed to have a secretary who embodied its more reassuring, governmental character. Maroni tried to strengthen the party's image as the defender of the North's interests by proposing that 75% of taxes paid went to Regional Governments, and coining the expression "First the North" (Cento Bull 2012, pp. 104–5). This strategy did not work, however, as the League's supporters remained disenchanted and in disarray. The anti-politics from below that had always been present among the party's electorate took its toll by penalising the party at the polling stations. At the 2013 general election, the League performed extremely poorly, obtaining just 4% of votes, half as many as those gained, with great effort, at the previous election, and managing to get only 33% of those who had voted for the party at the 2008 election to go and vote this time (compared with 78% between 2006 and 2008) (De Sio and Paparo 2014, p. 144). The League's electorate no longer felt that a party that was about to implode could safeguard their interests. In order to get out of this corner and survive as such, the League needed to change strategy once again and return to its anti-political origins, freshen up the leadership and invest once again in its image as a political movement. This was the only option the party had if it were to get its electors and activists motivated once again, and to preserve its strong territorial structure – its real strong point compared to other highly personalised parties in Italy (Vercesi 2015) – before the party became completely mummified.[14]

In the meantime, however, a new challenger party stepped into the arena of anti-politics, namely the 5SM led by a well-known professional comedian and entertainer, Beppe Grillo. As we shall see in Chapter 5, Grillo and his Movement focused heavily on challenging the existing political class and were much more credible, in this regard, than the other traditional anti-political "entrepreneurs": Berlusconi had been involved in politics (and also in judicial matters, given the considerable number of legal proceedings filed against him) for 20 years, while Bossi had been overwhelmed by the aforementioned scandals. As Piero Ignazi has pointed out: "The wind of anti-politics raging fiercely just as it did during the years of Tangentopoli (and perhaps even more so), this time did not benefit the League, since on questions of anti-politics, the leaders of the Five Star Movement were considered more credible than those of the League. The League preserved its role as the foremost anti-immigrant party" (2018, p. 206).[15]

Consequently, the League decided to alter its strategy: it put the question of separatism on the back burner and embraced an approach that was nationalistic, *sovereigntist*, as well as openly xenophobic, racist and ethnic-identity-centred (Passarelli and Tuorto 2018a). This approach was one that Bossi himself had attempted to make his own, but at a time when the national and European cultural and political climate was not exactly favourable to such a line. To be credible and effective, this change in direction needed a new face to come forward, that is, someone capable of getting people to forget the political scandals involving its historical leaders. That new face was to be Matteo Salvini, a young member of the League who had been in the party from a very young age and had previously represented it institutionally at various levels. While not exactly a "young clone of the early Bossi" (Tarchi 2015, p. 270), Salvini nevertheless reinterprets well the role that the League's founder played 30 years earlier. Following Maroni's resignation, who in the meantime had been elected President of the Lombardy Regional Government, Salvini became national party secretary in December 2013, beating Bossi himself at the party's primaries (only the 17,000 registered members of the League left at that time, just one-tenth of the number of members only two years beforehand, could vote at these primaries) (McDonnell and Vampa 2016, p. 120). Just like the early Bossi, Salvini focused heavily not only on racism and social egoism but also on anti-politics, the form of which he adapted to meet the rules of politics as a public spectacle. This focus on anti-politics was a necessity deriving from a fundamental difference between Salvini and Bossi: while Bossi emerged in the 1980s and 1990s as a typical example of the anti-political outsider, to use the terminology introduced in Figure 2.2 (Chapter 2), Salvini had to disguise the fact that after years in the country's institutions he was a political insider. Having rejected Maroni's political line comparable to that of a mainstream insider, Salvini aimed to build, for himself and as a result also for his party, a new image of the anti-political outsider. Thus, the League, under Salvini's leadership, was ready once again to take on the anti-political mantle which, as the 5SM's considerable success at the 2013 general election showed (we shall be examining this in Chapter 5), was something that Italy's electors continued to value highly.

Rebuilding the League, demolishing politics

Salvini's 82% share of the votes cast at the League's primaries, when he was up against the founder and spiritual leader of the party, Umberto Bossi, marked the end of the old Northern League. It was replaced by a new League featuring figures and policies capable of getting people to quickly forget the recent scandals involving the party's leadership. In fact, the conditions for relaunching the party were ideal. As Robert Harmel and Kenneth Janda observe, "far from assuming that party changes 'just happen' or 'must happen', we suggest that party change is normally a result of leadership change, a change of dominant faction within the party and/or an external stimulus for change" (1994, p. 262). In the League's case, both of the prerequisites for change were present: a clear change in leadership and in the dominant faction, and an external stimulus for change (the scandal involving Bossi, his family and his inner circle). Thus, the League's primary goal changed. It was no longer one of the four goals indicated by Harmel and Janda, namely vote maximisation, office maximisation, policy advocacy and intraparty democracy maximisation (ibid., p. 269) – which to different degrees had guided the actions of the party's leadership during the League's 20-year existence – but rather the very survival of the party itself.

The changes made to the party represented the principal strategy by which to repair the damage caused by the scandal that had previously engulfed the League. The first step in this strategy was represented by the overwhelming victory of the "new" secretary, Salvini, over the "old" leader, Bossi, in the aforementioned 2013 primaries. As Cucchi and Cavazza have observed, summarising the finding of studies concerning this matter, "a political scandal is damaging to people' trust in, and opinion of, the party or of the political class in general, but can be lucrative for individual politicians who may gain an advantage from the comparison with the corrupt politician(s) concerned" (2017, pp. 734–5). In becoming party secretary, Matteo Salvini undertook to change the identity and the image of the party he inherited from Bossi and Maroni, in particular by changing two specific aspects thereof.

The first is the image of the party's leadership. In this regard, Salvini has moved away from the mainstream insider leadership characterised by the previous party secretary Maroni and created one of the anti-political outsider. In view of the highly personalised nature of modern parties and politics, it is assumed that the leader's image is one that is readily associated with the party itself. The second thing that Salvini decided to do in order to save himself and the party was to abandon the rhetoric and battle in favour of the North – albeit rather ambiguously (Mazzoleni and Ruzza 2018) – and to embrace a national, nationalist philosophy (Vampa 2017, p. 33). In doing so, it was the only western regionalist party to do so (Albertazzi *et al.* 2018, p. 646). To this end, in 2014, the Northern League was flanked by a list of candidates bearing the title "We are with Salvini" who stood for election in the South of Italy. At the 2018 general election, the party adopted one symbol for the entire nation and became the "League for Salvini Premier". In addition to this change in name, the transformation of the party's identity and public image was pursued in two main ways: by radicalising the League's traditional hostility towards immigration and by exacerbating the anti-Europeanist transformation of the League's position undertaken in the early 2000s (Chari *et al.* 2004). Both of these strategies were portrayed as designed to safeguard national interests. By dropping the slogan "The North first" and replacing it with the highly successful "Italians first" – which echoed Trump's "America first" slogan – Salvini not only tried to maintain votes in the North of Italy but also attempted to win over voters in the regions of central and southern Italy. This was a highly ambitious project, particularly in the South, given that not only had the League been totally absent from that part of Italy but was also viewed with a certain hostility due to its previous campaigns against southerners, a characteristic of the original Northern League that had survived to some degree. Given that the League could not depend on support from established party structures or a local core of League politicians in the Centre or South, in order to succeed in his aims, Salvini had to wager everything on his own public image.

Salvini invests in anti-politics

Salvini found that adopting anti-political attitudes and behaviour helped conceal the fact that he himself was a professional politician and made it easier for him to be taken for an anti-political outsider rather than an anti-political insider. By emphasising his diversity compared to mainstream politicians, he was also able to counter the success of the 5SM, which had made anti-politics its leitmotiv, and which at the 2013 general election (as we shall see in more detail in Chapter 5) won a great many votes in the South. With the polls showing the League on an upward trajectory, Forza Italia losing support (Vampa 2017, p. 42) and encouraged by the League's showing at the European elections in 2014 (6.1%) and at the regional elections in 2015 (when Luca Zaia was re-elected as President of the Veneto Regional Government, with 50% of the vote), Salvini went ahead with his plan to transform the party as well as his own personal style of leadership. Leaving aside all the other strategies and actions for the moment, we are now going to take a closer look at the way in which the anti-political attitudes and behaviour were used by Salvini to sustain this project for change.

As with Berlusconi in 1994, there was nothing new about Salvini wanting to rebuild the party and launch his own leadership. While Berlusconi "Americanized" Italian politics by resorting to the massive, unscrupulous use of television and opinion polls, Salvini introduced certain methods of political communication to Italy that were already being employed elsewhere, in particular in the English-speaking world. Both leaders, at different moments in time, have represented the clearest example of the process of mediatisation of politics that has spread throughout western democracies (Mazzoleni and Schulz 1999). As we shall see in the third section of Chapter 4 concerning Matteo Renzi, Salvini was not the only one to have realised the importance of, and implemented, the new techniques of political marketing and leadership image construction. Nevertheless, he is without doubt the politician who has employed such techniques in the most professional, convincing and, for a certain period at least, successful manner. Such strategies aim principally to personalise, popularise and celebratise politics, which as the vast number of classical studies concerning this matter acknowledge (Street 2004, Van Zoonen 2005, Stanyer 2013, Wheeler 2013), are fairly common ways of creating the image of a political leader and, at the same time, of polarising the political sphere.

This personalisation, popularisation and celebritisation of the figure of Salvini is pursued through a clear strategy followed in a professional manner thanks to the support of a team of young advisors and experts (Albertazzi *et al.* 2018, p. 651, Centorrino and Rizzo 2019, p. 21). The use of aggressive, divisive, provocative language,[16] the clever choice of those enemies to be targeted, the growing political and institutional importance he attained after taking over the leadership, all render Salvini well suited to the logic of the media. Salvini can thus be situated at the centre of a communicative phenomenon combining his constant presence in the papers and on TV, his extreme activism on social media,[17] and a thorough campaign involving his presence at public events all over Italy (Zulianello 2021). In a short space of time, the League's leader has become a classic case of the celebrity politician.[18] In order to strengthen his new image and to conceal the fact that he is himself a professional politician and a party member – both figures highly criticised in modern Italy – Salvini has to do things that the much-hated politicians do not usually do. For example, he reveals aspects of his private life, which are published in certain gossip magazines (Mazzoni and Mincigrucci 2021). In doing so, he makes frequent mention of his children and of his role as father. He has also encouraged gossip about his personal relationships, in particular with a well-known journalist, and later with the daughter of a long-standing member of Forza Italia. To show that he is "just like us" (Wood *et al.* 2016), Salvini gives over part of his daily social network messages to what he has eaten for lunch or dinner, accompanied by photos of simple, wholesome dishes that are 100% Italian, in keeping with the *sovereigntist* character he has given the party (Terracciano 2019).

The way he dresses and presents himself in public is yet another way of concealing the fact that he is a professional politician himself and gives him the aura of an outsider and innovator. As has been remarked, "followers attribute higher charisma to those leaders who wear clothing that contrasts their organization's cultural norms and lower charisma to their conforming counterparts" (Maran *et al.* 2021, p. 87). Not wearing ties, dressing casual, and in the summer letting yourself be photographed bare-chested (a variation on Bossi's singlet), are all ways of distinguishing yourself from other politicians. However, the truly innovative aspect of Salvini's public appearances is the number of times he has appeared wearing a sweatshirt or a police uniform, even when he was Minister for the Interior. The sweatshirts are deployed to convey a political message ("no to the Euro", "Renzi go home", "No to sanctions for Russia" etc.); or sometimes they bear the name of the city where Salvini is holding his rally, designed to galvanise the citizens and activists of that city. The police uniforms, together with the Carabinieri and fire brigade uniforms he has recently worn in public, are designed to make the headlines, elicit the reactions of observers and political adversaries, and underscore Salvini's support for the "law and order" approach that characterises the new League. It has been transformed from a regionalist party to a "far-right party of government" (Passarelli and Tuorto 2018a). Finally, among the other aspects of the construction and divulgation of the leader's public image, there is the utilisation of religious symbols, clearly designed to solicit the support of the catholic electorate. At certain rallies or public meetings – covered by the papers, TV and social media – the leader of the League has been shown displaying a rosary, kissing it and invoking the Madonna's protection. On another occasion – and there were many such circumstances – Salvini was filmed praying live on television together with a highly popular TV presenter.

As well as concealing his true identity as a political insider, all of these strategies aimed at the personalisation, popularisation and celebritisation of the party's leadership are employed by Salvini to gain the support of a politically unsophisticated public with little interest in political affairs, and hostile to the symbols of politics such as professional politicians, political parties and political representatives. In fact, thanks to the construction of an anti-political outsider leadership style, Salvini manages to appeal to an electorate that is hostile to professional politicians and political parties in general (Passarelli and Tuorto 2018a, pp. 97–8).[19] Paradoxically, the anti-political outsider style is pursued with greater conviction and determination not when the League is sitting on the opposition benches, but when it is in government, and its leader, Matteo Salvini, is at one and the same time Minister of the Interior, Deputy Prime Minister and National Secretary of the League. In these circumstances, as well as pursuing the aim of further increasing his own popularity and votes for the League, the political outsider gambit is played out in order to impose his own political line on the governing majority of which he is part, and of which he is a junior coalition partner in virtue of the seats his party holds in parliament.

In short, the attitudes and behaviour indicative of the personalisation, popularisation and celebritisation of Salvini's leadership have furthered the combination of political outsider and anti-politics, and in doing so, have resulted in the League's moving away from its position as a dangerous, difficult mainstream insider under Maroni's leadership, to a more profitable position as anti-political outsider. This clear change in the party's image, together with the anti-EU, anti-immigration rhetoric, its courting the support of the Catholic electorate, and in winning over existing political networks in the South of Italy (Brancaccio *et al.* 2021), has proven a successful way of repairing the damage caused by the scandals and avoiding the party's disappearance form the political scene. The fact of Berlusconi's personal and political decline, together with Salvini's taking on of important governmental offices which guarantee him considerable media visibility, have undoubtedly made it easier to achieve the primary goal the party had set itself, namely to re-launch the League and thus avoid its eventual demise. For a party that in 1996 had gained 10% of the votes cast, but that had seen its share of votes drop from 8% in 2008 to 4% in 2013, the 17.5% share it obtained at the 2018 general election can in fact be considered an extraordinary achievement. Confirmation of the success of Salvini's new approach was given by the party's incredible 34.3% share of votes cast at the 2019 European elections. In fact, it won over 20% of the electorate that in 2018 had voted for the 5SM, and 30% of those who had voted for Forza Italia (Chiaramonte *et al.* 2020, p. 10). The League was also highly successful in the South, where it obtained 23.5% of the vote (22.4% in Sicily and 27.6% in Sardinia), and was the most voted-for party in many provinces. Nevertheless, despite this historical success, the League has failed to establish solid local roots in Italy's southern regions, and in fact, did not even present a list of candidates at many municipal elections. Even when it did present lists, it gained very few votes. The difference between the party's success at "distant" elections such as general elections and European elections, and its lack of success at "nearby" elections such as the municipal and regional elections, shows that it is not the League that is nationalised, but rather its leadership under Salvini (Brancaccio *et al.* 2021). His has been a transformative leadership (Burns 1978, p. 4), given that his rhetoric has succeeded not only in exacerbating the League's electorate's hostility towards immigrants, but indeed, has managed to get them to declare their support for the "Nation" and for "national unity" (Passarelli and Tuorto 2018a, p. 48), two facets of politics that never gleaned any support among the Northern League's electorate in the party's early days.

Not only emboldened by his own popularity and by the growing support for the party reported by the opinion polls, but also as a result of the growing conflict within the governmental alliance with the 5SM (Cotta 2020), in the summer of 2019, Salvini took a huge gamble and brought down the League-5SM coalition government that had only been formed just over a year before. He did this in order that an early election be called so as to capitalise, in terms of parliamentary seats and power, on his own popularity. This proved to be a mistake however, as shortly afterwards the 5SM formed an alliance with certain centre-left parties, thus marking the advent of a new government led by Giuseppe Conte, and relegating the League to the opposition ranks (see Chapter 5). His excessive self-belief, together with his overly zealous use of anti-political strategies (the announcement of the League's withdrawal from the government coalition was made from a discotheque on the Romagna coast, where Salvini, Minister of the Interior, posed for photos as a bare-chested DJ), thus deceived the League's leader. As we shall see in the next chapter, only three years earlier, this very same problem had led to the political demise of Matteo Renzi, another leader boasting strong anti-political views.

Notes

1 The history of the Northern League (now simply "The League") is a well-known one. There are several fundamental works regarding the foundation of the party and the rise of its unchallenged leader, Umberto Bossi. See, for example: Vimercati (1990), Mannheimer (1991a) and Diamanti (1993). With regard to the League's more recent history and its role in the Italian political system, see the works by Gianluca Passarelli and Dario Tuorto (2012, 2018a). In English, of specific note are the following works: Gilbert (1995, ch. 4), Tarchi (1998), Cento Bull and Gilbert (2001), Tambini (2001), Albertazzi (2016), McDonnell and Vampa (2016), Biorcio (2017), Albertazzi *et al.* (2018) and Albertazzi and Vampa (2021).

2 Italians have always had a significant aversion to politicians and political parties, as we saw in the preceding chapter. Renato Mannheimer and Giacomo Sani (2001, p. 83), basing their findings on a number of opinion polls, reported that in 1985 the Italians' feelings towards politics were as follows: anger 17%, disgust 10.4%, diffidence 13.9%, indifference 21.1%, boredom 12%. By 1990, during the period of the League's first electoral successes, but prior to the Tangentopoli bribery scandal, the shares of such feelings had become: anger 15.1%, disgust 9.5%, diffidence 17.7%, indifference 20%, boredom 12.2%. By the end of the 1990s, after Tangentopoli and the successes of anti-political parties like the League and Forza Italia, people's disgust with politics had more than doubled (22.8%).

3 The story recounted by the League of an Italian North exploited by a centralist State has been driven by, and in turn, has fed, a deep sense of injustice that produces a "politics of resentment", the dynamics of which is very similar to that described by Katherine Cramer in her account of a rural community in Wisconsin (Cramer 2016). In her study, Cramer points to the fact that the formation of political opinions and positions among ordinary people is strictly correlated to their sense of territorial identity, and to the opposition between "us" and "them".

4 Despite being an important aspect of the identity of the regional Leagues that came together to form the Northern League, this anti-southerner stance appears to become less important than the League's criticism of the country's political parties. In 1991, and thus before the Tangentopoli scandal, a national survey found that "50.3% perceive the existence of the Leagues in a positive light, and only 15% declare themselves openly hostile to them". The support for the Leagues is of course greater in the North of Italy, although appreciation for them is also significant in the South (42.5%). The reasons given by interviewees for their positive opinion of the Leagues include the following: "they break the parties' stranglehold" (28%), followed by 25.5% who believe that the Leagues "speak in clear terms". At this stage in their development, the Leagues were seen more as a movement against the existing political parties ("a form of protest against the parties" – 25.6%) than against southerners or foreigners ("the manifestation of the North's intolerance towards southern Italians" – 22.5%) (Colarizi 2005, p. 151). With regard to anti-political and anti-party opinions of the Leagues' voters and supporters, see also (Mannheimer 1991b, pp. 144–5).

5 For a pioneering comparative study of the Lombardy League and the Common Man Movement, which situates the actions and successes of the two parties in their respective historical-political contexts, see the volume by Antonio Costabile (1991).

6 For an analysis of the figure of Umberto Bossi, his personal traits and his presumed charismatic character, see Richard Barraclough (1998).

7   Information on the results of the European, General, Regional, Provincial and Municipal elections and of the various referenda, detailed to different degrees, can be found on the Ministry for the Interior's website (https://elezionistorico.interno.gov.it/).

8   Di Pietro left the judiciary in 1994 and went into politics two years later: first as an independent Minister in Prodi's first government, and then as a member of the new party he himself set up, pointedly named the "Italy of Values" party. Di Pietro was clearly the leading figure in the Tangentopoli affair. As the investigating magistrate, he came across as the genuine, real hero successfully battling against the corrupt, haughty political class of old. On the figure of Di Pietro, his party and his political life, see among others: Newell (2015).

9   "I will ask you to vote in a popular manner, that is by a show of hands, as to whether we should join the Government". The wording of Bossi's speech given at the rally can be found at: https://www.leganord.org/phocadownload/ilmovimento/Presidente_Federale/discorsi_pontida/1994_10aprile.pdf.

10 "Rome" was the symbol of the old corrupt, centralist political system; the "Pole" meant the "Pole of Liberties", that is, the centre-right coalition that the League had withdrawn from; "The Olive Tree", on the other hand, was the name of the centre-left coalition governing the country at that time.

11 An analysis of electoral flows shows that of 100 electors who voted for the League in 1996, only one-third voted for Bossi's party again in 2001. This is the lowest percentage of all parties concerned, and as such, is a sign of the widespread dissatisfaction with the change in the party's political line. Overall, 31% of those who had previously voted League now voted for the centre-left coalition, just over 10% for other centre-right parties, and almost 13% for miscellaneous other parties. Finally, 13% decided to abstain (Schadee and Segatti 2002, p. 358).

12 A first warning bell rang regarding the excessively personalised, family-based direction of the party when Umberto Bossi fell ill. Rather than replacing him in office with other party representatives, it was his wife who took on a leading role. Furthermore, at the time of his first public appearance after his illness, Bossi appointed his children to be his political heirs, despite their youth (Ignazi 2018, p. 199). In fact, in 2010, at the age of only 21, Bossi's son Renzo became the youngest regional counsellor to be elected in the Lombardy region. The scandals concerning the improper use of public funds earmarked for the party began to emerge at the beginning of 2012. The details were truly embarrassing and shook public opinion: the purchase of diamonds in Tanzania, connections with the Calabrian mafia ('ndrangheta), payment for the false graduation of his son Renzo from an Albanian university. The legal action brought against the Northern League's treasurers and other party leaders, resulted in a conviction in appeal which was largely invalidated because time-barred. In addition to the individual criminal liability of those convicted, the League as such was ordered to return 49 million Euro to the Italian State. Details of the funding received by the League during the period 1993–2016 are offered by Passarelli and Tuorto (2018a, p. 53).

13 The judiciary called the investigation "The Family", after the title of a file seized from the League's Treasury Office, containing documents concerning irregular spending by the family of the League's founder and leader.

14 There were clear signs of militants leaving the party and of the party's organisation crumbling following the scandals that rocked the League's leadership. By 2018, the number of party branches has fallen to 437 from the 1,451 present in 2011 (Passarelli and Tuorto 2018a, p. 45); party membership, which in the entire history of the League had never fallen below 110,000, plummeted from

173,044 in 2011 to 56,074 in 2012 (McDonnell 2016, p. 731); the accounts, which in 2011 showed a surplus of over 6 million Euro, revealed a deficit of over 10 million Euro in 2012 (McDonnell and Vampa 2016, p. 122).

15 At the 2013 general election, 10% of the votes cast for Five Star Movement candidates standing for election to the Chamber of Deputies came for electors who in 2008 had voted for the League (De Sio and Paparo 2014, p. 132). Furthermore, as Passarelli and Tuorto have pointed out, at the 2018 elections, the hostility towards career politicians and political parties was greater among Five Star Movement voters than among those of the League (2018a, p. 143).

16 His call for bulldozers to be brought in to resolve problems is emblematic of his style of communication, as they metaphorically destroy the old political system and politicians, but also physically destroy, for example, the Roma camps situated in Italy's cities (Hopkin 2020, p. 239). As we shall see in the following chapter, the metaphor of destruction and demolition is something that Matteo Renzi also uses, and in fact, he has been referred to as "demolition man" (Zulianello 2019a, p. 152).

17 Salvini is connected to all of the main social networks, although his preferred medium is Facebook. He has almost 5 million FB followers (August 2021), the most of any Italian political leader (Giuseppe Conte has almost 4.7 million, Luigi Di Maio around 2.6 million, Giorgia Meloni 2.2 million, Matteo Renzi just over 1.1 million, and indeed more than any other European leader) (Emmanuel Macron has almost 4.1 million followers, Angela Merkel, before closing her account in 2019 had around 2.5 million; Boris Johnson has around 2.1 million, Pedro Sánchez nearly 400,000). For an analysis of the popularity of Facebook posts, depending on their content, see Giuliano Bobba (2019). A very detailed analysis of the language used by Salvini on Twitter has been conducted by Fabrizio Macagno (2019).

18 An example of the celebritisation of Salvini, which clearly reveals the politicising fandom process undertaken by the League's leader (Dean 2017), is the organisation of two editions of a competition, with prizes awarded, entitled "win Salvini". In short, the competition gives prizes to those social media users who are the quickest to share and divulge Salvini's contributions. The prizes awarded consist of: once a day, a post with the photo of the winner to be shared on all social media, and a telephone call from Salvini; once a week, a personal encounter with Salvini himself. The first edition of this competition was launched prior to the 2018 general election (https://www.youtube.com/watch?v=FMXfO_pW1hM); the second edition, prior to the European elections of 2019 (https://www.youtube.com/watch?v=OuWimbUC9Eo).

19 Passarelli and Tuorto (2018a, p. 97) report that in 2018, the League's voters were in above-average agreement with the following three statements: "Members of Parliament must follow citizens' wishes" (72% compared to a mean of 58%); "Citizens, rather than politicians, should make the important decisions" (37% compared to 28%); "Politicians talk a lot but do very little" (69% compared to 59%).

4 The centre-left

Between democratic innovation and the "scrapping" of the old political class

Participation induced by the institutions

In Italy's political history, criticism of political parties, professional politicians and the country's representative institutions has mainly been the prerogative of the right. As the second chapter of this volume points out, Guglielmo Giannini and Giuseppe Maranini were two such critics from the conservative and moderate areas of the political sphere, respectively. More recently, Berlusconi and his Forza Italia party, together with the League – firstly under the leadership of Bossi and subsequently under that of Salvini – have offered further examples of the right's predilection for anti-politics. Anti-political rhetoric, moreover, is used much less by mainstream parties and leaders, as noted in Chapter 1, than it is by populist parties and politicians, not only in Italy but also elsewhere. Therefore, when these two aspects come together, that is, when we are faced with populist right-wing parties and leaders, it is almost inevitable that they adopt language, attitudes, behaviour and also legislative proposals and public policies, of an anti-political nature. In view of this, it may be interesting to examine the other side of the coin, that is, the relationship among anti-politics and left-wing and mainstream parties. In other words, it is a good idea to try and establish how it is that these parties manage to survive and operate in a social and political environment, like that of Italy, characterised by the ubiquitous anti-political sentiments and ideas of its citizens and politicians. Do these parties reject and fight against the denigration of politicians, parties and political institutions by the anti-political right, or do they adapt to the spirit of the time and thus adopt anti-political attitudes and behaviour themselves? If the latter, then what type of anti-political behaviour do they adopt, and how do they go about doing so?

In order to answer these questions, this chapter shall examine certain matters concerning the line-up of the centre-left in Italy in the last 20 years. The analysis conducted here will focus principally on the major centre-left party, the Democratic Party (*Partito Democratico* – PD). The PD was founded in 2007 as a combination of the inheritances left by two of the country's historical political traditions: on the one hand, the Italian Communist Party (PCI), and on the other, left-wing Catholicism as previously encapsulated

DOI: 10.4324/9781003109273-5

in the Christian Democratic Party (DC). The DC was the large, politically moderate denominational party which governed Italy for the entire duration of the First Republic.[1] The resulting hybrid PD is typically progressive yet mainstream. The political cultures that this new party inherited placed great importance on the role of politics, of political representation, of the nation's institutions, of political parties as such – considered to form the backbone of democracy – and of social and political participation as an expression of citizenship. These political cultures appreciate the value of universalism and benevolence, for example (Catellani and Milesi 2010, p. 236), and are opposed to those of success and power, which are more characteristic of right-wing populist forces and their anti-political rhetoric.[2] As a result of this cultural inheritance and of the different sensitivity of its own electorate, the PD's leadership cannot openly play the anti-political game: on the one hand, this is because the political scene is constantly populated by actors whose anti-political stances are far more credible; on the other hand, many of the PD's activists and voters would be disorientated and disappointed by such behaviour. Nonetheless, the anti-politics of Italians is something that exists and is a strong topic of public debate[3] and thus cannot be ignored by anyone hoping to win people's support and votes. The PD (and the centre-left as a whole) thus found itself caught between the Scylla of anti-politics widely present among the electorate and the Charybdis of its own political tradition that it cannot unashamedly repudiate.

The strategy adopted by the party's leadership in order to navigate between the two in this hazardous political "sea" was to try and combine grassroots participation – a traditional watchword of both the left and of democratic Catholicism – with a renewed image of the party and its leaders.[4] The foundation of a new party itself, whose very name is more a homage to the USA than to European social democracy, with any reference to "left" deleted now (Pasquino 2009, p. 22), clearly marks a departure from the "old politics". This departure was pursued with conviction by testing out certain democratic innovations, such as participatory and deliberative democracy practices, and by introducing primary elections. Once the innovative force of these democratic innovations – which shall be discussed in the present and following sections – began to wane, the PD relied on the renewal of the party's leadership to sustain its electoral appeal. Its choice of new leader was the outsider Matteo Renzi, who we shall be discussing in the third section of this chapter. We are now going to take a closer look at certain events that have involved the PD and the centre-left as a whole over the course of the last two decades, with the aim of identifying any anti-political implications of such.

Italy's "deliberative turn"

The first democratic innovation introduced by the centre-left parties and politicians, in particular at local and regional levels, regards certain new forms of citizen participation.[5] In the early 2000s, these participatory practices could be seen as the Italian version of the "strong deliberative turn" (Dryzek 2000, p. 1) witnessed in several western democracies during those years. Deliberative polls, citizens juries, consensus conference, open space technology, community dialogue, participatory budgeting, town meetings, are just some of the ways, that in different countries around the world, increased citizen participation was pursued together with the renewal of democracy which, it was claimed, was in crisis. This shift in direction can also be seen as the response from citizens, politicians and political parties to the grassroots demands that emerged within the context of the large-scale protests of the global justice movement (GJM), which forced its way onto the political stage in the late 1990s. These protests, which were of a pluralist, international nature,[6] criticised the character of economic globalisation and the workings of politics and democracy. The movements involved ascribed the incapacity to govern the on-going process of economic and cultural globalisation to the politicians, political parties and governments of the western democracies, who they claimed were held hostage by global economic interests. For the parties and politicians on the left, supporting and encouraging new forms of participation could thus be a way of shielding themselves from the criticism from the left itself, that is, from the world of social and political movements, and of trying to intercept part of those movements' opinions and consensus. In other words, deliberative practices, as Donatella della Porta has pointed out, can be seen "a renewed and more sophisticated, strategy of consensus building" (quoted in: Freschi and Mete 2009, p. 6).

Without going into the details of this endless debate,[7] we can establish the principal aims that the promoters and supporters of such new forms of participation had in mind. Firstly, they wished to extend citizens' political participation beyond mere voting at elections. Thus the new forms of participation impacted the mechanisms of political delegation by reclaiming space for the exercise of power from the elected representatives. Participatory practices of a deliberative nature aim to challenge the majoritarian, competitive principle's domination of the workings of democracy (Mouffe 1999), as this goes no further than simply aggregating citizens' previous political positions. The deliberative forms of democracy, on the contrary, aim to elicit a change in participants' opinions, through regulated discussion, where what counts is not the force of numbers but Habermas' principle of the "force of the best arguments". At the same time, in deliberative processes, participants should not seek to see their own individual or group interests prevail but should pursue the common good. From this point of view, the new forms of participation also play an educational role by shaping democratic practices, and by generating social capital, among the population. Participatory practices can also be employed to resolve specific conflicts within society, for example with regard to the construction of large-scale engineering works. Certain participatory mechanisms can offer invaluable input to political decision-makers, to a greater and better degree than surveys; this input, consisting in opinions and points of view, can be taken into account in decisional processes or in the implementation of public policy. They also operate to provide output, when political decision-makers involve or delegate to citizens in regard to the decisions or policy actions to be taken. In short, unlike the direct democracy perceived by the 5SM which we shall discuss in greater depth in the following chapter, these forms of participation are designed to be in addition to, rather than as a replacement for, representative democracy.

The centre-left parties, by importing certain participatory practices utilised in other political contexts, and by embarking on the gradual institutionalisation of participation (Hartz-Karp and Briand 2009), thus acknowledged (implicitly at least) the difficulties and limits of representative democracy. In order to overcome such limits, those same parties' local and regional authorities' actions subscribed to what has been described as a "folk theory of democracy", whereby: "the cure for the ills of democracy is more democracy" (Achen and Bartels 2016, p. 14). Consequently, as Clarke *et al.* point out: "mainstream politicians have tended to respond to [the] lack of confidence, trust, and perceived efficacy with 'democratic innovations', e. g. lowering the voting age, devolving power to regions/localities, or participatory decision-making" (Clarke *et al.* 2018, p. 1).

By availing itself of the solutions offered by the aforementioned "deliberative turn", the democratic medicine administered to Italy's sorry democracy was of various kinds. Certain local authorities led by the centre-left paved the way by introducing participatory budgeting along the lines of Porto Alegre in Brazil (Bassoli 2012). In Montaione, a municipality situated in "red" Tuscany, a sort of French *débat public* was tried out for the first time (Floridia 2012, p. 85). Deliberative processes were employed in an attempt to intervene in conflicts over large-scale public works or "NIMBY" protests such as the one concerning the siting of a waste dump and incinerator in the province of Turin (Bobbio 2002), or the construction of a large motorway section designed to stretch across the city of Genoa (Bobbio 2010).[8] These are just some examples from a very long list.[9] The point is that from the early 2000s onwards, local administrators on the centre-left widely availed themselves of forms of participation prompted by the institutions. In many cases, such practices involved the use of IT instruments and online platforms designed to facilitate contact and cooperation between users/citizens and the public authorities, giving rise to various forms of open government (De Blasio 2018).

In addition to Italy's municipalities, the country's regional administrations led by centre-left coalitions have invested considerably, both politically and, to a lesser degree, financially, in the new participatory and deliberative practices.[10] The forerunners in this regard have been the three so-called "red" regions – Emilia-Romagna, Tuscany and Umbria – together with the Puglia region which between 2005 and 2015 was governed by Nichi Vendola, a left-wing politician close to the GJM. In an attempt to institutionalise such participatory practices, these four Italian regions adopted a regional law on participation, while many other regions began to discuss whether or not to introduce such a law (Brunazzo 2017). The Tuscany region's law on participatory practices was formulated on the basis on a large-scale participatory event, namely an "electronic town meeting" lasting an entire day and involving over 400 participants (Freschi and Mete 2009, Cellini *et al.* 2010, Lewanski 2013). Furthermore, in 2009 the Lazio Regional Government passed a regional law on participatory budgeting, and the Sicily Regional Government did likewise in 2011 on the basis of a project advanced by the 5SM's group of regional councillors.[11] The reasons underlying such endeavours on the part of the aforementioned centre-left regional governments include the attempt to counter the anti-political feelings commonly expressed by their citizens, and to resolve conflicts with organised groups of citizens challenging the institutions' decisions. This intention is clearly evident in the President of the Tuscany Regional Government's account of the origins of the regional law on participatory practices:

> The years of my first electoral term were problematic. A significant part of the electorate and many activists criticized the top PD politicians. There were academics, social leaders, and also film directors who publicly criticized the competence and the strategies of their political representatives. At the same time, many citizen committees were sprouting up to protest against anything and everything: incinerators, highways, railways, etc. (...) Reacting to this situation, I decided to set up a link between institutions and movements. I started with the 'San Rossore meetings', which were organized every year in mid-July, in order to talk directly to the movements and citizen committees on various issues. But the relationship was complex, and there were clashes. I realized that we needed an institutional framework in order to be able to better manage the relationship with citizen committees and movements. The San Rossore model was not enough, we needed to go beyond the spontaneity of such assemblies; we needed to create a more structured way of participating. That's the reason for my idea of a law on public participation.
>
> (quoted in Ravazzi 2017, p. 7)

The anti-political significance of participatory practices driven by the institutions

Regardless of the intentions of those proposing such measures, the introduction by municipal and regional governments led by the centre-left of the participatory and deliberative instruments outlined here produced other effects in addition to those specifically pursued.[12] Such effects may conceal anti-political messages and meanings, which we are now going to examine. As we shall see, this form of anti-politics is not the direct, coarse, at times, vulgar version adopted by the populist right-wing parties, but is a subtler, more sophisticated variety, and perhaps for this reason less easily recognisable and more insidious.

First of all, at the theoretical level deliberative processes appear to be radically anti-political because, in proposing to resolve disputes through argumentation, they negate the very nature of politics, which consists of legitimately irreconcilable political positions, personal and collective interests and power asymmetries among those concerned (Mouffe 1999, Shapiro 1999, Walzer 1999). Participation organised and promoted by the nation's institutions, on the other hand, aims to render conflict sterile by stripping citizens of their identity and interests and encouraging a discussion pursuing agreement through the transformation of individual opinions and preferences. The lack of agreement among participants is reduced to a mere problem of a lack of information on the matter under discussion, or a lack of communication among participants, rather than one of genuinely contrasting interests and values. In other words, once citizen-participants have been depoliticised, then public decisions – and thus politics as such – can also be depoliticised.

Secondly, on a more practical level, those participatory processes fostered by the institutions have anti-political implications per se, in that they go against professional politicians, political representatives and political parties. In fact, on closer examination, the need for ordinary citizens chosen at random, who are not bearers of any specific interests, in order to re-lay a town square's paving, to provide guidelines for a regional law, or to settle a dispute concerning a large-scale public work, means, implicitly at least, sending the message that said citizens govern better than the elected representatives and professional politicians, and that artificial, ad hoc arenas work better than elected assemblies populated by costly, inefficient career politicians. Thus politics is brought down to the mere administration of public interests, and as Giannini suggested, good administration can be provided by any "good accountant". In other words, a person with no specific skills is a person, who does not have to worry about creating public consensus, and who renders professional politicians and representative assemblies superfluous. For the very reason that politics is commonly portrayed as the realm of quarrelling, partisanship, corruption and lack of effectiveness – this would appear to be the message sent out by the centre-left politicians and institutions promoting these new forms of participation – there is a need for wise, responsible, collaborative, disinterested common citizens capable of changing their opinions and of operating for the collective good.

The impact that the participation fostered by the institutions has on political parties is even clearer. When parties were strong and firmly-rooted, particularly in the aforementioned "red" regions of Italy, local authorities responded in full to the party's bodies. Gradually this close relationship weakened, particularly following the previously-mentioned reform in 1993 introducing the direct election of mayors, which furthered the importance of said mayors to the detriment of Italy's political parties and local assemblies. The spread of participatory practices through the creation of ad hoc assemblies, which were to become the "official", legitimate bodies coordinating with local politicians, marked a definitive separation of party activism from local administration. Parties were increasingly split between the management by professional politicians and a scattered group of sympathisers momentarily brought together in the deliberative arenas "created" at the time by local and regional administrations controlled by the party in public office. There were undoubted benefits to be had for party heads from replacing aggressive party militants with "deliberative" groups of citizens. As well as narrowing discussions to the sole issue for which the group of participants was created, the party leaders ran very little risk of being challenged and replaced by citizens who, for the simple reason that they are part of a temporary, artificial group, are less capable of coalescing and getting organised than are traditional activists with a stable place for discussion located within the party.

The instruments conceived to reinvigorate participation, threatened to backfire on the principal traditional channel of democratic participation, paradoxically. As Peter Mair has pointed out in this regard: "Parties are failing because the zone of engagement – the traditional world of party democracy where citizens interact with and felt a sense of attachment to their political leaders – is being evacuated" (Mair 2013, p. 16). These forms of participation thus hollow out the party from within. It cannot be argued that those proposing and sustaining them are against political parties. However, it is true to say that by doing so, they contribute towards hollowing out the organizational kernel of said parties and transforming them in the sense of strengthening their institutional roles to the detriment of their representative functions (Bartolini and Mair 2002). Furthermore, the implicitly anti-political significance of these new forms of participation inevitably affects democracy as such, of which the parties continue, for better or worse, to bear the burden: "the renewal of interest in democracy and its meanings at individual and institutional levels is not intended to open up or reinvigorate democracy as such; the aim is rather to redefine democracy in such a way that it can more easily cope with, and adapt to, the decline of popular interest and engagement" (Mair 2013, p. 9). Ultimately, as Piero Ignazi has pointed out in his volume of the transformation of political parties: "The same innovations that have been recently devised – deliberative polls, web participation, ballot recall, public jury, referendum, citizens' initiatives of different sorts, and so on – intend to bypass political parties. These alternatives seem to suggest a pragmatic way out of the present parties' deadlock. In reality, this search reveals an underground sentiment of the fundamental 'illegitimacy' of political parties, well beyond their present malpractice" (Ignazi 2017, pp. 1–2).

Finally, in addition to legitimising the political class and representative assemblies, and to contributing towards hollowing out parties by removing their more militant elements, these new forms of participation have an anti-political significance insofar as they risk driving down political participation as such. This apparently paradoxical outcome arises because participation driven by the institutions – which is already far from inclusive (Ryfe and Stalsburg 2012) – then represents the only legitimate channel of engagement with the country's political representatives. The other, pre-existing forms of participation, which are often more conflicting and better organised, are implicitly delegitimised, more or less, from the establishment of deliberative practices organised and endorsed by the institutions. Once again, the model of the engaged, reasonable citizen prepared to change opinion, clashes with the "noisy minorities" of dissatisfied citizens intending to have their demands heard through mobilisation operations and demonstrations. This attempt at regulating participation has led certain civil society groups, and even certain sections of the political class, to denounce the "hoax" of those forms of participation driven by the institutions.[13]

The "invention" of party primaries

The centre-left parties' prime choice of democratic "medicine" (considered even more important than the aforementioned new forms of participation), which they administer both to themselves and, consequently, to Italy's ailing democracy, is the primary election.[14] The primaries accompany and drive Italian voters' involvement in decisional processes, both in practical terms and, more importantly, from the symbolic point of view. Their design means that they enable party sympathisers (in fact, anyone who declares that they are such) to enter what has been called "the secret garden of politics" (Gallagher and Marsh 1988). In other words, they promise to bring a breath of fresh air into the party's smoke-filled rooms where the party heads at central office have traditionally decided on the names of electoral candidates. With regard to the questions covered in this chapter and in this volume in general, the same considerations made in the previous section concerning the new forms of participation also apply to the primaries. This form of citizen involvement, which is unprecedented in Italy, takes on the same subtle, paradoxical anti-party, anti-political careerist significance. A rapid reconstruction of the main events concerning primaries in Italy will help to clarify the anti-political character and consequences of this democratic innovation.

Local primaries, national primaries

Primaries were first introduced into Italy in the early 2000s (taking the American political system as a template), together with the participatory practices examined in the previous section. Once again, this democratic innovation, which in other countries as well has been adopted more by left-wing parties than those of a centre/centre-right persuasion (Shomer 2014,

p. 537), was partly in response to the large-scale mass movements of those years. It marked a shift in the way political candidates and party leaders are chosen and has gradually gained currency in other European countries as well. As Marco Valbruzzi has pointed out: "it was Italy, especially thanks to some left-wing parties, that opened the way in Europe to the introduction of more inclusive mechanisms (such as 'open' primary elections) for the selection of leaders and candidates" (2021, p. 20).

The first important experiment with primaries in Italy was conducted, perhaps unsurprisingly, in Tuscany. This is a region that has long been a stronghold of the left, and as we have seen is also the most active region, together with Emilia-Romagna, in terms of participatory practices. Following the debate on institutional reforms in the early 1990s, and after a number of rather tentative local experiments (Fusaro 2005, pp. 444–5), a regional law was passed in 2004 offering parties the opportunity to utilise primary elections to select candidates for the Regional Council and for the Presidency of the Regional Government. In Tuscany, primaries are perceived as a corrective instrument, which was designed to adjust an electoral system that was introduced almost at the same time as the primaries, and which envisaged blocked lists and the abolition of preferences. This electoral system, which considerably limited voters' freedom of choice, who were simply called upon to "endorse" the choice made by the parties' leaders, had been introduced, in turn, to remedy the battle for preferences witnessed at the previous regional elections (Floridia 2006, p. 95). This had been a hard battle requiring the investment of personal resources rather than those of the party, and as such was viewed by certain politicians and commentators as representing the degeneration of politics. The proponents of the electoral law and of the primary elections wanted to avoid the destabilisation of Italy's political parties, in particular those on the centre-left that had traditionally held power in the Tuscany region, and to avoid the emergence of forms of corruption due to the need to procure the resources required to win votes (ibid., p. 96).

Following this initial experiment which, while important, had generated limited interest beyond the regional level (of Tuscany), subsequent primary elections held to choose the centre-left coalition's candidate for the regional elections in Puglia generated interest at national level. Contrary to expectations, the winner of the latter primaries was Nichi Vendola, an MP and leader of a left-wing party that continued to call itself "communist". His declared homosexuality, together with his wearing an earring, made him a political outsider by the standards of Italian politics at the time. Nichi Vendola not only defeated the principal centre-left parties' chosen centrist candidate, but he also defeated, just as unexpectedly, the centre-right candidate, that is, the incumbent President of the Regional Government (Vassallo and Passarelli 2016, pp. 4–5). This dual victory by a political outsider, which was a very unlikely achievement for the leader of a small party with a communist heritage, made possible by the introduction of the primaries, caused a considerable stir in the political world and generated great public surprise and interest in Italy.

The ultimate consecration of the primaries as a means of selecting political representatives was witnessed in the autumn of 2005. These primaries were held to choose the person who would become Prime Minister in the event that the centre-left won the subsequent general election. Unlike on previous occasions, however, these primaries were not really competitive but simply served to endorse a choice already made. "The Prodi primaries", as they were pointedly called, served in fact to strengthen the legitimacy of one candidate – Romano Prodi, the former Prime Minister (1996–8) and President of the European Commission between 1999 and 2004 – who was not the direct representative of any one party (Pasquino and Valbruzzi 2016, p. 2). In terms of participation, the primaries held by the Union (the name of the centre-left coalition standing at the 2006 general election) proved highly successful. They also represented the mobilisation of the centre-left against the Berlusconi government which had been in office since 2001: more than 4 million electors voted at these primaries, at least four times the figure the organisers had foreseen (Hopkin 2005, p. 77). Thanks to this incredible success, the primaries became an easily recognisable "trademark" of the centre-left and of the PD (Cerruto and Facello 2014, p. 84), the party that was about to be founded and that was to include open primaries in its own statute.[15] In doing so, the centre-left embraced the issue of participation, presenting itself as a more open and inclusive coalition than the centre-right, which on the contrary was mainly composed of top-down, plebiscitary, personalised parties.

At the national level, the "Prodi primaries" were followed by another five primaries for the direct election of the PD's national secretary over a period of 15 years or so, In 2007, rather predictably, Walter Veltroni, a senior leader of the Left Democrats (*Democratici di sinistra*) and Mayor of Rome at the time, won the primaries and became the new party's first secretary. When he resigned in 2009, further primaries were held, which were won by Pier Luigi Bersani, another politician from the same party. In 2013, as a result of the rather unsatisfactory performance at the general election, Bersani resigned; and at the end of that year, further primaries were held which were won by Matteo Renzi. Renzi resigned as party leader in February 2017, having "lost" the referendum on "his" proposed reform of the Italian Constitution (which shall be discussed in greater detail in the following section). However, he stood for re-election at the subsequent primaries in April 2017 and won. Following the party's poor performance at the 2018 general election, Renzi resigned once again, and in March 2019 further primaries were held which were won by Nicola Zingaretti, President of the Lazio Regional Government. As a result of disagreements within the party, Zingaretti also resigned, and Enrico Letta was elected national secretary, but without recourse to open primaries involving the PD's supporters.[16] As we have seen, primaries have been a key feature of Italian political life, and of the centre-left in particular, over the last 15 years.[17]

The anti-political consequences of the primaries

Having briefly outlined the main points of the primaries held in Italy in recent years, let us now consider what exactly led the country's centre-left parties and politicians to introduce, and have such massive recourse to, this important democratic innovation. The literature regarding this question points to various different reasons for the introduction of new methods of selecting candidates. These include: the greater legitimation of the candidates themselves; the mobilisation of the electorate, increased democracy within the party, having a wider public get to know the candidates and so on. Of these reasons, perhaps the most pertinent in the Italian case are the following two: "improving the public image of parties by promoting new inclusive methods to involve citizens, and re-defining the relationship of the party with members/supporters who had a new incentive for their involvement" (De Luca 2018, p. 400). Thus the introduction of the primaries was an attempt to change things both within the party and externally, that is, in terms of the party's relations with its members and supporters.

Internally, the party leaders promoting primaries decided to officially open the gates of the aforementioned "secret garden" to everyone. This opening was greater than the literature imagined, given that the most inclusive hypothesis comprised the entire electorate (Rahat and Hazan 2001, p. 301); in the case of certain elections, on the other hand, the PD and the centre-left coalition lowered the minimum voting age to 16 and gave the right to vote to resident immigrants as well (Corbetta and Vignati 2013a, p. 83). This thus marked a clear departure from, and transformation of, the party model implying the Americanisation of the European left (Lipset 2002). The dividing line between inside and outside the party was now evanescent. Party sympathisers gained power, while activists and militants saw their powers decline. Thus the transformation of Italian parties, which had been on-going for some time, now intensified:

> The parties are actually making a careful and conscious distinction between different elements within the party on the ground (...): it is not the party congress or the middle-level elite, or the activists, who are being empowered, but rather the 'ordinary' members, who are at once more docile and more likely to endorse the policies (and candidates) proposed by the party leadership and by the party in public office (...). Ordinary members, often at home, and via postal ballots, are increasingly being consulted by the party leadership, and are increasingly involved in legitimizing the choices of the party in public office (...) the activist layer inside the party, the traditionally more troublesome layer, becomes marginalized. Nor is this necessarily a problem for the party leadership, for, in contrast to the activists, these ordinary and often disaggregated members are not very likely to mount a serious challenge against the positions adopted by the leadership.
>
> (Mair 1994, p. 16)

In addition to strengthening the party leadership, the primaries also atomise the membership, just like the deliberative practices examined in the previous section fragment participation, making any grassroots challenge to the party in public office more difficult, arduous and uncertain. The anti-party message that is subtly divulged within the party (among its activists, sympathisers and voters) is that the political parties we knew – those that channelled participation and bore the weight of representative democracy, and which in truth are viewed with a certain degree of retrotopia (Ignazi 2020), are in fact obsolete and unsuited to contemporary politics. In other words, they are worthless. What we need are leaders as the sole protagonists of the political scene: leaders that their followers are occasionally called upon to acclaim, rather than choose, given the non-competitive nature of many primaries or direct elections of party secretaries. On closer examination, therefore, the primaries represent a break with a cultural tradition whereby political leaders and the centralisation of power was viewed with suspicion by the left.[18] Having broken for good the taboo against the personalisation of politics, the primaries now offer a "left-wing" approach to the *celebritisation* of politics: party debate no longer focuses on alternative political or programmatic approaches, but on the personal qualities and characteristics of the aspiring leaders competing for office. Even in a party that is the product of 20th-century ideologies, it has become normal to disagree with regard to people rather than to the political programmes and aims to be pursued. The primaries not only send out an anti-party message, but an anti-political careerism message as well. Political leaders, in abdicating their role as selectors of electoral candidates and of the party's national secretary, implicitly acknowledge that they are not suited to their recognised role. They admit, symbolically, that any citizen who declares him/herself to be a party sympathiser, is capable of making wiser, more balanced, less conflictual choices than a professional politician. In short, the political class does not come out very well from such a situation.

Up to this point we have considered the anti-political consequences of the primaries within the party itself. There are also certain anti-political messages given out by the primaries that concern citizens in general, be they sympathisers of the left or otherwise. First of all, the primaries are not held on the basis of the rules and guarantees established for elections organised by the State, and are thus susceptible to problems of fairness, transparency and even fraud (Cross *et al.* 2016, p. 9, Kenig and Pruysers 2018, p. 42); they are often blighted by clientelism and manipulation, and in some cases election rigging.[19] These improper, or indeed illegal, practices mark the adaptation of certain areas of the centre-left to the new rules which, on paper, exalt free, spontaneous, impartial participation. The practices adopted by certain wings of the party and by party leaders who fictitiously signed up unknown individuals as party members, which in the "old" parties had been designed to enable such factions and leaders to dominate party congresses, have now re-emerged in new forms which "domesticate" and manipulate any democratic innovation introduced. The emergence of election rigging practices thus generates further disillusionment with, and anger at, parties and politicians. In addition to the aforesaid vote rigging, the primaries also send out a further message against the phenomenon of political careerism. The message in question is that what counts is not so much the political line a candidate adopts, that candidate's career within the party or in the country's institutions (even though this continues to be of importance in reality), but rather his/her individual, not strictly political, characteristics. In other words, what is considered important are candidates' communicative capacities, their discontinuity with the "old politics", their rapport with the political and non-political spheres, and their status as political outsiders.

In more general terms, deliberative practices and, more importantly, primary elections encouraged citizens' participation and raised their expectations and demands in terms of their counting for something in political decision-making processes. This was to pave the way for Beppe Grillo to sow the seeds of his own anti-politics, which subsequently gave rise to the emergence of the 5SM. As we shall see in the following chapter, the principal cornerstone of the 5SM's political project was its call for spontaneous, atomised participation, and the rejection of political careerism and political parties as such. In other words, the 5SM appropriated the issue that the centre-left had created and promoted in the early 2000s and became more credible than the PD in relation to said issue, with the latter calling non-competitive, random primaries or primaries characterised by vote rigging. Thus the 5SM sent out the message of its pursuit of grassroots participation, forcing the centre-left to play catch-up in this regard.[20] In practice, the 5SM used the weapon of popular participation against the established parties that had introduced it in the first place and had encouraged it by launching participatory practices, and by symbolically offering citizens the keys to the secret garden of politics. After having fostered for years, citizens' expectations of counting for something when it came to making both major and minor decisions, the persistence of primaries characterised by "high inclusiveness and low competitiveness" (Valbruzzi 2021, p. 42), and the decision not to hold them at all, as in the case of Letta's appointment as national secretary of the PD in 2021, resulted in disenchantment among the centre-left's electorate. This resulted in a gradual decline in participation in the party's primaries (Sandri and Seddone 2018, p. 321). As the following chapter shows, the disenchantment of voters with the PD was similar to that which was to affect the 5SM's activists and supporters, who when faced with the narrative of the miraculous powers of direct democracy, repeatedly found themselves having to endorse decisions already taken by the party's oligarchy.

Finally, mention should be made of a further anti-political consequence of the primaries, namely the creation of a window of opportunity for the emergence of marginal politicians or those at an initial disadvantage in electoral terms. Such politicians, who cannot count on the party's support in the primaries, can however focus on their status as outsiders in order to distinguish themselves from other candidates and prevail in a highly personalised competition basically devoid of political content. As we have seen, this is what happened in the case of Nichi Vendola for example. Despite being a mainstream insider according to the typology illustrated in fifth section of Chapter 2, he played the role of outsider up against the voting recommendations offered by the principal parties from his own coalition. This was also the case of Matteo Renzi who, despite his curriculum as a mainstream insider, played the part of the anti-political insider behaving as an outsider in order to distance himself from the stereotyped image of the professional politician, which his own party was full of. The primaries, by personalising the challenge and distracting attention away from any political content, led Renzi to embrace the rhetoric of the anti-political outsider. As we shall see in the following section, Renzi was in fact largely successful in this venture, both within his own party and at the institutional level, thanks to the public's perception of him (a perception encouraged and promoted by Renzi himself) as the young "scrapper" of the old political leaders from his own party.

The rise and fall of an "outsider" leader

On 8 December 2013, the day after Matteo Salvini had been directly elected as the new leader of the League, the "people of the primaries" crowned Matteo Renzi secretary of the PD.[21] This marked the completion of his transformation from a "leftist Berlusconi" (Bordignon 2014a), an "inside enemy" or "foreign body" within the party (Vicentini 2015), into the acclaimed, legitimate leader of the PD. Renzi's hegemonic hold on the PD and the entire centre-left meant that the sophisticated, insidious anti-politics that for at least a decade had characterised this political area, as we saw in the previous two sections, gave way to a full-blown, proudly touted form of anti-politics. Under Renzi's leadership, therefore, the types of anti-politics characteristic of the Italian right began to contaminate and conquer the centre-left as well and spread to the entire sphere of Italian politics.

Renzi's political development is strictly linked to the democratic innovations adopted and promoted by the centre-left and the PD in the years prior to his rise to power. Without such innovations, it is unlikely he would have been as successful as he was. While the 2013 primaries resulted in his election as national party secretary, Renzi had already successfully negotiated the primaries held in 2009 for the choice of mayoral candidate for the city of Florence. This was a key moment in a political career that had begun at a very early age, when Renzi became an active member of the Italian Popular Party (*Partito Popolare Italiano* – PPI). This party was one of the heirs to the defunct Christian Democratic Party (DC), before merging into the centrist "Daisy" (*Margherita*) party. Thanks to his political militancy, Renzi became the provincial secretary of the PPI, and subsequently of the

Daisy Party. This role guaranteed his candidacy and election as President of the Florence Provincial Government in 2004, when he was still only 29. Up until that point, his political career in the party and in the institutions had followed a conventional, albeit rapid and precocious, path. However, the introduction of the primaries, which occurred during the period of Renzi's first term of office as provincial president, changed the rules of the game. In fact, the primaries made it possible to circumvent those party rules requiring candidates to "wait their turn in the queue", as Renzi was allegedly informed by one of the PD's leaders at the time (Renzi 2011, p. 23). The queue in question was organised and monitored by the party's leaders. It was customary for ambitious politicians to gradually and patiently move from the political periphery towards the centre, and from the lower levels of the political system (local government) upwards (towards national level) (Recchi and Verzichelli 2003). When primaries are not simply designed to endorse choices already made by the party leadership, but are genuinely competitive, then they represent a challenge to the principle of waiting one's turn, since they enable impatient, ambitious politicians to jump the queue and forge ahead in their career development.[22] This is what Renzi did in 2009, when he declined a comfortable second term of office as President of the Florence Provincial Government, which he would certainly have obtained, in order that he could challenge the leadership of his own party and participate in the primaries held to select the party's mayoral candidate for the city of Florence.

The primaries: standing out from the other candidates – a successful strategy

In addition to utilising the political and relational capital accumulated as President of the Provincial Government, in order to defeat adversaries with greater political clout and supported to a greater degree by the party's leadership, Matteo Renzi needed to adopt a distinctive approach. He would surely have lost had he decided to play on the same political-party level as those weightier adversaries, and so he decided to adopt a strategy designed to conceal his membership of the category of professionals politicians so despised by Italy's citizens, and to hide the fact that he had grown up among the party's ranks. In order to distinguish himself from the popular perception of the mainstream politician, which is actually what he was, he focused on various aspects of his person. The first of these was his youthful age, given that when he contested the primaries for mayor of Florence he was only 34. The second factor, which is in keeping with the first, was his adoption of a simple, direct communicative style unlike the difficult, often incomprehensible style generally adopted by professional politicians. The third factor, which was combined with the first two and is the most important of all from our point of view, is Renzi's adoption of anti-political attitudes and rhetoric. The 2009 primaries thus resulted in a change in young Renzi who, to use the previously-described classification (see the fifth section in Chapter 2) from being a mainstream insider, was gradually transformed into an anti-political insider (who, however, tried to come across as an outsider).

As a young man going against the grain within his own party, Renzi's election as mayor of an important city like Florence lent him further visibility. He began to engender curiosity and interest among the population as a whole and within the political world. In 2012, on the back of this growing popularity, Renzi went one step further: not happy with accepting a second term of office as Mayor of Florence, a position he could probably have preserved until 2019, he decided to try once again to "jump the queue". The opportunity he was given again involved primary elections, this time for the centre-left coalition's candidate for the office of Prime Minister (in the event of it winning the 2013 general election). In order to beat his rivals, Renzi had to play the diversity card once again, by pointing out the aforementioned aspects: the need for a generational change; his standing as an anti-conformist politician; and his caustic, irreverent anti-political rhetoric. In fact, once politicians present themselves as "new", anti-political outsiders, it is not easy to then shed that guise, because should they do so then their political careers would be jeopardised.

Despite obtaining a healthy 35% of the vote at the first ballot, and an even more encouraging 39% at the second ballot, Renzi lost the coalition's 2012 primaries. The winner of those primaries was Pier Luigi Bersani, the PD's national secretary at the time. Nevertheless, the primaries were a further important opportunity for Renzi to appear in the public eye, which he gladly took in order to underscore his opposition to the "old guard" represented by Bersani. Furthermore, this was the same mechanism seen in the preceding chapter with regard to Salvini's election as federal secretary of the League, where the candidate in question self-proclaims his "newness" – based purely on his differences with the "old" leader, Bossi – on the media stage guaranteed by the primaries, rather than during any colourless party congress. The 2012 primaries, however, were only the first round of the fight within the party between the "old" and the "new". After the disappointing outcome of the 2013 general election, which was followed by political stalemate and a series of electoral defeats, Bersani resigned as national secretary. Consequently, further primaries were held, this time for the direct election of the PD's national secretary. These new primaries saw Renzi and Gianni Cuperlo contending the victor's prize. Cuperlo was considered to represent the "old politics" and the party apparatus. Following the difficulties encountered at the 2013 general election, and after having sustained Mario Monti's "blood, sweat and tears" government (Giannetti 2012), the PD found itself in great difficulty, and the young "new" Renzi was seen as the only person capable of pulling the party through its period of crisis.

What appears a particularly significant change was to take place between the 2012 primaries and those held in 2013: those voting for Renzi in the latter election were no longer prevalently young people and electors who had voted for centre and centre-right parties in the past. In 2013, Renzi also managed to appeal to more progressive, left-wing voters (Vicentini 2015, p. 10). This was a sign that by now his style and approach as an anti-political outsider had been accepted even by the more "traditional" PD electorate, that is, those who had previously considered him an internal enemy or foreign body. During this transitional period, Renzi injected the virus of plebiscitary democracy into the political culture of the left, which up until that moment had remained relatively unscathed by full-blown forms of leaderism. The extreme personalisation of political jousting imposed by Renzi thus affected the party in a way not dissimilar to that of Forza Italy and its leader Berlusconi. In other words, the party had become an instrument serving the advancement of the leader's political career. Strong in the knowledge of this unexpected concordance, Renzi easily won the 2013 primaries and was elected secretary, eventually displacing his fellow party member Enrico Letta as Prime Minister in February 2014. Thus Matteo Renzi, at the age of 39, became the youngest ever Prime Minister of Italy. He remained in office for over three years, and in addition to his relative youth, he also brought with him his style as an anti-political insider playing the part of the outsider.

As had previously been the case with Berlusconi (see the fifth section in Chapter 2) and subsequently with Salvini (see the third section in Chapter 3), the anti-politics of Renzi was to be an anti-politics of struggle, preached and practiced when in opposition, and of government. The two forms of anti-politics, as we have seen in part, have different purposes. When Renzi found himself in the minority within his own party, he used anti-politics to distinguish himself in order to first be elected as the party's candidate as mayor of Florence, then as the PD's national secretary, and ultimately as head of the Italian government. When leading his party and the country, anti-politics served to preserve his own personal support among the electorate, and to dominate any other representative of the same political colours. In the latter case, anti-politics were used as a way of going public (Kernell 1986), so as to impose his own political line on the MPs supporting the government, but who in the main had been selected previously, at the 2013 election, by the wing of the party led by his opponent Bersani. Furthermore, just as was true of Berlusconi and Salvini, when in government Renzi carefully chose his enemies. These included: the old guard of the PD and the other parties; the trade unions; the *"professoroni"* (academics considered pompous underachievers) and "jinxers" (pessimists, defeatists and bores), charged with being ideologically obdurate and with offering senseless criticism of the reforms he proposes or implements. By emphasising the differences between him and these enemies, who he claimed to be the supporters of the "old politics", Renzi recounted a simple, easily understandable tale that sets the good and the evil apart. The evil include, in fact, professional politicians surrounded by their party structures, supporting associations and intellectuals of a kindred spirit.

Renzi's anti-politics, however, cannot be accounted for simply in terms of the internal dynamics of the PD and its majority. The political period in which he operated, in fact, was that in which the 5SM unexpectedly rose to prominence. This latter movement party was to make anti-politics one of its distinctive traits (see Chapter 5). That same period was also characterised by the emergence of the "League for Salvini Premier" who, as we have seen, is one who plays the anti-politics card extensively. Therefore, the political-electoral marketplace was already populated by several individual and collective political actors who competed for the profitable issue of anti-politics.[23] The anti-political game being played out at the time had two principal effects. The first effect was to encourage the PD, led by Renzi, to move closer – in terms of the personalisation of politics, leadership style and the use of anti-politics – to the other key actors involved, resulting in a kind of contagion of the centre-left "by the right".[24] The second effect, which is related to the first, concerns the dynamics of competition among these actors which leads them to constantly attempt anti-political moves characterised by departures from political and institutional praxis. These distinguishing strategies are often accompanied by the denigration of professional politicians and political parties, and shows of contempt for democracy's representative institutions. The combination of these two effects was to result in a spiralling of anti-politics, which in turn has strongly impacted Italy's political life. In this regard, having examined in the previous chapter the forms of anti-politics that Salvini incarnates, and before focusing on those expressed by the 5SM, we shall conclude the present chapter with a more detailed look at Renzi's anti-political actions.

Renzi's multifaceted anti-politics

In analytical terms, Renzi's anti-politics can be broken down into the three conceptual categories examined in the third section of Chapter 1, namely: against professional politicians and political careerism; against political parties; against representative assemblies and their members. Of these three aspects of anti-politics, Renzi's preferred target is professional politicians. Making great play of his own youth, compared to the much higher average age of his opponents both within and outside the party, as early as 2010, Renzi declared that the time had come to "scrap" the old political leadership of his own party.[25] In Italian, the term used (*rottamare* – to scrap) has a very rough, brutal, offensive meaning, usually employed to describe the physical demolition of old cars, and as such is certainly an unusual term to use in the political sphere. The employment of such a politically and, even more so, humanly disrespectful, violent term, can be partly accounted for by the aforementioned anti-political competition, which intensified considerably following the growing popularity of Beppe Grillo and his 5SM. As we shall see more clearly in the following chapter, the joint founder of the 5SM, in a manner not dissimilar to that of the early Giannini, in fact used the derision of his political adversaries together with his blatant vulgarity as highly effective political weapons. Matteo Renzi thus gained the nickname of "scrapper", at the expense of further barbarising and poisoning the political climate both within and outside his own party. This nickname has stuck for the entire duration of Renzi's political career. It has proven highly popular with the media, and has strengthened his status as an anti-political outsider, due also to his targeting people like Massimo D'Alema, Rosy Bindi and Pier Luigi Bersani, who all represent the ideal type of professional politician in the collective imagination. Not unlike the aforementioned expression "the caste" (see the fourth section in Chapter 4), which became increasingly popular following the publication of a book of the same name by two Italian journalists (Rizzo and Stella 2007),[26] the terms "scrapping" and "scrapper" with their highly evocative, disdainful message also became part of everyday Italian in reference to both the political and other spheres.

In terms of communicative approach and leadership style, Renzi's strategy was not that different from Salvini's, consisting as it did in the personalisation, celebritisation and popularisation of politics. This combination of factors was designed to conceal – and to deny – his identity as a party and professional politician. Instead of wearing sweatshirts and police uniforms (like Salvini), Renzi's chosen "uniform" was a white shirt with rolled-up sleeves. When he was Prime Minister, as a guest on highly-popular TV programmes, aimed in particular at a public with little interest in politics, Renzi used to wear a trendy leather jacket. He was also filmed while jogging in the park, or riding his bicycle through the streets of Florence. The tabloids took a great interest in his private life (Ciaglia and Mazzoni 2015, Mazzoni and Mincigrucci 2021). From this point of view, the behaviour of the "two Matteos" was not that dissimilar, and as pointed out, it in fact triggered a competition to see who could produce the most hostile messages aimed at political careerism, which were divulged among the population and further strengthened the anti-political aspects of Italian political culture.

Among others, another powerful message to the detriment of professional politicians, that Renzi conveys to the electorate in the hope that they will reward him with their votes, is the promised reduction in the number of parliamentarians within the context of a broader reform of the Italian Constitution called for by Renzi. In fact, this reform foresees a reduction (from 350 to 100) in the number of Senate members, who were no longer to be elected by the country's citizens but rather nominated by the Regional Governments from among those regional counsellors and municipal mayors in office. In keeping with the rhetoric of reducing the cost of politics, this measure would "save" on the salaries of the senators, who would content themselves with the sums paid to them by their respective regional or municipal institutions. The same principle underlies the idea of eliminating, in the future, the figure of the senator for life appointed by the Italian President, to be replaced by other figures holding office for seven years only, however (Fusaro 2017, pp. 117–8). In this regard, it should be noted that

Renzi, in keeping with his call for the scrapping of the old guard, asked that his party's MPs be limited to three terms in office. This rule was introduced into the PD's statute, but according to Renzi had never been properly complied with (Renzi 2011, p. 185). These were exactly the same issues that the 5SM had embraced. As we shall see more clearly in the following chapter, the limitation of two terms in office is in fact one of the distinguishing traits of Grillo's party. The reduction in the cost of politics was put into practice, albeit not without certain challenges and scandals in this regard, through the 5SM's MPs giving up part of their salary. The reduction in the number of parliamentarians, on the other hand, was a constitutional measure promoted by the 5SM and approved, almost unanimously, by all parties in October 2019. A further proposal advanced by Renzi, inspired by another, very similar one promoted by the 5SM, was to abolish parliamentary pensions. Furthermore, upon Renzi's suggestion, during the period in which his fellow party member Enrico Letta led the Government (Letta's place was subsequently taken by Renzi following the latter's sleight of hand), and in order to subtract certain anti-political arguments from the domain of the 5SM's, which had increasingly become a key political player, the system of public funding of political parties was scaled down (Pizzimenti 2016, p. 79). Ultimately, the rather explicit message being sent out was that politicians constituted a privileged class, and it was time that someone dealt with this question and did the right thing by eliminating their privileges.[27]

The second aspect of Renzi's anti-politics is his anti-partyism. In this regard as well, several messages of hostility and intolerance towards political parties are clearly visible. The first, as previously mentioned, is Renzi's predilection for primary elections. He believes that political leaders should have a direct relationship with their sympathisers in an atomised, non-aggregated form, that is, without the presence of stable, organised arenas for political debate as with the political parties of the past. When he was mayor of Florence, rather than discussing politics in the party's branches, which continued to exist, he sustained a process of participatory democracy consisting in the municipal administration's direct encounters with citizens in 100 designated parts of the city.[28] Renzi also relaunched the most classical of anti-party targets: the abolition of public funding to political parties (Bordignon 2014a, p. 9). Furthermore, he proposed that financial subsidies to party newspapers be abolished.

Up to this point, Renzi's anti-party stance was not particularly innovative, consisting as it did in primaries, institutionally-encouraged participation and the abolition of public funding to political parties, all of which were ideas that had been adopted by a variety of other political actors. The truly innovative anti-party concept introduced by Renzi, which was to prove extremely appealing even to those who were traditionally uninterested in politics, was the establishment of a kind of party assembly or congress that ran parallel to, but was separate from, the party's official congress. In 2010, a few months after launching his idea to "scrap" the old political guard within his party, Renzi promoted a political, programmatic event held at the "Leopolda", an old railway station in Florence that had been converted into a congress centre. The encounters at the Leopolda, which have been held every year ever since, became "his 'personal' political space" (Ventura 2018, p. 189), and they served to foster a process of celebritisation of his leadership. The Leopolda is a place that is physically and symbolically different from the party's branches. It is here, at the Leopolda, in an atmosphere reminiscent of an American convention mixed with pseudo-participatory processes, that political debate and discussion take place instead of the previous arena constituted by the party's branches. The Leopolda has taken over this function traditionally performed by the parties; indeed, it stands in contrast to the "old parties" thanks to its modernity, technology, openness to civil society, innovation, youth and joy.

The third and final component of Renzi's anti-politics consists in his critical stance on certain forms of political representation. Renzi's rhetoric portrays the representative institutions as lethargic, bureaucratic, inefficient and antiquated. This image serves to underscore the fact that he, in contrast, was a youthful, determined, effective modern administrator of public interests. Hence, his proposal was to introduce an electoral law providing for the direct election of the head of government, which however tends towards presidentialism and the concentration and personalisation of political power. The chosen slogan is "let's elect the Mayor of Italy" (Salvati 2016, p. 10) who, as pointed out, has been directly elected by the nation's citizens since 1993. In this way, Renzi wanted to enhance the value of his past experience as mayor and administrator, that is, as a pragmatic person concerned with "getting things done". This proposal takes as it model the only institutional figure who, because of his vicinity to the populace, continues to enjoy the support of the Italian electorate and can be considered the only successful institutional innovation appreciated by the nation's citizens (Freschi and Mete 2020, p. 271). In more practical terms, as we have seen, Renzi introduced a change in the role of the Senate in the constitutional reform he promoted: he wanted it to be transformed into a chamber of autonomous local authorities. Once again, the reasoning behind this is the cumbersome nature of Italy's perfect bicameralism, which according to Renzi merely wastes time and serves solely to produce a proliferation of seats in parliament taken by career politicians.

The referendum: the voters "scrap" Renzi

The constitutional review methods establish that any changes, if approved by Parliament by anything less than a two-thirds qualified majority, have to be submitted to a referendum vote. In December 2016, following a lengthy, heated electoral campaign (Vicentini and Pritoni 2021), a referendum was held to confirm Renzi's proposed constitutional reform. The majority of Italians (59.1%) voted against the proposed package of reforms which, as we have seen, among other things had taken on an anti-political significance. Despite being at the height of his power, this vote was to mark the twilight of Renzi's political career. In fact, he had personalised the referendum issue to a considerable degree, to the point of declaring that if he were defeated at the ballot box, he would leave politics (the same promise was also made by the Minister for Constitutional Reform, the extremely loyal Maria Elena Boschi, a young politician from Tuscany just like Renzi). In fact, as Pasquino has pointed out, "a personalist party cannot avoid personalising the campaign of its leader and, with gusto, Renzi transformed the referendum into a plebiscite on his persona and leadership" (2018, p. 140).

Personalising the referendum vote and waging his political career on the outcome of the referendum, however, proved to be a fatal mistake. The anti-political feelings harboured by a significant portion of the population, and the dislike of politicians instilled by Renzi among others, with his rhetorical proposal to "scrap" the old guard, were waiting for just such an opportunity to be expressed openly.[29] After three years in government, during which Renzi was a constant, stifling presence on TV and in other media, he was suffering from over-exposure and appeared very different from the brilliant young politician rising to power just a few years earlier. He now appeared, in the collective imagination, to be the typical ambitious politician fighting more to preserve his own interests than to push through his party's political plans or to resolve the many problems concerning the citizens of Italy. In fact, as Patrick Öhberg points out, "People seem to have an innate aversion to those whom they associate with ambition for power" (2017, p. 8). On the basis of this aversion, or perhaps simply to see how Renzi's plans would pan out, that is, to see whether a successful politician would resign after an electoral defeat, a large proportion of voters decided to vote not on the merits of the referendum, but to express their judgement of Renzi and his government (Pasquino and Valbruzzi 2017a, p. 289).[30]

Just a few hours after the votes had been counted, with 60% voting against the reform, thus certifying Renzi's personal defeat in the referendum, he announced that he was going to resign as Prime Minister. However, contrary to the solemn promise that he had made public and had used as a means of convincing the electorate to vote for his constitutional reform, Renzi did not leave politics altogether. He belatedly resigned as national secretary of the PD, but only in order to call further primaries in the spring of 2017, which he subsequently won (Sandri and Seddone 2018), thus becoming party secretary once again. The disappointing results of the 2018 general election, which marked the significant victory of the 5SM, the relegation of the PD to the opposition benches and the formation of an unprecedented coalition between the 5SM and the League, led Renzi to resign once again. His loss of power and of his key role in the PD, led him to leave the party and establish a new party, *Italia Viva*, all within the space of just over a year, although his new party has to date not managed to obtain more than 2% of the votes in any election.

Ultimately, Renzi's inglorious departure from the PD, with him going back on his promise to leave politics altogether in the event of defeat, further stoked anti-political feelings among the Italian people. In their eyes, this was yet another demonstration of the unreliability and insincerity of politicians, even those who declared themselves to be "new" and "different" from the professional politicians of old. Renzi's story, briefly described here, shows that playing with anti-politics can be extremely hazardous. As in the cases of Giannini and Bossi, and as we shall see of the 5SM, those citizens encouraged and mobilised by anti-political leaders are not easily domesticated. The anti-political beast that Renzi had pitted against the old political guard, starting with politicians from his own party, as soon as it gets the chance (in Renzi's case the aforementioned referendum), takes revenge against, and devours, its master. As a result, despite the fact that the PD and Italia Viva are part of the same majority that supported the second Conte government, and currently supports Mario Draghi's government, and despite their being allies in many different places, the PD's voters have a greater aversion to Renzi than to Giorgia Meloni, the current leader of the most right-wing of Italy's sovereigntist parties. In this specific ranking of those persons most despised by the PD's voters, Renzi is second only to the other Matteo (Salvini).[31]

Notes

1 The foundation and development of the PD have been the focus of many sociopolitical studies. For an overview of the party's origins and the various stages of its development, see, first and foremost: Bordandini *et al.* (2008), Lazar (2008), Pasquino (2009), Ventura (2018) and Floridia (2019).

2 The Five Star Movement (5SM) is another party that considers citizens' involvement in political life to be of fundamental importance, as we shall see in the following chapter. However, in the case of the 5SM, this participation is perceived as being opposed to the politicians, parties and institutions of representative democracy and designed to establish a form of direct democracy. The left-wing parties, on the other hand, have traditionally perceived citizens' involvement in politics as an additional aspect of representative democracy, rather than something designed to replace said democracy. As such, therefore, it also differs from the participatory practices of the populist and right-wing parties, which are generally of a plebiscitary nature.

3 In May 2007, a few months prior to the foundation of the PD, a book was published in Italy entitled "The Caste". Co-authored by two journalists, it recounted the squandering of public resources by Italy's politicians and political system, together with the privileges enjoyed by the political class. The book was a huge success and was to impact public debate by fanning the existing hostility towards politics, political parties and career politicians. Strangely enough, the highly successful title of the book was taken from a statement made by Walter Veltroni, the first secretary of the PD: "When parties become castes of career politicians, the principal anti-political campaign is the one waged by the parties themselves" (Rizzo and Stella 2007, p. 16). The social and political climate was particularly favourable to the publication of a book attacking a disapproved of, delegitimised political class. In a survey

conducted in 2004, which we shall return to in Chapter 6, 48% of respondents cited "anger" as one of the feelings evoked by politics (in 1985 the percentage had been 28.5%); 39% cited "diffidence" (compared to 30% in 1985), while 28% expressed their "disgust" with politics (compared to 21% in 1985) (Biorcio 2007, p. 197).

4 The foundation of the PD can be seen as a rebranding operation reminiscent, in certain ways, of the transition from Labour to Tony Blair's New Labour in the mid-1990s. The similarities in the transformation of the two parties became increasingly evident when the PD was led by Matteo Renzi, from 2013 on Bordignon (2014a, p. 8) and Salvati (2016, p. 12).

5 If democratic change is considered to be a "new practice or process consciously and purposefully introduced with the aim of improving the quality of democracy, irrespective of whether the innovation in question has already been tried out in another state" (Geissel 2012, p. 164), it could be argued that in Italy, where such practices had never been employed before, participatory and deliberative procedures, together with the holding of primaries, which we shall be looking at in the following section, constitute democratic innovations. For a discussion of the defining aspects, and a proposed classification, of the various forms of democratic innovation, see Elstub and Escobar (2019). This same volume also examines the links between democratic innovations and the diverse forms of anti-politics (Flinders *et al.* 2019).

6 In Italy, the social movements regarding globalisation were particularly strong in the early 2000s and as such had a substantial impact on political debate at the time. In fact, Italy's recent political history was marred by the "events in Genoa", meaning the huge international demonstration against the G8 meeting held in the city in July 2001, which ended with the death of one young demonstrator, Carlo Giuliani, killed by a Carabiniere officer. The demonstration saw numerous acts of violence perpetrated by the police against demonstrators. The Genoa events led to fierce disagreement between on the one hand the left and centre-left parties, who at the time were in opposition and who sympathised with the movement and the demonstrators, and the centre-right parties on the other hand, who criticised the demonstrators' actions and sided with the police. The police uniforms that Salvini wears, discussed in the previous chapter, can be explained also in view of these events and the deep, lasting political rift they created, with the right-wing parties claiming to be the political force of law and order. For an overview of the GJM, see, among others: della Porta and Tarrow (2004) and della Porta (2007). For a reflection on the use of deliberative practices within the social movements, and in particular within the GJM, see: della Porta and Rucht (2013) and della Porta and Doerr (2018).

7 From the late 1990s onwards, with public interest in participatory and deliberative practices on the increase, there was a boom in studies regarding this theme. On a theoretical level, there was a thorough, detailed discussion of the origins and principles of deliberative democracy, with the presentation of the principal classical and contemporary writers who have dealt with the question, by Antonio Floridia (2017). Various manuals and collective works have presented the methods and forms of public involvement and have gathered and analysed case studies conducted in various parts of the world. The latter works include for example: Gastil and Levine (2005), della Porta (2013) and Bächtiger *et al.* (2018).

8 In certain cases, however, the participatory processes were implemented on the basis of decisions that had already been taken. In such cases, participation was part of the DAD (decide-announce-defend) approach adopted by the institutions promoting a large-scale public work opposed by the movements in question (Algostino 2011, ch. 5).

9   To get an idea of the spread of participatory practices, one only has to con-
    sider the fact that participatory budgeting has been introduced in more than
    one half of Italian municipalities with a population of over 2,000. A list of
    said municipalities, together with other information regarding participatory
    budgeting projects, is provided by the Italian Observatory on Participatory
    Budgeting (https://oibp.bipart.it/intro). An observatory on participatory pro-
    cesses nationwide, set up by the Emilia-Romagna Regional Government, can
    be consulted at: https://www.osservatoriopartecipazione.it/ricerca-processi.

10 The role of Regional Governments in promoting deliberative practices is indi-
    cated by a recent analysis of participatory budgeting in Italy. This analysis
    shows that the introduction of a regional law on participatory budgeting has
    led to its increased diffusion among the nation's municipalities (Allegretti
    et al. 2021).

11 The message presenting the regional law, published on the website of the
    Tuscany Regional Government's website, clearly explains the significance
    of the law: "The idea of a regional law on participation originated from a
    widespread concern, namely: democratic representative institutions are expe-
    riencing a crisis of legitimacy, that is, they are fully entitled to take decisions,
    but they increasingly do so in a vacuum and in the 'solitude' surround the
    decision-makers, in the absence of effective channels of communication with
    society. Those called upon to decide often feel that they are operating in a
    climate of mistrust, and cannot perceive the degree and quality of agreement
    with the decisions they are called upon to make. The general feeling is that
    the occasional election is not enough to legitimise such decisions. What is
    needed are permanent occasions and channels for mediation between politi-
    cians, the institutions and society, and yet *such channels are often unclear or
    indeed obstructed.* Hence the need to look for new forms of participation that
    can overcome such limits and difficulties" (https://www.regione.toscana.it/-/
    legge-regionale-sulla-partecipazione-l-r-27-dicembre-2007-n-69) (our italics).

12 There is a discussion of the political meaning of deliberative practices together
    with an empirical analysis of selected important participatory experiences in
    Italy, in Freschi and Mete (2009). The same issue of the journal containing
    the aforesaid essay also includes three articles commenting on the essay, plus
    a response from its authors. A detailed critical analysis of the new forms of
    decision-making, containing many references to Italian experiences, has been
    developed by Giulio Moini (2012).

13 As the Green Party's spokesperson in the Tuscany Regional Council said of
    the Regional Law on participation: "What has happened is that we have new
    instruments with which to sound out and analyse consensus, doing in a new
    way what marketing agencies or public opinion polls already do. This is not a
    law on participation, but a form of political control over what is going on in
    the community, a law against participation. It is based on the logic of the opin-
    ion poll. It is a blatant operation to annul participation. Today [six months
    after its adoption] enthusiasm for the law is dead. This is a dangerous law.
    Participation works if it is self-organized, not if it is organized" (Freschi and
    Mete 2009, p. 39).

14 Public and political debate, as well as academic discussion, in regard to the
    Italian primaries is extremely broad. It should be pointed out that the terms
    "primaries" is not always used correctly in the Italian context. As Pasquino
    and Valbruzzi observe, "the Italian experience has paved the way for a dele-
    terious case of 'conceptual stretching': any and all selection procedures are
    defined as primaries, and such usage has to some extent been 'accepted', if
    not promoted, by politicians and scholars alike" (2016, p. 2). Marino De Luca

(2018) offers an overview of the Italian experiences in this regard. Municipal primaries are very common (Pasquino and Venturino 2009, Sandri and Venturino 2016), while provincial, regional (De Luca and Rombi 2016) and national primaries (for parliamentary candidates) are less frequent (Regalia and Valbruzzi 2016). With regard to the 2005 primaries for the centre-left candidate for the subsequent 2006 general election, see Corbetta and Vignati (2013a). In regard to the direct election of the national secretary of the PD, which have been improperly termed "primaries", see: Fasano and Seddone (2016) and Seddone *et al.* (2020). The centre-right parties hold municipal primaries less often, on the other hand (De Luca 2018, p. 413). Only the League has directly elected its federal secretary, as we have seen, and once again it called these elections "primaries". As regards the 5SM, which we shall be discussing in the following chapter, primary elections are an important part of their strategy for the greater involvement of members and activists. A detailed, well-documented diachronic analysis of the processes of party leader selection in Republican Italy, including such primaries, has been developed by Valbruzzi (2021).

15 In truth, the mechanism for the selection of the party's national secretary envisaged an initial primary election among members of the party, followed by another primary open to all party supporters. For a detailed analysis of the PD's statute which governs, among other things, the way the primaries are conducted, see the work by Fulvio Venturino (2015).

16 In addition to these primaries, there were also the centre-left coalition's primaries, consisting of two ballots, held in 2012 in view of the 2013 general election (Corbetta and Vignati 2013a). These primaries were won, predictably, by the PD's secretary Bersani, although they also marked the emergence of Matteo Renzi, who the following year was elected party secretary as a result of further primaries.

17 According to Pasquino, focusing to such a large extent on the primaries, to the point where they become an important part of the party's identity, has prevented or impeded a broader reflection on the political culture of the PD: "Most of the energies of the party, its leaders, its activists went (and continue to go) into the organisation and holding of primary elections and, apparently, were exhausted by those demanding activities/tasks. Indeed, the Charter of the PD places much more emphasis on primary elections than on any specific aspect of the political culture the party might consider essential" (Pasquino 2018, p. 137).

18 In 1968, only 5.5% of left-wing voters, compared to 14.6% of those on the right, looked principally at the leader of the party when deciding how to vote. In 2004, the year of the introduction of the centre-left's primaries, these figures were now 11.2% and 28.2%, respectively (Barisione 2007, p. 171).

19 The news reports various cases of the clear improper, instrumental use of the primaries. In certain cases, activists and militants from opposing parties "infiltrated" the centre-left's primaries. In other cases, the number of votes obtained by the PD or by the centre-left lists at the elections was lower than those cast at the primaries, thus clearly pointing to the "spurious" mobilisation of the electorate in the latter case. There was a huge uproar in 2011 at the primaries organised to choose the candidate for the position of mayor of Naples. Following claims of vote rigging, and indeed of mafia involvement, the result of the primary election was annulled and the Naples branch of the PD was put under a commissioner. More recently, at the Bologna municipal primaries (held in June 2021), one of the candidates was blatantly supported by the 5SM, that is, by a party allied with, but separate from, the PD.

20 For example, immediately prior to the 2013 general election, the 5SM organised primaries for the selection of parliamentary (Mosca *et al.* 2015a), "forcing" the centre-left parties to do likewise (Regalia and Valbruzzi 2016, p. 2).

21 For a number of years, in particular between 2012 and 2017, Renzi was the most
important figure in Italian politics. Understandably, there have been numerous
studies of the figure of Matteo Renzi, many of a journalistic or polemical character, and others of a more academic nature. The latter have concerned various
aspects of his political career: his rapid, unconventional rise to the position of
national secretary of the PD and to governmental office (Vicentini 2015); the
changes he brought about in the party (Guidi 2014, Pasquino and Valbruzzi
2017a), his leadership style and his political communications, characterised by
the personalisation and celebritisation of his role as leader (Bordignon 2014a,
Ciaglia and Mazzoni 2015, Salvati 2016); his governmental actions (Fabbrini
and Lazar 2015); and the question of the constitutional referendum which was
to mark the beginning of his political decline (Bull 2017, Ceccarini and
Bordignon 2017, Fusaro 2017, Pasquino and Valbruzzi 2017b).

22 The "confirmative" rather than competitive logic of the primaries is clearly
described by Renzi, when back in 2011 he rather irreverently wrote: "The invo-
lution of the species has led the [PD's leadership] to hypothesise a model of
primaries which we could describe as 'confirmative': the [party leaders] choose
a name, and that person becomes the sole candidate, the one who *must* win:
then a fake competition is organised around that candidate. The only thing
that voters have to do is to endorse the result already decided by the leaders
in Rome. The whole story of the electors lining up at the gazebos to put their
signatures to a result has already been decided, acting as the extras in a drama
already written by the party leaders, who already have the press releases ready
in the draw, while toasting the 'massive popular turnout, a triumph of participation'" (Renzi 2011, p. 32 – the italics are from the Italian original).

23 One episode symbolising the countermeasures taken by the PD and the centre-left to defend itself and counter the 5SM's anti-politics regards the election
of the Speakers in the Italian Chamber of Deputies and Senate following the
2013 general election. The two successful candidates were Laura Boldrini,
the former spokesperson for Southern Europe of the United Nations High
Commissioner for Refugees (UNHCR), and the former National Anti-Mafia
Prosecutor Pietro Grasso. For both of them this was their first parliamentary
appointment. Both were figures from outside of politics and of any specific
party, and as such they reflected the proliferation of "points of entrance"
to the Italian political class (Lo Russo and Verzichelli 2015, p. 48). The centre-left parties supporting their appointment aimed to create a break from
the "old politics" and mark an opening up to civil society. During their first
public appearance as guests on a popular TV talk show, the two speakers
announced, as the first point in their working programme, that they would
reduce their salaries and lower Parliament's operating costs. They also added
that they intended to get MPs who had worked too little to work longer hours
and for more days a year. They also wanted to cut what they deemed to be the
excessively high salaries of the employees working in the two chambers of Parliament, and to review the system of reimbursement of MPs' expenses. Each
proposal was applauded by the public in the studio (https://www.youtube.
com/watch?v=sKN5sxcyIiM). Another way that the centre-left attempted to
encroach on the terrain of, and subtract votes from, the 5SM was by naming its coalition standing for election in 2013 *"Italia bene comune"* (Italy. A
Common Good). Less than two years earlier, in 2011, a referendum had
been called against the privatisation of the water supply, which had led to

mass mobilisation and intense debate regarding the question of "common goods" (Carrozza 2011). One of the five pillars of the movement created by Grillo – one each for the five points of the party's symbolic star – had in fact been its defence of the public water supply.

24 As well as often being called the left-wing Berlusconi, his detractors referred to him as "the other Matteo", a clear reference to the similarities between Renzi's political style and that of the League's Matteo Salvini.

25 In an interview given to the "la Repubblica" newspaper, published on 29 August 2010 and entitled "The new Olive Coalition makes people yawn: it's time to scrap out leaders", Renzi argued that: "If we want to get rid of granddad Silvio [Berlusconi], we need to remove an entire generation of my party's leaders (...). Enough's enough. The time for scrapping has come".

26 Renzi recognised, and was pleased with, the fact that the political provocation had achieved its intended effects, namely: distinguishing himself and establishing a position on the political scene, thus forcing his opponents within the party to react. Renzi wrote, in a book of his: "The terminological dispute over the expression 'scrapping' will accompany me for some time now. It's a sign that the expression hit home. If I had simply expressed a desire for a generational turnover, nobody would have taken any notice of me (...). The term 'scrapping', on the other hand, works. For better or for worse, is has become something of a literary topos. My fellow citizens use it, when they write on the walls of buildings to be demolished: 'Renzi, look to scrap this at the very least!'. My political opponents use it when something bad happens to me: 'Let's scrap the scrapper'. Journalists use it very often, even when discussing other questions. And of course, it's used by all those who don't know me personally when they see me outside of Florence" (Renzi 2011, pp. 187–8).

27 It is opportune to cite what Renzi himself had to say about the reduction in the cost of politics back in 2011, in a book he wrote at the time: "The leaders of my party (...) continue to underestimate the vital importance of [the question of the cost of politics]. And yet we should tackle this issue, by making a few, clear, easily understood proposals. I dream of a group of party leaders who are not afraid to say with conviction 'Half a parliament at half the price'. Because the problem is the cost of politics, and above all the number of political offices. Too many people live off politics, and this excessive number is invariably detrimental. There are a thousand parliamentarians. This number needs to be halved straight away (...). Not to mention pensions and life pensions: a parliament lacking the force to reform pensions results in a fast track system [to get a pension] after just a few years [in Parliament]. While regional councillors won't give up their life pensions not even when the public protest against this system (...). I think it's so unfair that an oncologist earns one third of what a regional councillor earns, it incenses me. Does that make me anti-political? Perhaps it does. Although I think those who fail to respect any hierarchy of values can be considered more anti-political" (Renzi 2011, pp. 66–9).

28 This project, launched in 2010, involved 100 citizens' assemblies being held on the same evening in 100 different places in and around Florence, including the railway station, an abandoned barracks, a square awaiting renovation, and so on. In keeping with the deliberative and participatory rhetoric very much in vogue at the time (see the first section in Chapter 4), each assembly discussed the problems and future of that place, with the intervention of a representative from the City Council. For a brief presentation of this project, together with a discussion of other forms of citizen participation promoted by Renzi when Mayor of Florence, see the work by Fabio Bordignon (2014b).

29 In distinguishing "elite discontent", which is believed to have led people to vote "no" to the constitutional reform, from "systemic discontent", which is believed to have led people to vote "yes", Matthew Bergman and Gianluca Passarelli find that the former type of discontent weighed more than the latter form on the outcome of the vote (2021, p. 13). For a further analysis on the role played by political disaffection and by judgement of the Renzi Government's performance in regard to the outcome of the referendum, see also Bergman (2019).

30 Renzi himself, in one of his books, tells a story which illustrates this point very well. At a public meeting held during the electoral campaign for the Florence primaries, and thus several years prior to the constitutional referendum, a woman asked Renzi whether he would really leave politics if he were defeated in the primaries. Having already made this promise publicly, Renzi answered that he would, thinking that by doing so he had gained a new supporter. However, the woman replied, saying: "No, listen, you've not understood anything. I'm not going to vote for you. It's true that I share practically all of your ideas, and I like your way of proposing those ideas. But you've said that if you lose the primaries you're going back to work. And as I believe your decision would be an important sign to the nation, not only am I not going to vote for you, but I also hope you lose the primaries; that way you can keep your promise. Goodbye" (Renzi 2011, pp. 30–1). With regard to the decisional processes of voters in a situation of low confidence in politicians, see the observations concerning the 2016 Brexit referendum made by Clarke *et al.* (2021).

31 https://www.repubblica.it/politica/2021/06/15/news/sondaggio_youtrend_ elettori_pd_meloni_meglio_di_renzi-306101573.

5 The Five Star Movement

Anti-politics in the form of a new party

A new anti-political party

The Five Star Movement (5SM) has been on the political scene for over a decade now and can be considered the purest, most direct, explicit and politically fruitful expression of anti-politics in Italy. Just like the other parties and politicians analysed previously, the 5SM feeds off the anti-politics widely found in Italy's political culture and in turn drives said anti-politics through its own leaders' rhetoric and behaviour both within and outside of the institutional framework. The singularity of the Movement's anti-politics is that it is richer, more intense and more variegated than that expressed by other political parties. In fact, as we shall see in the present chapter, the 5SM's anti-politics ranges from the more direct, explicit forms accompanied by verbal attacks characteristic of the League to the subtler, more sophisticated forms adopted by the Democratic Party and the centre-left in general.

The origins, development and characteristics of the 5SM have been widely examined in the sociological and political science literature.[1] Nevertheless, in order to analyse the anti-politics of this ground-breaking new political actor, we are going to briefly examine the origins and nature of the movement. The party's entire, incredible political success centres around the figure of Beppe Grillo, an entertainer and comedian who was already well known to the Italian public as a result of his regular appearance on the TV screen.[2] Thanks to his exuberant character and the satirical, hard-hitting nature of his shows, which increasingly concerned environmental, economic and political questions, Grillo became hugely popular with the Italian public. With support and advice from a businessman operating in the field of web communications, Gianroberto Casaleggio, in 2005, Grillo created a blog bearing his name (www.beppegrillo.it). He used this blog to wage various social and environmental battles, together with campaigns on behalf of consumers and small shareholders. His role as a battle-hardened, irreverent critic quickly resulted in a massive following on the Internet, and within a few years, his blog had become one of the most popular in Italy and among the most influential in the world (Vignati 2015, p. 16).

DOI: 10.4324/9781003109273-6

Thus, it was that various groups of Grillo supporters sprung up around Italy, and they took his blog as their point of reference. One of the most successful campaigns conducted via Grillo's blog was entitled "Clean Parliament", which denounced the presence of more than 20 MPs who had been charged with, and convicted of, criminal offences. In order to render this campaign for the moralisation of political life more effective, in September 2007, Grillo organised a national meeting, in Bologna, of the various groups throughout the country that followed his blog. The meeting was named "V-Day" where the "V" stands for various things, but principally for the unequivocal vulgar Italian expression "*vaffanculo*" [fuck off], a message addressed to all politicians. This V-Day event, which was subsequently repeated in other towns and cities around the country, represented the transformation of what was just a discussion on Grillo's blog, to a full-blown countrywide popular protest. This was to have political repercussions as early as January 2008, when Grillo announced the creation of "Civic Five Star lists" of electoral candidates, where the "Five Star" represents the five key common points of these lists' programmes: "1) Water – [the] public management of local water systems; 2) Environment – [the] environmental protection of local territory; 3) Transport – [the] promotion of public transport against [rather than] private mobility; 4) (De-)growth and connectivity – [a] long-term conception of social and economic development open to the notion of de-growth and with free Internet connectivity for all citizens; 5) Energy – renewable sources of energy and wide-ranging rubbish [waste] recycling" (Mastruzzo 2019, p. 142). This announcement marked the beginning of a process of institutionalisation of Grillo's political movement. The movement's lists of candidates were successful, to a limited degree, at the local elections held shortly thereafter. One important stage in this process of institutionalisation was the drafting, in March 2009, of the "Florence Charter": a programmatic document setting out 12 points shared by the "Five Star lists". In October of that same year, Grillo and Casaleggio officially founded the 5SM.

Electoral success and entry into Italy's institutions

In officially creating the 5SM, and having that movement stand for election, Grillo himself was also transformed, from entertainer and social rabble-rouser to anti-political outsider (as defined in Figure 2.2). Thanks to the enormous popularity of his blog and the massive attendance of his rallies in theatres and squares up and down the country, his status as a leading public communicator continued to grow. Grillo reinvested his enormous visibility in the political sphere. In view of the pending regional elections to be held in September 2012 in Sicily, at the age of 64, Grillo decided to help his movement "land" on the island of Sicily by actually swimming himself across the Straits of Messina (around 3 km in just over 1 hour), then ascending Mount Etna where he held a rally at an altitude of 2,000 m, and subsequently campaigning around the Sicily region. Somewhat unexpectedly, his list of candidates obtained 14.9% of the votes cast in Sicily, becoming the most voted party at the regional elections. Some months prior to this triumph in Sicily, the 5SM had already gone from being a politically irrelevant movement to one that was now successful at the local level, when it took the Municipality of Parma, a city traditionally governed by the left (Vignati 2012).

The time was therefore ripe to launch the 5SM at a national level. Indeed, at the February 2013 general election, the 5SM surprised everyone by winning an astonishing 25.6% of votes for the Chamber of Deputies, 23.8% of those for the Senate, and getting 163 members of parliament elected in the two houses. After Italy's political system had been dominated by two political groupings for around 20 years, the unforeseen success of the 5SM transformed it into a tripolar system (Pasquino 2014, p. 432). Thus, 2013 was a triumphal year for the 5SM, and it also marked the return of anti-politics in grand style. While it is certainly true that the 5SM fed into other concerns and policy priorities expressed by Italian voters (Conti and Memoli 2015), nevertheless, as Gianfranco Pasquino has observed: "The conspicuous amount of votes won by the 5SM in the 2013 national elections and in almost all subsequent elections can be explained satisfactorily with reference to another element of the (Italian) political culture or lack of it: anti-politics" (Pasquino 2018, p. 138). This was a triumph for anti-politics in terms not only of the rhetoric used by Grillo, Casaleggio and other leaders of the 5SM in the public eye but also in terms of the nature of the political class entering parliament. In fact, these were people who by definition had no significant previous political experience, who were not previously members of other political parties and who repudiated political careerism.[3] Furthermore, as we shall see later, the 5SM's MPs undertook to forego part of their salaries, and to return the public moneys that their party was entitled to.

After the election, despite being invited by the centre-left coalition to join the majority and be part of government, the 5SM decided to remain proudly in opposition. This decision was to pay dividends at the subsequent 2016 administrative elections, when the 5SM won power in two of Italy's most important cities, Rome and Turin, where the newly elected mayors were both young women. At the 2018 general election, Grillo's party was very different from the original movement-party, being much more institutionalised than before. While in 2013, the 5SM was the European party that won the largest share of the vote the first time it stood for election, in 2018, it went one step further, obtaining 32.3% of votes, and as such was the only party in Europe that bettered its performance at the previous election (Chiaramonte and Paparo 2019, p. 254). This time round, after a lengthy period of deadlock following the election, the 5SM decided to form part of the governing coalition, despite certain members of the party being opposed to what they saw as a contrived, unnatural alliance. The coalition in question was the one formed with Matteo Salvini's League in June 2018. The coalition was led by Giuseppe Conte, a lawyer and university professor chosen by the 5SM. In addition to selecting the Prime Minister, the 5SM also indicated Luigi Di Maio as Deputy Prime Minister, together with numerous governmental ministers, and it also elected one of its members, Roberto Fico, as Speaker of the Chamber of Deputies.

However, the new government only lasted just over a year. In a political U-turn designed to avoid new elections and the risk of the League coming out on top (given that it was performing very strongly at the time in all opinion polls), the 5SM chose to join forces with the centre-left. Thus, it was that in September 2019, a second Conte government was formed, and this government was subsequently tasked with dealing with the Covid-19 emergency during the early months of 2020. Severely tested by this difficult task, and despite substantial funding from the European Union (EU) for the post-Covid reconstruction of the economy, the handling of which was something that the other political parties were not prepared to forego, in February 2021, the second Conte government also fell, to be replaced by a coalition of all parties – with the sole exception of the sovereigntist "Brothers of Italy" (*Fratelli d'Italia*) – led by Mario Draghi, the former President of the European Central Bank. From the viewpoint of the 5SM, the fall of the second Conte government, which had been caused by the defection of the small *Italia Viva* party led by Matteo Renzi, coincided with a deep rift between the supporters of Conte, who wanted him to become leader of the party, and the supporters of Beppe Grillo, who had no intention of foregoing the key political role he has always played in the movement.

The social and political grounds for the emergence of the Five Star Movement

The considerable political and electoral importance of the 5SM, both in Italy and Europe, together with the unique way in which it emerged, the original leadership style of Beppe Grillo and its ground-breaking organisation and programmes have led scholars to ponder how this unusual political being ought to be classified. The considerable interest in the movement has inevitably led to a number of different views in regard to this matter. Firstly, it should be pointed out that the 5SM, in order to distinguish itself from the much-despised political parties, and in keeping with the generalised rejection of the "party" label witnessed over the last 30 years in Italy (with the exception of the Democratic Party), calls itself a "movement". As a result not only of this rhetorical choice of the term but in particular of its proximity to other major social movements (Mosca 2015), first and foremost the one opposing the construction of the high-speed train link between Turin and Lyon (della Porta and Piazza 2008, Fabbri and Diani 2015, Biancalana 2020), certain scholars have classified the 5SM among the so-called movement parties (della Porta *et al.* 2017, Mosca 2020). In fact, considering the model originally proposed by Kitschelt (2006), the 5SM possesses some of

the characteristic traits of this type of party. Its organisational arrangements, participatory practices and style of institutional representation,
which we shall examine shortly, have been likened to those introduced back
in the 1980s by certain movement parties such as the German Greens and
other left-libertarian parties (Biorcio 2014, p. 50).

Grillo's rhetoric, which compares the wise, honest populace with the
corrupt governing politicians, and his outbursts targeting the economy's
"major powers", his anti-intellectualism and other aspects of his being have
led many other observers to define the 5SM as a populist party, indeed as
an expression of "unadulterated populism" (Tarchi 2015, p. 333). The party
founded by Grillo is in fact regularly included in the list of populist parties (Zulianello 2019b, Taggart and Pirro 2021), while its affairs are dealt
with in collective works on populism, often as a particularly significant case
study (Borriello and Mazzolini 2019, Briquet 2019, Agnew and Shin 2020).
Furthermore, attempts have been to classify this populism as specifically
"polyvalent" (Pirro 2018), "eclectic" (Mosca and Tronconi 2019) or as an
example of "valence populism" (Zulianello 2019b). In this regard, in order
to underscore the central role played by web communications in the foundation, development, organisation and decision-making of the 5SM, it has
been defined as "web-populism" (Corbetta 2013), "digital populism" (Dal
Lago 2017) and, with the emphasis on the technological aspects of its practices rather than any political ideology, as "techno-populism" (Bickerton
and Accetti 2018). The importance of the web to the party's daily operation
and public image has led Paolo Gerbaudo (2019) to consider the 5SM as one
of the most important examples of his "digital party" model.

As well as being considered a populist party, the 5SM is usually described
as an "anti" party of one sort or another[4]: anti-system (Hopkin 2020, ch.
7), anti-establishment (Cotta 2020), anti-party (De Petris and Poguntke
2015) or challenger (Ignazi 2021). Furthermore, the party set up by Grillo
can be seen as an actor in the monitoring democracy envisaged by Keane
(2009) and previously mentioned in Chapter 2. The movement of opinion
that gave rise to the 5SM aimed to monitor and criticise political representatives, adopting a "post-representational" logic and rejecting the idea
of electoral, intermittent democracy, in favour of "continuous democracy"
(Rodotà 1997, p. 4) based on the web, which in turn is seen as an expression
of collective intelligence. Clearly the aforementioned labels, together with
others proposed, interweave with the populist aspects generally attributed
to the party. In any case, all of the proposed definitions include a healthy
dose of anti-politics as defined in Chapter 1, consisting in the hostile attitudes towards professional politicians, political parties and representative
assemblies, expressed by the movement's political leaders, supporters and
militants.

Discussion of the reasons for the emergence and incredible success of the
5SM is even broader and more detailed than that of its intrinsic nature and
identity. These reasons, which are not mutually exclusive, regard the social,

political, cultural, technological and other levels. Thus, the 5SM's development can be associated with various known phenomena that for some time have impacted Western democracy. These include the process of individualisation (Beck 1986); the post-materialist, anti-authoritarian transformation of citizens' values (Inglehart 1977); cognitive mobilisation, which renders the electorate less deferent to, and more demanding of, their political representatives (Dalton 1984). On a political level, the replacement of a competitive logic with a more collusive one when it comes to relations between political parties (Katz and Mair 1995) has widened the divide between parties and the electorate (Mair 2013), rendering the latter increasingly disorientated and dissatisfied. Changes in political communication, through the mediatisation, personalisation and celebritisation of political life previously mentioned (see Section "Rebuilding the League, demolishing politics" in Chapter 3), also help account for the emergence of the 5SM and other similar parties in diverse democracies. Finally, but only for the sake of brevity, mention ought to be made of the economic reasons for the Movement's emergence and success. The globalisation process and the major economic and financial crisis that struck in 2007 and 2008, and the consequent austerity measures, gave rise to the emergence of various other oppositional parties in southern Europe, such as Podemos in Spain and SYRIZA in Greece (Kriesi and Pappas 2015, della Porta *et al.* 2017, Morlino and Raniolo 2017, Norris and Inglehart 2019).

These long-term structural factors, together with others which we cannot go into here, help account for the foundation and subsequent success of the 5SM. Alongside these basic reasons, which are largely shared by other advanced democracies, there are certain additional factors that are more specific to the Italian context. Although they are in some way connected to the aforementioned macro-factors, they are of a more contingent nature. This does not mean, however, that their explanatory potential is limited. On the contrary, the extraordinary success of the 5SM may indeed be seen in the light of the combination of these two sets of factors. On the one hand, there are the basic factors shared by all Western democracies and, on the other hand, those unique to the Italian case that result in a political crisis and a strong sense of political discontent and thus offer opportunities for new parties to emerge and embrace the popular protest. In the aftermath of the grave economic crisis, and given the presence of political parties seemingly impotent to rectify matters, the 5SM capitalised on this political discontent and transformed it into votes for the Movement. In other words, the 5SM was seen as the only way out of the evident crisis of the Italian political system.

On closer examination, the emergence and success of Grillo's party closely resembled that of Bossi's Northern League. In their early days, both of these political movements were derided and adjudged folkloristic and thus were relegated to the margins of political life for years, that is, until the historical and political conditions were ripe for their subsequent electoral success.[5] In the case of the League, as we saw in Chapter 3, the Tangentopoli bribery scandal was a disruptive event that generated considerable hostility towards the country's political parties and politicians and opened a considerable window of opportunity. In the case of the 5SM, on the other hand, anti-politics became the prevailing, politically exploitable sentiment as a result of a series of circumstances and situations that discredited Italy's principal political actors, and which we shall now examine in greater detail.

The mainstream parties' failings as a window of opportunity

In the mid-2000s, at the time of the emergence of Beppe Grillo's famous political blog and the movement of opinion was taking form that was to subsequently result in the 5SM, Italy had a bipolar political system. The centre-right was monopolised by Silvio Berlusconi and his party, while the centre-left was highly fragmented and riven by internal conflict. The conflict between supporters and opponents of Berlusconi, which was to dominate the political scene from 1994 onwards, resulted in a climate of weariness and repetitiveness: Berlusconi's unscrupulous, unconventional political style generated strong political and social opposition, which gave rise first to the "*Girotondi*" movement (2002–3) (Ceri 2009) and then to that of the "Purple People" (2009–12), which made ample use of the Internet to aid its activities (Coretti and Pica 2015). Grillo initially began dialoguing and cooperating with this left-wing, anti-Berlusconi movement.

During those years, Italian democracy increasingly suffered and faltered as a result of the departures from institutional praxis initiated by Berlusconi. In 2005, the governing centre-right majority approved a proportional electoral law at the end of the legislature, against the will of the opposition parties, thus representing a forcing of democratic practices. This law established closed lists, a majority premium system and thresholds (Renwick *et al.* 2009). Therefore, this was a law that restricted electors' options and in practice empowered parties to nominate MPs. If it is true that more open electoral systems offering electors a greater choice and are generally correlated to greater satisfaction with the workings of democracy (Farrell and McAllister 2006), the 2005 Italian electoral reform, which reduced such options, must have been the source of further political discontent.[6] The political trajectory of Berlusconi, the main actor in the political life of the nation during that period, was closely interwoven with the judicial problems plaguing him from the very start of his political career. These problems concerned his business affairs in particular, although he was also involved in a series of sex scandals as well, which were of great interest to the public, which followed the relative news reports with morbid fascination (Gundle 2009). On several occasions, Berlusconi's personal and judicial affairs spilled over into the institutions he was a part of, and into the political life of Italy as a whole. The leader of Forza Italia, who for a considerable period was also the Prime Minister of Italy, was accused of using his political power to safeguard the financial position of his family's business group, and in particular his judicial position.[7] This moral decline of Berlusconi and the centre-right was accompanied by a political defeat. In April 2010, a live TV debate between Berlusconi and Gianfranco Fini, at the time Speaker of the Chamber of Deputies, signalled the end of the "Freedom Party" (the PDL) of which Forza Italia was an integral part.

The centre-right was having a rather rough time of things, and the aforementioned judicial proceedings had discredited Italian politicians, parties and representative institutions, thus further fostering the population's political disenchantment and hostility. During that very same period, in which Beppe Grillo had succeeded in mobilising popular opposition to the existing system, the centre-left was also blighted by political problems and identity concerns of its own. The massive turnout for the "primaries for Prodi" in 2005, as mentioned in Section "The 'invention' of party primaries" in Chapter 4, saw more than 4 million people vote, and this facilitated the victory of the centre-left coalition led by Prodi at the 2006 general election. However, its victory was a marginal one: it obtained the majority premium in the Chamber of Deputies by only 25,000 votes (out of 38 million going to the polls). In the Senate, on the other hand, the centre-right obtained approximately 430,000 votes more than the centre-left. However, as a result of the electoral system offering majority premium at a regional level, the centre-left still ended up with 158 Senators, that is, two more than the 156 of the centre-right. With a very slim, heterogeneous and litigious majority (in terms of policy preferences), and with Berlusconi continuing to claim that the elections had been rigged, thus delegitimising the elected majority and increasing the tension present within the country (Andrews 2006, Lioy 2021), the government struggled to govern, and in fact lasted just two years, thus bringing the legislature to a premature end. In the meantime, the Democratic Party was founded in 2007. This party, as we saw in Chapter 4, represented the "cold" merger – through an operation conducted by the two leading centre-left parties' apparatuses – of Italy's two major political traditions: Communism on the one hand, and Christian-Democracy on the other. Once again, primaries were held and Walter Veltroni was elected the new party's first national secretary by over 3.5 million citizens (with 76% of the votes cast). Despite this large-scale popular investiture, Veltroni was to resign just a couple of years later, in 2009, following the PD's defeat in the Sardinian regional elections. In both cases (the election of Prodi and that of Veltroni), the primaries were non-competitive, with outcomes that were foregone conclusions, and the primary purpose of which was to legitimise the choice of leader. In both cases, the great enthusiasm with which the primaries played out was followed by the bitter blow of the respective government's demise and the resignation of the party secretary. So disillusionment with, and hostility towards, political leaders and parties were increasingly felt on the left as well as on the right.

Furthermore, at the 2008 general election, the PD's electoral campaign appealed to those politically to the left of the party to cast "useful votes" in favour of the PD. In virtue of an electoral system that assigned a substantial majority premium, the aim of Veltroni (who called the PD a party with a "majoritarian vocation") was to win one more vote than the centre-right coalition. However, the electoral system also envisaged a minimum threshold for the allocation of seats: this threshold was 4% for the Chamber of Deputies, and 8% for the Senate. The "useful" votes cast for the PD by those voters who in 2006 had voted for left-wing parties[8] did not enable the left-wing coalition to reach the said minimum threshold. Thus, for the first time in the history of the Italian Republic, the left had no members of parliament. This operation meant that the left-wing parties' voters were now orphaned and consequently viewed their "cousins" in the PD with increasing resentment, as they held them responsible for the left-wing parties' exclusion from parliament following the appeal to cast "useful votes" for the PD.[9] This same operation also orphaned activists from citizens' committees and social movements. These people considered the left-wing parties to be their institutional point of reference, and after the failure of the left coalition, they went in search of new forms of representation and new political organisations that could defend their interests and help them pursue certain social and political aims.

From the PD's viewpoint, nevertheless, the hostility from the left was a minor worry. What it was really concerned about during that period was the damage to its image caused by a series of corruption and mismanagement scandals concerning party finances, involving various national leaders who were very much in the public eye. These affairs increased the anger and disillusionment of the party's militants and supporters, as well as the hostility of citizens in general, and the credibility of the PD was undermined as a consequence.[10] In the public's mind, these scandals offer further confirmation of the inadequacy, immorality and greed of politicians as a whole, as clearly emerged in public debate following the publication and popularity of the previously mentioned volume *"La Casta"* (The Caste) (Rizzo and Stella 2007). The financial scandals and those concerning the embezzlement of public funds shone the spotlight once again on the cost of the political system and the nation's representative institutions; prior to the 5SM's unexpected success at the 2013 general election (Rizzo and Stella 2012), the movement unsurprisingly focused its electoral campaign on a more morally worthy, more affordable political system. Indeed, the 5SM held rallies in Italy's town squares and in front of government buildings, during which the old style of politics was lambasted, and the movement's leaders and supporters called out loud for "honesty, honesty, honesty!".

The technocratic government of austerity and the anti-establishment parties' difficulties

One further key factor that increased the disenchantment of the electorate with all parties, both centre-left and centre-right, was the support those parties gave to the technocratic government led by Mario Monti.[11] In forming the Monti government, "the broad center-right and center-left coalitions had broken up, the 'personal' party had become weaker, and the pro-/ anti-Berlusconi split had lost some of its intensity. Meanwhile, the distance between voters and parties had grown wider, marking the revival of an 'anti-political' mood in the country" (Ceccarini *et al.* 2011, p. 58). The only parties to remain outside of the majority supporting this government, which was tasked with putting Italy's public finances in order by adopting highly unpopular policies,[12] were the League and Di Pietro's "Italy of Values". However, both of these parties, despite traditionally taking advantage of the population's discontent with politics, were at that time concerned with a number of internal problems which were to lead to the radical transformation of the League, as mentioned in Chapter 3, and to the demise of the Italy of Values party. The League, after many years in government, faithfully allied with an increasingly discredited Berlusconi, began to lose its appeal. Indeed, it began to suffer the revenge of anti-politics itself, as a result of the scandals involving Bossi and the rest of the party leadership. When the 5SM moved up a gear or two – first at the administrative elections in 2012 and then in the 2013 general election – the League appeared doomed to political marginalisation: not only was it no longer capable of attracting new voters but also a significant number of those who had previously voted League now turned to the 5SM.[13]

As previously mentioned, the other party opposing the Monti government, Di Pietro's Italy of Values, was also really struggling at the time. Di Pietro, the most well-known of the magistrates involved in the "Clean Hands" operation, had gone into politics with a moralising purpose: however, through no fault of his own, he became the source of yet another wave of anti-political fervour. It was two MPs from Di Pietro's party who, at the end of 2010, went against the party line and endorsed the Berlusconi government in a confidence vote, thus permitting it to survive a little longer. The two MPs in question, Razzi and Scilipoti, became symbols of the worst kind of politics as a result of their action, when they were called arrogant, opportunist turn-coats. The final blow to Di Pietro's party and its political credibility was dealt with in 2012 by a popular current affairs TV programme. This programme denounced the mismanagement of the party's funds and accused Di Pietro himself of having used such funds for his own personal ends. At the 2013 general election, the Italy of Values party allied itself with the left-wing coalition led by another former magistrate, Antonio Ingroia but failed to get any of its candidates into parliament and, shortly afterwards, disappeared from the political scene.

The disappearance of all left-wing parties from parliament following the 2008 election, and the scandals that overwhelmed Italy of Values and the League, significantly changed the political choices available to Italians. The crisis experienced by all of them left three important issues unaddressed. The first such issue was the penal populism symbolised in particular by Di Pietro's Italy of Values party (Anastasia and Anselmi 2020). The second question, of which Italy of Values and the League were the principal advocates, was the moralisation of politics and the battle against the politician "caste". The third was the relationship with the citizen's committees and social movements, which, as we know, boast a powerful political ally in Italy's left-wing parties. The vacuum left by the disappearance of these parties was subsequently filled by the 5SM, the rhetoric of which focused precisely on reducing the costs of politics, denouncing politicians' privileges and ineptitude, emphasising the value of legality, honesty and transparency in politics, and on support for the battles fought by social movements and local committees.[14]

Summing up the discussion of the various affairs described in this section, the beginnings and development of the movement of opinion that coalesced around the figure of Beppe Grillo and his blog as from 2005, and which was to lead to the foundation and success of the 5SM, accompanied the decline and failure of the mainstream parties as well as consolidated populist parties such as the League, Forza Italia and Italy of Values. This circumstance altered the political opportunity structure, making it easier for a new party to succeed (Lucardie 2000), like the niche party that the original 5SM was.[15] The persistent difficulties of Italy's political parties, and the onset of the economic crisis, were to lead, as we all known, to the centre-right government led by Berlusconi being replaced by a technocratic government headed by Mario Monti. The latter government had to take a series of unpopular decisions in order to meet austerity demands, with a view to balancing the nation's accounts to some degree, and which in fact quickly lost the popularity it enjoyed when first appointed. At the beginning of 2013, at the end of the legislature, the Monti government was substantially opposed by Italians (Giannetti 2012, p. 146) who at that point had lost all faith in both traditional parties and technocrats. As a consequence, the citizens' anti-political feelings grew, and yet there was no political party or individual politician capable of credibly advocating the moralisation of politics.

Thus, the conditions were ripe for Grillo's niche party, derided and ignored by the political mainstream, to take up the cause of all those citizens dissatisfied and disenchanted with what was deemed to be a bankrupt political class.[16] The remarkable and unexpected success of the 5SM at the 2013 general election was due also to this, as well as to the underlying causes outlined at the beginning of this section. The paradoxical aspect of this is that the 5SM's policy proposals constitute a real collage of the anti-political attitudes and behaviour of the movement's political adversaries. In other words, the 5SM blends the explicit, unrefined anti-political attitudes of the centre-right, with the more refined and subtler ones of the centre-left. Grillo's party did not create its anti-politics from scratch, but rather it recycled, underscored and took to the extreme the catalogue of anti-political attitudes and behaviour adopted by others, which, in truth, are an integral part of Italian political culture. The following section shall examine in more detail the nature of said catalogue of anti-political attitudes and behaviour, and how they were employed to guarantee the success of the 5SM.

The anti-politics of the Five Star Movement: inside, and outside of, the institutions

The 5SM, as we saw in the preceding two sections of this chapter, represents a complete novelty for the Italian political system. Indeed, its organisational and policy-related originality stands out from the political scenarios seen in other Western democracies. Even years after its emergence, its creator Beppe Grillo continues to skilfully vaunt its newness and originality, qualities that are invariably remunerative in the electoral marketplace (Sikk 2012). This is particularly true when the other parties have lost all credibility and are considered morally and politically bankrupt in the eyes of the nation's citizens, even if for non-contingent reasons (Ignazi 2021). The newness of the 5SM is based on various factors, particularly the fact that prior political experience is not required for those aspiring to political office from within the party's ranks. Furthermore, this is reiterated by the movement's fierce opposition to old politics and traditional political parties. This opposition between the new and the old reveals the various forms of anti-politics discussed in Chapter 1. In short, by accusing all political adversaries of belonging to the same privileged "caste", the 5SM finds it easy to present itself as a new political actor aiming to eliminate the old, corrupt political class.

So what exactly is genuinely new about the 5SM's anti-politics? On closer examination, its anti-politics feature three novel aspects which can be summed up by three adjectives: extreme, tangible and multiform. The first novel aspect consists in the occasionally violent intensity of its anti-political preaching. If we exclude Umberto Bossi and the early version of the League, which as we have seen took the unprecedented step of waving a hangman's noose in parliament, none of the political figures described in the previous chapters has ever railed so strongly against political parties, professional politicians and the arenas of political representation, as Beppe Grillo and the other 5SM militants have. To give but one example: "Grillo generally refers to politicians as 'corpses' or 'zombies'" (Cosenza 2014, p. 93). The second aspect of the 5SM's anti-politics is the transformation of its previous anti-political rhetoric into tangible action, and once in government, into political decisions. While the anti-politics of other political actors remain intangible, and consist of speeches and attitudes, the 5SM's anti-politics consists of tangible actions: in fact, the 5SM has adopted rules of conduct governing its political representatives, together with mechanisms for the operation of the party and its parliamentary groups; it has also proposed bills of a constitutional nature pertaining to the workings of the political system and democracy as such. The third characteristic feature of the anti-politics of Grillo's party regards its capacity to interpret and blend the principal forms of anti-politics that have emerged during Italy's political history. As pointed out at the beginning of this chapter, the 5SM in fact updates and takes to the extreme both the unrefined, explicit anti-political messages of the centre-right parties and their leaders and the more sophisticated, nuanced anti-politics of the centre-left. This is why the 5SM's anti-politics is of a multiform nature, and during its early days in particular, it permeated almost every action the party took.

We shall now try to more precisely identify the specific anti-political repertoire of the 5SM, and to link each item of this repertoire with the political actors that introduced it or have made ample use thereof in the past. This will also enable us to identify certain similarities between the affairs of other anti-political politicians and parties, and those of the 5SM. This does not mean, of course, that history repeats itself. Nevertheless, by identifying certain similarities or regularities may inform our understanding of the risks and opportunities of those who choose to adopt an anti-political approach. This exercise also enables us to more accurately trace the trajectory of the 5SM which, as we shall see, is also characteristic of other movement parties and other parties that play the anti-political game.

The Five Star Movement and the Common Man Movement

The first comparison made by various scholars is that between Giannini and Grillo, and thus between the Common Man Movement experience and that of the 5SM.[17] It is clear that the two movements, due to the different historical and political contexts, are not directly comparable. However, they do share certain common traits and directions, which we shall now look at. The two leaders Grillo and Giannini were both entertainers, although their respective political development and characteristics differ somewhat. Thus, they were both used to being centre stage and addressing a public expecting to be entertained, and if possible, to get excited about something. Their central role as founders of movements of opinion, and of the parties originating from such movements, was underlined by the fact that Giannini was referred to as "the Founder" (Setta 2005, p. 86), while Grillo, who shared the role with Casaleggio, was the "Co-founder" (Bordignon and Ceccarini 2013, p. 439) of their respective movements. Giannini often mispronounced the names of his political adversaries, with a clearly comical, but also caustic, often offensive intent. Furthermore, "Giannini patented the 'method' of launching personal attacks on his adversaries, without restraint, even at the cost of encroaching on, and denigrating, their private lives, in an ironic manner at times amusing and effective, and at other times insulting and trivial" (Setta 2005, p. 59). Grillo acted likewise, giving denigratory nicknames to the country's principal politicians, often based on their physical features. As Giovanna Cosenza has pointed out:

> The insolent nicknames that Grillo attributes to politicians have exactly [this] purpose: they either reduce human beings to their physical traits and defects, or they highlight their folly, stupidity, and advanced age. In

any case, politicians are so belittled that even the most ordinary human being – who, unlike politicians, has nothing to do with power, social status and wealth – looks down on them, and ends up feeling better than them: more attractive, more intelligent, stronger and younger. Hence Silvio Berlusconi becomes the "Psiconano" (Psychodwarf) (...) Mario Monti becomes "Rigor Montis", owing to his austerity politics and his cold communication style (...). When Grillo wants to be more brutal, instead of these nicknames, he makes use of metaphors combined with swear words. For example, he once defined Giuliano Ferrara, editor-in-chief of the newspaper Il Foglio, as a "container full of liquid shit". In some cases, the nicknames he invents can be extremely offensive – so much so that they become unacceptable, even when not combined with foul language.

(Cosenza 2014, pp. 92–3)

As we saw in Section "The advent of anti-politics: the Common Man" in Chapter 2, one of the main targets of Giannini's rhetoric was the category of professional politicians whom he contemptuously referred to as "upp" [*uomini politici di professione*]. In order to ridicule the entire category, Giannini claimed that a "good accountant" would suffice to govern Italy. Grillo and the 5SM were to exalt this very same amateurism and political inexperience some 60 years later. In fact, Grillo declared that he would rather have "a housewife with three kids" as Minister of Finance than an economics professor (Bickerton and Accetti 2018, p. 140), since that housewife, despite the innumerable difficulties she faces, would never see her family go bankrupt. Consequently, self-sacrifice, honesty, a spirit of commitment and a healthy dose of common sense are preferable to master's degrees from the most famous universities, according to Grillo. As mentioned, one of the characteristics of the 5SM's anti-politics is its tangibility and consistency. Once Grillo had entered the nation's political institutions and gained political power, he did not decide to entrust the Ministry of Finance to a housewife with three kids, although his choice of Minister was not that far removed from such a figure: in fact, Luigi Di Maio, the 5SM's most important governmental figure (previously the political head of the 5SM, and now the Minister for Foreign Affairs), prior to entering parliament for the first time, had only ever worked as a steward (or according to some, a simple drinks seller) at San Paolo football stadium during Naples F.C. matches (Gerbaudo 2019, p. 2).[18]

Two more important things render the 5SM's idea of the ideal administrator of public affairs similar to that of Giannini's "good accountant". As previously mentioned, a lack of prior political experience is an essential prerequisite for electoral candidacy or selection as a minister in the view of the 5SM. This "rule" is only relaxed by the provision establishing a possible second term of office, beyond which, however, no activist or political representative may venture according to the 5SM's original line. Giannini had established that the "good accountant" should remain in office for one year only and could not be immediately re-elected. The 5SM is not quite as drastic, but the principle of the limitation on the term of office remains the same. A good accountant, furthermore, is paid little or in any case does not benefit from any particular financial privileges. The proposed reduction in MPs' salaries, which Grillo initially wanted to be no higher than the salary of a normal office clerk (around 1,400 euro a month) (Pinto and Pedrazzani 2015, p. 104), is the second aspect of the 5SM's conception of political personnel that resembles that of the Common Man Movement. Furthermore, foregoing part of one's salary and returning the public funds made available to the party's MPs are rules that "can be also interpreted as representing a form of delegitimisation of the political elites, described by the 5SM as a clique" (*ibid.*). Ultimately, the powerfully anti-political message that emerges is that the lack of previous political experience on the part of the 5SM's MPs and ministers is proof of the fact that anyone can act politically. From this anti-political message stems the popular consideration of the harmfulness, or in any case the worthlessness, of professional politicians and traditional political parties.

Another expression of anti-politics that is shared by the 5SM and the Common Man Movement is their refusal to define themselves along the left-right spectrum. Just like many other anti-political leaders and parties, both proudly boast of not belonging to either left or right: "neither right nor left, but forwards" was what Giannini said of his movement (Setta 2005, p. 202), while Grillo and his party have always maintained an eclectic position in this regard (Mosca and Tronconi 2019). Neither right nor left, because in their view of the political sphere, there is no substantial difference between left-wing and right-wing professional politicians, or between left-wing and right-wing parties acting collusively. During the years immediately after the Second World War, when the wound inflicted by Fascism had yet to heal, and the anti-Fascist parties began to dominate the political scene, Giannini provokingly and scandalously proclaimed the equal distance separating him from the two factions: "[he] explained that he was not at all neutral in regard to Fascism and anti-Fascism, 'but an enemy: a bitter enemy and convinced despiser of both. No neutrality, but enmity and hostility towards both of them with strict equanimity. To simply adopt a neutral position vis-à-vis two forms of parasitism would be too easy – too easy for the parasites, that is'" (Setta 2005, p. 59). During the second half of the 2000s, when the most important political opposition was between supporters and opponents of Berlusconi, Grillo took a similar stance, refusing to join either grouping. In one of his more successful linguistic expressions, he called the PD (the Democratic Party), the "PD without the L" in reference to the party led by Berlusconi, which at that time was called the "PDL" (*Popolo della Libertà* – the People of Freedom).

Finally, the anti-partyism of the Common Man Movement and 5SM is also evident in the idea that their leaders have of the nature and destiny of their own parties. Both parties negate (in theory at least) Michels' classical idea of the transformation of a political party, which from being a means to an end becomes an end in itself (Michels 1915, p. 394), since they consider themselves as being of a transient nature. They see their own organisation as a necessary means by which to conduct a salvific mission and believe that once that mission has been accomplished, the organisation itself is destined to disappear. Consequently, Giannini was to claim that the Common Man Movement was like an umbrella, that is, a thing to be put away once the sun comes out again (Setta 2005, p. 166); the 5SM, on the other hand, considers itself a "biodegradable party" (Gerbaudo 2019, p. 87) that will vanish once its aims have been achieved.

The Five Star Movement and centre-right anti-politics

The 5SM shares a number of features not only with Giannini and his Common Man Movement but also with Berlusconi, Forza Italia and the anti-politics that they embody and express. This similarity is paradoxical, given that the 5SM has always considered Berlusconi a bitter rival. In fact, it was opposition to Berlusconi's unscrupulous political style and disdain for the rules (resulting among other things in Berlusconi being accused of a series of offences) that led to the emergence and growth, in the mid-2000s, of the movement of opinion, which subsequently became the 5SM. The similarities regard both the leaders of the two parties and the latter's organisational framework. Grillo and Berlusconi can both be considered anti-political outsiders, since they both went into politics after successful careers in the worlds of entertainment and business, respectively. Their previous non-involvement in politics is thus a resource rendering their anti-political stance credible in the long term. Indeed, the fact of never having been involved in politics before made it very easy for both of them to take aim at professional politicians. Likewise, it was easy for them to denigrate political parties of which they were not a part. Both leaders are considered good, histrionic, persuasive orators: Grillo, thanks to his career as a comedian, and Berlusconi, because he has managed to make the very most of the expertise and professionals present in his TV companies, to learn how to cleverly employ communication techniques in the political field.

Despite the rhetoric regarding the importance of participation, accountability and power sharing, summed up in the obsessive, yet highly successful slogan "everyone counts as one", Grillo's party, just like Berlusconi's, is strongly hierarchical, oligarchical and centralised.[19] In fact, the origins and the process of institutionalisation of the two parties are similar in various ways, particularly as regards the personalised, charismatic strategy adopted by their respective leaders (Panebianco 1988b, pp. 52–3). Both parties were created in a top-down fashion, based on pre-existing corporate organisations (Berlusconi's companies in the case of Forza Italia, and Casaleggio's IT consultancy firm in the case of the 5SM), and some years later they continued to remain the property of their founders. This notwithstanding,

Berlusconi has always concealed the party character of Forza Italia, claiming it to be a movement. Grillo has done exactly the same, choosing the term "movement" for his party, whose activities were for a long time governed by a "non-statute".[20]

One further thing that Forza Italia and the 5SM have in common is strictly related to their anti-political character. This concerns their conception of political representation and the space given over to representative assemblies and society's other intermediary bodies. Both parties have adopted a plebiscitary style, which in Berlusconi's case involves the use of opinion polls and the claim that the majority enjoys a form of omnipotence. In Grillo's case, plebiscitary democracy is based on the surveying of the "general will", which in practice consists of the votes that the movement's members cast during the regular polls organised by the party's leadership (Vittori 2021, p. 14). These polls of the "membership", as we shall see shortly, pursue the chimera of direct democracy. They force MPs to vote not according to their conscience, but in line with the will of members. In doing so, they belittle parliament itself and introduce, in practice, a form of imperative mandate. It therefore comes as no surprise to find that Grillo, on several occasions, has criticised the Italian Constitution's prohibition of the imperative mandate (Lanzone and Tronconi 2015, p. 68).

The 5SM also utilises the anti-political strategies adopted by Bossi and the League, which were examined in detail in Chapter 3. These include a plebiscitary style; the use of direct, vulgar language; acting as an outsider; large-scale popular rallies during which he uses violent tones when criticising other politicians and parties. They are all aspects shared by the two parties and their respective leaders. Even the successful play on words "PD less the L" mentioned above, with which Grillo aimed to underline the irrelevance and misleading nature of the distinction between left and right, echoes another equally successful slogan coined ten years earlier by Umberto Bossi, namely *"Roma-Polo e Roma-Ulivo"* ("Rome–the Pole of Liberties and Rome-The Olive Tree Coalition"), designed to underscore the collusive tolerance of corruption of all parties, accused of concentrating power in the political centre (Rome). In using this phrase, Bossi wished to emphasise his belief that there was no genuine difference between the centre-right (*Polo delle Libertà*) and the centre-left (*L'Ulivo*), by alluding to collusion, rather than rivalry, between the two coalitions.

Anti-politics as a moralising force

Riding the extensive wave of discontent created by the Tangentopoli bribery scandal, and occasionally fanned thereafter by other political scandals and the publication of the previously mentioned volume "The Caste", Grillo and the 5SM set great store in the moralising of politics. The moralising campaign was transformed, almost automatically, into a generalised accusation of the immorality of professional politicians, political parties and, consequently, Italy's national, regional and local representative bodies. Using a tried-and-tested approach (Achen and Bartels 2016, ch. 5), politicians were blamed for things that were clearly beyond their control and responsibility. They thus became the perfect scapegoats for all the forms of dissatisfaction present in society. The 5SM's moralising anti-politics – which was also referred to as "justicialism" (the exploitation of the legal system to persecute political figures), taking this name incorrectly from Argentina's Justicialist Party – clearly derive from the professional and political affairs of Antonio Di Pietro and are fed by the constant face-off between supporters and opponents of Berlusconi (Cento Bull 2016, p. 227, Di Maggio and Perrone 2019, p. 471). The 5SM, for a long time initially at least, seemed to be acting as a collective public prosecutor denouncing politicians' misdemeanours and investigating them and the parties they belong to. During this early phase, prior to the foundation of his own party, Grillo lent his support to the political positions adopted by Di Pietro, who was to use Casaleggio's consultancy firm for communication purposes (Vittori 2021, p. 7). In keeping with Di Pietro's political undertaking, which as we have seen ended badly, Grillo and the 5SM became obsessed with the question of the moralisation of politics. This started with the rules governing the operation of their own party. As well as establishing a limit of two terms of office, designed to combat the corruption and careerism deemed characteristic of professional politicians, the 5SM paid special heed to the judicial affairs of those standing for election and those elected. Consequently, stringent rules were applied to candidacies: Article 7 of the "non-statute" established that would-be candidates "must have no criminal record and must not be subject to any pending criminal proceedings, regardless of the nature of the offence with which they may be charged". Furthermore, the 5SM's "Code of Ethics" establishes (Art. 6) that the movement's bodies may sanction any candidate or elected member who is simply charged with a criminal offence. Elected members, moreover, undertake to resign from office should they be expelled from the 5SM for any reason (Art. 3).

The honesty of politicians was thus the battle that the 5SM took over from Di Pietro, in an attempt to moralise a political class portrayed as intrinsically corrupt. Compared to Di Pietro's "analog" party, Grillo's digitalised 5SM added a number of innovative features in the pursuit of this objective. Not only the criminal records (or rather, the absence thereof) of politicians but also their conduct within the country's institutions were examined. To do this, Grillo and the 5SM utilised the technology made available on the web and decided to guarantee the transparency of their own operations through the live streaming of meetings and encounters. While the traditional political parties remained enclosed in their smoke-filled rooms, and their decisions remained rather opaque, the 5SM decided to open up to society by rendering public the various phases of the party's everyday life, including those of a delicate nature, which were not generally accessible to the nation's citizens, or indeed to the party's members.[21] To sum up, the practices of a monitored democracy introduced by the 5SM not only imply diffidence towards, and mistrust of, politicians but are also fed by the theatrical representation of an entire political class humiliated, ridiculed and accused by the people's genuine representatives who, on the contrary, are honest, hard-working, new and uninterested in power games. Grillo came up with yet another successful linguistic device, when he described MPs as "our employees", which was specifically designed to invert the power relationship between citizens and political representatives, an objective that the 5SM intended to pursue.

Just as convincing, in the electors' eyes, were the harsh words that Grillo and the other leaders of the 5SM had for the power and the collusive actions of political parties, and for the suffocating presence of partitocracy as a whole. The arguments they use echo certain polemical points made by Maranini (see Section "Against partitocracy" in Chapter 2) and subsequently reiterated by the Radical Party and its leader, Marco Pannella. The narrative fed by the 5SM is that of a civil society interested in the common good and the future of society, opposed by a political class the only real concern of which is the preservation of its own privileges; a political class rooted in outdated political methods and a slave to the powerful. This narrative is highly effective in generating electoral support among the population. Once again it is easy to identify, in Italy's recent political history, certain precedents of this kind of opposition. The first that comes to mind concerns the early 1990s, when the principal actors were what was called "civil society", part of which at a certain point was transformed into a party – "The Network" (*La Rete*) – an ephemeral organisation headed by the Mayor of Palermo, Orlando (Saresella 2016). At that time, there was no such thing as live streaming, although its equivalent existed in the form of live TV debates, involving politicians and "ordinary people". The latter were interviewed in the street by journalists, present in the television studios together with the compere and other guests, consulted by means of instant surveys conducted in real time. In this manner, representatives of civil society were given a rare opportunity to talk with politicians on an equal footing. These discussions often resulted in the politicians in question being criticised and accused of wrongdoings. Due also to the cultural and political atmosphere created by the Tangentopoli bribes scandal, the politicians struggled to defend themselves and their public image, either on a personal level or as representatives of the category of professional politicians and generally came out very badly from such live debates.

Participatory anti-politics

As has already been mentioned, in addition to the radical, explicit forms of anti-politics that characterised right-wing populism in Italy, the 5SM offered subtler, more sophisticated expressions thereof, initially introduced into Italy by the centre-left and which, in any case, share an emphasis on the importance of grassroots involvement (see Chapter 4). As several scholars have pointed out (Biorcio 2014, p. 38, Pinto and Pedrazzani 2015, p. 104, Gerbaudo 2019, p. 16, Mosca 2020, p. 358), the 5SM's organisational framework, its participatory practices and its style of political representation are all reminiscent of the actions of the libertarian parties in the 1970s and 1980s, in particular those of the German Green Party (Poguntke 1993) and, more recently, of the northern European pirate parties (Hartleb 2013). Initially, for example, the elected municipal and regional representatives of the 5SM went to the electors and submitted their mandate, somewhat symbolically, to the party's activists (Gualmini 2013, p. 16). Leadership of the parliamentary groups is of a collective nature and follows a system of rotation. The party's elected representatives are considered mere spokespersons for the membership, and they undertake to comply with the decisions taken by members following specific consultations. The party's MPs refuse to be called "Honourable", demanding that they be referred to simply as "citizen" or, in fact, "spokesperson". Furthermore, they themselves curtail their own salaries and are selected in a more participatory manner than the MPs of other parties. Unlike the libertarian left parties, however, the 5SM does not hold regular large-scale assemblies (Mosca 2020, p. 358) but organises large open-air rallies (such as V-Day) or meetings when Grillo is up on stage (like the "tsunami tour" organised prior to the 2013 general election). Finally, the 5SM only allows registered members to participate in the decisions regarding the life of the party.

In short, the answer offered by the 5SM, which is against professional politicians, against ossified political parties, against meetings of idle, privileged MPs strictly obedient to party directives, is the promotion of grassroots involvement in the party's life through the Internet. Unlike in northern European countries, in particular Germany, the Italian green party's innovative participatory and organisational methods have never really taken off (Rhodes 1995, Biorcio 2002). The grassroots movements that emerged from the late 1990s onwards in Italy, described in detail in Chapter 4, were what prepared the ground for the 5SM's subsequent success. In fact, there are clear similarities between the participatory practices of the centre-left, borrowed in part from the global justice movement, and those of the 5SM. Participatory budgeting, which is one of the primary instruments already promoted by centre-left local authorities some years prior to the emergence of the movement of opinion centred on the figure of Beppe Grillo, has been systematically adopted by the 5SM as soon as it has entered the country's political institutions, as in the case of Sicily, for example (Allegretti *et al.* 2021, p. 33). The first local organisational hubs, called "meetups", formed spontaneously after Grillo's appeal to the followers of his blog (Lanzone and Tronconi 2015, pp. 55–8), closely resembled the groups participating in the decision-making experiments launched by local and regional authorities governed by the centre-left during that same period.

However, the primaries introduced by the centre-left in the mid-2000s and subsequently employed widely by the PD were what offered a model of participatory democracy to Italy's citizens even before the 5SM's leadership followed their example. The 5SM was to use primaries widely, not only to select the "head of the party" but also to choose parliamentary, regional governmental and mayoral candidates. Members were also called on to nominate the 5SM candidate for the office of Italian President (who under the Italian Constitution is elected by MPs and a select group of other representatives nominated by the country's regional governments), the names of the "lay" members (non-magistrates) of the Supreme Council of the Judiciary (another parliamentary prerogative) and in regard to the 5SM's participation in Italy's governments, as well as a number of other important issues (Gerbaudo 2019, p. 134). Ultimately, Grillo's recipe for righting the ills of Italian democracy was very similar to that of the centre-left, namely administering more democracy to the democratic system. However, Grillo's recipe was far more radical than that of the centre-left. It went as far as envisaging, and hoping for, a form of direct democracy in which citizens express their will in regard to every single important question, and where MPs have no decisional autonomy but simply implement the will of the people. As Grillo stated: "We want instruments of direct democracy in the hands of the citizens. I dream of my son voting yes or no on a computer from his home, deciding whether to go to [to war in] Afghanistan or not, whether to stay in Europe or not, whether to leave the euro or not. This is what I want" (della Porta *et al.* 2017, p. 131).

Despite this radical participatory project, the 5SM's primaries and the other grassroots consultation practices have been less inclusive than those promoted by the PD and the centre-left. In fact, while the latter's primaries are open, on occasion even to those under the age of 18 and to immigrants resident in Italy, the 5SM's primaries and other consultations have been reserved for party members only. Apart from this significant difference, it can be argued that the subtly anti-political outcomes and implications of the centre-left's primaries, mentioned in Chapter 4, also apply to the 5SM's consultations. For example, the results of many such consultations are a foregone conclusion and simply reflect the positions that the party's leadership hopes for. This was the case when Di Maio was elected the head of the party. Said election was principally a process of legitimation of a decision made by others, and perhaps unsurprisingly other party leaders did not submit their own candidacies, while just a limited number of members bothered voting (Gerbaudo 2019, p. 3). As with the PD, the 5SM's primaries result in the atomisation of the party's members, which prevents them from challenging the leadership and renders them powerless to oppose the leaders' decisions. By negating the basic principle of deliberative processes, namely that the best arguments prevail following an orderly discussion thereof, the 5SM's members are simply called upon to say "yes" or "no" to proposals formulated by the party's leadership in an episodic, contingent manner. Consequently, the 5SM's participatory practices, like those of the centre-left, are of a plebiscitary, manipulative nature.

Normalisation: anti-politics gets sucked into politics

From its very earliest electoral successes, the 5SM's development has been the subject of analysis by various scholars, all of whom have emphasised the process of institutionalisation and normalisation of the party witnessed during this latter period (Bordignon and Ceccarini 2015, 2019, Ceccarini and Bordignon 2016, Tronconi 2018, Biorcio and Sampugnaro 2019, Di Maggio and Perrone 2019, Biancalana 2020, Vittori 2021). This path of development, moreover, is one followed by many movement parties, such as the previously mentioned green parties (Frankland *et al.* 2008). Putting to one side this broad debate for one moment, and without delving into the political positions and governmental actions of the 5SM, this final section is going to examine how this process of institutionalisation has necessarily affected the 5SM's anti-political features which have always been a key factor in the party's success. This factor has been of crucial importance to the life of the party because, as we saw in previous chapters, the anti-political theme is a red-hot one. As a result of Italians' widespread aversion to politics in general, by focusing on this matter permits political parties and entrepreneurs to quickly, and rather easily, scale the heights of political power. However, at the same time, the inability to preserve an anti-political line, or worse still, betraying such a line, will quickly result in a party biting the dust and being ridden roughshod over by a disenchanted, even angrier populace. Knowing that its very survival and room for manoeuvre depend on its anti-political line, the 5SM has constantly tried to conceal the inevitable process of normalisation impacting the party and its leadership. However, while being part of government speeds up the institutionalisation and normalisation processes, it also offers resources that can be used to foster its anti-political self-image. This is the direction that the 5SM took, operating on two different fronts. Firstly it was to take advantage of the visibility it gained through its involvement in government, in order to underscore its unconventional political style and invest in the symbolism of anti-politics. Secondly, it conducted various battles of a patently anti-political nature, which were to have a significant impact on the institutional framework, and even the constitutional framework, of the Italian political system.

Of course, the 5SM's entire political existence, particularly having governed the country for over three years, cannot be summed up simply in terms of an anti-political crusade. Once in government, in fact, the party has pursued numerous important actions having a genuine and symbolic impact on the country. These include the introduction of the "citizen's income" (Nizzoli 2018, Di Ruzza 2020). In regard to other important issues such as immigration, relations with the EU and Italy's cooperation with

China, the position of the 5SM has wavered in recent years. With regard to these questions, given the substantial continuity of Italian policy (Giugliano 2020), the 5SM has tried to distinguish its own position from the clearer positions of the right-wing parties and also from the more flexible stances adopted by the PD. The question of anti-politics, nevertheless, remains the key to the construction of the party's image, and thus this is the question we ought to focus on, while not losing sight of the importance of the 5SM's other political initiatives during its period as a governing party.

The crumbling pillars of anti-politics: everybody does not count as one

The 5SM's lengthy presence as a member of the Italian government and in the country's institutions, together with its consequent inevitable institutional-isation, undermine the three pillars of the party's anti-politics, namely par-ticipatory egalitarianism as highlighted by the slogan "everybody counts as one", its opposition to professional politicians and its rejection of the party format for its own political organisation. We shall now examine the ways in which each one of these aspects of the 5SM's anti-politics has changed, such changes being clearly interconnected with one another. These changes, interpreted as a series of contradictions, inconsistencies and indeed acts of betrayal of the party's original promises, have ended up clouding the 5SM's anti-political development in the eyes of its electorate and militants, as well as of the Italian population as a whole.

The first patent contradiction perceived by the country's citizens regards the participatory rhetoric the 5SM has expounded since its earliest days. As was foreseeable, the spontaneity of the "friends of Beppe Grillo" groups, together with the movement-like character of the initial meet-ups, were grad-ually transformed by the internal structuring of the organisation, reveal-ing clear imbalances in the status and power of its militants. In fact, some of them, particularly those who managed to enter the nation's institutions, stopped being simple activists to become party leaders with decision-making powers. Michels' iron law of oligarchy derived from his observation of the German Social Democratic Party a century before – "Who says organization, says oligarchy" (Michels 1915, p. 401) – seemed to quickly apply to the 5SM. The words of their slogan – "everyone counts for one" – exclaimed as they attacked the "Winter Palace" of old parties and corrupt politicians, sounded increasingly hollow to the ears of Italy's citizens and the 5SM's own activists. Conflict, defections and expulsions inevitably followed as a result of, among other things, this process of internal stratification (Tronconi 2018, p. 165).

The consultation of party members via the 5SM's digital platforms, which according to Grillo and Casaleggio would have guaranteed the exercise of full direct democracy, increasingly became simply a means of legitimising the party leadership's own decisions (Gerbaudo 2019, p. 140). Moreover, the instruments employed for the purposes of such consultations have not escaped criticism either. The software programmes and the digital platforms used during the course of the 5SM's existence, in fact, have not permitted any control over the authenticity of voting, and the procedures concerned have only been certified twice, by a third party (a Norwegian company specialised in online security: ibid., p. 125). At all other times, the leadership called for members to vote, they duly did so, and the persons in charge of the platform notified the results, without any internal or external checks being carried out. Furthermore, the firm owned by Casaleggio, which for a considerable time held information on the members of the 5SM and took care of electoral procedures, has no specific skills in the field of voting security. Therefore, on several occasions, questions have been raised regarding the correctness of voting and on the risk of votes being manipulated both by the 5SM's leadership and hackers (ibid., p. 119). The truth is that the voting platform, which has been pointedly named "Rousseau", was only used intermittently, with no guarantee of the soundness of the vote, before eventually being abandoned as a result of conflict within the party.[22]

The same fate awaited the streaming of political meetings and encounters. The flag of transparency which Grillo flaunted and used against Matteo Renzi and the old political class, as we have seen, was quickly taken down. The confidentiality and secrecy of party debate and the opaqueness of decisional processes, which Grillo and the 5SM had accused other parties of, became the norm for the 5SM as well, as soon as it entered the nation's political institutions, and in particular when it became a member of the Italian government. An eloquent example of this is the different ways of selecting candidates for the 2013 and 2018 general elections. In 2013, candidates were chosen by means of primaries only open to registered members (Mosca *et al.* 2015a, p. 170). In 2018, on the other hand, the majority of candidates were chosen by the 5SM's political head, Luigi Di Maio, while the remaining candidates put their own names forward, although he had the last word on their candidacy (Marino *et al.* 2019, p. 276). In addition to guaranteeing personal loyalty, this selection method probably served also to permit the re-candidature and re-selection of numerous outgoing MPs, which was greater in the case of the 5SM than in that of other parties (Tronconi and Verzichelli 2019, p. 214). Article 7 of the "non-statute", stating that "discussions regarding candidatures shall be conducted in a public, transparent, direct manner", was clearly not being complied with here. Furthermore, the appointment of Giuseppe Conte as Prime Minister in the first government, in which the 5SM was allied with the League, and in the second government, when the 5SM was allied with the centre-left, took place in an oligarchical manner, subject to ratification, in both cases, by the members' votes. The fact that Conte did not stand for election at the 2018 general election, and therefore was not voted for from any 5SM list, further damaged the participatory, egalitarian philosophy that had been professed by the party from the very beginning.

To conclude, mention should be made of the circumstance that perhaps more than any other made it apparent that the "everyone counts for one" slogan was purely utopian. The circumstance in question, which was unfortunately of a tragic nature, was the sudden death in 2016 of Gianroberto Casaleggio, the co-founder of the 5SM. His place was immediately taken by his son, Davide, as if it were a dynastic office. This affair was very similar to that of the "old" Bossi who, after falling ill, was first replaced as the head of the League by his wife, and who subsequently designated his very young and inexperienced son, Renzo, as his political heir. Thus, family links are important for the 5SM as much as they are for Italy's other parties, and this is one of the features of Italian politics that most annoys the electorate. In sum, when it came to testing government and the nation's institutions, the plan to demolish representative democracy in the name of anti-politics, and replace it with direct democracy capable of removing power from politicians, political parties and parliament, whilst giving it back to the people, proved unsuccessful. It was simply one huge act of deception or, at the very least, was seriously misleading. This may have been due to naivety, as Grillo and Casaleggio failed to realise that their utopian project required an anthropological, rather than a political, transformation of the Italian people. As Achen and Bartels have observed:

> The folk theory of democracy celebrates the wisdom of popular judgments by informed and engaged citizens. The reality is quite different. Human beings are busy with their lives. Most have school or a job consuming many hours of the day. They also have meals to prepare, homes to clean, and bills to pay. They may have children to raise or elderly parents to care for. They may also be coping with unemployment, business reverses, illness, addictions, divorce, or other personal and family troubles. For most, leisure time is at a premium. Sorting out which presidential candidate has the right foreign policy toward Asia is not a high priority for them
>
> (Achen and Bartels 2016, p. 9)

The professionalization of the political class

The idyllic world of egalitarian, grassroots participation theorised by the 5SM thus revealed its many limitations and was very quickly shattered. Its members' actions and representative style when part of the institutions – which constitute the second cornerstone of their anti-political preaching – followed a similar path of normalisation and produced the same disenchantment with the party's inability to remain faithful to its original ideals. The basis for the party's negation of political careerism, that is, the limit of a maximum of two terms of office, was questioned on several occasions. The first of these was when an awkward attempt was made to add a "zero term" to the aforesaid two terms in the case of local government posts only. This was immediately ridiculed by observers and critics alike. Thereafter, once the floodgates had been opened, the debate over the abandonment of the two-term limit became a focal point of the conflict between the two factions within the 5SM: on the one hand, there were the "orthodox members" who, together with Grillo, wanted to preserve said limitation, and on the other hand, there were Conte's followers who wanted to eliminate it.

Not only was there a desire to hold on to office – and this is the message that is ultimately conveyed to the 5SM's voters and activists – like all elected representatives, the 5SM's members of parliament at a certain point also wanted to keep their entire salary, rather than halve it as had originally been promised. Furthermore, many MPs refused to pay 300 euro a month to the company run by Casaleggio, for the services said company provided to the 5SM (Bordignon and Ceccarini 2019, p. 154), in particular the aforementioned online voting service. Once again, there was an argument between the party's purists on the one hand, and those who wanted to see the rule requiring MPs to return one half of their salary and make periodic payments to Casaleggio, abolished. In a lot of cases, the intention not to give up part of their salary led MPs and sSenators to jump ship for another parliamentary group. This circumstance fuelled this switching from one parliamentary group to another that Grillo had so strongly opposed and stigmatised, and which is seen as one of the principal negative aspects of Italian politics and a source of political discontent and disaffection.[23] Furthermore, the way in which certain 5SM MPs pretended to return part of their salary (by arranging a bank transfer, generating a receipt for said transfer and subsequently cancelling the transfer itself) made a laughing stock of the party. In an attempt to defend itself against the accusation of being just like every other party, with MPs solely interested in power and money, the leadership of the 5SM subsequently expelled from the party all those having breached the established rules[24] (Mosca *et al.* 2015a, p. 170).

As the process of institutionalisation advanced, the positions of power within the 5SM became increasingly consolidated. At the same time, certain practices characteristic of movement parties was gradually abandoned. For example, during the course of the legislature that began in 2018, the party stopped selecting the head of the group in the Chamber of Deputies on a rotational basis. Furthermore, political careers now followed the standard path, with the most important leaders always taking on the key political and ministerial posts. As occurs in other political parties, there was a segmentation of the political class within the 5SM (Sampugnaro and Gozzo 2019). The movement's internal hierarchies are what count when it comes to assigning posts, as is clear in the case of the 5SM's two most high-profile figures: Luigi Di Maio, who in the transition from the first Conte government to the second one, took on the key post of Foreign Minister (and this post was subsequently confirmed in the Draghi government) and Roberto Fico, who following the party's 2018 electoral success, was appointed Speaker in the Chamber of Deputies.

The construction of an organised, mainstream party

As usually happens with personal parties, Grillo's power within the 5SM has never been seriously questioned. In fact, the uniqueness of the political organisation created by Grillo and Casaleggio, the third cornerstone of the

5SM's anti-politics, also gradually began to tarnish. It very quickly became evident that the fluid, spontaneous organisation seen in the party's early days was inadequate when the great number of newly elected 5SM MPs, regional councillors and mayors began to take their places in the nation's institutions. Taking great care to avoid the classical terminology of political and party life, such as "party functionary", "regional secretary" and "national leadership", in 2014, the 5SM set up a "Directory" comprising the party's more important party leaders (ibid. p. 21). Subsequently, as generally happens in highly organised parties, the 5SM created a kind of national secretariat consisting of 18 "facilitators": 6 of them were to deal with party organisation, while the other 12 were each entrusted with a theme to follow (the environment, the economy, justice etc.). A further 90 "regional facilitators" were appointed, tasked with liaising with the party's elected representatives in the European Parliament, the Italian Parliament and Regional Governments (Vittori 2021, p. 12).

The 5SM was subsequently forced to abandon its principle of non-alliance with other political parties. In Giuseppe Conte's first government (2018), the 5SM formed a majority coalition with the League; in Conte's second government (2019), the 5SM formed a governing coalition with the centre-left; and in 2021, it was to sustain the "government of national unity" led by Mario Draghi. Thus, within the space of three years, the 5SM managed to ally itself with all the parties present in parliament – even with arch-enemy Silvio Berlusconi's Forza Italia – with the exception of the sovereigntists "Brothers of Italy" (*Fratelli d'Italia*), but only because the latter refused to join the governing majority. Consequently, even its much flaunted ideological neutrality – another cornerstone of anti-politics – has in fact been repudiated by the 5SM's alliances with other political parties. Initially, when governing together with the League, the 5SM did not deny being a populist movement. Indeed, it claimed to be just that, with Conte proclaiming himself as the "people's advocate" (Marangoni and Verzichelli 2019, p. 267). Then after the stormy end to its coalition with the League, the 5SM constructed this image of itself as a centre-left party and even presented lists of candidates in conjunction with the Democratic Party, at municipal and regional elections.

Lastly, the 5SM had to admit that being part of government and being involved in the political life of the nation was a costly business. Consequently, the 5SM finally decided to accept the public funding of the party (these funds were principally employed in financing parliamentary activity and party communications[25]). Thus, it was that the final pillar of the 5SM's anti-politics fell.

The process of institutionalisation, together with its experiences as part of government, led the 5SM to reconsider another of its intransigent, clearly anti-political traits, namely its harsh attitude to offenders: from demanding the resignation of any politician standing trial, the 5SM gradually moved towards less intransigent, more understanding positions. This also occurred when its best-known local politicians, the mayors of Rome and Turin, were placed under investigation and eventually prosecuted (Zampano 2017). On the aforesaid occasions, the 5SM's leadership did not demand the resignation of those concerned.

The presence of the party at various levels of government has also been accompanied by its gradual turning away from the country's social movements and their respective battles, often aimed at the political class and mainstream parties, which are accused of collusion with large financial powers (Mosca 2020). Of the many social battles that Beppe Grillo and the 5SM had initially supported (the battles against the construction of a new motorway in Genoa, against a US military base in the Veneto region, against the building of a bridge over the Straits of Messina, against the construction of a gas pipeline in Puglia etc.), the most important one, in which the 5SM had invested heavily in terms of the party's identity, was the battle against the construction of the Turin-Lyon high-speed train line. The 5SM's responsibility as a governing party eventually resulted in it abandoning this battle as well (Biancalana 2020).

In short, there is a clear parallel between these matters and those concerning the Common Man Movement. We do not know whether Grillo, like Giannini, believes that having created a new party was "the biggest mistake of [his] life" (Setta 2005, p. 83). Nevertheless, we would agree with Setta when he sums up the development of the Common Man Front in the following words: "In short, the antiparty party was to adopt membership cards and badges, hierarchical bodies and disciplinary committees tasked with guaranteeing compliance with the latter's will; in other words, it was exactly like all other parties, including its leadership's desire for power" (ibid., p. 87).

Institutional resources serving the anti-political cause

The relentless process of party normalisation and institutionalisation saw all of the anti-political pledges made at the beginning of the movement's life, which had largely accounted for the party's electoral success, abandoned one by one. Grillo's party has since tried to remedy matters. Being in a position of power within the country's institutions, including its government, has offered the party a number of resources, as we know, which have enabled it to curb its withdrawal from the anti-political battle. Such resources are essentially of two kinds: the party's public visibility and its legislative potential. The former was to be used to distinguish its own politicians from the political "caste", at least symbolically; its legislative potential, on the other hand, was to be employed in order to force its governmental allies to adopt anti-political provisions so as to allay its supporters' disappointment and discontent regarding the direction the party had gone in.

Certain symbolic aspects, such as its MPs' refusal to accept being called "Honourable", have been examined above. Here we are simply going to offer a few examples which better emphasise the counter actions employed by the 5SM to safeguard its own anti-political credibility. One of the targets of people's criticism of politicians and their privileges is the use of governmental cars (the so-called blue cars used by leading politicians). The 5SM decided not to avail itself of these vehicles, which in Italy's recent history have often been used for purposes having nothing to do with political service and have been at the centre of various scandals for this very reason. The 5SM's MPs declared that they preferred travelling on foot, by train or bus instead. There was a great stir, for example, when the newly elected Speaker of the Chamber of Deputies, Roberto Fico, arrived for work by bus.[26] Another example of the communication strategy adopted by the 5SM in order to distance itself from the old, self-important rituals of Italian politics was the celebrations of the principal ministers, consisting in terrace-like chanting, after a governmental agreement had been reached regarding the budget deficit. On that occasion, the ministers in question went out onto the balcony of Government House, while in the meantime, their MPs had gathered in the square below, to celebrate "the abolition of poverty" (sic!) no less.[27]

The strongest, ground-breaking action taken to counter the disappointment, of electors and activists alike, at the betrayal of the original anti-political promises made by the 5SM, was not simply symbolic however; in fact, it concerned a proposed amendment to the Italian Constitution. This amendment consisted in the reduction of the number of MPs, which had always been one of the declared aims of the party, and reflected the hostility displayed towards political careerism and the role of parliament. This is a measure that the 5SM determinedly called for during the course of the legislature starting in 2018. Approval of the constitutional reform in question was included in the "government contract" signed by the League and the 5SM when the first Conte government was formed (Bordignon and Ceccarini 2019, p. 143) and was re-submitted for discussion during negotiations with the centre-left parties prior to the formation of the second Conte government. The centre-left, despite its fierce opposition to this measure during the preceding three votes when it sat on the opposition benches, voted together with the 5SM on the occasion of the fourth and final vote, which ultimately approved the amendment in question. Anti-political feelings among the public were so strong that no political party had the courage to vote against the amendment. The resulting constitutional reform, which as from the next legislature will see the number of Deputies reduced from 630 to 400, and the number of enators from 315 to 200, was passed with 553 votes in favour, 14 against and 2 abstentions. The fact that the reform was not voted for by a qualified majority of two-thirds in one of the votes, meant that it was subjected, in September 2020, to a confirmative referendum. Just over one-half of those entitled to vote in the said referendum, which was held right in the middle of the Covid-19 epidemic, did so: of those who voted, 70% were in favour of the reduction in the number of parliamentarians. All of the principal political parties asked their electors to vote in favour of the reform.[28]

Despite the ground-breaking result achieved by the 5SM, consisting firstly in the end to MPs *"vitalizi"* (special parliamentary pensions), and then in the reduction of the number of members of the two houses of parliament (the Chamber of Deputies and the Senate), the 5SM, after three years in government, has almost completely exhausted its initial anti-political, anti-establishment charge. As has been said of green parties and socialist parties in many Western democracies (Rihoux and Frankland 2008, p. 284), politics has changed the 5SM more than the 5SM has changed politics. This transformation was sealed by the approval of a new party statute in August 2021, formulated at length by Giuseppe Conte, and the object of conflict with Beppe Grillo. Said conflict regarded the positions of power within the party: Conte demanded sole leadership, whereas Grillo did not want to lose his personal power over the party as its co-founder. This conflict was resolved by a compromise solution: Conte was proposed as party leader, while Grillo was to be the party's "guarantor". This decision was officially ratified by a membership vote, which saw some 67,000 voting out of a total of 115,000 entitled to do so: 92.8% voted for Conte as the 5SM's leader. This vote was organised through a new platform different from Casaleggio's "Rousseau" system (the party had acrimoniously broken all ties with Casaleggio prior to this). However, the new platform still proved unable to guarantee the authenticity of the vote. By approving the party's new statute, the 5SM abandoned all claims to being a movement-party, becoming a party as such, albeit with certain plebiscitary traits (Vittori 2021, p. 14).[29]

Summing up then, the failure to maintain the party's original promises (Ceri and Veltri 2017, pp. 359–60) was a source of further political frustration and discontent among Italians. These feelings account for the disappointing results achieved at the 2019 European elections, when the 5SM lost half of the votes it had obtained the year before (Chiaramonte *et al.* 2020), and at the subsequent regional elections, when the 5SM won 7.4% of votes in Umbria, 4.7% in Emilia-Romagna, and 6.3% in Calabria (Tronconi and Valbruzzi 2020, p. 10). Rather than domesticating anti-political feelings, the 5SM's path to date has exacerbated such among the population and legitimised the anti-political conduct of Italy's politicians. Ultimately, the 5SM has injected fresh anti-political lymph into the Italian political system. It is no coincidence that before the Covid-19 emergency monopolised public and political debate, new collective actors had appeared on the political scene, like the "Sardines" who, although opposing Salvini's League and presenting themselves as an anti-populist (Caruso and De Blasio 2021, Hamdaoui 2021), also adopted anti-political, movement-party practices and arguments. This they did in reaction against the "old political class", which they considered to include the 5SM at this point. Like a restless sea, anti-politics advances and withdraws, its waves breaking on the coasts of Italy's battered democracy, eroding it significantly at every storm.

Notes

1 The most important, empirically wealthy studies of the 5SM are the works edited by Corbetta and Gualmini (2013), Tronconi (2015) and Corbetta (2017), together with the volumes by Biorcio and Natale (2013, 2018), Ceri and Veltri (2017), Chiapponi (2017) and Vittori (2020). Local developments have also been thoroughly studied (Biancalana 2017a, Lanzone and Morini 2017, Macaluso and Montemagno 2019, Mete 2019, Minaldi and Soare 2019). As regards

communications strategy and the use of the web, see Mosca *et al.* (2015b), Biancalana (2017b) and Musso and Maccaferri (2018); the party formula, its evolution and ideological character are analysed in Bordignon and Ceccarini (2013, 2015), Ceccarini and Bordignon (2016), Tronconi (2018), Di Maggio and Perrone (2019), Mosca and Tronconi (2019) and Vittori (2021); the electorate, militants and electoral performance are analysed in Bordignon and Ceccarini (2014), Biorcio (2015), Russo *et al.* (2017), Passarelli and Tuorto (2018b), Brancaccio and Fruncillo (2019), De Falco and Sabatino (2019) and Pratschke *et al.* (2021); while candidates, its political class and its parliamentary activity are examined in Lanzone and Rombi (2014), Pinto and Pedrazzani (2015), Montesanti and Veltri (2017, 2019) and Borghetto (2018).

2 Various scholars and observers liken Grillo to Coluche, the French comic actor whom Grillo met in the 1980s on the set of a film in which they both starred (Biorcio 2014, pp. 38–9, Vignati 2015, pp. 13–4). In fact, the arguments, plays on words and at times vulgar sarcasm that Coluche directed towards France's politicians, was used by Grillo some 25 years later to attack Italian politicians and political parties. In the early 1980s, Coluche announced that he was standing for the French Presidency (his candidature was later withdrawn). Thanks in part to the support he received from intellectuals like Bourdieu, Deleuze, Guattari and Touraine, his political adventure became extremely well known both in France and abroad.

3 None of the 5SM's MPs elected in 2013 had any previous political experience, while only 0.9% had some experience in the field of local administration (Pinto and Pedrazzani 2015, p. 108). Likewise, 100% of the 5SM's candidates standing at the 2013 general election were chosen by means of online primaries (Mosca *et al.* 2015a).

4 For a conceptual breakdown, and a discussion of the proliferation, of the "anti" labels attached to contemporary parties, see Zulianello (2019a, pp. 25–9).

5 In this regard, Natale observed as follows: "Twenty years on from the rise of the Lega, a comedian who for years had railed against the dark and perverse aspects of globalised capitalism, the banks and multinational companies – without achieving very much – started a blog that, step by step, became a key site for debate and discussion for an increasing number of citizens in an attempt to create 'a real democracy, without a blank cheque for politicians'. And it is this last element that has become, slowly but surely, a crucial aspect for the success of the new movement of the 'Friends of Beppe Grillo'. As with the Lega, in the initial phase, candidates standing under the banner of the Genoese comedian were – with only a few localised exceptions – only moderately successful. The impact of the M5S was little more than symbolic, attracting little more than a few thousand votes. It was only when this central theme became clear – a ferocious attack on the 'political class' – that the boom really began. There is a widespread belief that the success of the M5S can be attributed largely to its ability to channel protest against the parties and, in part, the government. This belief has remained its hold over time – including among the voters who have backed the Movement thus far. And indeed, despite the increasing sophistication of the proposals in the Movement's programme, it is the crisis of traditional parties and a ferocious and constant condemnation of current politicians that are the two main factors explaining the success of Grillo and the M5S" (Natale 2014, p. 18).

6 Taking a cue from a statement made by the League's representative who had designed the electoral law and who had called it "*una porcata*" (meaning "crap" – the term derives from "*porco*" – pig), Sartori jokingly nicknamed the law "*porcellum*" from the Latin, and this name stuck. After being used in the general elections held in 2006, 2008 and 2013, the law was deemed unconstitutional by the Constitutional Court in 2014 (Massetti and Farinelli 2019).

7   Among the most important affairs capable of generating political discontent, there was the vote in the Chamber of Deputies regarding the records of proceedings brought against Berlusconi for having had sex with an under-age prostitute. The vote in the Chamber, which attested to the fact that Berlusconi honestly believed the girl in question to be the niece of the Egyptian President Mubarak (sic!), was designed to shift jurisdiction over the case from the Milan Court to the Court of Ministries. The instrumental nature of this vote, the humiliation of Parliament and the total absence of the MPs' intellectual integrity further discredited the institutions, political parties and politicians concerned. In 2013, at a hearing of one of the legal proceedings deriving from this affair, the MPs from Berlusconi's party "occupied" the Milan courtroom in which proceedings were being conducted against Berlusconi. The significance of this event, which was already considered of a very serious nature by politicians and observers, was emphasised further by the fact that a film about Berlusconi, directed by the well-known director Nanni Moretti, had recently come out. The film, which was shown in Italy some months prior to said event, was entitled "The Cayman", and the final scene of the film shows Berlusconi being convicted by the criminal court, and then instigating the public who, gathered on the steps of the court building, throw Molotov cocktails at the judges who had just handed down their sentence (Brook 2009).

8   Of the 3.9 million who had voted for left-wing parties in 2006, only 1.6 million voted for the left coalition in 2008. It has been estimated that 1.3 million voters chose to follow Veltroni's recommendation to cast a "useful vote" as he called it (D'Alimonte and De Sio 2010, p. 100).

9   Just a few days after the election, Oliviero Diliberto, one of the left coalition's leaders, declared: "We have been murdered. There is a name and surname for the murderer: Walter Veltroni. He has cannibalized us. He destroyed the left without winning a single vote from the center. He used weed killer against us, inflicting an even worse defeat on him-self – delivering the country to our enemy" (Corbetta 2008, p. 71).

10 Shortly after the foundation of the PD, in July 2008, the then President of the Abruzzo Regional Government, a former Senator and Minister, previously President of the Parliamentary Anti-Mafia Commission, and at the time a member of the PD's national leadership, was arrested on charges of bribery concerning the healthcare sector. In July 2011, quite a stir was caused by the news that Filippo Penati, a former leader of the Italian Communist Party and of those parties that emerged after the PCI's demise, former Chairman of the Milan Provincial Council and a regional counsellor in Lombardy, had been charged with corruption (for which he was acquitted however). Furthermore, in January 2012, Luigi Lusi, treasurer of the *Margherita* (the Daisy), a centre party and successor to the Christian Democrat Party (DC) which subsequently merged with the PD, was accused of embezzling public funds. That same year, Vasco Errani, another member of the PD and President of the Emilia-Romagna Regional Government, was implicated in a question concerning a loan granted by the Regional Government to a cooperative headed by his brother. His conviction in 2014 led to him resigning from office. Errani's conviction was subsequently quashed, but the affair had a significant impact on public opinion and people's voting intentions: at the regional elections called following Errani's resignation, the voter turnout was only 37.7%, compared to 68.1% at the previous elections (Tuorto 2015). During those years, the PD was not only negatively impacted by matters of corruption and mismanagement but also by sex scandals which were extremely newsworthy, just as those involving Berlusconi had been. In October 2009, public opinion was monopolised by the news that

the President of the Lazio Regional Government, Piero Marrazzo of the PD, had been blackmailed by four Carabinieri officers who had found him in an apartment in the company of a Brazilian transsexual. This scandal, which led to Marrazzo's resignation and his immediate withdrawal from public life, was also fuelled by the discovery of drugs in the apartment and by the use of a government vehicle and an official escort for the purposes of the secret meeting.

11 As Valbruzzi has pointed out, not all technocratic governments are technocratic to the same degree. The government led by Monti may be considered a "Full Technocratic Government", that is, possessing all of the following three characteristics: "The prime minister is a technocrat; the majority of ministers are technocrats; and they have a mandate to change the status quo" (Valbruzzi 2020, p. 126).

12 The Monti government's main actions, all based on the principles of economic and financial austerity, were: "Massive reduction in the budget deficit; introduction of property taxes; increase in the retirement age; cuts in the size and costs of administrative bodies; 'liberalization' of closed professions, labour market reform" (Valbruzzi 2020, p. 124).

13 Rinaldo Vignati, in reporting that around a quarter of the votes obtained by the 5SM at the 2012 local elections came from former League voters, notes that: "It is plausible to argue – even if there is no data to support it – that the transfer of votes from the League has intensified particularly after the outbreak of the scandal involving the LN's treasurer, Francesco Belsito, and the organizational problems that have hit Umberto Bossi's party" (Vignati 2012, p. 80). According to another estimate, at the 2013 general election, nearly 7 out of 100 people who voted for the 5SM had previously voted League at the 2008 general election, while 6 had voted for the Italy of Values party and 13.5% had abstained (Russo *et al.* 2017, p. 54).

14 At the 2012 local elections, a substantial share of the votes obtained by the 5SM came from centre-left parties as well as from the League. One of the reasons for this shift, according to Vignati, was the transformation, in an anti-political direction, of the left-wing electorate generated by the anti-Berlusconi movements of the previous decade: "These movements, I would argue, are going beyond even the intentions of their promoters, helping to fuel and legitimize in the center-left electorate a general lack of confidence in the political class, in politics in general, and in the need to compromise that follows. Thanks to technological and organizational tools, and to his unquestionable skills and unscrupulous rhetoric, Grillo has been able to take advantage of all this and become a political entrepreneur. Arguably, some elements that make implicit reference to the usual practices of 'anti-politics' (unwillingness to compromise, tendency to see political competition in terms of good and bad, generalized distrust of the political class) have in the last 20 years spread through the center-left electorate. This may have contributed to the loss of votes by historically center-left parties in favor of the political forces – the IdV previously and the M5S today – that have approached these issues with greater resolve and have been more vigorously opposed to the 'privileges' of the political class. The current success of the M5S, I argue, can therefore be indicative of deeper cultural transformations that have not yet been appraised" (Vignati 2012, p. 81). At the 2013 general election, it was estimated that 27.4% of those voting for the 5SM had previously voted PD at the 2008 elections, while another 6% had voted for other left-wing parties (Russo *et al.* 2017, p. 54).

15 According to the definition originally proposed by Bonnie Meguid, a niche party is characterised by three main aspects: "First, niche parties reject the traditional class-based orientation of politics. Instead of prioritizing economic

demands, these parties politicize sets of issues that were previously outside the dimensions of party competition (...). Second, the issues raised by the niche parties are not only novel, but they also often do not coincide with the existing, 'left-right' lines of political division. Niche parties appeal to groups of voters that may crosscut – and undermine – traditional patterns of partisan alignment (...). Third, niche parties further differentiate themselves by limiting their issue appeals. They eschew the comprehensive policy platforms common to their mainstream party peers, instead adopting positions on and prioritizing only a restricted set of issues" (Meguid 2008, pp. 3–4). While it is true that the moralisation of politics and environmental issues are not something new within the framework of Italy's politics and party system, however, during the period in which the 5SM emerged, none of these questions was being credibly addressed by an Italian party. If it is true, as Meguid claims, that "each of these parties is best known for one issue" (ibid., p. 4), the issue for which the 5SM is best known is without a doubt that of anti-politics, that is, its criticism of politicians, political parties and the arenas of political representation.

16 In an opinion poll conducted in 2012, the 5SM's electors displayed less faith in political parties, parliament and local councils than the electors of the other Italian parties did (Biorcio 2014, p. 41). The following year, the customary post-electoral survey conducted by the ITANES research team revealed that the 5SM's electors agree to an above-average degree with the following statement: "Referenda should be used to decide important questions", and to a below-average degree with the following statement: "Without parties there can be no democracy" (ibid., 49).

17 Nadia Urbinati has observed in this regard: "some of the themes originally raised by Giannini can be found in the program of the M5S, which is perhaps the most mature anti-party movement, structurally shaped to speak for 'the citizens' not even 'the people', thus for 'la gente' or 'the crowd'. The difference between then and now – between 1948 and 2018 – is that anti-party-ism was then the name of a peripheral idea and movement, while it is now the style of politics and of thinking about politics that is somehow the common denominator of all parties (or what remains of them). We would say that today, Uomo qualunque è dovunque – everyman is everywhere" (Urbinati 2020, p. 77). Other scholars who compare the two political undertakings and their principal actors and promoters include Baldini (2013, p. 489), Corbetta and Vignati (2013b, p. 514), Gualmini (2013, p. 19) and Ceccarini and Newell (2019, p. 6). A more detailed comparison of the two undertakings has been provided by Antonio Costabile (2019).

18 For a description of the 5SM's ministers and MPs, see among others: Farinelli and Massetti (2015), Pinto and Pedrazzani (2015) and Tronconi and Verzichelli (2019).

19 This is exactly the opposite of what the 5SM's unofficial anthem claims: "There is a leaderless and ownerless movement/ You can find it by searching for the word 'non-association'/ A network of directly-connected people/ We are the web multitude, live now on our webcams/ (...)/ everybody counts as one, everybody counts as one, everybody counts as one" (Mosca *et al.* 2015b, p. 128).

20 In the 5SM's first statute, dated 2009, which the movement called a "non-statute" to distance itself from the statutes of the traditional Italian parties, Article 4 reads: "The Five Star Movement is not a political party nor is it going to become one in the future" (https://www.politicalpartydb.org/wp-content/uploads/Statutes/Italy/IT_M5S_2009.pdf).

21 The most emblematic, best-known example of this was the meeting between Grillo and Renzi during the discussions held regarding the formation of the

government led by Renzi in 2014. The meeting was a tense one, as Renzi unsuccessfully tried to take the floor, due to the constant invective from Grillo, who accused him as follows: "You represent the banks, the strong powers. You say something and then you deny it the following day. You're a young man, but at the same time you're also old. I made fun of you, and I'm sorry if you were offended (…). You're not credible, so anything you say is not going to be believed (…). You're the TV entertainer, not me. You know, every time I change channel there you are, the comic character (…). You're no longer credible because you represent people who are our long-standing enemies (…). I'm here to show you my, our total contempt for what you represent, the system you represent. We make mistakes, but at least we're consistent: we decided to forego 42 million [Euro of public funding] (…). We've foregone our salary [as MPs], we've halved it. I don't even want to explain our programme, as you've already appropriated half of it. Good luck if you can manage to implement it (…). You've joined forces with a previous offender from the Florentine freemasonry. You're a decent chap who represents a rotten power that we want to change completely". An exasperated Renzi tries to say his piece, and turning to the camera exclaims: "Get out of this blog Beppe! Get out of this stream!" (https://www.youtube.com/watch?v=4Sm6dF_moqc).

22 Indeed, in 2017, Grillo went as far as invalidating the result of the primaries held to choose the 5SM's candidate for mayor of Genoa, Grillo's home town. The party's members had selected Cristina Cassimatis (Vittori 2021, p. 11). Grillo offered no explanation for this move but simply asked the electors and party activists to trust his judgement.

23 To deal with this phenomenon, the 5SM's leadership introduced a much disputed, arguably unconstitutional clause (Art. 5) into the party's Code of Ethics. This clause provided for a 100,000 euro fine to be levied on anyone within the party who changes parliamentary group, is expelled from the 5SM parliamentary group or who resigns without just cause, prior to the end of their term of office (Bordignon and Ceccarini 2019, p. 143). In August 2021, three and a half years after the 2018 election, of the 227 Deputies and 111 Senators elected from the 5SM's lists of candidates, only 160 and 74, respectively, are still members of their corresponding parliamentary groups, as a total of 104 have changed parliamentary group in the meantime. During the course of the legislature that commenced in 2013, the 5SM lost 21 out of 109 Deputies, and 19 out of 53 Senators. The rules governing the 5SM Group in the Chamber of Deputies establish that MPs who have not been elected as members of the 5SM can join the party's Group provided that "they have no criminal record, are not members of another party, have not already served more than one term of office in addition to the current one, and have accepted and signed the 'Code of Ethics'" (https://www.camera.it/application/xmanager/projects/leg18/attachments/statuti/file_pdfs/000/000/020/MOVIMENTO_5_STELLE-NUOVA_VERSIONE-per_sito_10-11-2020.pdf).

24 The problems that a party new to the nation's political institutions, like the 5SM, has had in managing its parliamentary groups are reminiscent of those that the League experienced during the legislature starting in 1994 and mentioned in Section "The original anti-politics of the Northern League" in Chapter 3. In that case as well, following the League's decision to leave the governing majority and thus see the Berlusconi government fall, many League MPs changed parliamentary group, mostly for the Forza Italia group. Much earlier still, Giannini himself had difficulty keeping his parliamentary group together. In fact, Giannini "realised his initial naivety and decided to get a firm grip on the party's organisation, by bureaucratising it and undertaking a

thorough purge of its membership, consisting in suspensions, expulsions, and the appointment of commissioners bearing 'orders from on high'" (Setta 2005, pp. 86–7). For legal observations regarding the expulsions from the 5SM, see Caterina (2016). For an overview of moves from one parliamentary group to another, which were at their height in the 1994–6 and 2013–8 legislatures, see Russo and Verzichelli (2020, p. 59).

25 https://www.repubblica.it/politica/2021/07/25/news/m5s_tesoro_di_15_milioni_per_i_gruppi_parlamentari-311581314/.

26 https://www.youtube.com/watch?v=XArZRPzqzO4. The unusual decision to travel by bus rather than taxi, however, needs to be seen in the context of Fico's previous spending, as during the preceding legislature, when he was just an MP, Fico spent something like 15,000 euro on taxis (https://www.repubblica.it/politica/2018/03/26/news/camera_fico-192304582/).

27 https://www.youtube.com/watch?v=tN1p4R_3J-Q.

28 The reduction in MPs' numbers had been preceded by another highly symbolic battle of a clearly anti-political nature. One of the first measures that the 5SM developed as soon as it entered the governing majority in 2018 was to cut the parliamentary pensions paid to MPs. In order to emphasise the importance of this event which the 5SM considered "epoch-making", and to show its electors and militants that it had honoured one of its electoral promises (Mosca and Tronconi 2019, p. 11), the Deputies and Senators of Grillo's party met up to celebrate in front of parliament (https://www.youtube.com/watch?v=cEF-bqU2D06g). This measure was subsequently challenged by the association of former MPs who did not consider it a "hateful privilege" as the 5SM called it, but rather an acquired right that cannot be questioned *a posteriori*. In fact, in June 2020, following the filing of an appeal by around 600 parliamentarians, the Senate decided to return the parliamentary pensions even to those former parliamentarians who had been convicted of an offence (https://www.rainews.it/dl/rainews/articoli/vitalizi-ex-parlamentari-Senato-annullamento-delibera-taglio-Paniz-Crimi-Caliendo-Lega-Pillon-Riccardi-911256a8-6e3a-49be-8a17-be2765856ea7.html).

29 The "5 Star Movement's Statute" consists of 39 pages and establishes not only the office of Leader and Guarantor but also a National Council, various committees, a Board of Auditors, a Disciplinary Board, a Treasurer and Supervisory Bodies. It also provides for a penalty procedure, an arbitration clause in the event of disputes and a procedure for the suspension or self-suspension of members. Unmindful of the earlier "vaffa-days" (fuck-off days), one of the aims of the association is to "take care over the use of words". This section of the statute establishes that "Aggressive expressions shall be considered on an equal footing with violent behaviour". The full wording of the statute can be found at: https://www.movimento5stelle.eu/wp-content/uploads/2021/07/NUOVO-STATUTO-TESTO-DEFINTIVO.pdf.

6   A socio-political profile of anti-political citizens

Are Italians more anti-political than the citizens of other democracies? A comparative analysis

The events described in the previous chapters would suggest that Italy is a particularly interesting and stimulating testing ground for the various forms of anti-politics that exist. Leaving aside for the moment the different expressions of anti-politics encountered over the years, we are now going to take a closer look at the citizens of Italy themselves. This final chapter, in fact, is going to offer two in-depth analyses of the diffusion and nature of anti-political attitudes and feelings among the Italian population. The first analysis regards the place that Italians' anti-politics have within a broader framework, and this shall be determined by means of a comparison with the anti-politics of certain other Western democracies' citizens. This operation will enable us to establish whether Italy represents an exception to the rule, or whether it behaves in a similar manner, more or less, to that of other comparable democracies. The second analysis aims to better characterise, both socially and politically, those Italian citizens harbouring anti-political sentiments. Thus, we shall try to establish the existence or otherwise of those subjective conditions typically associated with the development of anti-political attitudes, or whether such attitudes are common to all social strata. The remaining part of this section shall be taken up by the aforementioned international comparison. The last two sections of this chapter are given over to a closer empirical investigation of the socio-demographic and political characteristics, and the values, of those Italians expressing anti-political attitudes.

In search of anti-politics: indicators and indexes

A number of possible indicators of the concept of anti-politics were mentioned at the end of the terminological and conceptual analysis presented in Chapter 1. The formulation of indicators of anti-politics, which are of fundamental importance for the various units of analysis considered, has been somewhat neglected by the sociological and political science literature on

DOI: 10.4324/9781003109273-7

this subject. This conceptual-methodological operation, however, is of vital importance for any comparison of different political systems and developing an empirically-grounded investigation of citizens' anti-political attitudes. In the first chapter, three different units of analysis were identified, namely citizens/voters; leaders (or in any case, representatives of the political class); the political system as a whole. Different indicators were formulated for each analytical unit (see fourth section in Chapter 1). At the citizens/voters level, anti-political attitudes were distinguished from anti-political behaviour. Mention was made, for example, of the feeling of trust in politicians, political parties and institutions; abstention from voting; returning a blank or spoilt ballot paper. For the purposes of the second analytical unit – political leaders and political class – the behaviour of such leaders and other senior political figures was taken into consideration; this included, for example, the frequency of anti-political speeches and statements, both at public events and in the media. The third analytical unit comprises phenomena aggregated at the level of the political system as a whole, such as voter abstention, the presence and electoral force of anti-political parties and leaders and the recurrence of referenda with anti-political implications. Many of these aspects have been studied by scholars concerned with other questions, rather than by those specifically interested in the question of anti-politics per se: questions such as voter abstention and electoral volatility, for example, or the analysis of leaders' political language, or of party manifestos. Given the impossibility of documenting all of these aspects empirically and comparatively, I decided that I would focus on the first analytical unit, that is, on citizens/voters. Despite this self-imposed limitation, as we shall see the exploration of individual anti-political attitudes and behaviour still provides useful information about the other two units of analysis.

Unlike in the case of populism, a concept which overlaps to a certain degree with that of anti-politics as we saw in Chapter 1, there are very few studies offering an international comparison of anti-politics. On the other hand, there are several reflections on, and comparative empirical analyses of, related concepts or concepts of a more specific nature – that is, concepts lower down the ladder of generality – such as anti-partyism (Torcal *et al.* 2002, Bélanger 2004, Kestilä-Kekkonen 2009), political disaffection (Pharr and Putnam 2000, Torcal and Montero 2006a) and the lack of trust in politics and politicians (Dogan 2005, Citrin and Stoker 2018). As previously mentioned, there are very few transnational studies framing and analysing the concept of anti-politics. The large-scale international studies based on surveys – such as the European Social Survey (ESS), the European Election Studies (EES), the European Values Study (EVS), the World Values Survey (WVS), the surveys conducted by Eurobarometer on behalf of the European Commission and the Comparative Study of Electoral Systems (CSES) – contain no trace of any lists of questions or indexes designed to identify the existence of anti-politics. It is true that with a little imagination one can see questions contained in these studies that partly cover the meaning of anti-politics as a concept. However, in practice, it seems difficult to formulate a credible definition of the concept that can then be satisfactorily employed in a comparative territorial and/or diachronic analysis.[1]

The only two exceptions to this rather desolate picture of international anti-politics studies are Module 5 of the CSES (2016–21), which focuses specifically on citizens' perceptions of political elites and out-groups, and the implications for electoral democracy in 28 countries,[2] and the study conducted by Eri Bertsou and Daniele Caramani into technocratic attitudes among the citizens of 9 European countries.[3] Thanks to the public availability of the datasets from these two research projects, it is possible to construct two indexes of anti-politics[4] with which to investigate, essentially, two different aspects of anti-politics, namely the diffusion of anti-politics in Italy, compared to other countries; the degree to which Italy's anti-political citizens are similar to, or different from, those of other countries.

Italians and the citizens of other democracies

In their study, Bertsou and Caramani (2020b, p. 6) build a simple additive index of anti-politics resulting from the following items: "The best political decisions are taken by experts who are not politicians"; "Political parties do more harm than good to society"; "Politicians just want to promote the interests of those who vote for them rather than the interests of the country as a whole"; "Politicians spend all their time seeking re-election instead of fixing problems". Interviewees classified themselves on a scale of 1–7, where 1 means "disagree completely" and 7 means "agree completely". With regard to the conceptualisation presented in Chapter 1, it was deemed a better idea to partially modify the index proposed by the two authors. More specifically, the item "The best political decisions are taken by experts who are not politicians" was excluded, as this exalts the role of the experts rather than offering a negative take on politicians as such, while two classical items were added, namely "trust in national parliament" and "trust in political parties". Furthermore, another item that Bertsou and Caramani use as an indicator of populism has been added, namely: "The people, not the politicians, should make our most important policy decisions". Interviewees were also given the opportunity to respond on a scale of 1–7 to these three further items. Consequently, after inverting the polarity of the two items regarding trust in the national parliament and political parties, a simple additive index was formulated with a range of between 1 and 7, and the average of which is 4.8. Table 6.1 shows the mean values of the index for each country concerned.

As one can see, Italy lies just behind Greece and ahead of Romania and Poland. Thus Italy holds a similar position to the other southern European democracy (Greece) experiencing a dramatic period in its history following the economic crisis of the mid-2000s. In fact, the two countries have followed similar paths in the intervening years (Verney and Bosco 2013). In this ranking, Italy and Greece are part of a group of countries that also includes the

Table 6.1 Mean values of the anti-political index by country (*Citizens' Technocratic Attitudes*)

Country	Mean	N
Greece	5.41	1,008
Italy	5.24	1,037
Romania	5.10	1,067
Poland	4.93	1,013
France	4.87	1,046
Great Britain	4.74	1,069
Germany	4.45	1,090
The Netherlands	4.28	1,096
Sweden	4.23	1,023
Total	4.80	9,449

Source: The author's processing of the Citizens' Technocratic Attitudes dataset.

other two new, troubled democracies of Eastern Europe. In anti-political terms, Italians differ significantly from the citizens of the other consolidated democracies of western and northern Europe.

As previously mentioned, the CSES provides a second source of information for a comparative analysis of citizens' anti-political attitudes. Those surveys conducted within the context of Module 5 and concerning the 2016–21 period contain a number of questions which when put together may be utilised to build an index of anti-politics. They specifically include a set of items which in the study are referred to as "attitudes about elites", comprising the following questions to which the interviewees could respond by choosing one of five alternative answers, ranging from "strongly agree" to "strongly disagree": "What people call compromise in politics is really just selling out on one's principles"; "Most politicians do not care about the people"; "Most politicians are trustworthy"; "Politicians are the main problem in [country]"; "The people, and not politicians, should make our most important policy decisions"; and "Most politicians care only about the interests of the rich and powerful".[5] By inverting the polarity of the item "Most politicians are trustworthy", a simple additive index was created and then normalised so that its range was between 0 and 1. Table 6.2 shows the mean values of the anti-political index by country. Of the 24 countries considered, Italy was ranked sixth. The five democracies ranked higher than Italy are all countries experiencing significant political and social upheaval, with countries like Brazil and Hungary[6] governed by blatantly populist leaders. In any case, in this specific classification, Italy is ranked higher than all the other consolidated Western democracies. In some cases the gap between Italy and the other country is small, as in the case of Portugal (another country severely impacted by the 2008 economic and financial crisis and by the austerity policies introduced as a consequence); in other cases, it is considerable, as with the countries of northern Europe which are all ranked at the bottom of the classification.[7]

Table 6.2 Mean values of the anti-political index by country (*CSES*)

Country	Mean	N
Brazil	0.78	2,292
Hungary	0.68	1,047
Costa Rica	0.67	1,250
Montenegro	0.66	1,031
Chile	0.66	1,539
Italy	0.65	1,885
Portugal	0.64	1,270
Lithuania	0.63	1,137
Taiwan	0.62	1,477
Turkey	0.61	954
France	0.59	1,687
United States of America	0.58	3,602
Belgium	0.55	1,746
Australia	0.55	1,988
Great Britain	0.53	873
Austria	0.50	1,096
Switzerland	0.50	4,486
Germany	0.49	1,860
Canada	0.49	2,675
New Zealand	0.47	1,423
Finland	0.42	1,377
Norway	0.42	1,777
Iceland	0.39	2,764
Total	0.56	41,236

Source: The author's processing of the CSES – Module 5 (2016–21).

A comparison of the socio-political profiles of anti-political citizens

Anti-politics, as defined and empirically investigated in the aforementioned two studies, is a relatively common phenomenon in today's Italy. It now remains to be seen whether those Italian citizens with anti-political feelings are socially and politically similar to, or different from, those of other countries, and also which other democracies' anti-political citizens are similar to, or different from, those of Italy. In an attempt to respond to these questions, a more detailed analysis was made of the survey conducted by Bertsou and Caramani which, unlike the CSES, resulted in a specific index of anti-politics (although, as previously mentioned, we have partially modified this index for the purposes of our secondary analysis). Figures 6.1–6.4 compare the levels of anti-politics in the various countries considered, in relation to three socio-demographic variables – age, gender and level of education – together with a political variable, that is, an individual's self-placement along the left-right ideological spectrum.[8]

Let us examine the results in more detail. The analysis concerning gender (Figure 6.1) reveals that compared to the anti-political citizens of other countries, anti-political views in Italy are more common among men than among

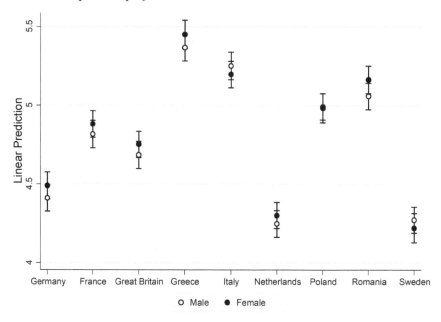

Figure 6.1 Predictive probabilities for anti-politics: country and gender

Source: The author's processing of the Citizens' Technocratic Attitudes dataset.

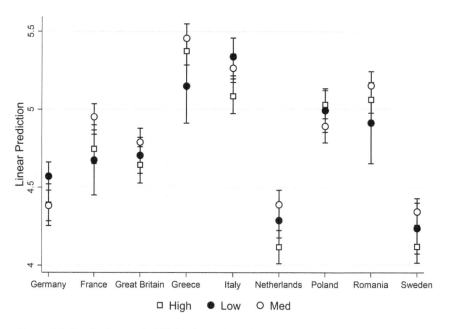

Figure 6.2 Predictive probabilities for anti-politics: country and education

Source: The author's processing of the Citizens' Technocratic Attitudes dataset.

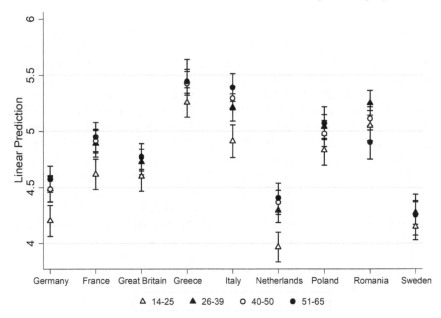

Figure 6.3 Predictive probabilities for anti-politics: country and age

Source: The author's processing of the Citizens' Technocratic Attitudes dataset.

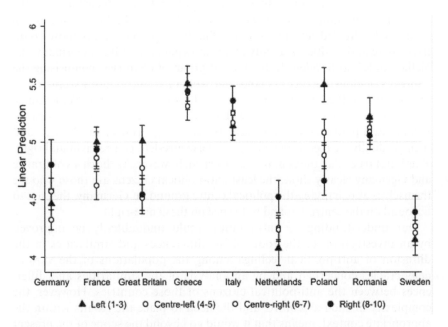

Figure 6.4 Predictive probabilities for anti-politics: country and left-right position

Source: The author's processing of the Citizens' Technocratic Attitudes dataset.

women. In all of the other countries, with the exception of Sweden and, to a certain degree, Poland, women tend to be more anti-political than men. With regard to citizens' levels of education (Figure 6.2), Italy's uniqueness is even more pronounced. In fact, anti-political attitudes are on average more common among low-educated Italians and are less frequently found among the country's highly-educated citizens. In all other countries, the greatest concentration of citizens classifiable as anti-political is among those with an intermediate level of education: Poland is an exception in that the most anti-political group is indeed that of the highly-educated, albeit to a very slight degree; Germany is the other exception, in that anti-politics is more common among the low-educated, as it is among low-educated Italians. However, unlike in Italy, the presence of anti-political sentiments among Germans with intermediate or higher educational qualifications is roughly the same. As regards age, there is greater homogeneity among the nine countries examined (see Figure 6.3). Italy is like the other countries concerned, in that the older generations are the ones that display the strongest anti-political sentiments. On the other hand, younger people tend to embrace anti-political sentiments to a lesser degree. The only exception to this general rule is Romania, where the strongest anti-political feelings were expressed by those in the 26–39 age group at the time the survey was conducted (2017). Furthermore, unlike in the other eight countries, anti-political feelings are lowest among the older generations of Romanians. Greater variation exists in terms of the relationship between the anti-politics and the political self-placement along the left-right continuum of the interviewees (see Figure 6.4). The countries can basically be divided into two groups. The first group contains those countries where anti-politics is mainly of a right-wing nature: Italy, Germany, the Netherlands and Sweden. In the second group of countries, comprising the United Kingdom, Greece, Poland and Romania, anti-politics seems to be the preserve of the left. In some cases, such as Poland and the Netherlands, the differences are more evident, while in others they are more nuanced. In Poland, anti-politics follows a linear trend, being stronger on the left, and then gradually weaker as one moves to the centre-left, centre-right and right. This is not true of all the countries concerned, however. As the cases of France and Germany clearly show, the least anti-political citizens are those who see themselves as occupying the political centre ground: in Germany, they are to be found on the centre-left and in France on the centre-right.

Our understanding of anti-politics would undoubtedly be improved by an investigation of the roots of the differences and similarities in the diffusion of anti-political feelings among the populations of the various democracies concerned and by an analysis of the similarities and differences between the anti-political citizens of those countries. However, the complexity of such a venture, and the need to place the results within the appropriate context, means that it would go beyond the scope of the present study which is basically concerned with the Italian case. Consequently, we are simply going to conclude that, as has been emphasised by the studies of anti-partyism, political disaffection, populism and the other phenomena related to anti-politics mentioned previously, the shape and diffusion of anti-political feelings vary from one democracy to another. The analysis carried out in this section, based on two significant, recently conducted comparative studies, reveals that Italy ranks high among those countries most affected by the anti-political "syndrome". The other countries keeping it company at the top of the ranking, however, are not the other major Western democracies, but rather countries where democracy remains rather fragile. These are countries governed by populist leaders, or as in the case of Greece, seriously affected by the 2008 financial crisis which subsequently led to considerable social tensions and massive anti-austerity demonstrations throughout southern Europe (della Porta *et al.* 2017). Furthermore, the socio-demographic and political characteristics of anti-political citizens vary from one country to another. These two points call for a couple of brief observations: the first is that just as "The populist voter does not seem to exist" (Rooduijn 2018, p. 353), there does not seem to be any typical anti-political voter either: that is, a voter, who on the international scale, possesses the same socio-political characteristics, or who votes for parties from the same side of the ideological spectrum. The second observation concerns the anti-political research agenda. Given that each country (or group of countries) "produces" its own unique type of anti-political citizen, we need to examine the social, political, economic and institutional dynamics shaping each country in order to identify any similarities and differences.

Having established, insofar as the available information permits, the considerable geographical variability of anti-politics, we may now proceed to examine its variability over time. Focusing on Italy, the next section will be looking at the characteristics of anti-political citizens in the mid-1980s, that is, before the break-up of the existing party system brought on by the Tangentopoli bribes scandal, and then again in the 2000, by which time the reorganised political system had taken on a stable, bipolar character.

The anti-political citizens of the First and Second Republics

The analysis in the preceding section offers an indication of the diffusion of anti-political sentiments and ideas in Italy compared with other European and non-European democracies. At the same time, it examines the nature of those Italians harbouring anti-political attitudes and sentiments compared to their counterparts in a number of other European countries. I shall now focus once again on Italy's anti-political citizens, this time looking at the question from a diachronic viewpoint as well. Certain scholars, some of whom were mentioned in Chapter 1, have in truth offered various ideas for a reflection on the transformation of the Italians' hostility towards politics and politicians. Paolo Segatti, for example, has reconstructed a time series covering the period 1959–2001, based on the few international studies available and the surveys conducted by the ITANES, of the traditional set of items regarding the subjective feeling of political efficacy. His study reveals that over the course of the aforesaid 40-year period, political disaffection was more common among the more socially and economically marginal sectors of the population (those with a lower level of education, less political awareness and no ideological traits), and among those less interested in politics in general. Segatti concludes his analysis as follows: "the percentage of disaffected citizens has changed dramatically when major political events (such as scandals, or political turmoil, or opportunities for a new beginning) threw the actual working of political systems into question. Therefore, our (...) conclusion is that political disaffection is both a culturally rooted predisposition and a response to current events" (Segatti 2006, p. 270).

From this point of view, as we all know the most significant political upheaval in the history of the Italian Republic was that brought on by the Tangentopoli bribery scandal in the early 1990s, which has been covered in some detail in the preceding chapters of this volume. It is therefore interesting to see the extent and characteristics of anti-politics in Italy prior to, and following, Tangentopoli, an event that had an enormous effect on Italy's political system and political culture. To assess whether, to what extent and how the Italians' anti-political attitudes changed at the time of the Tangentopoli scandal, we are going to conduct a secondary analysis based on two surveys provided by the ITANES research team. The first of these surveys was carried out in 1985, during the so-called First Republic. In other words, it was conducted seven years prior to the emergence of the political scandal in question, at a time when the League was still a marginal presence on the political scene, and there were no major leaders or parties advancing specifically anti-political views. The second survey was conducted in 2004, ten years after Silvio Berlusconi's entry into politics, 15 years after Bossi and the League's first appearance on the political stage and nine years after Di Pietro's move from the judiciary to politics (at that time, Di Pietro had symbolised the battle against bad politics and corrupt politicians). However, this second survey was conducted immediately prior to the emergence of Beppe Grillo and his movement of opinion, which in 2009 was to give rise to the Five Star Movement (5SM).[9]

Fortunately, the two surveys enable us to build the same index of anti-politics, so that the comparison between the two surveys, at least as far as this concerned, can be based on solid methodological foundations. In order to create this index, two variables regarding the feelings evoked by politics were taken into consideration. The interviewees in both surveys were asked to indicate, in order of importance, the first and second feelings that best describe their relationship with politics. The feelings that they could choose from were as follows: boredom, enthusiasm, anger, interest, indifference, passion, disgust, commitment and diffidence. Table 6.3 shows the frequency distributions of the interviewees' responses.

It is clear from the data presented here that over the course of the 20 years before and after Tangentopoli (i.e. 1985–2004), anger was the one feeling

Table 6.3 The feelings evoked by politics in 1985 and 2004
(percentage values)

	1985		2004	
	First choice (N = 2,017)	Second choice (N = 1,503)	First choice (N = 1,867)	Second choice (N = 1,790)
Passion	0.9	2.3	1.7	3.0
Enthusiasm	1.4	2.8	1.2	1.7
Interest	19.1	10.5	18.5	8.4
Commitment	4.0	8.5	3.2	6.5
Indifference	21.1	11.2	11.1	10.1
Boredom	12.1	10.5	8.5	9.2
Diffidence	13.9	22.8	15.9	24.3
Disgust	10.4	14.9	11.8	17.2
Anger	17.1	16.4	28.1	19.7

Source: The author's processing of the data from the Political Culture of Southern Europe (1985) and ITANES (2004) surveys.

that increased significantly (taking the first and second feelings together, feelings of anger rose from 33.4% in 1985 to 47.8% in 2004). Feelings of disgust rose from 25.3% to 29%, and even those of diffidence rose slightly during that same period. Positive feelings (passion, enthusiasm, interest, commitment) remained more or less stationary, while the frequency of indifference fell from 32.3% in 1985 to 21.2% in 2004. No simple conclusions can be drawn from the available data, and in any case such conclusions would fail to take account of the well-known "ecological fallacy" problem. However, it would seem that during the 20-year period considered here, those who previously looked upon politics with detachment and indifference, subsequently adopted a more critical, negative approach, expressed by their increased anger and disgust. In other words, those who were initially apathetic and indifferent gradually adopted a more aggressive take on politics and politicians.

On the basis of the aforementioned feelings evoked by politics, a weighted anti-politics index was created for each of the two surveys. More specifically: 2 points were assigned to any strongly negative feelings about politics, such as "anger" and "disgust"; 1 point was assigned to those slightly negative feelings, such as "boredom", "indifference" and "diffidence"; while 0 points were assigned to the remaining feelings implying a more positive relationship between the citizens concerned and the world of politics, such as "enthusiasm", "interest", "passion" and "commitment". In order to take account of the diverse significance of the first-choice and second-choice terms, the number associated with the former has been multiplied by 2, and then summed to the number associated with the second feeling indicated.[10] In this way a new variable was created with a value ranging from 0 to 6. By normalising the variable, that is, by dividing the values by the theoretical

Table 6.4 Class distribution of the anti-political indexes in 1985 and 2004

	1985 (N = 2,107)	*2004 (N = 1,852)*
Low (from 0 to 0.33)	29.4	27.5
Medium (from 0.34 to 0.67)	47.5	37.7
High (from 0.68 to 1)	23.1	34.8
Total	100	100

Source: The author's processing of data from the Political Culture of Southern Europe (1985) and ITANES (2004) surveys.

maximum value, an index of 0–1 was obtained. The distributions of the two indexes are shown in simplified form in Table 6.4.

As a reading of Table 6.3 already suggests, the distribution of the two indexes would seem to indicate that feelings about politics became increasingly negative over the course of the period in question. While in 1985, 29.4% of those interviewed expressed a limited degree of anti-political feelings, this category had fallen to 27.5% by 2004; on the other hand, while those expressing a strongly negative sentiment as their first choice, and a strongly or mildly negative sentiment as their second choice, represented 23.1% of the sample in 1985, this percentage had risen to 34.8% by 2004. In general, the mean value of the anti-political index rose from 0.52 in 1985 (with a standard deviation of 0.30) to 0.58 in 2004 (a standard deviation of 0.32).

The social and political characteristics and values of anti-political citizens

Over a period of 20 years covering the years prior and subsequent to the reorganisation of Italy's political system in the early 1990s, the negative feelings expressed by Italians towards the country's politics increased. This finding is in keeping with what Clarke *et al.* note in regard to the British case (Clarke *et al.* 2018). Their study, based on a combination of qualitative and quantitative methods, also reveals that the social basis of anti-politics had broadened over time, taking in an increasing number of different social categories. In other words, from a phenomenon mainly restricted to the more marginal sections of the population, anti-politics has increasingly come to involve the whole of society.

A closer examination of the 1985 and 2004 datasets enables us to establish the socio-demographic and political profiles of anti-political citizens in the mid-1980s and mid-2000s. Among other things, this analysis enables us to better understand whether the social basis of those citizens with anti-political views had broadened in Italy, as it had in the United Kingdom. Therefore, in the case of both datasets, a series of linear regressions were carried out between the anti-politics indexes and the main socio-demographic and political variables. Table 6.5 presents two regression models regarding the 1985 survey, while Table 6.6 presents the same analysis conducted on the

Table 6.5 Linear regression of the anti-politics index with respect to socio-demographic and political covariates (1985)

Anti-politics index	Model 1 (N = 2,007)			Model 2 (N = 1,986)			Model 3 (N = 1,876)		
	Coef.	St.Err.	St.Err.	p-value	St.Err.	p-value	p-value	St.Err.	p-value
Age									
Base category: 18–24	0			0			0		
25–34	−.002	.023	.928	.014	.024	.546	.019	.024	.437
35–44	−.015	.023	.528	.012	.024	.628	.015	.025	.536
45–54	.014	.025	.587	.040	.026	.122	.044	.027	.098
55–64	.007	.027	.797	.032	.027	.244	.037	.029	.200
Over 64	.019	.028	.504	.040	.028	.160	.048	.030	.107
Education									
Base category: Low	0			0			0		
Low-intermediate	−.031	.018	.096	.008	.018	.667	.010	.019	.611
High-intermediate	−.087	.020	0	−.015	.02	.464	−.017	.021	.433
High	−.173	.025	0	−.054	.025	.034	−.050	.026	.056
Gender									
Base category: Male	0			0			0		
Female	.042	.013	.002	.013	.013	.307	.018	.014	.196
Territorial area									
Base category: North-West	0			0			0		
North-East	−.016	.023	.490	−.021	.022	.335	−.026	.023	.264
Red belt	−.014	.019	.462	−.011	.019	.556	−.007	.019	.725
Centre	.041	.022	.061	.037	.021	.074	.038	.021	.073
South	−.017	.018	.35	−.028	.017	.109	−.030	.018	.093
Interest in politics									
Base category: not at all				0			0		
Not very much interested				−.025	.016	.116	−.024	.017	.154

(*Continued*)

Table 6.5 Linear regression of the anti-politics index with respect to socio-demographic and political covariates (1985) (*Continued*)

Anti-politics index	Model 1 (N = 2,007)			Model 2 (N = 1,986)			Model 3 (N = 1,876)		
	Coef.	St. Err.		p-value	St. Err.	p-value	p-value	St. Err.	p-value
Fairly interested				−.205	.019	0	−.200	.019	0
Very interested				−.334	.030	0	−.328	.031	0
Party voted									
Base category: PCI				0		.	0		.
PSI				−.021	.024	.368	−.018	.025	.467
Other *laici*				−.007	.030	.819	−.008	.031	.802
DC				−.034	.020	.097	−.032	.021	.125
MSI				.060	.042	.156	.031	.044	.488
Others				−.007	.029	.800	−.009	.030	.776
Blank ballot paper				−.059	.044	.179	−.029	.047	.536
Don't remember or don't wish to answer				−.01	.019	.592	−.009	.020	.648
Opinion about democracy									
Base category: "A democratic system is preferable to any other form of government"							0		.
Whether authoritarian or democratic, it makes no difference to people like me							.020	.022	.376
In certain circumstances, an authoritarian regime, a dictatorship, may be preferable to democracy							.064	.020	.001

Source: The author's processing of the data from the 'Political Culture of Southern Europe' (1985) survey.

Table 6.6 Linear regression of the anti-politics index with respect to socio-demographic and political covariates (2004)

Anti-politics index	Model 1 (N = 1,860)			Model 2 (N = 1,764)			Model 3 (N = 1,722)		
	Coef.	St. Err.	p-value	Coef.	St. Err.	p-value	Coef.	St. Err.	p-value
Age									
Base category: 18–24	0			0			0		
25–34	-.013	.039	.750	.007	.039	.856	.004	.040	.913
35–44	.033	.039	.390	.048	.038	.214	.048	.039	.220
45–54	.008	.039	.845	.037	.038	.339	.036	.039	.352
55–64	-.036	.040	.363	.005	.040	.891	.001	.040	.987
Over 64	.008	.040	.846	.053	.040	.187	.054	.041	.183
Education									
Base category: Low	0			0			0		
Low-intermediate	-.051	.022	.023	-.024	.023	.293	-.029	.023	.217
High-intermediate	-.129	.022	0	-.061	.023	.008	-.065	.023	.005
High	-.229	.029	0	-.116	.031	0	-.121	.031	0
Gender									
Base category: Male	0			0			0		
Female	.087	.014	0	.047	.015	.002	.048	.015	.002
Territorial area									
Base category: North-West	0			0			0		
North-East	.027	.025	.280	.032	.025	.207	.029	.026	.266
Red belt	.046	.023	.041	.058	.023	.011	.058	.023	.012
Centre	.051	.023	.030	.076	.024	.001	.073	.024	.002
South	.060	.020	.003	.056	.020	.005	.049	.020	.015
Interest in politics									
Base category: not at all				0			0		
Not very much interested				-.038	.019	.043	-.042	.019	.029

(*Continued*)

Table 6.6 Linear regression of the anti-politics index with respect to socio-demographic and political covariates (2004) (*Continued*)

Anti-politics index	Model 1 (N = 1,860)			Model 2 (N = 1,764)			Model 3 (N = 1,722)		
	Coef.	St.Err.	p-value	Coef.	St.Err.	p-value	Coef.	St.Err.	p-value
Fairly interested				-.209	.022	0	-.213	.022	0
Very interested				-.331	.035	0	-.335	.036	0
Party voted									
Base category: Communist Refoundation and Italian Communists				0			0		
Left Democrats				.041	.034	.232	.039	.035	.260
The Daisy Party				.029	.038	.444	.032	.038	.405
Italy of Values				-.009	.059	.873	-.012	.061	.842
Forza Italia				-.024	.032	.464	-.025	.033	.454
Lega				.053	.058	.360	.052	.058	.371
National Alliance				-.015	.036	.679	-.012	.037	.748
Others				-.012	.041	.764	-.011	.042	.791
Blank or invalid ballot papers				.097	.062	.119	.106	.064	.097
Cannot remember, or do not wish to answer				.024	.033	.469	.026	.034	.449
In a true democracy, the majority is responsible for protecting the rights of all minorities									
Base category: Strongly agree							0		
Agree							-.003	.015	.837
Disagree							-.017	.035	.623
Strongly disagree							.050	.053	.345

Source: The author's processing of the data from the ITANES (2004) survey.

2004 dataset. The first model considers the socio-demographic dimension only and is circumscribed to age, education, gender and geographical area of residence. In the second model, a further two variables have been added to these four, namely: a person's interest in politics and the party voted for at the previous general election.[11]

A reading of the analytical findings set out in Tables 6.5 and 6.6 reveals the principal features of anti-politics in the mid-1980s and mid-2000s, and thus the degree to which this changed over the course of what was a period of considerable political upheaval in Italy.[12] First of all, anti-politics pervades all age groups but appears to increase slightly as people get older judging by the results of the two surveys in question. However, there was one important exception to this general rule in both surveys: in 1985, the least anti-political age group was that of the 35–44 year olds, while in 2004, the least anti-political Italians were those aged 55–64. In other words, this was the same age cohort (in 2004, they were 20 years older) whose attitude to politics and politicians seems to have survived the Tangentopoli scandal unscathed: this bribery scandal and the fallout from it had cancelled the political and party-based points of reference which had accompanied that generation's introduction to the world of politics. However, this was a particular generation of Italians – the "68 generation" born between 1941 and 1950, who in 1968, the year of large-scale student protests in many of the world's major cities, were aged between 17 and 28.[13] Despite the social, economic and cultural unrest and the consequent acceleration of political change characterising the modern era, the importance of political generations underscored by Karl Mannheim in his classic study (1952) still appears to ring true.

As was to be expected, people's educational qualifications were negatively correlated to their anti-political feelings both in 1985 and 2004. In other words, possession of the cultural means by which to obtain a more complete understanding of social and political affairs represents a powerful antidote to negativity towards politics. On the other hand, those who possess a simpler view of society due to the lack of the cultural capital accumulated through education, tend to see politicians, parties and representative assemblies as scapegoats for all of society's ills (or for those aspects of society that fail to live up to their expectations). Rather than the gap, in terms of anti-political attitudes, between those with a limited education and the more highly educated members of society narrowing as a result of the expansion of mass education, over a period of 20 years, this gap in fact widened even further. The same could be said with regard to gender. While perhaps not a foregone conclusion, in both surveys the anti-political attitudes of women were stronger than those of men. The long-term transformation of the Italian family (Naldini 2003), together with the increasing involvement of women in the workplace and society as a whole, do not seem to have narrowed the difference between the anti-political feelings of women and men over the course of the 20-year period in question. Finally, as with educational qualifications, an interest in politics would seem to significantly reduce the likelihood of a person adopting anti-political attitudes. A better understanding of, and a feeling of greater involvement in, political life means taking fewer cognitive shortcuts that can lead to such anti-political attitudes.

As regards the geographical areas that Italy is generally subdivided into, both socially and politically, in the 1985 and 2004 surveys greater anti-political hostility was expressed by those residing in the country's central regions. In the earlier survey, those areas where the two political-geographical subcultures were still strong – the North-East as far as concerns the Catholic subculture and the central "red belt" (Emilia-Romagna, Tuscany, Umbria and Marche) as far as regards socialist subculture – tended to be characterised by the presence of less negative attitudes towards politics than was the case elsewhere. Rather surprisingly, the same is true of southern Italy, which has always been considered an area distinguished by its extensive political rebelliousness, endemic clientelism and the less ideological attitudes of its citizens (Allum 1973, Chubb 1982). In regard to the anti-political character of the various different geographical areas in question, things appear to have changed with the advent of the Second Republic and the disappearance of the two political parties representing the aforesaid two subcultures: the Christian Democrats (DC) in the North-East and the Italian Communist Party (PCI) in the central "red belt". Anti-political attitudes increased in those areas where the two subcultures dominated, as well as in the South albeit to a more limited degree. In the North-East, the Christian Democrat Party's place had been taken by Forza Italia and its anti-political leader Silvio Berlusconi, who together with the League had made anti-politics one of their distinguishing marks. In 2004, anti-politics assumed greater significance in Italy's "red belt". The citizens of that area of Italy, traditionally more inclined to vote for, and associate with, the nation's left-wing parties, were probably paying the price of a twofold delusion: on the one hand, the left's historical and ideological narrative had come to an abrupt end with the fall of the Berlin Wall, leading among other things to the break-up of the PCI, which in these regions of Italy had enjoyed political hegemony up to that point; the second delusion derived from the expectations fostered, and partly betrayed, by the first experience in government of those parties that had inherited the Communist Party's mantle. This experience was characterised by a series of internal conflicts and unexpected surprises between 1996 and 2001 (Fabbrini 1998, Massari and Parker 1998, Pasquino 2000).

This interpretation appears to be supported by a more detailed analysis of the anti-political feelings of the electorates of the various parties concerned. As can be deduced from the regression models, those people who at the 1983 general election had voted for the two parties at the extremes of the political spectrum – the PCI to the left, and the MSI to the right – were the ones who ranked highest on the anti-political index. The persistent exclusion of these two parties from government, which derives from Italy's "imperfect bipartism" (as mentioned in the first section of Chapter 2) as regards the PCI, and from the *conventio ad excludendum*, an agreement precluding any form of cooperation with the neo-Fascist MSI (Colarizi and Panvini 2017), generated hostility towards politics and governmental policy among the electorates of these two excluded parties.

The situation changed significantly over the course of the following 20 years. On the right, those voters harbouring anti-political sentiments were attracted towards the League rather than the National Alliance (AN) – the party that following the 1995 party congress in Fiuggi became heir to the MSI (Ignazi 1996b). On the left, probably as a result of the aforementioned twofold delusion as exemplified by developments in the "red belt", substantial negative attitudes towards the political sphere persisted. The centre-left electorate's higher scores on the anti-political index in 2004 can also be accounted for by another factor. As was the case in 1985 when the voters of the left and right opposition parties scored highest on said index, in 2004, it was the opposition parties' supporters who expressed the strongest anti-political sentiments of anger and disgust, probably aimed at the policy of government and Silvio Berlusconi and his party. The *Girotondi* and Purple People movements, described in second section of Chapter 5, whom Tarchi describes as populist (Tarchi 2015), are good examples of the anger aimed at Berlusconi during that period. Within the 20-year period considered here, another important change took place as well: while those who handed in blank ballot papers in 1985 had been the least anti-political voters according to our analysis, in 2004, this category of voter had become the most anti-political. This reflects the transformation discussed in relation to the figures shown in Table 6.3, whereby the Italians, from generally adopting a lukewarm, indifferent view of politics during the First Republic, subsequently became a lot more angry with, and disgusted by, that same politics following the transition to the Second Republic.

One further and final consideration ought to be made here with regard to the relationship between anti-politics and attitudes to democracy. Unfortunately, the 1985 and 2004 surveys do not contain directly comparable questions in this respect. Notwithstanding this, the inclusion in the regression models of a variable covering this aspect, albeit in different ways, results in convergent findings. In 1985, anti-political attitudes were strongly correlated to the statement "in certain circumstances an authoritarian regime, a dictatorship, may be preferable to democracy". In 2004, anti-politics was just as strongly inversely correlated to people's agreement with the following statement: "In a true democracy, the majority is responsible for protecting the rights of all minorities".[14] These empirical findings, which deserve specific analysis in order to better understand the relationship and interdependency of the two aspects, are in line with the results of our analysis of the CSES dataset presented beforehand.

Today's anti-political citizens

To complete the analysis of the social and political profile of those Italian citizens driven by anti-political sentiments, we ought to move on from the situations in the mid-1980s and the mid-2000s described in the preceding section, to take in more recent developments. Once again, in order to do so, we shall be performing a secondary analysis of another post-electoral survey. The most recent and substantial survey from the viewpoint of the questions dealt with in this chapter was the one conducted by the ITANES research team at the time of the constitutional referendum held in September 2020, concerning the proposed reduction in the number of parliamentary representatives in Italy. As pointed out in the fourth section of Chapter 5, this referendum was of a strongly anti-political nature and it represented the achievement of one of the 5SM's key aims. In fact, the 5SM was one of the promoters of the constitutional reform, which means that the number of parliamentarians will in fact be reduced from 935 to 600 as from the next legislature.

Compared to 2004, the political situation and the anti-political actors in 2020 had radically changed. Silvio Berlusconi, who in the mid-2000s had been the unrivalled leader of Italian politics and had been considered "the knight of anti-politics", was now relegated to the political fringe and his creation, Forza Italia was no longer considered a populist, anti-political party. His rival, Antonio Di Pietro, who in his own particular way was an anti-political actor as well, was also out of the mix, and his "Italy of Values" party was now just a distant memory. The Democratic Party (PD), founded in 2007 with the aim of expressing a "majoritarian vocation", had suppressed the radicalism of the PCI of which it was to an extent the heir, in order to play the part of the established centre-left party. In addition to the PD, there were basically two other leading actors on the political stage at the time of the constitutional referendum: the 5SM, which thanks to its success at the 2018 general election, was the largest party in parliament; and Salvini's League, which in theory at least had foregone its role as defender of the interests of Northern Italy, to become a nationalist, sovereigntist party. At the institutional level, the mid-2000s financial crisis had given rise to the technocratic government led by Mario Monti which, like other governments in Southern Europe, adopted austerity measures to tackle the crisis. These measures were met with public demonstrations, protests and political hostility, as elsewhere in Southern Europe. This government consequently had a significant impact on voting behaviour (Lewis-Beck and Nadeau 2012). The health and social crisis brought on by the Covid-19 pandemic, on the other hand, favoured the establishment of another technocratic government, this time led by Mario Draghi. Said government comprises all of

Italy's parties with the sole exception of Giorgia Meloni's Fratelli d'Italia (Brothers of Italy[FdI]). This party, heir to the neo-Fascist Italian Social Movement (MSI), and of marginal importance until quite recently, is the one that now appeals most to the many Italians unhappy with the way the country is going. In this much-changed social and political context, one may wonder what has happened to anti-politics. Have anti-political attitudes increased or decreased in intensity, and what kinds of citizen are now driven by anti-political feelings?

As with all of the other secondary analyses presented in this chapter, a number of questions have been identified covering the semantic field of anti-politics. The survey conducted on the occasion of the 2020 constitutional referendum contains questions which unfortunately differ from those used in the 1985 and 2004 surveys of anti-political attitudes. Consequently, the diachronic comparison should be treated with due caution.[15] Nevertheless, it is precisely because the 2020 survey centred on a political event of a clearly anti-political flavour that ITANES' researchers included certain questions about people's hostile attitudes to politics and politicians in general. Thus it proved possible to create a satisfactory index of anti-politics on the basis of six items, four of which come from the same set of questions and the remaining two from another set.

The first 4 items were as follows: "Politicians in Parliament must follow the will of the citizens"; "Citizens rather than politicians should make the most important political decisions"; "I would rather be represented by the man or woman in the street than by a professional politician"; "Politicians talk a lot but do very little". The interviewees were given the choice of responding to the aforesaid statements on the basis of a traditional Likert scale of 1–5, ranging from "strongly agree" to "strongly disagree". The other two items constituting the anti-politics index were formulated differently: one question asked the interviewee about the degree to which they agreed with certain possible meanings attributable to the referendum, on a scale of 1–10. The two responses which were believed to indicate a clearly anti-political stance were: [in regard to the reduction in the number of parliamentarians] "It rightly cuts the costs of politics" and "It sends a strongly critical message to politicians". In order to ensure that each item carried the same weight when constructing the anti-politics index, regardless of the response options available, all variables were normalised. In this way it was possible to construct a simple additive index, in turn normalised so that its range varied between 0 and 1. The measure of the internal consistency of the six items (Cronbach's alpha test) gave a very high score of 0.90.

The frequency distribution of the index, shown in simplified form in Table 6.7, reveals the persistent, strong anti-political propensities of Italians. Suffice it to say that up to the 15th percentile there is not even one case present, while the last percentile, comprising those who in response to all six questions chose the option with the clearest anti-political meaning,

Table 6.7 Class distribution of the anti-politics index in 2020

	Percentage
Low (from 0 to 0.33)	2.1
Medium (from 0.34 to 0.67)	29.1
High (from 0.68 to 1)	68.8
Total	100

Source: The author's processing of the data from the 2020 ITANES survey.

contained 10.8% of the sample as a whole. Consequently, the mean was also very high (0.75), while the standard deviation was 0.18.

As a result of the different nature of the instruments used to survey anti-political attitudes among Italian citizens, it is difficult to say whether such attitudes have grown or diminished since the time of the surveys conducted in the mid-1980s and mid-2000s. Regardless of any other considerations, it is clear that such attitudes are extremely common among the Italian population. Whilst bearing in mind the aforementioned methodological caveats, we shall now see examine the possible similarities and differences between the socio-demographic and political characteristics of anti-political citizens in the year 2020, and those of 15–35 years ago. As in the case of the secondary analyses conducted on the previous two surveys, a linear regression was performed on the 2020 survey in order to reveal, in a simple, easily comprehensible manner, the relationship between the variables taken into consideration and the anti-politics index. The results of the statistical analysis, comprising three models, are set out in detail in Table 6.8.[16]

Let us start with the age factor. Contrary to common public criticism of young people's lack of involvement and interest in politics (Beck 2000), the age group that expresses anti-political feelings to the least extent is that of young people (aged 18–24).[17] The central age categories, accounting for those Italians aged between 35 and 64 who witnessed the traumatic end to the First Republic and/or who first took an interest in politics during, and lived through, the Berlusconi years, are the ones who on average express the strongest anti-political feelings. What would seem surprising is that the oldest age group (those over 65), comprising the somewhat aged "68 generation" who have not given up on politics completely however, is the one that expresses the weakest level of anti-political feelings. Despite the fluidity of political convictions, the volatility of voting behaviour, the changing, highly-fragmented party political scenario, it would seem that the processes of socialisation among young people, which the American school of political socialisation had greatly emphasised (Hyman 1959), continue to operate effectively.

Table 6.8 Linear regression of the anti-politics index with respect to socio-demographic, political and attitudes towards immigration, civil rights and EU covariates (2020)

Anti-politics index	Model 1 (N = 3,063)			Model 2 (N = 3,063)			Model 3 (N = 2,035)		
	Coef.	St.Err.	p-value	Coef.	St.Err.	p-value	Coef.	St.Err.	p-value
Age									
Base category: 18–24	0			0			0		
25–34	.018	.014	.209	.014	.014	.322	.005	.018	.776
35–44	.040	.014	.005	.03	.013	.026	.034	.017	.047
45–54	.056	.014	0	.048	.013	0	.050	.017	.003
55–64	.044	.014	.002	.047	.014	.001	.040	.017	.020
Over 64	.011	.014	.403	.027	.013	.042	.027	.017	.112
Education									
Base category: Low	0			0			0		
Low-intermediate	−.031	.011	.006	−.014	.011	.184	−.010	.013	.447
High-intermediate	−.081	.014	0	−.045	.013	.001	−.049	.016	.003
High	−.091	.012	0	−.048	.012	0	−.05	.014	.001
Gender									
Base category: Male	0			0			0		
Female	.018	.006	.004	.012	.006	.048	.017	.008	.025
Territorial area									
Base category: North-West	0			0			0		
North-East	0	.011	.989	−.003	.010	.767	−.01	.012	.401
Red belt	.001	.010	.948	.005	.010	.574	0	.012	.987
Centre	.006	.010	.555	−.002	.010	.802	.010	.012	.385
South	.039	.009	0	.029	.008	0	.041	.010	0
Interest in politics									
Base category: not at all				0					
Not very much interested				−.003	.018	.867			

(Continued)

Table 6.8 Linear regression of the anti-politics index with respect to socio-demographic, political and attitudes towards immigration, civil rights and EU covariates (2020) (*Continued*)

Anti-politics index	Model 1 (N = 3,063)			Model 2 (N = 3,063)			Model 3 (N = 2,035)		
	Coef.	*St.Err.*	*p-value*	*Coef.*	*St.Err.*	*p-value*	*Coef.*	*St.Err.*	*p-value*
Fairly interested				−.020	.017	.253			
Very interested				−.033	.018	.068			
Don't know or don't answer				−.082	.053	.119			
Party voted									
Base category: Communist Party and The Left				0		.			
PD				.016	.016	.331			
5MS				.170	.017	0			
Forza Italia				.078	.021	0			
Lega				.146	.017	0			
Brothers of Italy				.110	.021	0			
Others				.033	.018	.066			
Abstained or blank/null ballot paper				.108	.017	0			
Prefer not to answer				.091	.019	0			
Attitudes towards the European Union							.062	.013	0
Attitudes towards immigrants							.007	.002	0
Attitudes towards civil rights							−.002	.002	.198

Source: The author's processing of the data from the 2020 ITANES survey.

The education and gender factors appear to count in much the same way as in the previous two analyses. Women and those with low educational qualifications continue to display strong anti-political feelings.[18] The differences with other categories, however, are not as great as they were in the past. This could be seen as a sign of anti-political attitudes spreading to other social categories, as found by Clarke *et al.* in the case of the United Kingdom. The correlation between an interest in politics and the expression of anti-political feelings is also similar to that found in the 1985–2004 surveys: the higher the educational qualifications of those interviewed, the more limited tend to be their negative views on politics and the principal symbols of politics. Again, however, the relationship between variables does not appear to be a particularly close one. This would seem to indicate that even those people more interested in politics are not safe from the wave of anti-political feeling sweeping across Italy.

Together with these aspects of continuity with the past, the analysis of the 2020 survey also reveals a very different situation as regards the geographical distribution of anti-political attitudes and feelings. While in 1985–2004, the most anti-political citizens were those living in central Italy, in 2020, it was the inhabitants of Italy's southern regions who boasted this primacy. In the previous surveys, southern Italians had not really stood out for their anti-political attitudes. However, in the 2020 survey, they were the only ones with above-average scores on the anti-politics index. Political discontent in the South is obviously the result of various different causes, and this is not the appropriate place for a full analysis of such causes. However, broadly speaking the economic crisis that hit the entire country hard in the latter half of the 2000s, together with the consequent austerity measures, affected the South's economy, society and welfare services even more so than elsewhere, as this is the most economically backward, least dynamic part of Italy. As also happened in other parts of Europe (Kriesi 2012), social desperation in Italy's south quickly turned into disenchantment with, and hostility towards, the traditional political parties, who were blamed, rightly or wrongly, for the economic crisis and the management of that crisis. This helps explain the incredible success in that part of the country of the only truly new party – the 5SM – at the 2013 general election, together with its even better performance at the subsequent 2018 general election. This political desperation would also explain the large number of votes cast by southern Italian voters for Salvini's League at the 2018 election, and in a truly surprising fashion at the 2019 European elections when the League was the most voted party in many of the South's provinces. In fact, it only needed a swift, rather rough restyling of the League's political line, to transform it from a regionalist party to a nationalist one; and in the South of Italy, it offered to liaise with certain consolidated clientelist networks (Brancaccio *et al.* 2021), in order to get voters on board who had previously been its staunchest critics. In the absence of alternatives, with politics generally discredited and the 5SM beginning to show signs of "ageing" and "institutionalisation", the South's voters were ready to embrace Salvini's anti-political rhetoric and pretend to forget the anti-southerner prejudices that the leaders of the League and its supporters in the North of Italy have never truly put aside.

Significant changes ought to be mentioned (again with the aforementioned methodological provisos) also with regard to the anti-politics of different parties' voters. The appearance of a new political party (the 5SM), the distinctive feature of which is in fact its anti-politics, has resulted in the more anti-political sections of the electorate being attracted towards it, thus shifting their allegiances away from other parties or returning to the ballot station after a period of absence (in the case of those previously abstaining from voting). This new development, together with the generational renewal of the electorate and the evolution of the other parties' programmes, have contributed towards changing the anti-political character of the electorate of Italy's political parties. The analysis has indicated that 5SM's voters are predictably the most anti-political of all, closely followed, unsurprisingly yet again, by those voting for Salvini's League. In third place in the anti-political stakes lies the FdI's electorate. The novelty here lies in the fact that this electorate's profile is very different from that of the AN, the party that subsequently begat Giorgia Meloni's FdI. In the 2004 survey, AN's electorate was not characterised by anti-political attitudes. For the sake of comparison, the anti-political level of Meloni's party is comparable to that of those who abstain from voting or who spoil their ballot papers or leave them blank.

This circulation and mixing of anti-political voters necessarily lead to a change in the character of the left-wing and centre-left parties. While in the mid-1980s, the PCI, just like the MSI, won over those voters most unhappy and disgusted with politics; in 2020, those voting for parties to the left of the PD were the least anti-political of all. The PD itself, which in electoral terms was much more important than Italy's left-wing parties as such, was characterised by a relatively limited degree of anti-politics. It may thus be true that the 5SM, with its eclectic positioning along the left-right spectrum (Mosca and Tronconi 2019), had attracted voters from other parties disappointed and angry with the political sphere, politicians and political parties, but who did not wish, for ideological and policy reasons, to vote for the right-wing anti-political parties like Forza Italia in its prime or the League thereafter. In other words, the 5SM had "cleansed" the anti-political sphere of the other parties, in particular those on the left.

Finally, in order to establish not only the social and political profile of anti-political citizens but also to characterise them in terms of their values, the third linear regression model reported in Table 6.8 includes three variables regarding attitudes to the EU, immigrants and civil rights.[19] The analysis shows that there are negligible differences in people's attitudes to these three important issues. Only anti-EU feelings appear correlated, to a slight extent, to anti-political attitudes. The reason for this may be that also the EU, its representatives and its institutions are seen as part of that "politics" – comprising politicians, parties and representative assemblies – which citizens display hostility towards. The inclusion of these three issues in the 2020 questionnaire may be accounted for by the fact that they were among the most divisive political issues being debated at the time. These are issues that the political parties and their respective electorates disagree on. The absence of any significant variations in terms of the spread of anti-politics through groups holding different values, further confirms the fact that in contemporary Italy, anti-political feelings are widespread throughout society and are not simply identifiable with certain specific social groups.

Notes

1 In a survey of political discontent in Britain, Will Jennings and colleagues formulated a number of items that they believed cover the concept of anti-politics. The statements contained in the survey were as follows: "Politicians have the technical knowledge needed to solve the problems facing Britain today"; "Politicians in government can make a difference to the major social and economic issues facing Britain"; "Politicians possess the leadership to tell the public the truth about the tough decisions that need to be made"; "Politicians are too focused on short-term chasing of headlines"; and "Politics is dominated by self-seeking politicians protecting the interests of the already rich and powerful in our society" (Jennings et al. 2016, pp. 882–3). Their proposal seems sufficiently convincing, although the survey only covered Great Britain, and as such no international comparison can be made using this survey.

2 The CSES is a vast international research project concerning citizens' political opinions and the electoral systems in numerous different countries. This project was launched in the mid-1990s and makes public the datasets and corresponding documents of numerous national surveys conducted using the same questionnaire. At present, data are available for the first five modules. Unfortunately, the data contained in the various modules are not always comparable. Furthermore, Italy has only participated in Modules 2 and 5. The data processed and presented in this chapter are taken from this latter module, which covers the period from 2016 to 2021, and which in the case of Italy concerns the year 2018 (post-electoral survey). Further information concerning the project, including a list of the publications resulting from it, can be found at the following URL: https://cses.org. The dataset, codebook and other information on Module 5 can be found at the following link: https://cses.org/data-download/cses-module-5-2016-2021.

3 The study *"Citizens' Technocratic Attitudes: A Survey of Nine European Countries"* was funded by the Department of Political Science at the University of Zurich and carried out in 2017 based on representative samples from the following countries: Germany, France, Great Britain, Greece, Italy, the Netherlands, Poland, Romania and Sweden. At present, the main works published in regard to this study are Bertsou and Caramani (2020b) and Bertsou (2022). The dataset made available by the authors and employed in the secondary analysis conducted in this chapter can be found, together with the codebook and other documents illustrating the methods and procedures adopted, at the following URL: https://doi.org/10.7910/DVN/0MOPI4.

4 Although the two indexes have been created on the basis of different questions, I believe that they both cover the diverse semantic aspects of the concept of anti-politics to a sufficient degree. In order to assess their reliability, a test of internal consistency (Cronbach's alpha) was conducted on both: the results

are a satisfactory 0.76 in the case of Bertsou and Caramani's study and 0.78 in the case of the CSES.

5   The set of items also included the following: "Having a strong leader in government is good for [country] even if the leader bends the rules to get things done". However, for reasons of semantic consistency with the concept of anti-politics, it was decided not to use this item when building the index. In a study of France based on the 2017 French Election Study, Camille Bedock and Jean-Benoit Pilet (2021) use some of these same questions to create an index of "political trust". In particular, the two authors consider the following items: "How widespread is corruption such as bribe taking among politicians in France"; "Most politicians are trustworthy", "Most politicians do not care about the people", "The politicians are the main problem in France"; and "The majority of politicians are only interested in the rich and the powerful".

6   Just like Italy, and also Greece and Romania, the two countries ranked either side of Italy in Table 6.1, Hungary as well witnessed the advent of a technocratic government as a consequence of the economic crisis in the second half of the 2000s (Bertsou and Caramani 2020c, p. 91).

7   If certain other variables are introduced into the analysis, such as gender, age, level of education, interest in politics and satisfaction with the working of democracy, then the ranking of countries shown in Table 6.2 changes slightly. The linear regression that holds these variables together shows Italy maintaining sixth place, but being overtaken by Taiwan (which takes Chile's place) in the group of countries characterised by the highest level of anti-politics. The USA is now close behind Italy, whereas the gap between Italy and the other European countries widens. The analysis also shows that considering all countries taken together, anti-politics is equally common among men and women, it tends to be concentrated in the central age bracket (from 26 to 65 years of age), and is negatively correlated to people's level of education, their interest in politics and their satisfaction with the working of democracy in their country.

8   The interviewees' ages ranged from 14 to 65. In an attempt to establish numerically balanced classes, the sample was subdivided into the following four age groups: 14–25 (20.9%); 26–39 (29.1%); 40–50 (30.4%); and 51–65 (19.6%). The "education" variable was aggregated into three categories: Low (Primary and Secondary; 19.8%); Medium (High school or practical apprenticeship, Technical degree; 43.9%); and High (University bachelor's degree, master's degree, PhD; 36.3%). The political self-placement variable was subdivided into four categories: Left (positions 1–3; 18.7%); Centre-left (positions 4 and 5; 35.5%); Centre-right (positions 6 and 7; 27.8%); and Right (positions 8–10; 18.0%). Men constituted 51% of the sample, women the remaining 49%.

9   "The Political Culture of Southern Europe, a Four Nations Study" was coordinated by Giacomo Sani, José Santamaria and Renato Mannheimer. The survey sample consisted of 2,074 cases, and the study was based on the face-to-face interview. The survey was conducted in May 1985, around two years after the 1983 general election. The 2004 survey was conducted by ITANES and was part of a panel comprising three surveys: the first one, conducted in the spring of 2001, immediately after the general election, was based on 3,209 cases interviewed face-to-face; the second survey involved 1,882 interviewees (representing 58.6% of those participating in the first survey in 2001) and was conducted in the spring of 2004, using the face-to-face technique once again; and the third survey involved 1,048 interviewees (32.7% of those involved in 2001 and 55.6% of those interviewed in 2004) and was conducted using the CATI method in the spring of 2006. Further details of the surveys, together with the two datasets concerned, may be requested from the ITANES association through the following URL: http://www.itanes.org/dati/.

10 In the 1985 survey, 571 interviewees failed to respond to the second question; in 2004, their number fell to 92. In order to avoid attributing only the value of their response to the first question to those who failed to answer the second question, it was decided that they would be assigned, as a second value, the same value as that associated with their first answer. Following this procedure, there were only 57 'absent' cases in 1985 and 15 in 2004.

11 In the 1985 survey, the age of interviewees ranged from 18 to 90. This variable was reclassified into six age groups: 18–24 (14.2% of the sample); 25–34 (18.9%); 35–44 (20.3%); 45–54 (18.2%); 55–64 (14.3%); and over 64 (14.1%). The variable "education" was subdivided into four categories: "low", that is, primary school education only (46.1%); "low-intermediate", i.e. middle school diploma (23.9%); "high-intermediate", high-school diploma (19.0%); and "high", attends university or has a degree (10.5%). Women represented 50.1% and men the remaining 49.9%. Italy's regions were subdivided into five groups: North-West (Piedmont, Lombardy and Liguria, comprising 28.3% of the cases considered); North-East (Trentino-Alto Adige, Veneto and Friuli-Venezia Giulia, 11.5%); Red Belt (Emilia-Romagna, Tuscany, Umbria and Marche, 19.6%); Centre (Lazio, the Abruzzo and Sardinia, 13.9%); and South (Campania, Puglia, Basilicata, Calabria and Sicily, 26.7%). The frequency distribution of answers to the question regarding an interest in politics is as follows: "not at all" 30.6%; "not very much" 35.7%; "fairly" 26.9%; and "very" 5.8%. Finally, the parties for which the interviewees voted in the 1983 general election accounted for the following percentages: DC 23.4%; PCI 18.2%; PSI 11.3%; and MSI 2.6%. The smaller *laici* parties (PSDI, PLI, PRI) have been aggregated into a single group; this group together obtained 5.7% of the interviewees' votes in said election. Other parties accounted for 6.4%; those who turned in a blank ballot paper represent 2.9%, while the remaining 29.5% of the sample either did not remember who they voted for or did not wish to answer the question. In the case of the 2004 survey, the same categories were maintained in respect of age, area of residence and education, and the following distributions emerged: 21–24 (4.0%; the minimum age is 21 because the sample is part of a panel the first part of which regards the year 2001), 25–34 (16.6%), 35–44 (20.3%), 45–54 (19.1%), 55–64 (17.0%), and over 64 (23%); North-West (22.2%); North-East (11.9%); Red Belt (17.8%); Centre (15.5%) and South (32.6%); and in terms of education, "low" (23,3%); "low-intermediate" (28,1%); "high-intermediate" (39,1%); and "high" (9,1%). Men constituted 50.4% of the sample and women 49.6%. The interviewees' declared interest in politics (or lack thereof) was distributed as follows: "not at all" 25.0%; "not very much" 42.7%; "fairly" 26.7%; and "very" 5.6%. The parties they voted for at the 2001 general election were distributed as follows: Refounded Communists and Italian Communists 5.6%; Left Democrats 14.9%; The Daisy Party 8.2%; Italy of Values 1.8%; Forza Italia 25.4%; the League 1.9%, AN 10.5%; other parties 5.6%; blank or invalid ballot papers 1.5%; cannot remember, or do not wish to answer the question 19.3%; and missing cases 5.2%.

12 Not all of the relations between the variables contained in the linear regression models featured in this chapter are statistically significant. This does not mean, however, that the results are weak or misleading. To grasp the meaning of these relations, account always has to be taken both of the force of the variables' effects and the statistical significance concerned. In fact, on occasion, it may be misleading to consider statistical significance alone. For a concise examination of this question, see Hoem 2008. With regard to this same argument, Fabrizio Bernardi *et al.* (2017) have examined 356 articles using regression models published in the European Sociological Review during the periods 2000–4 and 2010–4. They found that in approximately one half of the

articles they examined, the authors of those articles had wrongly interpreted low statistical significance as a sign of the ineffectiveness of the variables.

13 Analysing five surveys conducted in Italy between 1983 and 2001, Piergiorgio Corbetta found that the 1968 generation – whom he considered as comprising those born between 1946 and 1955 – continued to vote in the main for left-wing parties (Corbetta 2002, p. 85).

14 The question contained in the 1985 questionnaire was as follows: "Let us now consider various forms of political system. Which of the following statements do you agree with most?" Those who agreed with the statement "a democratic system is preferable to any other form of government" revealed the lowest degree of anti-political feelings. A medium level of anti-political feeling was expressed by those who chose "whether authoritarian or democratic, it makes no difference to people like me". Much higher levels of anti-political feelings were expressed by those who said that dictatorship was sometimes preferable to democracy, as previously mentioned. In the 2004 questionnaire, the interviewees were asked to express the degree to which they agreed with a set of statements regarding democracy, their responses being ranked from 1 to 5 on the Likert scale. One of the items was the aforementioned statement concerning the protection of minorities.

15 Strictly speaking, not even the use of the same questions in different contexts can guarantee that the meanings associated to the indexes will be equivalent, and that they will thus result in a good comparison. In fact, the sense of the questions may change both over the course of time and from one place to another. Consequently, when operating in diverse contexts, the researcher needs to take care to build indicators and indexes, as we have tried to do when developing this secondary analysis, that have the same significance as far as possible; that is, they need to refer to the same concept. Despite the fact that the 2020 ITANES survey was carried out shortly after the survey conducted by Bertsou and Caramani presented in the first section, their comparability is not perfect. The main difference between the two surveys is the age range of the interviewees: in the ITANES survey their ages ranged from 18 to 90, whereas in the international study they ranged from 14 to 65.

16 The variables considered in the analysis were re-coded in a similar manner to those of the 1985–2004 surveys. The six age groups were as follows: 18–24 (8.9% of the sample); 25–34 (12.7%); 35–44 (15.8%); 45–54 (19.6%); 55–64 (17.4%); and over 64 (25.0%). As regards education, given the general increase in the level of schooling of the population, and the different importance of educational qualifications in 2020 compared to 1985 and 2004, the four categories of educational achievement were created on a slightly different basis: "low", those schooled up to the middle school diploma (10.7%); "low-intermediate", those having attended high-school and/or possessing a high-school diploma (46.3%); "high-intermediate", those attending university or possessing a 3-year university degree (16.9%); and "high", those with a 5-year university degree or a PhD (26.1%). Women constituted 51% of the sample, men the remaining 49%. By geographical area: North-West (27.7%); North-East (12.5%); Red Belt (15.2%); Centre (15.8%); and South (28.8%). When asked whether they were interested in politics, the responses were: "not at all" 4.3%; "not very much" 21.8%; "fairly" 52.4%; and "very" 20.4%. The parties they voted for at the 2019 European elections were distributed as follows: Communist Party and The Left 3.9%; PD 22.7%; 5SM 17.4%; Forza Italia 4.2%; The League 17.7%, FdI 4.4%, other parties 8.6%; and abstained or blank/null ballot paper 13.0%, prefer not to answer 8.1%.

17 García-Albacete and Lorente (2021) carried out a secondary, longitudinal analysis of Eurobarometer data and found that over the last 10 years, among

young Italians – compared to their Greek, Spanish and Portuguese peers – the largest increases were recorded in the number of such individuals expressing high satisfaction with democracy and characterised by their significant political involvement.

18 The conclusion that women tend to be more anti-political than men is not what emerges from the analysis conducted by Bertsou and Caramani, commented on in the first section of Chapter 6. As has been pointed out, the comparability of that study and the ITANES surveys presented here is not guaranteed, given the use of different indexes, and also given the diverse age composition of the sample, which in Bertsou and Caramani's study ranges from 14 to 65 years. This discrepancy in findings may be partly the result of such differences.

19 Attitudes towards the EU were gleaned from the positive, negative or neutral opinions given on the role of the EU, on the single European currency, and on the EU's capacity to deal with the Covid-19 crisis. The answers given to four questions were used to build an additive index, which was then included in the linear regression model. Attitudes to immigrants were based on the responses to the following question: "Some people say we take in too many immigrants. Others say that this is not true. Others still say that we could easily take in more immigrants than we do. Where do you stand on this issue?" The question concerning civil rights, on the other hand, was as follows: "Some people think that the law should recognise the new forms of family, such as unmarried couples. Others think that the law should safeguard and defend the traditional model of the family. Where do you stand on this issue?" The interviewees were asked to respond to each of the two questions by rating their position on a scale of 1–7, where 1 equates to the least open-minded position and 7 to the most open-minded position, on the question in hand. Despite the fact that at times it is preferable, from a statistical-analytical perspective, to use other ways of processing the Likert scale, it was decided to adopt the linear regression approach since this is in keeping with the other analyses presented in this chapter.

Conclusions

The reflections and analysis presented in this volume all centre on the question of anti-politics. As we have seen, the conceptual confines of anti-politics are somewhat blurred, overlapping as they do with other forms of disaffection with, and hostility towards, politics and its principal symbols, namely: professional politicians, political parties and representative assemblies. In recent decades, anti-political attitudes and feelings appear to have grown, involving broader social categories than before. Together with other phenomena that have been extensively examined in the literature and with which anti-politics is strictly interrelated – to name but two, the mediatisation of politics and the diffusion of populist leadership styles – the spread of anti-politics has helped change the relationship between citizens and the political sphere. Consequently, reflecting on the causes, effects and forms of anti-politics implies, among other things, questioning the path taken by democracies at the beginning of the 21st century.

The analysis of anti-politics presented here consists in three main phases: the conceptual, terminological and methodological analysis conducted in Chapter 1; the detailed survey of manifestations of anti-politics in Republican Italy, in particular over the last 30 years, set out in Chapters 2–5; and the empirical and comparative analysis of the anti-political feelings of Italians from the mid-1980s to the present day contained in Chapter 6. Briefly running through each of these three phases, we see which findings emerge, and consequently the contribution that this volume offers to the advancement of our understanding of contemporary anti-politics, as well as the directions in which future research can hopefully go.

The conceptual, terminological and methodological analysis

In view of the terminological confusion regarding the various forms that anti-politics has taken, I decided to try and clarify the meaning of the term "anti-politics" as a preliminary measure. Therefore, following Sartori's classical recommendations concerning the analysis of concepts (Sartori 1984), the first chapter offers an overview of the everyday and academic uses of the term "anti-politics". Among other things, the diachronic analysis of

DOI: 10.4324/9781003109273-8

the diffusion of this term among speakers of different languages (English, French, Spanish, Italian and German) reveals that the term is much more commonly used in Italy than elsewhere (see Figure 1.1). Although this is not a true indicator of the presence of the phenomenon, the broader thematisation of anti-politics within the Italian context helps justify the decision to focus on Italian political affairs. Furthermore, the diachronic analysis of the circulation of the term shows that, while its use has increased in all of the countries considered, in Italy the debate over anti-politics took a leap forward in the early 1990s, at the time that the Tangentopoli bribery scandal emerged, when in fact the Italians' relationship with the political world worsened significantly.

During that period, as Figure 2.1 clearly shows, this hostility towards politics and politicians was better expressed as "partitocracy", a term that had been revived and made popular by the jurist and intellectual, Giuseppe Maranini, as far back as the late 1950s. As regards its circulation, the term "anti-politics" gradually made up ground on "partitocracy" before catching up with and overtaking it in the latter half of the 2000s. This was not simply a contest between two different terms: in fact, words are never used randomly, particularly not in politics. As Sartori puts it, view "words are not simple means for identifying objects. Words intervene in our *perception* of objects and indeed convey *interpretations* and attach *significance* to their referents" (Sartori 1975, p. 14 – emphasis in original). Consequently, the semantic shift from "partitocracy" to "anti-politics" marked a significant change that we shall now briefly discuss.

As long as parties were the principal actors on the political stage, and society was organised in a capillary manner on the basis of membership of this or that party, political anger was aimed mainly at the parties themselves. In that particular cultural and political context, the widespread circulation of the term "partitocracy", used in a disparaging, contemptuous way, is fully understandable. When, in the early 1990s, the traditional political parties became weaker or disappeared altogether, they were replaced by corporatised or personalised parties (like Forza Italia), and the surviving or new parties' grip on society was no longer so strong. Consequently, the nature of society and politics' problems had to be rethought. The issue was no longer the excessive power and self-referential character of political parties. The main target of the hostility of a growing number of citizens, observers and, in a manner only apparently paradoxical, also of politicians was now politics as a whole. This is how "anti-politics" replaced "partitocracy".

In conceptual terms, the broad survey of the uses of the word "anti-politics" reveals serious problems of homonymy (Figure 1.2) and of synonymy (Figure 1.3), which render any theoretical or empirical analysis of the question more complicated and confused. In fact, it is difficult to make any headway in this terminological jungle, where the problems are twofold: on the one hand, the same term has a variety of meanings and indicates diverse empirical referents (homonymy); and on the other hand, several terms have the same meaning and indicate the same empirical referents (synonymy). In the light of this, it is hereby proposed that the meaning of the concept of anti-politics be reconstructed. The result of this operation, which is summarised in Figure 1.4, bridges a gap in the literature and brings some order to the variegated uses of the term. In doing so, different terms such as "anti-partyism", "anti-establishment" and "anti-politicians" are distinguished and related to one another: these terms are considered to be internal aspects of the concept of anti-politics, and are all positioned lower down the ladder of abstraction (Sartori 1970, p. 1040) (or to put it more accurately, the ladder of generality). This process of conceptual reconstruction also proposes to define the link between anti-politics and the difficult, elusive concept of "populism", by arguing that the two concepts semantically overlap to a certain extent. To put it simply, it is argued that anti-politics is one aspect of populism. In fact, the rhetoric and behaviour of those leaders and parties commonly considered "populist" nearly always contain a healthy dose of anti-politics. Vice versa, not all expressions of anti-politics can be considered populist.

Going back to certain previously formulated conceptual distinctions among the anti-politics expressed by political leaders, the political class in general and other élites within society (anti-politics from above) and the anti-politics of the people (anti-politics from below) (Mete 2010), Chapter 1 of this volume examines selected methodological aspects of the empirical study of anti-politics. Despite the existence of various studies focusing on the concept of anti-politics (or that consider it explicitly) (Clarke *et al.* 2018, Bertsou and Caramani 2020b), the literature does not offer any specifically tailored indicators of anti-politics in society. In order to bridge this gap, at least in part, some possible indicators of the concept of anti-politics have been identified. More specifically, I decided that these indicators could be organised around three units of analysis: political leaders or other representatives of the political class; the political system as such; citizens-voters. Our methodological reflections on the phenomenon of anti-politics need to be strengthened if we are to produce a research agenda reflecting the complexity and importance of the object of study. This can also be done by having recourse to less frequently used qualitative research methods (Boswell *et al.* 2019).

What we learn from the Italian case

Once the terminological and conceptual aspects of anti-politics have been examined, and having pondered the methodological approach to the question, I decided to identify a political context within which the various manifestations of anti-politics could be observed. Italy was the nation chosen for this purpose, since it represents a particularly interesting case; one characterised by multiple anti-political dynamics both at the level of political leaders, political parties and the political class as a whole and at that of citizens-voters. There are a number of reasons for this choice. In Italian, the use of the term *"antipolitica"* goes back some way in history; and more recently, this term has been utilised to an increasing degree in Italy. Openly anti-political Italian leaders and parties have been more successful than their equivalents in other countries: Silvio Berlusconi and the Five Star Movement (5SM) are good examples of this success. Compared to other democracies, Italy has experienced the clearest break from its political past, as a consequence of the 1990s bribery scandal (*Tangentopoli*), which generated a great deal of anger and hostility towards the political sphere. Let us look at how the analysis of such an interesting case of anti-politics can help further our understanding of the phenomenon itself.

The post-war Common Man Movement, the fragments of the earliest opinion polls conducted in the 1950s and 1960s, the polemical campaign against partitocracy launched by Maranini during that same period, all testify to the far from idyllic relationship that Italians have had with politics. Like Britain (Clarke *et al.* 2018), Italy has never experienced any golden age of this relationship. This simple fact, which may appear rather banal to those who are fully acquainted with Italy's Republican history, has often been obscured by the Italians' intense involvement in the political life of their country, by the large-scale mobilisation of the masses and by the organisational capabilities of Italy's political parties, which have been key figures in the political life of the nation from the post-war years onwards. The conclusion that can be drawn from this is that the considerable presence of anti-political sentiments and attitudes is not incompatible with substantial political mobilisation. Hostility towards, and disaffection with, politics may thus coexist with a strong degree of political participation.

What effects have the aforementioned early forms of anti-politics had on politicians, and on the political culture of the Italian people, over the course of the last 30 years? Or put more simply: can any historical continuity of anti-politics be said to exist? A careful consideration of Italy's political history would suggest that the answer to this question is no. Despite being driven by polemical and political intentions in many cases, political actors, opinion-makers and even scholars have on several occasions claimed that there are direct links between the Common Man Movement and certain more recent manifestations of anti-politics, such as the League, the politics of Berlusconi and the 5SM. Moreover, Maranini's criticism of partitocracy 70 years ago has been uncritically employed to analyse the collapse of Italy's traditional parties in the early 1990s.

Although there does not appear to be any direct link between such distant and diverse phenomena, this does not mean that the earlier forms of anti-politics could not have had a role to play in the more recent political dynamics presented in Chapters 3–5. The actions taken by Giannini and others critical of politics, such as the representatives of civil society in the early 1990s, contributed towards the formulation and circulation of anti-political language. These are the same social and political actors who gave a name to a thing that already existed and in doing so performed an action that was to be key to the subsequent development of the phenomenon. As Sartori points out, "if a language does not provide a name for an object, the object passes unnoticed" (Sartori 1975, p. 14).

Therefore, it would be rather naive to think that the anti-political "objects" of the post-war years (Giannini, Maranini etc.), those of the early 1990s (civil society, Bossi, Berlusconi etc.) and those of the last 15 years (Salvini's League, Renzi, the 5SM etc.), were all expressions of the same phenomenon. As we know, history never repeats itself, due among other things to the simple fact that the social context and meanings attributed to politics vary considerably from one period to another. However, the earliest manifestations of anti-politics were to coin the names given to the object; when many years later, similar objects arose, the same names were used once again, whether rightly or wrongly. At times this was done unwittingly, but more often than not it was done with more or less explicit political intentions. Thus, a complicated sleight of hand was performed, fostered by the attractiveness to the media of the anti-political narrative, and by the investment in this theme on the part of certain "political entrepreneurs of anti-politics".

From the early 1990s onwards, as a result among other things of the growing importance of the media, who were revolutionising the political environment, a succession of entrepreneurs of anti-politics appeared on the political scene. They were not a complete novelty, although the Tangentopoli bribery scandal certainly opened a window of opportunity guaranteeing them visibility and success. The analysis of political developments in Italy presented in Chapters 3–5 shows, in fact, that adopting an anti-political line pays in the short-term. In other words, wagering on the impact of anti-politics enables politicians to achieve political aims that are often highly ambitious and difficult to achieve otherwise. Of course, anti-politics is just one ingredient in a much richer political, programmatic and communicational recipe deployed by the various political actors concerned. Other ingredients include the extreme personalisation of politics; the scapegoating of immigrants, the European Union (EU) and large multinationals; nationalism; the promise of giving power back to the people. All of these are ingredients that get blended in various ways by political leaders pursuing their own political ends. Anti-politics, however, remains an important, strong ingredient that makes the proposed recipe immediately recognisable. The chapters of this volume dealing with the Italian case reveal why embracing the anti-political sentiments commonly felt by the Italian people has proven to be a politically successful strategy.

First of all, by playing the anti-political card – and of course using other ploys such as encouraging tax resistance and denigrating Southern Italians – Bossi's Northern League was able to emerge from the shadows in the late 1980s. Twenty years later, Salvini's League embraced the language and ideas of anti-politics, and this enabled it to avoid the complete demise of the party following the scandals concerning the fraudulent management of public funds by Bossi, Bossi's political entourage and his close circle of friends and family.

Criticism of political careerism and political parties is also something that strongly characterised Berlusconi's political rhetoric. His political outsider leadership style, in addition to his personal wealth, acquaintances and communicative resources, enabled Berlusconi the successful businessman to be elected Prime Minister of Italy in 1994. Aware of the rewards of investing in anti-politics, Berlusconi was to preserve his clear anti-political stance for some considerable time thereafter.

As we have seen, however, anti-politics is not the exclusive prerogative of the centre-right and its leaders, parties and voters. The centre-left has also employed anti-political means, albeit in different ways and with diverse aims in mind. In the early 2000s, a subtler, more sophisticated expression of anti-politics took the form of participatory and deliberative practices introduced by local and regional authorities governed by the centre-left. The large-scale diffusion of such practices, and the accompanying political emphasis on such, served to shield the centre-left parties and leaders from criticism from the people and groups involved in the global justice movement: while the watchword of these movements was participation, the authorities led by the centre-left undertook to facilitate and organise such participation.

Another important democratic innovation went in this same direction. This was the introduction of primaries and the direct election of the secretary of the principal centre-left party. Chapter 4 examines the anti-political consequences, specifically in terms of the message that citizens receive, of these forms of democratic medicine administered to a democracy in a sorry state. To put it briefly, the message being sent out was that certain functions that had been traditionally assigned to the parties, such as political recruitment, could be better performed (with better results, that is) by the citizens themselves. At the same time, allowing those citizens who declare themselves to be party supporters to choose the head of the party, implies that they are more capable of doing so than the party's own members and militants are.

Chapter 4 also reveals how the primaries have resulted in the somewhat surprising emergence of a young political leader, Matteo Renzi, who, in order to fast track his own political career, waged an internecine war within the PD. His employment of an anti-political strategy consisting in calls for the "scrapping" of the party's "old" guard, together with other similar ploys, enabled him to stand out from the crowd and to win primaries: first of all, the primary for the post of mayor of Florence, and then that for the national secretary of his party, the PD. This was to be the prelude to his subsequent appointment as Prime Minister of Italy. With the advent of Renzi, as we have seen, the more explicit forms of anti-politics, traditionally the preserve of the right, were gradually adopted by Italy's left-wing parties and leaders as well.

Finally, anti-politics represents the most important political resource invested in by Grillo and Casaleggio, the co-founders of the 5SM. The recipe they adopted in order to achieve their incredible electoral success was doubly anti-political: it consisted in a combination of primitive, explicit, irreverent and, at times, violent right-wing anti-politics, and the subtler and more sophisticated anti-politics of the left designed to guarantee the democratic participation and involvement of the nation's citizens. Thus, the 5SM's anti-politics can be considered the mature product of anti-political preaching and practices that emerged following the Tangentopoli bribes scandal. Its anti-political recipe was so well thought out that it saw the transformation of a movement of opinion vaunting the intrinsic value of political inexperience, into the most voted-for party at the Italian general election held in 2018, and thus a member of the majority sustaining three different governments during the course of the legislature that began in 2018.

In view of the success of Italy's anti-political leaders, we have to conclude that waging on anti-politics does in fact pay. In politics, however, wagers are not always won completely. Furthermore, having won a wager it cannot be automatically assumed that subsequent wagers are going to be won as well. In fact, if we take a closer look at the aforementioned developments, we discover that while anti-politics has helped political parties and leaders achieve their own immediate or short-term aims, in the medium and long-term, however, anti-political strategies have proven a weakness for those having recourse to them. Indeed, once anti-politics has been embraced, it needs to be constantly nurtured, and those who have used it to create their own image are forced to continually launch new drives in order to sustain that image. If, for whatever reason, anti-political actors fail to maintain a convincing anti-political profile, then anti-politics will exact its revenge by annihilating the "traitor". This is precisely what happened to Umberto Bossi, the "father and master" of the Northern League. When the scandals emerged regarding him and the party, he was immediately tossed aside and humiliated by some of those who had been among his most ardent supporters. The anti-politics of the League's grassroots could not stand the idea that Bossi, the political moraliser, had been responsible for the purchase of diamonds in Tanzania using the party's funds, and that he had used those same funds to pay for his son's university degree from an Albanian university. A similar end befell Antonio Di Pietro, the judge made famous by the political corruption investigations he led in the early 1990s. Di Pietro was another who had entered politics with moralising intentions; however, his political career was short-lived, and his personal party disintegrated when the people he himself had selected were guilt of the worst variety of political transformism and careerism.

Anti-politics was also to ruin the political career of the young, anti-political Matteo Renzi who for three years had been the leading figure in Italian politics. His greatest political mistake was not that of losing the constitutional referendum he had so strongly campaigned for but of promising to leave politics in the event of defeat in that referendum. Renzi did not keep his promise following his defeat and thus fell victim to the double standards which people usually adopt when judging ordinary people on the one hand and politicians on the other (Hatier 2012). Instead, he left the PD, the party he was national secretary of, and created his own small party. By doing so, he gave people the idea that despite his proclamations, promises and grand ideals, the one thing he really cared about was his own political status. This is why Renzi quickly went from being a highly esteemed, extremely popular politician, to a despised symbol of the old politics characterised by deception, arrogance and lies.

Ultimately, as Chapter 5 shows, the process of normalisation and institutionalisation that inevitably affected the 5SM once its representatives had set foot in the country's political institutions and government was accompanied by the "betrayal" of many of the original movement's anti-political promises. One by one the characteristics that had distinguished the 5SM from the much criticised "old" parties were lost. The party's experience in parliament and government was characterised by a series of expulsions and splits, and by the fostering of personal ambition: in fact, the aim of transforming its representatives into the mere spokespersons for the general will as expressed by the web consultations, quickly revealed itself to be a utopian ideal. Even the rule prohibiting representatives from holding parliamentary office for more than two terms, which had expressed a simple, yet strong principle, was increasingly questioned. The characterising, mobilising slogan of "everyone counts as much as any other" (in Italian: *uno vale uno*) was quickly deflated as the first internecine struggles emerged within the movement, while the ongoing judicial inquiries demolished the myth of the inherent honesty of those coming into politics with no prior political experience.

To sum up, at least two of the various outcomes of these political dynamics centred on anti-politics merit emphasising here. The first concerns the political class, while the second regards citizens and their political culture. In terms of the political class, while the Italian case shows that waging on anti-politics can be a way for politicians to further and fast track their careers, it also shows that these careers can quickly come to an end as a consequence. The same could also be said of those political parties voicing citizens' anti-political feelings. So anti-politics is like a bundle of wood thrown onto a fire: for a while the fire burns with renewed vigour, offering light and warmth; however, it very quickly burns out, leaving only a pole of ash. Those political leaders and parties who decide to play the anti-political card are taking an enormous risk, since while this may lead them to rapid success, it can also bring them down just as quickly. At the political system level, this dynamic implies a rapid turnover of anti-political leaders and creates the right conditions for the foundation and success of new (or renewed) anti-political parties, which will significantly impact the quality of the political class.

In terms of the population's political culture, the constant letting down of people's expectations due to the failings of anti-political leaders and parties inevitably generates further mistrust, disaffection and anger with regard to the symbols of politics. Bottom-up anti-politics then becomes more radical, more desperate and increasingly diversified involving a broader section of society. Thus, the anti-politics deriving from contingent situations (a political scandal, the failure to keep a political promise etc.) is transformed into a deep-rooted form of mistrust and hostility vis-à-vis the world of politics. As our analysis of the Italian case would seem to suggest, anti-politics becomes an endemic feature of political culture, which in turn permits the emergence and success of new actors who decide to play the anti-politics game. This creates a spiral of anti-politics that it is difficult to put an end to, and the development of which, in the medium term, inevitably impacts the selection of the political class and the quality and preservation of democracy.

Anti-political Italians

The central chapters of this volume described a number of events testifying to the considerable importance of anti-politics in the history of Republican Italy. Although anti-politics from below and anti-politics from above are intrinsically bound together, the analysis focuses principally on the former, that is, on those phenomena concerning political leaders and politicians, rather than on the bottom-up variety regarding the attitudes, beliefs and behaviour of the nation's citizens. In an attempt to render this analysis more comprehensive, the final chapter examines the diffusion and characteristics of the anti-politics of the Italians in greater depth. To this end, a secondary analysis has been conducted of selected national and international surveys covering a period from the mid-1980s to the year 2020, in order to investigate three principal aspects of anti-politics. The first consists of an international comparison designed to establish whether in fact Italians are more anti-political than the citizens of other European and non-European democracies. This secondary analysis also enables us to assess whether the socio-demographic and political characteristics of anti-political Italians are similar to, or different from, those of other nations' anti-political citizens. The second in-depth investigation consists in a diachronic comparison of Italians' anti-political attitudes and behaviour prior to, and after, the early 1990s Tangentopoli bribery scandal. The comparison between the mid-1980s and the mid-2000s enables us to establish whether anti-political attitudes among Italians grew during that period, and whether at those times anti-politics attracted voters with different socio-demographic and political characteristics. Based on the analysis of a survey conducted in 2020, the third and final aspect examined regards the social and demographic characteristics, the values and the political nature of modern-day anti-political Italians. We shall now briefly examine the main results of the analysis of these three aspects of Italians' anti-politics discussed in greater detail in Chapter 6.

The comparison with other democracies based on two different surveys sees Italy ranked among those countries where anti-political attitudes are most commonly found (Tables 6.1 and 6.2). These findings are in keeping with the broader circulation of the term anti-politics than in other major western democracies (Figure 1.1), and with other indicators of anti-politics relating to the political system. These indicators include the electoral weight and political relevance of clearly anti-political leaders and parties. The comparative analysis also shows that in terms of the diffusion of anti-politics, Italy ranks closer to those countries where democracy is struggling, which are characterised by substantial social inequality, and are sometimes dominated by populist leaders, than to those where democratic life proceeds smoothly as far as is possible. Italy, in fact, is ranked alongside Greece, a country that has recently come out the worse for wear from the severe economic and financial crisis suffered in the latter half of the 2000s; and it ranks close to Jair Bolsonaro's Brazil, Donald Trump's USA and Viktor Orbán's Hungary. It comes in some way behind the social democracies of Northern Europe, on the other hand.

Another finding that emerged from this initial comparative analysis is that those citizens holding the strongest anti-political views differ in terms of their socio-demographic and political profiles from one country to the next. Consequently, just as there is no such thing as a typical populist voter (Rooduijn 2018, p. 353), likewise there is no such thing as a typical anti-political voter. In this regard, compared to the citizens of the other eight European countries considered in the 2017 survey, anti-political Italians are over-represented among men, the low-educated, the elderly and right-wing voters (Figures 6.1–6.4).

In order to investigate the anti-politics of the Italians, a second comparison was carried out, this time of a diachronic rather than a geographical nature. The secondary analysis of two surveys – one conducted in 1985 and the other in 2004 – made it possible to investigate the changes in people's anti-political attitudes at the time of the significant rift in the Italian political system during the early 1990s. An anti-politics index based on the same questions regarding people's feelings about politics reveals that anti-political feelings grew significantly during the period in question. More specifically, the index shows that an increased number of Italians felt anger, disgust or distrust in regard to politics. At the same time, those indifferent to politics decreased in number (Table 6.3). Anti-political feelings not only rose during the 20-year period in question, in keeping with similar developments in the United Kingdom (see Clarke *et al.* 2018) but were now expressed by a broader section of the population, that is, by people with different socio-demographic and political characteristics and values.

Both surveys seem to show a positive correlation between anti-politics and age. One important exception to this trend – and something that is of considerable importance with regard to our understanding of the evolution of anti-political feelings – is the generation that first took an interest in politics during the late 1960s. This was the so-called 68 generation, and the people from this generation proved less critical of politics and politicians in both the 1985 and 2004 surveys. Moreover, both surveys revealed a negative correlation with educational qualifications. Somewhat surprisingly, and unlike in the case of the aforementioned 2017 comparative survey, the 1985 and 2004 surveys revealed that women were more angry and disgusted with politics than were men. As far as the geographical distribution of anti-political feelings is concerned, such feelings were less intense in those regions where in the mid-1980s the political subcultures associated with the Christian Democrat party (in the North-East), or with the Italian Communist Party (PCI) (the red belt of central Italy), prevailed. Twenty years later, with those historical parties now just a memory, the intensity of anti-political feeling in those areas of Italy increased. An increase in anti-political sentiment was also witnessed in the regions of Southern Italy.

As regards the relationship between anti-political feelings and the parties that people support, in 1985 the most anti-political people were those who voted for parties with more well defined ideological positions, namely the PCI on the left, and the neo-Fascist MSI on the right. The voters of these two parties (sworn enemies) were equally distrustful and disdainful of the political sphere that both parties had been excluded from (for different reasons). By 2004 the situation had changed significantly. On the right, the most anti-political citizens were no longer those who voted for the party's heir to the legacy of the MSI, but rather those voting for Bossi's Northern League. On the left, a distrust of politics persisted, probably as a result of the disappointing experience of government during the 1996–2001 legislature, contrary to voters' high expectations; and perhaps also due to the fact that at that time, politics was embodied by the hated figure of Silvio Berlusconi, who had a firm grip on the government of Italy in 2004. Finally, although the questions concerned differed somewhat, both in 1985 and in 2004 anti-political feelings were positively correlated to people's dissatisfaction with the functioning of democracy, and in the case of the 1985 survey, to dictatorial solutions being viewed with some favour.

The third and final investigation, which was conducted in the form of a secondary analysis of a 2020 survey, concerns the characteristics of those current-day Italians harbouring anti-political feelings. While the anti-politics index was created in a different way from those of the 1985 and 2004 surveys, in 2020 anti-political attitudes appeared to be much commoner than in the past. Anti-politics continues to be positively correlated to age. The only exception to this rule is that of the 1968 generation. Although by now comprising people aged over 70, it continues to be the category that views politics in the least negative light compared to other generations. The analysis also confirms the greater anti-political propensity of women and of the low-educated, even though the differences are less evident than they were 15 or 35 years before. As previously mentioned, this could be a sign of the fact that the social base of anti-politics has broadened over time, and is no longer restricted to the more marginal sections of the population.

The most important novelty that emerges from an analysis of the 2020 survey is the advance of anti-politics in South Italy. This is the area of the country where the mid-2000s economic crisis hit hardest, leaving in its wake a desolate economic and social situation which has generated further hostility towards, and anger with, politics. It therefore comes as no surprise to find that it was in these southern regions that the 5SM, acting as an anti-political party, obtained record levels of votes at the 2013 and 2018 general elections. However, as soon as the process of institutionalisation began to take the shine off Grillo's "five stars", the political desperation of these southern regions punished the 5SM. In fact, at the 2019 European elections, voters in Italy's South shifted their allegiances to Salvini's League, a political party that only a few years earlier had been viewed as the enemy by the majority of the citizens of those regions.

By 2020, the party affiliations of the anti-political electorate had also changed. In addition to the League, which continued to act as a party of protest (despite being the party present for the longest time in parliament), anti-political voters were attracted en masse towards the 5SM. The concentration of anti-political hardliners in Beppe Grillo's party had the effect of "cleansing" the electorates of other parties (particularly those on the left) of their anti-political elements. Unlike in the past, those voting for these parties now displayed a below-average level of anti-politics. Finally, there does not appear to be any correlation between anti-political feelings and certain politically important values, such as people's attitudes towards immigrants, towards the EU or their views on moral questions such as euthanasia. This last piece of the analysis further confirms the fact that anti-politics is a phenomenon that now concerns the entire Italian electorate.

New research directions

This volume aims to contribute towards academic reflection on the question of anti-politics. It endeavours to bridge certain gaps in the existing literature. While part of this endeavour has already been accomplished, there still remains a lot to be done. These final observations shall therefore look at possible directions in which I hope research can go from here. This would, in turn, enable us to further our understanding of the role played by anti-politics in today's democracies.

One item that deserves further investigation is the concept of anti-politics. Notwithstanding the terminological and conceptual clarification offered in Chapter 1, the problems of homonymy and synonymy remain. This results in a confusing use of "anti-politics" as a term and concept, and of its empirical referents, rendering it elusive and difficult to analyse. In turn, this conceptual vagueness makes it difficult to develop a separate, independent field of study, which at present appears somewhat fragmented and encumbered by the presence of other concepts such as populism and anti-partyism. At the terminological, conceptual level, it would also be a good idea to investigate the linguistic differences between the diverse national contexts, in order better understand why it is that different terms are employed to indicate similar phenomena. In this regard, the Italian case is highly instructive: while the replacement of the old term "partitocracy" with the less-used "anti-politics" marked a change in the way the problem was perceived and defined, so other linguistic uses can signal changes and rifts in the political system and culture of a given country. One also needs to bear in mind that these terminological shifts are probably not random but are associated with the political uses made of anti-politics mentioned at various points in the present volume.

This lack of conceptual clarify entails another problem, namely the identification of pertinent indicators of the concept of anti-politics. Once again, the analysis set out in Chapter 1 has made it possible to partly bridge the gaps in the existing literature. However, a broader, more systematic reflection is called for; one that takes account of the various units of analysis to be studied in depth. Once the indicators have been precisely identified for the diverse units in question, it would be a good idea to conduct a study that considers all of them (or as many as is possible) together. Rather than focusing exclusively on the organisation or electoral successes of populist (and anti-political) parties, on the analysis of the anti-political leaders' political language, on the study of the anti-political content of party manifestos, on the characteristics of anti-political voters, on the anti-political grounds for abstaining and so on, as often is the case (for understandable reasons), it would be a good idea to combine these various aspects in one single study of a comparative nature if possible.

With regard to a comparative study of different nations, the analysis conducted in Chapter 6 concludes that citizens with anti-political views living in different countries are not necessarily from the same social-demographic category, or possess the same political outlook or moral values. Consequently, one question that ought to be investigated carefully is the following: why do different countries "produce" anti-political citizens of different kinds? In other words, why is it that in certain countries, those who hate politics and politicians tend to be from the right, whereas in other countries they tend to be from the left? Why is it that in certain countries they tend to be those with a better education, whereas in others they are predominantly the low-educated? Once the social and political characteristics of anti-political citizens in a large set of democracies have been mapped more precisely, the countries could then be subdivided into homogeneous groups based on the anti-political profiles of their citizens. This would make it easier to investigate the various sources of anti-political feelings, together with the diverse social and political mechanisms that generate political discontent: this could be done, for example, by checking whether there is any correlation with the forms taken by capitalism in those countries, and with the social inequalities that exist therein (Trigilia 2020); or whether anti-politics is in any way related to the nature of the relationship between the media and politics (Hallin and Mancini 2004). This would help broaden and render more specific an examination of the contingent or long-term nature of the widespread anti-political views held by the country's citizens, which has already been performed in relation to concepts similar to anti-politics and mentioned at various points in this volume.

One further finding that emerged from the secondary analysis conducted in Chapter 6 concerns the positive correlation between dissatisfaction with the way democracy works, and the strength of anti-political feelings at the individual level. The relationship between the two is perhaps hardly surprising, given that they are two separate, yet interrelated, forms of political discontent. From this point of view, one promising line of research could be to try and establish, more precisely, the causal link between the two phenomena. In other words, it would be interesting and helpful to establish whether it is the lack of trust in democracy that casts its shadow over the principal symbols of democracy, or whether, on the contrary, it is the poor opinion of political leaders, political parties and representative institutions that carries with it a general dissatisfaction with the workings of democracy as a whole.

However, to carry out such a research project would require more than just surveys – the commonest tools used to study people's political opinions and beliefs. As has been mentioned on several occasions in this volume, other qualitative methods have been employed to get a close-up view of people's relationship with politics. Unfortunately, such methods continue to be used sparingly, whereas they ought to be developed further and combined with other methods of analysis and sources of information. This is the only possible way of uniting further study, designed to render results of a more representative nature, with in-depth study of a complex phenomenon like anti-politics.

As regards the case of Italy, which has been used here to study the phenomenon of anti-politics, while a considerable amount of research has been conducted so far, there is still a lot to do. There has never been a golden age of relations between Italian and politics, and the Tangentopoli bribes scandal undoubtedly stoked resentment and disaffection towards professional politicians, political parties and political institutions. However, certain deeper, less obvious roots of this growing anti-political hostility in Italy remain to be studied and understood more fully. For example, it would be interesting to examine in greater depth the seven-year period during which the Italian President was Sandro Pertini (1978–85), whose presidential style was less formal than that of his predecessors. While there are numerous studies of the figure and leadership of Socialist Party politician Bettino Craxi, a key player in Italian politics right through the 1980s who ended up involved in the Tangentopoli scandal, it would be interesting to further investigate the impact he had on both anti-politics from below and anti-politics from above. Finally, it would be interesting to examine the degree to which Achille Occhetto – the PCI's national secretary who, following the fall of the Berlin Wall, led the party towards the Second Republic – subscribed to the positions adopted by the protest movements and civil society in the early 1990s. In fact, it was this that sowed the seeds of the sophisticated, subtle forms of anti-politics subsequently expressed by the centre-left and discussed in Chapter 4.

Finally, a word about the role of the scholars who, perhaps as much if not more than other social actors, contribute towards establishing the public's perspective of the nature and causes of, and the possible remedies for, anti-politics. As previously mentioned, anti-politics is positively correlated to dissatisfaction with the functioning of democracy. In fact, anti-politics targets democracy's individual figures and institutions. By doing so anti-politics corrodes democracy, and in the long-term this corrosive action inevitably weakens democracy. Given this, in my opinion, those scholars who care about democracy's state of health have got to do two things. Firstly, they need to bridge the gap between people's unrealistic expectations of politics on the one hand, and what politicians can realistically do to resolve society's problems on the other. As Flinders has stated in this regard, "any defence of democratic politics must to some extent seek to defend politicians" (Flinders 2021, p. 498). This can be achieved by representing the job of politicians and the workings of democracy, in an as realistic, non-idealised manner as possible. In other words, people need to understand the limitations of an instrument which, while preferable to other forms of political governance, is far from perfect, starting with its unsatisfactory method of selection of those entrusted with highly important political roles. Secondly, as scholars, we possess all of the means needed to disclose the political uses of anti-politics which, while they may be considered legitimate within an electoral context, tend to foster false beliefs, and in the end, to mislead and manipulate voters, particularly those more socially marginalised. The destiny of democracy does not lie in the hands of social scientists of course, but it would be far worse if we were to stand there and do nothing.

Bibliography

Aalberg, T., Esser, F., Reinemann, C., Strömbäck, J., and de Vreese, C.H., eds., 2016. *Populist political communication in Europe*. New York: Routledge.

Abedi, A., 2004. *Anti-political establishment parties. A comparative analysis*. London; New York: Routledge.

Achen, C.H. and Bartels, L.M., 2016. *Democracy for realists. Why elections do not produce responsive government*. Princeton: Princeton University Press.

Agger, R.E., Goldstein, M.N., and Pearl, S.A., 1961. Political cynicism: measurement and meaning. *The Journal of Politics*, 23 (3), 477–506.

Agnew, J.A. and Shin, M.E., 2020. *Mapping populism: taking politics to the people*. Lanham: Rowman & Littlefield.

Albertazzi, D., 2006. 'Back to our roots' or self-confessed manipulation? The uses of the past in the Lega Nord's positing of Padania. *National Identities*, 8 (1), 21–39.

Albertazzi, D., 2016. Going, going,... not quite gone yet? 'Bossi's Lega' and the survival of the mass party. *Contemporary Italian Politics*, 8 (2), 115–130.

Albertazzi, D., Brook, C., Ross, C., and Rothenberg, N., eds., 2009. *Resisting the tide: cultures of opposition under Berlusconi (2001-06)*. New York; London: Continuum.

Albertazzi, D., Giovannini, A., and Seddone, A., 2018. 'No regionalism please, we are Leghisti !' The transformation of the Italian Lega Nord under the leadership of Matteo Salvini. *Regional & Federal Studies*, 28 (5), 645–671.

Albertazzi, D. and McDonnell, D., 2005. The Lega Nord in the second Berlusconi government: in a league of its own. *West European Politics*, 28 (5), 952–972.

Albertazzi, D. and McDonnell, D., 2015. *Populists in power*. Abingdon: Routledge.

Albertazzi, D., McDonnell, D., and Newell, J.L., 2011. Di lotta e di governo: the Lega Nord and Rifondazione Comunista in office. *Party Politics*, 17 (4), 471–487.

Albertazzi, D. and Vampa, D., 2021. *Populism in Europe. Lessons from Umberto Bossi's Northern League*. Manchester: Manchester University Press.

Aldrin, P., 2003. S'accommoder du politique. Economie et pratiques de l'information politique. *Politix*, 16 (64), 177–203.

Aldrin, P., 2010. The invention of European public opinion: intellectual and political genesis of the Eurobarometer (1950-1973). *Politix*, 89 (1), 79–101.

Aldrin, P., 2020. Des petits actionnaires du système. *Actes de la recherche en sciences sociales*, 232–233 (2), 50–69.

Aldrin, P. and de Lassalle, M., 2016. Ce que faire parler de politique veut dire: Remarques sur la relation d'entretien et le parler politique à partir d'une enquête sur le rapport ordinaire à l'Europe. *In*: F. Buton, P. Lehingue, N. Mariot, and S. Rozier, eds. *L'Ordinaire du Politique: Enquêtes sur les rapports profanes au politique*. Villeneuve d'Ascq: Presses universitaires du septentrion, 297–319.

Algostino, A., 2011. *Democrazia, rappresentanza, partecipazione: il caso del movimento No Tav*. Napoli: Jovene.

Allegretti, G., Bassoli, M., and Colavolpe, G., 2021. On the verge of institutionalisation? Participatory budgeting evidence in five Italian regions. *Financial Journal*, 13 (2), 25–45.

Allum, P., 1973. *Politics and society in postwar Naples*. Cambridge: University press.

Anastasìa, S. and Anselmi, M., 2020. Penal populism in the multi-populist context of Italy. *In*: P. Blokker and M. Anselmi, eds. *Multiple populisms: Italy as democracy's mirror*. London; New York: Routledge, 164–178.

Andrews, G., 2006. The Italian general election of 2006. *Representation*, 42 (3), 253–260.

Bächtiger, A., Dryzek, J.S., Mansbridge, J.J., and Warren, E.M., eds., 2018. *The Oxford handbook of deliberative democracy*. Oxford: Oxford University Press.

Baldini, G., 2002. The direct election of mayors. An assessment of the institutional reform following the Italian municipal elections of 2001. *Journal of Modern Italian Studies*, 7 (3), 364–379.

Baldini, G., 2011. The different trajectories of Italian electoral reforms. *West European Politics*, 34 (3), 644–663.

Baldini, G., 2013. Don't count your chickens before they're hatched: the 2013 Italian parliamentary and presidential elections. *South European Society and Politics*, 18 (4), 473–497.

Banack, C., 2021. Ethnography and political opinion: identity, alienation and anti-establishmentarianism in rural Alberta. *Canadian Journal of Political Science*, 54 (1), 1–22.

Barbera, A. and Morrone, A., 2003. *La Repubblica dei referendum*. Bologna: il Mulino.

Bardi, L. and Morlino, L., 1992. Italy. *In*: S.R. Katz and P. Mair, eds. *Party organizations: a data handbook on party organizations in western democracies, 1960–90*. London: Sage, 458–618.

Bardi, L. and Morlino, L., 1994. Italy: tracing the roots of the great transformation. *In*: S.R. Katz and P. Mair, eds. *How parties organize: change and adaptation in party organizations in western democracies*. London: Sage, 242–277.

Barisione, M., 2007. L'orientamento al leader: forme, effetti, dinamiche. *In*: M. Maraffi, ed. *Gli italiani e la politica*. Bologna: il Mulino, 157–186.

Barr, R.R., 2009. Populists, outsiders and anti-establishment politics. *Party Politics*, 15 (1), 29–48.

Barraclough, R., 1998. Umberto Bossi: charisma, personality and leadership. *Modern Italy*, 3 (2), 263–269.

Barrault-Stella, L., Gaïti, B., and Lehingue, P., eds., 2019. *La politique désenchantée? Perspectives sociologiques autour des travaux de Daniel Gaxie*. Rennes: Presses universitaires de Rennes.

Bartolini, S. and Mair, P., 2002. Challenges to contemporary political parties. *In*: L. Diamond and R. Gunther, eds. *Political parties and democracy*. Baltimora; London: Johns Hopkins University Press, 327–343.

Bassoli, M., 2012. Participatory budgeting in Italy: an analysis of (almost democratic) participatory governance arrangements. *International Journal of Urban & Regional Research*, 36 (6), 1183–1203.

Beck, U., 1986. *Risikogesellschaft: auf dem Weg in eine andere Moderne.* Frankfurt am Main: Suhrkamp.

Beck, U., 2000. Figli della libertà: contro il lamento sulla caduta dei valori. *Rassegna italiana di sociologia,* XLI, 3–27.

Bedock, C., 2017. *Reforming democracy. Institutional engineering in Western Europe.* Oxford: Oxford University Press.

Bedock, C., 2020. Citizens' contrasting aspirations about their political system: entrustment, participation, identification and control. *Frontiers in Political Science,* 2, 1–15.

Bedock, C. and Pilet, J.-B., 2021. Who supports citizens selected by lot to be the main policymakers? A study of French citizens. *Government and Opposition,* 56 (3), 485–504.

Bélanger, É., 2004. Antipartyism and third-party vote choice. A comparison of Canada, Britain, and Australia. *Comparative Political Studies,* 37 (9), 1054–1078.

Bellucci, P. and Segatti, P., eds., 2010. *Votare in Italia: 1968-2008. Dall'appartenenza alla scelta.* Bologna: il Mulino.

Belohradsky, V., 1999. Il conflitto presidente. Sistema dei partiti nel consolidamento della democrazia céca. *Studi politici,* 3, 71–92.

Benoit, W.L., 1997. Image repair discourse and crisis communication. *Public Relation Review,* 23 (2), 177–186.

Berger, S., 1979. Politics and antipolitics in Western Europe in the seventies. *Daedalus,* 108, 27–50.

Bergman, M.E., 2019. Rejecting constitutional reform in the 2016 Italian referendum: analysing the effects of perceived discontent, incumbent performance and referendum-specific factors. *Contemporary Italian Politics,* 11 (2), 177–191.

Bergman, M.E. and Passarelli, G., 2021. Conflicting messages of electoral protest: the role of systemic and elite discontent in the Italian 2016 constitutional referendum. *Politics,* (Early view: https://doi.org/10.1177%2F 0263395720974975).

Bernardi, F., Chakhaia, L., and Leopold, L., 2017. 'Sing me a song with social significance': the (mis)use of statistical significance testing in European Sociological Research. *European Sociological Review,* 33 (1), 1–15.

Berta, G., ed., 2008. *La questione settentrionale: economia e società in trasformazione.* Milano: Feltrinelli.

Bertsou, E., 2019a. Rethinking political distrust. *European Political Science Review,* 11 (2), 213–230.

Bertsou, E., 2019b. Political distrust and its discontents: exploring the meaning, expression and significance of political distrust. *Societies,* 9 (4), 72.

Bertsou, E., 2022. Bring in the experts? Citizen preferences for independent experts in political decision-making processes. *European Journal of Political Research,* 61 (1), 255–267.

Bertsou, E. and Caramani, D., eds., 2020a. *The technocratic challenge to democracy.* Abingdon: Routledge.

Bertsou, E. and Caramani, D., 2020b. People haven't had enough of experts: technocratic attitudes among citizens in nine European democracies. *American Journal of Political Science,* (Early view: https://doi.org/10.1111/ajps.12554).

Bertsou, E. and Caramani, D., 2020c. Measuring technocracy. *In*: E. Bertsou and D. Caramani, eds. *The technocratic challenge to democracy.* Abingdon: Routledge, 91–109.

Bhatti, Y., Hansen, K.M., and Leth Olsen, A., 2013. Political hypocrisy: the effect of political scandals on candidate evaluations. *Acta Politica*, 48 (4), 408–428.

Biancalana, C., 2017a. Dalla protesta al potere: il Movimento 5 stelle a Torino. *Polis*, 31, 329–356.

Biancalana, C., 2017b. Désintermédiation et populisme. L'emploi d'internet par le Mouvement 5 Étoiles. *Studia Politica. Romanian Political Science Review*, 17 (4), 541–559.

Biancalana, C., 2020. From social movements to institutionalization: the Five-star Movement and the high-speed train line in Val di Susa. *Contemporary Italian Politics*, 12 (2), 155–168.

Bickerton, C.J. and Accetti, C.I., 2018. 'Techno-populism' as a new party family: the case of the Five Star Movement and Podemos. *Contemporary Italian Politics*, 10 (2), 132–150.

Biorcio, R., 2002. Italy. *Environmental Politics*, 11 (1), 39–62.

Biorcio, R., 2007. Democrazia e populismo nella seconda repubblica. *In*: M. Maraffi, ed. *Gli italiani e la politica*. Bologna: il Mulino, 187–207.

Biorcio, R., 2010. Gli antecedenti politici della scelta di voto: l'identificazione di partito e l'autocollocazione sinistra-destra. *In*: P. Bellucci and P. Segatti, eds. *Votare in Italia: 1968-2008. Dall'appartenenza alla scelta*. Bologna: il Mulino, 187–211.

Biorcio, R., 2014. The reasons for the success and transformations of the 5 Star Movement. *Contemporary Italian Politics*, 6 (1), 37–53.

Biorcio, R., ed., 2015. *Gli attivisti del Movimento 5 stelle. Dal web al territorio*. Milano: Franco Angeli.

Biorcio, R., 2017. The Northern League. *In*: O. Mazzoleni and S. Mueller, eds. *Regionalist parties in Western Europe: dimensions of success*. Abingdon: Routledge, 135–151.

Biorcio, R. and Natale, P., 2013. *Politica a 5 stelle: idee, storia e strategie del Movimento di Grillo*. Milano: Feltrinelli.

Biorcio, R. and Natale, P., 2018. *Il movimento 5 stelle: dalla protesta al governo*. Milano-Udine: Mimesis.

Biorcio, R. and Sampugnaro, R., 2019. Introduction: the Five-star Movement from the street to local and national institutions. *Contemporary Italian Politics*, 11 (1), 5–14.

Bobba, G., 2019. Social media populism: features and 'likeability' of Lega Nord communication on Facebook. *European Political Science*, 18 (1), 11–23.

Bobbio, L., 2002. Come smaltire i rifiuti. Un esperimento di democrazia deliberativa. *Stato e mercato*, (1), 101–141.

Bobbio, L., 2010. Il dibattito pubblico sulle grandi opere. Il caso dell'autostrada di Genova. *Rivista Italiana di Politiche Pubbliche*, (1), 119–146.

Bogaards, M., 2005. The Italian First Republic: 'Degenerated Consociationalism' in a Polarised Party System. *West European Politics*, 28 (3), 503–520.

Borchert, J. and Zeiss, J., eds., 2003. *The political class in advanced democracies. A comparative handbook*. Oxford: Oxford University Press.

Bordandini, P., Di Virgilio, A., and Raniolo, F., 2008. The birth of a party: the case of the Italian Partito Democratico. *South European Society and Politics*, 13 (3), 303–324.

Bordignon, F., 2014a. Matteo Renzi: A 'Leftist Berlusconi' for the Italian Democratic Party? *South European Society and Politics*, 19 (1), 1–23.

Bordignon, F., 2014b. Dopo Silvio, Matteo: un nuovo ciclo personale? La democrazia italiana tra berlusconismo e renzismo. *Comunicazione politica*, (3), 437–461.

Bordignon, F. and Ceccarini, L., 2013. Five Stars and a Cricket. Beppe Grillo Shakes Italian politics. *South European Society and Politics*, 18 (4), 427–449.

Bordignon, F. and Ceccarini, L., 2014. Protest and project, leader and party: normalisation of the Five Star Movement. *Contemporary Italian Politics*, 6 (1), 54–72.

Bordignon, F. and Ceccarini, L., 2015. The Five-Star Movement: a hybrid actor in the net of state institutions. *Journal of Modern Italian Studies*, 20 (4), 454–473.

Bordignon, F. and Ceccarini, L., 2019. Five Stars, Five Years, Five (Broken) Taboos. *In*: L. Ceccarini and J.L. Newell, eds. *The Italian general election of 2018: Italy in uncharted territory*. Cham: Palgrave Macmillan, 139–163.

Borghetto, E., 2018. Challenger parties in Parliament: the case of the Italian Five Star Movement. *Italian Political Science*, 13 (3), 19–32.

Borriello, A. and Mazzolini, S., 2019. European populism(s) as a counter-hegemonic discourse? The rise of Podemos and M5S in the wake of the crisis. *In*: J. Zienkowski and R. Breeze, eds. *Imagining the peoples of Europe. Populist discourses across the political spectrum*. Amsterdam-Philadelphia: John Benjamins Publishing Company, 73–100.

Boswell, J., Corbett, J., Dommett, K., Jennings, W., Flinders, M., Rhodes, R.A.W., and Wood, M., 2019. State of the field: what can political ethnography tell us about anti-politics and democratic disaffection? *European Journal of Political Research*, 58 (1), 56–71.

Brancaccio, L. and Fruncillo, D., 2019. Il populismo di sinistra: il Movimento 5 Stelle e il Movimento Arancione a Napoli. *Meridiana*, 96, 129–158.

Brancaccio, L., Mete, V., Scaglione, A., and Tuorto, D., 2021. La Lega al Sud. Il difficile cammino di un insediamento annunciato. *SocietàMutamentoPolitica*, 12 (23), 227–239.

Briquet, J.-L., 2019. Le Movimento 5 Stelle en Italie: une entreprise de mobilisation antipolitique. *In*: A. Dieckhoff, C. Jaffrelot, and É. Massicard, eds. *Populismes au pouvoir*. Paris: SciencesPo les presses, 49–60.

Brook, C., 2009. The cinema of resistance: Nanni Moretti's *Il caimano* and the Italian film industry. *In*: D. Albertazzi, C. Brook, C. Ross, and N. Rothenberg, eds. *Resisting the tide: cultures of opposition under Berlusconi (2001-06)*. New York; London: Continuum, 110–123.

Brunazzo, M., 2017. Istituzionalizzare la partecipazione? Le leggi sulla partecipazione in Italia. *Le istituzioni del federalismo*, 38 (3), 837–864.

Brusattin, L., 2007. Late anti-communism as a shortcut: the success of Forza Italia in the 1994 Italian election. *South European Society and Politics*, 12 (4), 481–499.

Bull, M.J., 2017. Renzi removed: the 2016 Italian constitutional referendum and its outcome. *Italian Politics*, 32, 131–153.

Bull, M.J. and Newell, J.L., 1995. Italy changes course? The 1994 elections and the victory of the right. *Parliamentary Affairs*, 48 (1), 72–100.

Bull, M.J. and Rhodes, M., eds., 1997. *Crisis and transition in Italian politics*. London: Frank Cass.

Burnham, P., 2001. New labour and the politics of depoliticisation. *British Journal of Politics & International Relations*, 3 (2), 127–149.

Burns, J.M., 1978. *Leadership*. New York: Harper & Row.

Caciagli, M., 2004. Contro la partitocrazia: dalla critica alla retorica. *In:* S. Rogari, ed. *Istituzioni e poteri nell'Italia contemporanea: atti del Convegno di studi in memoria di Giuseppe Maranini a cento anni dalla nascita.* Firenze: Centro editoriale toscano, 243–256.

Caciagli, M., Cazzola, F., Morlino, L., and Passigli, S., eds., 1994. *L'Italia fra crisi e transizione.* Roma-Bari: Laterza.

Cafagna, L., 1993. *La grande slavina: l'Italia verso la crisi della democrazia.* Venezia: Marsilio.

Calise, M., 1994. The Italian particracy: beyond president and parliament. *Political Science Quarterly,* 109 (3), 441–460.

Calise, M., 2010. *Il partito personale: i due corpi del leader.* Roma-Bari: Laterza.

Calise, M., 2015. The personal party: an analytical framework. *Italian Political Science Review,* 45 (3), 301–315.

Campus, D., 2010. *Antipolitics in power: populist language as a tool for government.* Cresskill: Hampton Press.

Campus, D., 2016. *Lo stile del leader. Decidere e comunicare nelle democrazie contemporanee.* Bologna: il Mulino.

Capozzi, E., 2009. *Partitocrazia: il regime italiano e i suoi critici.* Napoli: Guida.

Capozzi, E., 2020. Antipartito. Opposition to the political class and the party system in 1970's Italy. *Journal of Modern Italian Studies,* 25 (1), 10–22.

Caprara, G.V. and Vecchione, M., 2016. *Personalizing politics and realizing democracy.* New York: Oxford University Press.

Carrozza, C., 2011. The June referendums: a partial victory. *Italian Politics,* 27, 244–261.

Cartocci, R., 1991. Localismo e protesta politica. *Rivista Italiana di Scienza Politica,* 21 (3), 551–581.

Caruso, L. and De Blasio, E., 2021. From the streets to the web: communication and democratic participation in the case of the 'Sardines'. *Contemporary Italian Politics,* 13 (2), 242–258.

Castanho Silva, B., Jungkunz, S., Helbling, M., and Littvay, L., 2020. An empirical comparison of seven populist attitudes scales. *Political Research Quarterly,* 73 (2), 409–424.

Catellani, P. and Milesi, P., 2010. I valori e la scelta di voto. *In:* P. Bellucci and P. Segatti, eds. *Votare in Italia: 1968-2008. Dall'appartenenza alla scelta.* Bologna: il Mulino, 213–245.

Caterina, E., 2016. Le espulsioni dal MoVimento 5 stelle davanti al giudice civile. *Quaderni costituzionali,* XXXVI, (4), 793–795.

Ceccarini, L. and Bordignon, F., 2016. The five stars continue to shine: the consolidation of Grillo's 'movement party' in Italy. *Contemporary Italian Politics,* 8 (2), 131–159.

Ceccarini, L. and Bordignon, F., 2017. Referendum on Renzi: the 2016 vote on the Italian constitutional revision. *South European Society and Politics,* 22 (3), 281–302.

Ceccarini, L., Diamanti, I., and Lazar, M., 2011. The end of an era: the crumbling of the Italian Party System. *Italian Politics,* 27, 57–77.

Ceccarini, L. and Newell, J.L., 2019. Introduction: the paradoxical election. *In:* L. Ceccarini and J.L. Newell, eds. *The Italian General Election of 2018: Italy in uncharted territory.* Cham: Palgrave Macmillan, 1–17.

Cellini, E., Freschi, A.C., and Mete, V., 2010. Chi delibera? Alla ricerca del significato politico di un'esperienza partecipativa-deliberativa. *Rivista Italiana di Scienza Politica*, XL (1), 113–144.

Cento Bull, A., 2012. When the magic wears off: Bossi loses his grip and the league its appeal. *Italian Politics*, 28, 95–111.

Cento Bull, A., 2016. The role of memory in populist discourse: the case of the Italian Second Republic. *Patterns of Prejudice*, 50 (3), 213–231.

Cento Bull, A. and Gilbert, M., 2001. *The Lega Nord and the Northern Question in Italian Politics*. New York: Palgrave.

Centorrino, M. and Rizzo, P., 2019. La costruzione dell'influenza nel cyberspazio: la seconda vita della Lega (Nord). *Humanities*, 8 (1), 19–37.

Ceri, P., 2009. Challenging from the Grass Roots: the Girotondi and the No Global Movement. *In*: D. Albertazzi, C. Brook, C. Ross, and N. Rothenberg, eds. *Resisting the tide: cultures of opposition under Berlusconi (2001-06)*. New York; London: Continuum, 83–93.

Ceri, P. and Veltri, F., 2017. *Il movimento nella rete: storia e struttura del Movimento 5 Stelle*. Torino: Rosenberg & Sellier.

Cerruto, M. and Facello, C., 2014. Il cambiamento dei partiti tradizionali al tempo dell'antipolitica. *Quaderni di Sociologia*, 65, 75–96.

Chari, R.S., Iltanen, S., and Kritzinger, S., 2004. Examining and Explaining the Northern League's 'U-Turn' from Europe. *Government and Opposition*, 39 (3), 423–450.

Chiapponi, F., 2017. *Democrazia, populismo, leadership: il Movimento 5 stelle*. Novi Ligure: Epoké.

Chiaramonte, A., De Sio, L., and Emanuele, V., 2020. Salvini's success and the collapse of the Five-Star Movement: The European elections of 2019. *Contemporary Italian Politics*, 12 (2), 140–154.

Chiaramonte, A. and Paparo, A., 2019. Volatile voters and a volatile party system: the results. *In*: L. Ceccarini and J.L. Newell, eds. *The Italian General Election of 2018: Italy in uncharted territory*. Cham: Palgrave Macmillan, 247–270.

Chiarini, R., 2004. Il disagio del Nord, l'anti-politica e la questione settentrionale. *In*: S. Colarizi, ed. *Gli anni Ottanta come storia*. Soveria Mannelli: Rubbettino, 231–265.

Chubb, J., 1982. *Patronage, power and poverty in Southern Italy: a tale of two cities*. Cambridge: Cambridge University Press.

Ciaglia, A. and Mazzoni, M., 2015. Political intimization as a key to bypassing traditional leadership selection procedures: The case of Matteo Renzi. *European Journal of Cultural Studies*, 18 (6), 656–671.

Citrin, J. and Stoker, L., 2018. Political trust in a cynical age. *Annual Review of Political Science*, 21, 49–70.

Claeys, G., 1989. *Citizens and saints. Politics and anti-politics in early British socialism*. Cambridge: Cambridge University Press.

Clarke, N., Jennings, W., Moss, J., and Stoker, G., 2018. *The good politician. Folk theories, political interaction, and the rise of anti-politics*. Cambridge: Cambridge University Press.

Clarke, N., Jennings, W., Moss, J., and Stoker, G., 2021. Voter decision-making in a context of low political trust: the 2016 UK EU Membership Referendum. *Political Studies*, (Early view: https://doi.org/10.1177/00323217211003419).

Cocco, M., 2018a. *Qualunquismo: una storia politica e culturale dell'uomo qualunque.* Firenze: Le Monnier.

Cocco, M., 2018b. Who's John Doe? The roots of 'Qualunquismo'and the populistic protest of the middle class in postwar-Italy. *In*: C. Chini and S. Moroni, eds. *Populism. A historioghaphic category.* Newcastle upon Tyne: Cambridge Scholars, 79–96.

Colarizi, S., 2005. La crisi del consenso e il tramonto della prima Repubblica. *In*: S. Setta, ed. *Italiani contro gli uomini politici: il Qualunquismo.* Napoli: Edizioni Scientifiche Italiane, 133–165.

Colarizi, S. and Panvini, G., 2017. From enemy to opponent: the politics of delegitimation in the Italian Christian Democratic Party (1945–1992). *Journal of Modern Italian Studies*, 22 (1), 57–70.

Conti, N. and Memoli, V., 2015. The emergence of a new party in the Italian Party System: rise and fortunes of the Five Star Movement. *West European Politics*, 38 (3), 516–534.

Corbett, J., 2016. Diagnosing the problem of anti-politicians: a review and an agenda. *Political Studies Review*, 14 (4), 534–543.

Corbetta, P., 2002. Le generazioni politiche. *In*: M. Caciagli and P. Corbetta, eds. *Le ragioni dell'elettore. Perché ha vinto il centro-destra nelle elezioni italiane del 2001.* Bologna: il Mulino, 79–111.

Corbetta, P., 2008. Chronicle of a Victory Foretold: the 13–14 April general elections. *Italian Politics*, 24, 59–80.

Corbetta, P., 2013. Conclusioni. Un web-populismo dal destino incerto. *In*: P. Corbetta and E. Gualmini, eds. *Il partito di Grillo.* Bologna: il Mulino, 197–214.

Corbetta, P., ed., 2017. *M5s. Come cambia il partito di Grillo.* Bologna: il Mulino.

Corbetta P. and Gualmini E., 2013, eds. *Il partito di Grillo.* Bologna: il Mulino

Corbetta, P. and Parisi, A., 1995. The referendum on electoral law for the Senate: another momentous April. *In*: C. Mershon and G. Pasquino, eds. *Italian Politics: ending the First Republic.* Westview Press: Boulder, 75–92.

Corbetta, P. and Vignati, R., 2013a. The primaries of the centre left: only a temporary success? *Contemporary Italian Politics*, 5 (1), 82–96.

Corbetta, P. and Vignati, R., 2013b. Beppe Grillo's first defeat? The May 2013 municipal elections in Italy. *South European Society and Politics*, 18 (4), 499–521.

Corduwener, P., 2017. Challenging parties and anti-fascism in the name of democracy: the Fronte dell'Uomo Qualunque and its impact on Italy's Republic. *Contemporary European History*, 26 (1), 69–84.

Coretti, L. and Pica, D., 2015. The Purple Movement: how Facebook's design undermined the anti-Berlusconi protest in Italy. *Journal of Italian Cinema & Media Studies*, 3 (3), 305–318.

Cosenza, G., 2014. Grillo's communication style: from swear words to body language. *Contemporary Italian Politics*, 6 (1), 89–101.

Costabile, A., 1991. *Il fronte dell'uomo qualunque e la lega lombarda: movimenti antipartito e crisi di legittimazione nel sistema politico italiano.* Messina: Armando Siciliano.

Costabile, A., 2019. L'Uomo Qualunque e il Movimento 5 Stelle: dal qualunquismo al populismo. *Meridiana*, 96, 183–206.

Cotta, M., 2015. Partitocracy: parties and their Critics in Italian Political Life. *In*: E. Jones and G. Pasquino, eds. *The Oxford Handbook of Italian Politics.* Oxford: Oxford University Press, 41–52.

Cotta, M., 2020. The anti-establishment parties at the helm: from great hopes to failure and a limited resurrection. *Contemporary Italian Politics*, 12 (2), 126–139.

Cramer, K.J., 2016. *The politics of resentment: rural consciousness in Wisconsin and the rise of Scott Walker.* Chicago; London: University of Chicago Press.

Crick, B., 1962. *In defence of politics.* London: Weidenfeld and Nicolson.

Croci, O., 2001. Language and politics in Italy: from Moro to Berlusconi. *Journal of Modern Italian Studies*, 6 (3), 348–370.

Cross, W.P., Rahaṭ, G., Kenig, O., and Pruysers, S., 2016. *The promise and challenge of party primary elections: a comparative perspective.* Montreal; Chicago: McGill-Queen's University Press.

Cucchi, S. and Cavazza, N., 2017. Scandali politici e opinione pubblica: Impatto e strategie di ripristino della reputazione. *Giornale italiano di psicologia*, XLIV (3), 727–758.

Curini, L., 2018. *Corruption, ideology, and populism: the rise of valence political campaigning.* Cham: Palgrave Macmillan.

Dal Lago, A., 2017. *Populismo digitale: la crisi, la rete e la nuova Destra.* Milano: Raffaello Cortina.

D'Alimonte, R. and De Sio, L., 2010. Il voto. Perché ha rivinto il centrodestra. *In*: R. D'Alimonte and A. Chiaramonte, eds. *Proporzionale se vi pare. Le elezioni politiche del 2008.* Bologna: il Mulino, 75–105.

Dalle Mulle, E., 2018. *The nationalism of the rich discourses and strategies of separatist parties in Catalonia, Flanders, Northern Italy and Scotland.* Abingdon: Routledge.

Dalton, R.J., 1984. Cognitive mobilization and partisan dealignment in advanced industrial democracies. *The Journal of Politics*, 46 (1), 264–284.

Dalton, R.J., 2020. *Citizen politics: public opinion and political parties in advanced industrial democracies.* Los Angeles: Sage, CQ Press.

Davies, J.A., 2015. A tale of two Italys? The 'Southern Question' past and present. *In*: E. Jones and G. Pasquino, eds. *The Oxford Handbook of Italian Politics.* Oxford: Oxford University Press, 53–67.

De Blasio, E., 2018. *Il governo online: nuove frontiere della politica.* Roma: Carocci.

De Falco, C.C. and Sabatino, P., 2019. Il voto del Movimento 5 Stelle nelle aree marginali. Le elezioni del 2018 a Napoli. *Meridiana*, 96, 105–127.

De Giorgi, E. and Marangoni, F., 2015. Government laws and the opposition parties' behaviour in parliament. *Acta Politica*, 50 (1), 64–81.

De Luca, M., 2018. The Italian style of intra-party democracy. A twenty-year-long journey. *In*: R.G. Boatright, ed. *Routledge handbook of primary elections.* London and New York: Routledge, 399–423.

De Luca, M. and Rombi, S., 2016. The regional primary elections in Italy: a general overview. *Contemporary Italian Politics*, 8 (1), 24–41.

De Petris, A. and Poguntke, T., eds., 2015. *Anti-party parties in Germany and Italy: protest movements and parliamentary democracy.* Roma: Luiss University Press.

De Sio, L. and Paparo, A., 2014. Elettori alla deriva? I flussi di voto tra 2008 e 2013. *In*: L. De Sio and A. Chiaramonte, eds. *Terremoto elettorale. Le elezioni politiche del 2013.* Bologna: il Mulino, 129–152.

De Vries, C.E. and Hobolt, S.B., 2020. *Political entrepreneurs. The Rise of Challenger Parties in Europe.* Princeton: Princeton University Press.

Dean, J., 2017. Politicising fandom. *British Journal of Politics & International Relations*, 19 (2), 408–424.

Debre, M., 1957. *Ces princes qui nous gouvernent...* Paris: Plon.

della Porta, D., 2007. *The global justice movement: cross-national and transnational perspectives*. Boulder: Paradigm Publishers.

della Porta, D., 2013. *Can democracy be saved? Participation, deliberation and social movements*. Cambridge: Polity Press.

della Porta, D. and Doerr, N., 2018. Deliberation in protests and social movements. *In*: A. Bächtiger, J.S. Dryzek, J.J. Mansbridge, and E.M. Warren, eds. *The Oxford handbook of deliberative democracy*. Oxford: Oxford University Press, 391–406.

della Porta, D., Fernández, J., Kouki, H., and Mosca, L., eds., 2017. *Movement parties against austerity*. Cambridge: Polity.

della Porta, D. and Piazza, G., 2008. *Voices of the valley, voices of the straits: how protest creates communities*. New York: Berghahn Books.

della Porta, D. and Rucht, D., eds., 2013. *Meeting democracy: power and deliberation in global justice movements*. Cambridge: Cambridge University Press.

della Porta, D. and Tarrow, S.G., 2004. *Transnational protest and global activism*. Lanham: Rowman & Littlefield.

della Porta, D. and Vannucci, A., 1999. *Corrupt exchanges: actors, resources, and mechanisms of political corruption*. Hawthorne: Aldine de Gruyter.

Deschouwer, K., ed., 2008. *New parties in government: in power for the first time*. London: Routledge.

Di Gregorio, L., 2021. *Demopathy and the democratic malaise: symptoms, diagnosis and therapy*. Cheltenham: Edward Elgar Publishing.

Di Maggio, M. and Perrone, M., 2019. The political culture of the Movimento Cinque Stelle, from foundation to the reins of government. *Journal of Modern Italian Studies*, 24 (3), 468–482.

Di Ruzza, A., 2020. Revenu de citoyenneté: la montagne accouche d'une souris. *Chronique Internationale de l'IRES*, 169–170 (1), 41–51.

Diamanti, I., 1993. *La Lega. Geografia, storia e sociologia di un nuovo soggetto politico*. Roma: Donzelli.

Diamanti, I., 2003. *Bianco, rosso, verde... e azzurro. Mappe e colori dell'Italia politica*. Bologna: il Mulino.

Diani, M., 1996. Linking mobilization frames and political opportunities: insights from regional populism in Italy. *American Sociological Review*, 61 (6), 1053–1069.

Dieckhoff, A., Jaffrelot, C., and Massicard, É., eds., 2019. *Populismes au pouvoir*. Paris: SciencesPo les presses.

Dogan, M., ed., 2005. *Political mistrust and the discrediting of politicians*. Leiden; Boston: Brill.

Doherty, D., Dowling, C.M., and Miller, M.G., 2011. Are financial or moral scandals worse? It depends. *PS: Political Science & Politics*, 44 (4), 749–757.

Donolo, C., 2000. Il buon uso dell'antipolitica. I confini mobili del politico nel regime democratico. *Meridiana*, 38–39, 83–99.

Donovan, M., 1995. The politics of electoral reform in Italy. *International Political Science Review*, 16 (1), 47–64.

Dowding, K.M., 2020. *It's the government, stupid: how governments blame citizens for their own policies*. Bristol: Bristol University Press.

Dryzek, J.S., 2000. *Deliberative democracy and beyond: liberals, critics, contestations*. Oxford: Oxford University Press.

Eder, C., Mochmann, I.C., and Quandt, M., eds., 2015. *Political trust and disenchantment with politics: international perspectives*. Leiden; Boston: Brill.

Eliasoph, N., 1998. *Avoiding politics: how Americans produce apathy in everyday life.* Cambridge: Cambridge UniversityPress.

Elstub, S. and Escobar, O., 2019. Defining and typologising democratic innovations. *In*: S. Elstub and O. Escobar, eds. *Handbook of democratic innovation and governance.* London: Edward Elgar Publishing, 11–31.

Fabbri, M. and Diani, M., 2015. Social movement campaigns from global justice activism to Movimento cinque stelle. *In*: E.G. Parini, G.A. Veltri, and A. Mammone, eds. *The Routledge handbook of contemporary Italy: history, politics, society.* London: Routledge, 225–236.

Fabbrini, S., 1998. From the Prodi Government to the D'Alema Government: continuity or discontinuity? *Italian Politics*, 14, 121–138.

Fabbrini, S. and Lazar, M., 2015. Renzi's Leadership between Party and Government. *Italian Politics*, 31, 40–58.

Farinelli, A. and Massetti, E., 2015. Inexperienced, leftists, and grassroots democrats: a profile of the Five Star Movement's MPs. *Contemporary Italian Politics*, 7 (3), 213–231.

Farrell, D.M. and McAllister, I., 2006. Voter satisfaction and electoral systems: does preferential voting in candidate-centred systems make a difference? *European Journal of Political Research*, 45 (5), 723–749.

Farrell, D.M., McAllister, I., and Studlar, D.T., 1998. Sex, money and politics: sleaze and the conservative party in the 1997 election. *British Elections & Parties Review*, 8 (1), 80–94.

Fasano, L.M. and Seddone, A., 2016. Selecting the leader, Italian style. *Contemporary Italian Politics*, 8 (1), 83–102.

Fawcett, P. and Corbett, J., 2018. Politicians, professionalization and anti-politics: why we want leaders who act like professionals but are paid like amateurs. *Policy Sciences*, 51 (4), 411–432.

Fawcett, P., Flinders, M., Hay, C., and Wood, M., 2017. Anti-politics, depoliticization, and governance. *In*: P. Fawcett, M. Flinders, C. Hay, and M. Wood, eds. *Anti-politics, depoliticization, and governance.* Oxford: Oxford University Press, 3–27.

Ferguson, J., 1990. *The anti-politics machine. 'Development', depoliticization, and bureaucratic power in Lesotho.* Cambridge: Cambridge University Press.

Fisher, W.F., 1997. Doing good? The politics and antipolitics of NGO practices. *Annual Review of Anthropology*, 26 (1), 439–464.

Fitzgerald, J., 2013. What does 'Political' mean to you? *Political Behavior*, 35 (3), 453–479.

Flinders, M., 2012a. *Defending politics: why democracy matters in the 21st century.* Oxford: Oxford University Press.

Flinders, M., 2012b. The demonisation of politicians: moral panics, folk devils and MPs' expenses. *Contemporary Politics*, 18 (1), 1–17.

Flinders, M., 2021. Democracy and the politics of coronavirus: trust, blame and understanding. *Parliamentary Affairs*, 74 (2), 483–502.

Flinders, M., Wood, M., and Corbett, J., 2019. Reconceptualising anti-politics. *In*: S. Elstub and O. Escobar, eds. *Handbook of democratic innovation and governance.* London: Edward Elgar Publishing, 148–160.

Floridia, A., 2006. Le primarie in Toscana: la nuova legge, la prima sperimentazione. *Quaderni dell'osservatorio elettorale*, 55, 91–132.

Floridia, A., 2012. *Democrazia deliberativa: teorie, processi e sistemi.* Roma: Carocci.

Floridia, A., 2017. *From participation to deliberation: a critical genealogy of deliberative democracy.* Colchester: ECPR Press.

Floridia, A., 2019. *Un partito sbagliato: democrazia e organizzazione nel Partito Democratico.* Roma: Castelvecchi.

Foot, J., 1996. The 'Left Opposition' and the crisis. Rifondazione Comunista and La Rete. *In*: S. Gundle and S. Parker, eds. *The New Italian Republic: from the fall of the Berlin Wall to Berlusconi.* London: Routledge, 173–188.

Frankland, E.G., Lucardie, P., and Rihoux, B., eds., 2008. *Green parties in transition. The end of grass-roots democracy?* Abingdon: Ashgate.

Freiman, C., 2021. *Why it's ok to ignore politics.* New York: Routledge.

Freschi, A.C. and Mete, V., 2009. The political meanings of institutional deliberative experiments. Findings on the Italian case. *Sociologica*, III (2–3), 1–55.

Freschi, A.C. and Mete, V., 2020. The electoral personalization of Italian mayors. A study of 25 years of direct election. *Italian Political Science Review*, 50 (2), 271–290.

Fusaro, C., 2005. La legge regionale toscana sulle primarie. *Le Regioni*, XXXIII (3), 441–458.

Fusaro, C., 2017. Yet another failed attempt to reform the Italian Constitution. *Italian Politics*, 32, 111–130.

Gallagher, M. and Marsh, M., eds., 1988. *Candidate selection in comparative perspective: the secret garden of politics.* London: Sage.

Galli, G., 1966. *Il bipartitismo imperfetto: comunisti e democristiani in Italia.* Bologna: il Mulino.

Galli, G. and Prandi, A., 1970. *Patterns of political participation in Italy.* New Haven; London: Yale University Press.

Gambarota, P., 2019. Uomo Qualunque: the transnational making of Italian postwar populism. *The Italianist*, 39 (1), 44–63.

Gangemi, G., 2008. *Italian antipolitics as a long run question: 'Bad civil societies' or 'bad elites'?* Giessen: Institut für Politikwiss.

García-Albacete, G. and Lorente, J., 2021. Has the great recession shaped a crisis generation of critical citizens? Evidence from Southern Europe. *South European Society and Politics*, (Early view: https://doi.org/10.1080/13608746.2021.1949672).

Garzia, D., 2011. The personalization of politics in Western democracies: causes and consequences on leader–follower relationships. *The Leadership Quarterly*, 22, 697–709.

Gastil, J. and Levine, P., eds., 2005. *The deliberative democracy handbook: strategies for effective civic engagement in the twenty-first century.* San Francisco: Jossey-Bass.

Gaxie, D., 1990. Au-delà des apparences… *Actes de la Recherche en Sciences Sociales*, 81 (1), 97–112.

Gaxie, D., 2001a. Vu du sens commun. *Espaces Temps*, 76 (1), 82–94.

Gaxie, D., 2001b. Les critiques profanes de la politique. Enchantements, désenchantements, réenchantements. *In*: J.-L. Briquet and P. Garaud, eds. *Juger la politique. Entreprises et entrepreneurs critiques de la politique.* Rennes: Presses universitaires de Rennes, 217–240.

Gaxie, D., 2001c. Sur l'humeur politique maussade des démocraties représentatives. *In*: O. Mazzoleni, ed. *La politica allo specchio.* Lugano: Casagrande, 109–136.

Gaxie, D., 2003. Une construction médiatique du spectacle politique? Réalité et limites de la contribution des médias au développement des perceptions négatives du politique. *In*: J. Lagroye, ed. *La politisation.* Paris: Belin, 325–356.

Gaxie, D., 2007. Les conceptions ordinaires de la démocratie. *In*: V. Champeil-Desplats and N. Ferre, eds. *Frontieres du droit, critique des droits: billets d'humeur en l'honneur de Daniele Lochak*. Paris: L.G.D.J, 177–181.

Gaxie, D., 2008. Le profanes en politique: réflexions sur les usages d'une analogie. *In*: T. Fromentin and S. Wojcik, eds. *Le profane en politique: Compétences et engagements du citoyen*. Paris: L'Harmattan, 289–301.

Geissel, B., 2012. Impacts of democratic innovations in Europe: findings and desiderata. *In*: B. Geissel and K. Newton, eds. *Evaluating democratic innovations: curing the democratic malaise?* London and New York: Routledge, 163–183.

Geissel, B. and Newton, K., eds., 2012. *Evaluating democratic innovations: curing the democratic malaise?* London and New York: Routledge.

Gerbaudo, P., 2019. *The digital party: political organisation and online democracy*. London: Pluto Press.

Giannetti, D., 2012. Mario Monti's technocratic government. *Italian Politics*, 28, 133–152.

Giannini, G., 2002. *La Folla. Seimila anni di lotta contro la tirannide*. [Original edition 1945]. Soveria Mannelli: Rubbettino.

Giddens, A., 1999. *Runaway world: how globalization is reshaping our lives*. New York: Routledge.

Giglioli, P.P., 1996. Political corruption and the media: the Tangentopoli affair. *International Social Science Journal*, 48 (149), 381–394.

Giglioli, P.P., 2001. Ritual degradation as public display: a televised corruption trial. *In*: L. Cheles and L. Sponza, eds. *The art of persuasion: political communication in Italy from 1945 to the 1990s*. Manchester: Manchester University Press, 298–311.

Gil, D.J., 2013. *Shakespeare's anti-politics: sovereign power and the life of the flesh*. Basingstoke: Palgrave Macmillan.

Gilbert, M., 1995. *The Italian revolution: the end of politics, Italian style?* Boulder: Westiew Press.

Ginsborg, P., 2004. *Silvio Berlusconi: television, power and patrimony*. London; New York: Verso.

Giugliano, F., 2020. Between bragging and reality: Italy's confusing place in a changing world order. *Contemporary Italian Politics*, 12 (2), 214–226.

Giuliani, M., 1997. Measures of consensual law-making: Italian "Consociativismo". *South European Society and Politics*, 2 (1), 66–96.

Giuliani, M., 2008. Patterns of consensual law-making in the Italian Parliament. *South European Society and Politics*, 13 (1), 61–85.

Gourgues, G., Mazeaud, A., Nez, H., Sainty, J., and Talpin, J., 2021. Les Français veulent-ils plus de démocratie? Analyse qualitative du rapport des citoyens à la politique. *Sociologie*, 12 (1), 1–19.

Grasso, A., 2019. *Storia critica della televisione italiana. 1980-1999*. Milano: Il Saggiatore.

Griffo, M., 2007. Sull'origine della parola 'partitocrazia'. *L'Acropoli*, VIII (4), 396–409.

Gualmini, E., 2013. Introduzione. Da movimento a partito. *In*: P. Corbetta and E. Gualmini, eds. *Il partito di Grillo*. Bologna: il Mulino, 7–28.

Guidi, M., 2014. The Democratic Party of Matteo Renzi. *Italian Politics*, 30, 51–66.

Guidorossi, G., 1984. *Gli italiani e la politica: valori, opinioni, atteggiamenti dal dopoguerra a oggi*. Milano: Franco Angeli.

Gundle, S., 2009. Berlusconi, sex, and the avoidance of a media scandal. *Italian Politics*, 25, 59–75.

Gundle, S. and O'Sullivan, N., 1996. The mass media and the political crisis. *In*: S. Gundle and S. Parker, eds. *The New Italian Republic: from the fall of the Berlin Wall to Berlusconi*. London: Routledge, 206–220.

Gurr, T.R., 1970. *Why men rebel*. Princeton: Princeton University Press.

Gusso, M., 1982. *Il Partito radicale: organizzazione e leadership*. Padova: CLEUP.

Habermas, J., 1998. *Die postnationale Konstellation: Politische Essays*. Frankfurt am Main: Suhrkamp.

Hallin, D.C. and Mancini, P., 2004. *Comparing media systems: three models of media and politics*. New York: Cambridge University Press.

Hamdaoui, S., 2021. A "stylistic anti-populism": an analysis of the Sardine movement's opposition to Matteo Salvini in Italy. *Social Movement Studies*, (Early view: https://doi.org/10.1080/14742837.2021.1899910).

Harmel, R. and Janda, K., 1994. An integrated theory of party goals and party change. *Journal of Theoretical Politics*, 6 (3), 259–287.

Hartleb, F., 2013. Anti-elitist cyber parties? Understanding the future of European political parties. *Journal of Public Affairs*, 13 (4), 355–369.

Hartleb, F., 2015. Here to stay: anti-establishment parties in Europe. *European View*, 14 (1), 39–49.

Hartz-Karp, J. and Briand, M.K., 2009. Institutionalizing deliberative democracy. *Journal of Public Affairs*, 9 (2), 125–141.

Hatier, C., 2012. 'Them' and 'us': demonising politicians by moral double standards. *Contemporary Politics*, 18 (4), 467–480.

Hay, C., 2007. *Why we hate politics*. Cambridge: Polity Press.

Hibbing, J.R. and Theiss-Morse, E., 2002. *Stealth democracy. Americans' beliefs about how government should work*. Cambridge: Cambridge University Press.

Hidalgo Tenorio, E., Benitez-Castro, M.A., and De Cesare, F., eds., 2019. *Populist discourse. Critical approaches to contemporary politics*. London: Routledge.

Hobsbawm, E. and Ranger, T., eds., 1983. *The invention of tradition*. Cambridge: Cambridge University Press.

Hoem, J.M., 2008. The reporting of statistical significance in scientific journals: a reflexion. *Demographic Research*, 18 (15), 437–442.

Holmberg, S. and Oscarsson, H., 2020. Party identification: down but not out. *In*: *Research handbook on political partisanship*. Cheltenham: Edward Elgar Publishing, 14–29.

Hopkin, J., 2005. From Federation to Union, from Parties to Primaries: The Search for Unity in the Center-Left. *Italian Politics*, 21, 67–84.

Hopkin, J., 2020. *Anti-system politics: the crisis of market liberalism in rich democracies*. Oxford, New York: Oxford University Press.

Howard, D., 2016. *Between politics and antipolitics. Thinking about politics after 9/11*. New York: Palgrave Macmillan.

Hyman, H.H., 1959. *Political socialization: a study in the psychology of political behavior*. Glencoe: The free press.

Ignazi, P., 1996a. The intellectual basis of right-wing anti-partyism. *European Journal of Political Research*, 29 (3), 279–296.

Ignazi, P., 1996b. From neo-Fascists to post-Fascists? The transformation of the MSI into the AN. *West European Politics*, 19 (4), 693–714.

Ignazi, P., 2017. *Party and democracy: the uneven road to party legitimacy.* Oxford: Oxford University Press.

Ignazi, P., 2018. *I partiti in Italia dal 1945 al 2018.* Bologna: il Mulino.

Ignazi, P., 2020. Party change and citizens' retrotopia. *Contemporary Italian Politics,* 12 (4), 498–515.

Ignazi, P., 2021. The failure of mainstream parties and the impact of new challenger parties in France, Italy and Spain. *Italian Political Science Review,* 51 (1), 1–17.

Imbriani, A.M., 1996. *Vento del Sud: moderati, reazionari, qualunquisti, (1943–1948).* Bologna: il Mulino.

Inglehart, R., 1977. *The silent revolution: changing values and political styles.* Princeton: Princeton University Press.

Jedlowski, P., 2015. Cinema and public memory. *In:* E.G. Parini, G.A. Veltri, and A. Mammone, eds. *The Routledge handbook of contemporary Italy: history, politics, society.* London: Routledge, 295–304.

Jennings, W., Stoker, G., and Twyman, J., 2016. The dimensions and impact of political discontent in Britain. *Parliamentary Affairs,* 69 (4), 876–900.

Jørgensen, K.E., 1992. The end of anti-politics in Central Europe. *In:* P.G. Lewis, ed. *Democracy and civil society in Eastern Europe.* Basingstoke: Macmillan, 32–60.

Katz, S.R., 2001. Reforming the Italian electoral law, 1993. *In:* M.S. Shugart and P.M. Wattemberg, eds. *Mixed-member electoral systems. The best of both worlds?* Oxford: Oxford University Press, 96–122.

Katz, S.R. and Mair, P., 1995. Changing models of party organization and party democracy: the emergence of the Cartel Party. *Party Politics,* 1 (1), 5–28.

Keane, J., 2009. *The life and death of democracy.* London and New York: Simon & Schuster.

Kenig, O. and Pruysers, S., 2018. The challenges of inclusive intra-party selection methods. *In:* X. Coller and G. Cordero, eds. *Democratizing candidate selection: new methods, old receipts?* Cham: Palgrave Macmillan, 25–48.

Kenney, C.D., 1998. Outsider and anti-party politicians in power: new conceptual strategies and empirical evidence from Peru. *Party Politics,* 4 (1), 57–75.

Kernell, S., 1986. *Going public: new strategies of presidential leadership.* Washington: Congressional Quarterly.

Kestilä-Kekkonen, E., 2009. Anti-party sentiment among young adults: evidence from fourteen West European countries. *Young,* 17 (2), 145–165.

King, A., 2002. The outsider as political leader: the case of Margaret thatcher. *British Journal of Political Science,* 32 (3), 435–454.

Kitschelt, H., 2006. Movement parties. *In:* R.S. Katz and W.J. Crotty, eds. *Handbook of party politics.* London: Sage, 278–290.

Klingemann, H.-D., 2014. Dissatisfied democrats: democratic maturation in old and new democracies. *In:* R.J. Dalton and C. Welzel, eds. *The civic culture transformed. From allegiant to assertive citizens.* New York: Cambridge University Press, 116–57.

Koff, S.Z. and Koff, S.P., 2000. *Italy, from the First to the Second Republic.* London and New York: Routledge.

Konrád, G., 1987. *L'antipolitique.* Paris: Èditions La Découverte.

Kriesi, H., 2012. The political consequences of the financial and economic crisis in Europe: electoral punishment and popular protest. *Swiss Political Science Review,* 18 (4), 518–522.

Kriesi, H. and Pappas, T., eds., 2015. *European populism in the shadow of the great recession.* Colchester: ECPR Press.

Lanzone, M.E. and Morini, M., 2017. Populists in power: from municipalities to (European) parliament, the case of the Italian Five Star Movement. *Chinese Political Science Review*, 2 (3), 395–409.

Lanzone, M.E. and Rombi, S., 2014. Who did participate in the online primary elections of the Five Star Movement (M5S) in Italy? Causes, features and effects of the selection process. *Partecipazione e conflitto*, 7 (1), 170–191.

Lanzone, M.E. and Tronconi, F., 2015. Between blog, social networks and territory: activists and grassroots organisation. *In*: F. Tronconi, ed. *Beppe Grillo's Five Star Movement: organisation, communication and ideology.* Farnham: Ashgate, 53–98.

Lazar, M., 2008. The birth of the Democratic Party. *In*: M. Donovan and P. Onofri, eds. *Italian politics. Frustrated aspirations for change.* New York: Berghahn Books, 51–67.

Le Gall, L., Offerlé, M., and Ploux, F., eds., 2012. *La politique sans en avoir l'air.* Rennes: Presses universitaires de Rennes.

Leonardi, R. and Kovacs, M., 1993. The Lega Nord: the rise of a new Italian catch-all party. *Italian Politics*, 8, 50–65.

Levitsky, S. and Ziblatt, D., 2018. *How democracies die: what history tells us about our future.* London: Viking.

Lewanski, R., 2013. Institutionalizing deliberative democracy: the 'Tuscany laboratory'. *Journal of Public Deliberation*, 9 (1), 1–16.

Lewis-Beck, M.S. and Nadeau, R., 2012. PIGS or not? Economic voting in Southern Europe. *Electoral Studies*, 31 (3), 472–477.

Lioy, A., 2021. The blank ballot crisis: a multi-method study of fraud in the 2006 Italian election. *Contemporary Italian Politics*, (Early view: https://doi.org/10.108 0/23248823.2021.1955190).

Lipset, S.M., 2002. The americanization of the european left. *In*: L. Diamond and R. Gunther, eds. *Political parties and democracy.* Baltimora and London: Johns Hopkins University Press, 52–65.

Lo Russo, M. and Verzichelli, L., 2015. Reshaping political careers in post-transition Italy. A syncronic analysis. *In*: M. Edinger and S. Jahr, eds. *Political careers in Europe. Career patterns in multi-level systems.* Baden-Baden: Nomos, 27–53.

Lopez-Rabatel, L. and Sintomer, Y., eds., 2020. *Sortition and democracy: history, tools, theories.* Exeter: Imprint Academic.

Louwerse, T., Otjes, S., Willumsen, D.M., and Öhberg, P., 2017. Reaching across the aisle: explaining government-opposition voting in parliament. *Party Politics*, 23 (6), 746–759.

Lucardie, P., 2000. Prophets, purifiers and prolocutors: towards a theory on the emergence of new parties. *Party Politics*, 6 (2), 175–185.

Lumley, R., 2001. The last laugh: cuore and the vicissitudes of satire. *In*: L. Cheles and L. Sponza, eds. *The art of persuasion: political communication in Italy from 1945 to the 1990s.* Manchester: Manchester University Press, 233–257.

Lupo, S., 2000. Il mito della società civile. Retoriche antipolitiche nella crisi della democrazia italiana. *Meridiana*, 38–39, 17–43.

Lupo, S., 2013. *Antipartiti. Il mito della nuova politica nella storia della Repubblica (prima, seconda e terza).* Roma: Donzelli.

Luzzatto-Fegiz, P., 1956. *Il volto sconosciuto dell'Italia: dieci anni di sondaggi Doxa.* Milano: Giuffrè.

Macagno, F., 2019. Analizzare l'argomentazione sui social media. Il caso dei tweet di Salvini. *Sistemi intelligenti*, XXXI (3), 601–632.

Macaluso, M. and Montemagno, F., 2019. The Five-Star Movement inside the institutions in Sicily: from 'swimming the Strait' to institutionalisation in local politics. *Contemporary Italian Politics*, 11 (1), 80–100.

Magnier, A., 2004. Between institutional learning and re-legitimization: Italian mayors in the unending reform. *International Journal of Urban and Regional Research*, 28 (1), 166–82.

Mair, P., 1994. Party organizations: from civil society to the state. *In*: S.R. Katz and P. Mair, eds. *How Parties Organize. Change and Adaptation in Party Organization in Western Democracies*. London: Sage, 1–22.

Mair, P., 2008. Concepts and concept formation. *In*: D. della Porta and M. Keating, eds. *Approaches and methodologies in the social sciences. A pluralist perspective*. Cambridge: Cambridge University Press, 177–197.

Mair, P., 2013. *Ruling the void: the hollowing of western democracy*. London; New York: Verso.

Mannheim, K., 1952. The sociological problem of generations. *In*: P. Kecskemeti, ed. *Essays on the sociology of knowledge*. London: Routledge & Kegan, 276–320.

Mannheimer, R., ed., 1991a. *La Lega Lombarda*. Milano: Feltrinelli.

Mannheimer, R., 1991b. Chi vota Lega e perché. *In*: R. Mannheimer, ed. *La Lega Lombarda*. Milano: Feltrinelli, 122–158.

Mannheimer, R. and Sani, G., 2001. *La conquista degli astenuti*. Bologna: il Mulino.

Maraffi, M., ed., 2007. *Gli italiani e la politica*. Bologna: il Mulino.

Maran, T., Liegl, S., Moder, S., Kraus, S., and Furtner, M., 2021. Clothes make the leader! How leaders can use attire to impact followers' perceptions of charisma and approval. *Journal of Business Research*, 124, 86–99.

Marangoni, F. and Verzichelli, L., 2019. Goat-stag, chimera or chameleon? The formation and first semester of the Conte government. *Contemporary Italian Politics*, 11 (3), 263–279.

Maranini, G., 1958. *Miti e realtà della democrazia*. Milano: Edizioni di Comunità.

Maranini, G., 1963. *Il tiranno senza volto*. Milano: Bompiani.

Marino, B., Martocchia Diodati, N., and Verzichelli, L., 2019. Members of the Chamber of Deputies. *In*: L. Ceccarini and J.L. Newell, eds. *The Italian General Election of 2018: Italy in uncharted territory*. Cham: Palgrave Macmillan, 271–295.

Markoff, J. and Burridge, D., 2019. The global wave of democratization. *In*: C.W. Haerpfer, P. Bernhagen, C. Welzel, and R.F. Inglehart, eds. *Democratization*. Oxford: Oxford University Press, 82–99.

Marradi, A., 1987. Linguaggio scientifico o torre di babele? *Rivista italiana di scienza politica*, XVII (1), 135–56.

Marradi, A., ed., 2020. *Percezione del sé e senso della natura. Un confronto tra Italia e Argentina*. Milano: Franco Angeli.

Martini, S. and Quaranta, M., 2020. *Citizens and democracy in Europe: contexts, changes and political support*. Cham: Palgrave Macmillan.

Massari, O. and Parker, S., 1998. The two lefts: between rupture and recomposition. *Italian Politics*, 14, 47–63.

Massetti, E. and Farinelli, A., 2019. From the *Porcellum* to the *Rosatellum*: 'political elite-judicial interaction' in the Italian laboratory of electoral reforms. *Contemporary Italian Politics*, 11 (2), 137–157.

Mastropaolo, A., 2000. *Antipolitica. All'origine della crisi italiana*. Napoli: L'ancora.

Mastropaolo, A., 2005. *La mucca pazza della democrazia. Nuove destre, populismo, antipolitica.* Torino: Bollati Boringhieri.

Mastropaolo, A., 2008. Politics against democracy: party withdrawal and populist breakthrough. *In*: D. Albertazzi and D. McDonnell, eds. *Twenty-first century populism. The spectre of western European democracy.* Basingstoke: Palgrave Macmillan, 30–48.

Mastropaolo, A., 2009. From the other shore: American political science and the 'Italian case'. *Modern Italy*, 14 (3), 311–337.

Mastropaolo, A., 2012. *Is democracy a lost cause? Paradoxes of an imperfect invention.* Colchester: ECPR Press.

Mastruzzo, G., 2019. Five Stars of change: the transformation of Italian protest publics through Grillo's blog. *In*: N. Belyaeva, V. Albert, and D. Zaytsev, eds. *Protest publics: toward a new concept of mass civic action.* Cham: Springer, 137–154.

Mauk, M., 2020. *Citizen support for democratic and autocratic regimes.* Oxford: Oxford University Press.

Mazzoleni, G. and Schulz, W., 1999. 'Mediatization' of politics: a challenge for democracy? *Political Communication*, 16 (3), 247.

Mazzoleni, O. and Ruzza, C., 2018. Combining regionalism and nationalism: the Lega in Italy and the Lega dei Ticinesi in Switzerland. *Comparative European Politics*, 16 (6), 976–992.

Mazzoni, M. and Mincigrucci, R., 2021. The representation of Matteo Salvini in gossip magazines: the Ordinary Super Leader. *Contemporary Italian Politics*, 13 (1), 49–63.

McCarthy, P., 1992. The referendum of 9 June. *In*: S. Hellman and G. Pasquino, eds. *Italian politics: a review (vol. 7).* London: Pinter Publishers, 11–28.

McDonnell, D., 2013. Silvio Berlusconi's personal parties: from Forza Italia to the Popolo Della Libertà. *Political Studies*, 61 (1), 217–233.

McDonnell, D., 2016. Populist leaders and Coterie Charisma. *Political Studies*, 64 (3), 719–733.

McDonnell, D. and Vampa, D., 2016. The Italian Lega Nord. *In*: O. Mazzoleni and R.R. Heinisch, eds. *Understanding populist party organisation: the radical right in Western Europe.* London: Palgrave Macmillan, 105–129.

Medvic, S.K., 2013. *In defense of politicians. The expectations trap and its threat to democracy.* New York: Routledge.

Meguid, B.M., 2008. *Party competition between unequals: strategies and electoral fortunes in Western Europe.* Cambridge: Cambridge University Press.

Meridiana, 1993. *Questione settentrionale, numero monografico.* Meridiana. Rivista di Storia e Scienze Sociali. 16.

Merkel, W. and Kneip, S., eds., 2018. *Democracy and crisis challenges in turbulent times.* Cham: Springer International Publishing.

Mete, V., 2010. Four types of anti-politics: insights from the Italian case. *Modern Italy*, 15 (1), 37–61.

Mete, V., 2019. Il Movimento 5 Stelle in Calabria, tra voto locale e nazionale. *Meridiana*, (96), 85–104.

Michel, J.-B., Shen, Y.K., Aiden, A.P., Veres, A., Gray, M.K., Team, T.G.B., Pickett, J.P., Hoiberg, D., Clancy, D., Norvig, P., Orwant, J., Pinker, S., Nowak, M.A., and Aiden, E.L., 2011. Quantitative analysis of culture using millions of digitized books. *Science*, 331 (6014), 176–182.

Michels, R., 1915. *Political parties: a sociological study of the oligarchical tendencies of modern democracy*. London: Jarrold & Sons.

Minaldi, G. and Soare, S., 2019. Tra innovazione e normalizzazione: la rappresentanza politica del Movimento 5 Stelle in Sicilia. *Meridiana*, 96, 63–84.

Mohan, S. and Dwivedi, D., 2019. *Gandhi and philosophy: on theological anti-politics*. London; New York: Bloomsbury Academic.

Moini, G., 2012. *Teoria critica della partecipazione: un approccio sociologico*. Milano: Franco Angeli.

Monina, G., 2012. Lelio Basso e il finanziamento pubblico dei partiti (1963-1974). *Parolechiave*, 20, (1), 71–94.

Montesanti, L. and Veltri, F., 2017. I sindaci di Grillo: ceto politico e selezione della rappresentanza locale nel M5S. *In*: D. Bianchi and F. Raniolo, eds. *Limiti e sfide della rappresentanza politica*. Milano: Franco Angeli, 215–47.

Montesanti, L. and Veltri, F., 2019. Il Movimento 5 Stelle e la personalizzazione alle elezioni regionali: un partito in trasformazione. *Meridiana*, 96, 39–61.

Monti, L., 2000. Antipolitica. *In*: R. Esposito and C. Galli, eds. *Enciclopedia del pensiero politico. Autori, concetti, dottrine*. Roma-Bari: Laterza, 27–28.

Morlino, L., 2001. The three phases of Italian parties. *In*: L. Diamond and R. Gunther, eds. *Political parties and democracy*. Baltimora and London: Johns Hopkins University Press, 109–142.

Morlino, L. and Raniolo, F., 2017. *The impact of the economic crisis on South European democracies*. Cham: Springer.

Mosca, L., 2015. The Movimento 5 Stelle and social conflicts: between symbiosis and cooptation. *In*: F. Tronconi, ed. *Beppe Grillo's Five Star Movement: organisation, communication and ideology*. Farnham: Ashgate, 153–177.

Mosca, L., 2020. The Five Star Movement's progressive detachment from social movements. *In*: C. Flesher Fominaya and R.A. Feenstra, eds. *Routledge handbook of contemporary European social movements. Protest in turbulent times*. Abingdon: Routledge, 357–371.

Mosca, L. and Tronconi, F., 2019. Beyond left and right: the eclectic populism of the Five Star Movement. *West European Politics*, 42 (6), 1258–1283.

Mosca, L., Vaccari, C., and Valeriani, A., 2015a. How to select citizen candidates: the Movimento 5 Stelle online primaries and their implications. *In*: A. De Petris and T. Poguntke, eds. *Anti-party parties in Germany and Italy: protest movements and parliamentary democracy*. Roma: Luiss University Press, 165–192.

Mosca, L., Vaccari, C., and Valeriani, A., 2015b. An internet-fuelled party? The Movimento 5 Stelle and the web. *In*: F. Tronconi, ed. *Beppe Grillo's Five Star Movement: organisation, communication and ideology*. Farnham: Ashgate, 127–151.

Mouffe, C., 1999. Deliberative democracy or agonistic pluralism? *Social Research*, 66 (3), 745–758.

Musso, M. and Maccaferri, M., 2018. At the origins of the political discourse of the 5-Star Movement (M5S): internet, direct democracy and the "future of the past". *Internet Histories*, 2 (1–2), 98–120.

Naldini, M., 2003. *The family in the Mediterranean welfare states*. London: Frank Cass.

Natale, P., 2014. The birth, early history and explosive growth of the Five Star Movement. *Contemporary Italian Politics*, 6 (1), 16–36.

Newell, J.L., 2000. Party finance and corruption: Italy. *In*: R. Williams, ed. *Party finance and political corruption*. Basingstoke: Macmillan Press, 61–87.

Newell, J.L., 2015. Magistrates going into politics: Antonio Di Pietro and Italy of Values. *In*: E.G. Parini, G.A. Veltri, and A. Mammone, eds. *The Routledge handbook of contemporary Italy: history, politics, society*. London: Routledge, 215–224.

Newell, J.L., 2019. *Silvio Berlusconi. A study in failure*. Manchester: Manchester University Press.

Newell, J.L. and Bull, M.J., 1993. The Italian referenda of April 1993: real change at last? *West European Politics*, 16 (4), 607–615.

Nizzoli, C., 2018. Le revenu de citoyenneté comme programme phare du Mouvement 5 étoiles. *Chronique Internationale de l'IRES*, 164 (4), 96–104.

Norris, P., ed., 1999a. *Critical citizens: global support for democratic governance*. Oxford: Oxford University Press.

Norris, P., 1999b. Introduction: the growth of critical citizens? *In*: P. Norris ed. *Critical citizens. Global support for democratic governance*. Oxford: Oxford University Press, 1–27.

Norris, P., 2011. *Democratic deficit: critical citizens revisited*. New York: Cambridge University Press.

Norris, P. and Inglehart, R., 2019. *Cultural backlash: Trump, Brexit, and the rise of authoritarian populism*. Cambridge: Cambridge University Press.

Novelli, E., 2012. Satira, politica e televisione in Italia. *Comunicazione politica*, XII, (1), 57–72.

Novelli, E., 2016. *La democrazia del talk show: storia di un genere che ha cambiato la televisione, la politica, l'Italia*. Roma: Carocci.

Nye, J.S., Zelikow, P., and King, D.C., eds., 1997. *Why people don't trust government*. Cambridge: Harvard University Press.

Ogden, C.K. and Richards, I.A., 1923. *The meaning of meaning: a study of the influence of language upon thought and of the science of symbolism*. New York: Harcourt Brace.

Öhberg, P., 2017. *Ambitious politicians: the implications of career ambition in representative democracy*. Lawrence: University Press of Kansas.

Orsina, G., 2014. *Berlusconism and Italy. A Historical Interpretation*. New York: Palgrave Macmillan.

Ost, D., 1990. *Solidarity and the politics of anti-politics: opposition and reform in Poland since 1968*. Philadelphia: Temple University Press.

Panebianco, A., 1988a. The Italian radicals: new wine in an old bottle. *In*: K. Lawson and P.H. Merkl, eds. *When parties fail: emerging alternative organizations*. Princeton: Princeton University Press, 110–136.

Panebianco, A., 1988b. *Political parties. Organization and power*. Ed. or. 1982. Cambridge: Cambridge University Press.

Pasquino, G., 2000. Premiership and Leadership from D'Alema to Amato and Beyond. *Italian Politics*, 16, 37–51.

Pasquino, G., 2007. The Five Faces of Silvio Berlusconi: the knight of anti-politics. *Modern Italy*, 12, 39–54.

Pasquino, G., 2009. The Democratic Party and the restructuring of the Italian party system. *Journal of Modern Italian Studies*, 14 (1), 21–30.

Pasquino, G., 2014. The 2013 elections and the Italian political system. *Journal of Modern Italian Studies*, 19 (4), 424–437.

Pasquino, G., 2018. The disappearance of political cultures in Italy. *South European Society and Politics*, 23 (1), 133–146.

Pasquino, G. and Valbruzzi, M., 2016. Primary elections between *fortuna* and *virtù*. *Contemporary Italian Politics*, 8 (1), 3–11.

Pasquino, G. and Valbruzzi, M., 2017a. The Italian Democratic Party, its nature and its secretary. *Revista Española de Ciencia Política*, 44, 275–299.

Pasquino, G. and Valbruzzi, M., 2017b. Italy says no: the 2016 constitutional referendum and its consequences. *Journal of Modern Italian Studies*, 22 (2), 145–162.

Pasquino, G. and Venturino, F., eds., 2009. *Le primarie comunali in Italia*. Bologna: il Mulino.

Passarelli, G. and Tuorto, D., 2012. *Lega & Padania: storie e luoghi delle camicie verdi*. Bologna: il Mulino.

Passarelli, G. and Tuorto, D., 2018a. *La Lega di Salvini: estrema destra di governo*. Bologna: il Mulino.

Passarelli, G. and Tuorto, D., 2018b. The Five Star Movement: purely a matter of protest? The rise of a new party between political discontent and reasoned voting. *Party Politics*, 24 (2), 129–140.

Pattyn, S., Van Hiel, A., Dhont, K., and Onraet, E., 2012. Stripping the political cynic: a psychological exploration of the concept of political cynicism. *European Journal of Personality*, 26 (6), 566–579.

Pauwels, T., 2017. Measuring populism: a review of current approaches. *In*: R. Heinisch, C. Holtz-Bacha, and O. Mazzoleni, eds. *Political Populism. A Handbook*. Baden-Baden: Nomos, 123–36.

Pechenick, E.A., Danforth, C.M., and Dodds, P.S., 2015. Characterizing the Google Books corpus: strong limits to inferences of socio-cultural and linguistic evolution. *PLoS ONE*, 10 (10), 1–24.

Petrocik, J.R., 1996. Issue ownership in presidential elections, with a 1980 case study. *American Journal of Political Science*, 40 (3), 825–850.

Pharr, S.J. and Putnam, R.D., eds., 2000. *Disaffected democracies: what's troubling the trilateral countries?* Princeton: Princeton University Press.

Piccio, D.R., ed., 2018. *Il finanziamento alla politica in Italia: dal passato alle prospettive future*. Roma: Carocci.

Pinto, L. and Pedrazzani, A., 2015. From 'Citizens' to members of parliament: the elected representatives in the parliamentary arena. *In*: F. Tronconi, ed. *Beppe Grillo's Five Star Movement: organisation, communication and ideology*. Farnham: Ashgate, 99–125.

Pirro, A.L.P., 2018. The polyvalent populism of the 5 Star Movement. *Journal of Contemporary European Studies*, 26 (4), 443–458.

Pizzimenti, E., 2016. The evolution of party funding in Italy: a case of inclusive cartelisation? *Modern Italy*, 22 (1), 71–85.

Pizzorno, A., 1992. La corruzione nel sistema politico. *In*: D. della Porta, *Lo scambio occulto*. Bologna: il Mulino, 13–74.

Pizzorno, A., 1993. Le difficoltà del consociativismo. *In*: A. Pizzorno, *Le radici della politica assoluta e altri saggi*. Milano: Feltrinelli, 285–313.

Poguntke, T., 1993. *Alternative politics: the German Green Party*. Edinburgh: Edinburgh University Press.

Poguntke, T., 1996. Anti-party sentiment – conceptual thoughts and empirical evidence: explorations into a minefield. *European Journal of Political Research*, 29, 319–344.

Poguntke, T. and Webb, P., 2005. *The presidentialization of politics. A comparative study of modern democracies*. Oxford: Oxford University Press.

Poli, E., 2001. *Forza Italia. Strutture, leadership e radicamento territoriale.* Bologna: il Mulino.

Pratschke, J., Vitale, T., Morelli, N., Cousin, B., Piolatto, M., and Del Fabbro, M., 2021. Electoral support for the 5 Star Movement in Milan: an ecological analysis of social and spatial factors. *Journal of Urban Affairs*, (Early view: https://doi.org /10.1080/07352166.2021.1886855).

Putnam, R.D., 2000. *Bowling alone. The collapse and revival of American community.* London and New York: Simon & Schuster.

Ragazzoni, D., 2020. 'Particracy'. The pre-populist critique of parties and its implications. *In*: P. Blokker and M. Anselmi, eds. *Multiple populisms. Italy as democracy's mirror.* Abingdon: Routledge, 86–105.

Rahat, G. and Hazan, R.Y., 2001. Candidate selection methods: an analytical framework. *Party Politics*, 7 (3), 297–322.

Raniolo, F., 2006. Forza Italia: a leader with a party. *South European Society and Politics*, 11 (3–4), 439–455.

Ravazzi, S., 2017. When a government attempts to institutionalize and regulate deliberative democracy: the how and why from a process-tracing perspective. *Critical Policy Studies*, 11 (1), 79–100.

Recchi, E. and Verzichelli, L., 2003. Italy: the homeland of the political class. *In*: J. Borchert and J. Zeiss, eds. *The political class in advanced democracies.* Oxford; New York: Oxford University Press, 223–244.

Regalia, M. and Valbruzzi, M., 2016. With or without parliamentary primaries? Some evidence from the Italian laboratory. *Contemporary Italian Politics*, 8 (1), 42–61.

Reinemann, C., Aalberg, T., Stanyer, J., Esser, F., and de Vreese, C.H., eds., 2019. *Communicating populism: comparing actor perceptions, media coverage, and effects on citizenship in Europe.* New York: Routledge.

Renard, J.-B., 2010. La construction de l'image des hommes politiques par le folklore narratif. Anecdotes, rumeurs, légendes, histoires drôles. *Mots. Les langages du politique*, 92, 11–22.

Renwick, A., 2006. Anti-political or just anti-communist? Varieties of dissidence in East-Central Europe and their implications for the development of political society. *East European Politics and Societies*, 20 (2), 286–318.

Renwick, A., 2010. *The politics of electoral reform. Changing the rules of democracy.* Cambridge: Cambridge University Press.

Renwick, A., Hanretty, C., and Hine, D., 2009. Partisan self-interest and electoral reform: the new Italian electoral law of 2005. *Electoral Studies*, 28 (3), 437–447.

Renwick, A. and Pilet, J.-B., 2016. *Faces on the ballot. The personalization of electoral systems in Europe.* Oxford: Oxford University Press.

Renzi, M., 2011. *Fuori!* Milano: Rizzoli.

Repp, K., 2000. *Reformers, critics, and the paths of German modernity: anti-politics and the search for alternatives, 1890-1914.* Cambridge: Harvard University Press.

Rhodes, M., 1995. Italy: greens in an overcrowded political system. *In*: D. Richardson and C. Rootes, eds. *The green challenge.* London and New York: Routledge, 124–141.

Rhodes, M., 1997. Financing party politics in Italy: a case of systemic corruption. *West European Politics*, 20 (1), 54–80.

Rhodes, M., 2015. Tangentopoli – more than 20 years on. *In*: E. Jones and G. Pasquino, eds. *The Oxford Handbook of Italian Politics*. Oxford: Oxford University Press, 309–324.

Ricolfi, L., 2006. *Tempo scaduto: il contratto con gli italiani alla prova dei fatti*. Bologna: il Mulino.

Rihoux, B. and Frankland, E.G., 2008. Conclusion: the metamorphosis on amateur-activist newborns into professional-activist centaurs. *In*: E.G. Frankland, P. Lucardie, and B. Rihoux, eds. *Green parties in transition. The end of grass-roots democracy?* Abingdon: Ashgate, 259–287.

Rizzo, S. and Stella, G.A., 2007. *La casta. Così i politici italiani sono diventati intoccabili*. Milano: Rizzoli.

Rizzo, S. and Stella, G.A., 2012. The costs of politics and reform: the year of 'Little Trims'. *Italian Politics*, 28, 59–77.

Rodotà, S., 1997. *Tecnopolitica: la democrazia e le nuove tecnologie della comunicazione*. Roma-Bari: Laterza.

Rogari, S., ed., 2004. *Istituzioni e poteri nell'Italia contemporanea: atti del Convegno di studi in memoria di Giuseppe Maranini a cento anni dalla nascita*. Firenze: Centro editoriale toscano.

Rooduijn, M., 2018. What unites the voter bases of populist parties? Comparing the electorates of 15 populist parties. *European Political Science Review*, 10 (3), 351–368.

Rooduijn, M., van der Brug, W., de Lange, S.L., and Parlevliet, J., 2017. Persuasive populism? Estimating the effect of populist messages on political cynicism. *Politics & Governance*, 5 (4), 136–145.

Rosenbluth, F.M. and Shapiro, I., 2018. *Responsible parties. Saving democracy from itself*. New Haven and London: Yale University Press.

Runciman, D., 2018. *How democracy ends*. London: Profile Books.

Russo, F. and Verzichelli, L., 2020. Representation in the Italian Parliament. *In*: A. Freire, M. Barragán, X. Coller, M. Lisi, and E. Tsatsanis, eds. *Political representation in Southern Europe and Latin America: before and after the great recession and the commodity crisis*. London: Routledge, 50–65.

Russo, L., Riera, P., and Verthé, T., 2017. Tracing the electorate of the MoVimento Cinque Stelle: an ecological inference analysis. *Italian Political Science Review*, 47 (1), 45–62.

Ryfe, D.M. and Stalsburg, B., 2012. The participation and recruitment challenge. *In*: T. Nabatchi, J. Gastil, G.M. Weiksner, and M. Leighninger, eds. *Democracy in motion: evaluating the practice and impact of deliberative civic engagement*. Oxford: Oxford University Press, 43–58.

Sabbatucci, G., 2005. Il trasformismo e i suoi critici. *In*: S. Setta, ed. *Italiani contro gli uomini politici: il Qualunquismo*. Napoli: Edizioni Scientifiche Italiane, 15–22.

Salvati, E., 2016. Matteo Renzi: a new leadership style for the Italian Democratic Party and Italian politics. *Modern Italy*, 21 (1), 7–18.

Sampugnaro, R. and Gozzo, S., 2019. The end of Gulliver's travels: MPs and leaderisation in the Italian parliament. *Contemporary Italian Politics*, 11 (1), 15–42.

Sandri, G. and Seddone, A., 2018. The Democratic Party between change and settlement. Chronicle of a particular year. *Contemporary Italian Politics*, 10 (4), 315–329.

Sandri, G. and Venturino, F., 2016. Primaries at the municipal level: how, how many and why. *Contemporary Italian Politics*, 8 (1), 62–82.

Saresella, D., 2016. *Tra politica e antipolitica. La nuova società civile e il movimento della rete (1985-1994)*. Firenze: Le Monnier.

Sartori, G., 1970. Concept misformation in comparative politics. *The American Political Science Review*, 64 (4), 1033–1053.

Sartori, G., 1975. The Tower of Babel. *In*: G. Sartori, F.W. Riggs, and H. Teune, eds. *Tower of Babel: on the definition and analysis of concepts in the social sciences*. International Studies Associations, Occasional Paper n.6, University of Pittsburgh, 15–85.

Sartori, G., 1982. *Teoria dei partiti e caso italiano*. Milano: SugarCo.

Sartori, G., 1984. Guidelines for concept analysis. *In*: G. Sartori, ed. *Social science concepts. A systematic analysis*. Beverly Hills: Sage, 15–85.

Sartori, G., 1994. *Comparative constitutional engineering: an inquiry into structures, incentives and outcomes*. Basingstoke: Macmillan.

Saunders, C. and Klandermans, B., eds., 2020. *When citizens talk about politics*. Abingdon: Routledge.

Scarrow, S.E., 1996. Politicians against parties: anti-party arguments as weapons for change in Germany. *European Journal of Political Research*, 29, 297–317.

Scarrow, S.E., 2015. *Beyond party members. Changing approaches to partisan mobilization*. Oxford: Oxford University Press.

Schadee, M.A.H. and Segatti, P., 2002. Informazione politica, spazio elettorale ed elettori in movimento. *In*: M. Caciagli and P. Corbetta, eds. *Le ragioni dell'elettore. Perché ha vinto il centro-destra nelle elezioni italiane del 2001*. Bologna: il Mulino, 339–369.

Schedler, A., 1996. Anti-political-establishment parties. *Party Politics*, 2 (3), 291–312.

Schedler, A., 1997a. Introduction: antipolitics – closing and colonizing the public sphere. *In*: *The end of politics*. Basingstoke: Macmillan Press, 1–20.

Schedler, A., ed., 1997b. *The end of politics*. Basingstoke: Macmillan Press.

Schmitt, H., 2009. Partisanship in nine western democracies. *In*: J. Bartle and P. Bellucci, eds. *Political parties and partisanship*. London: Routledge, 75–87.

Sciarrone, R., ed., 2017. *Politica e corruzione: partiti e reti di affari da Tangentopoli a oggi*. Roma: Donzelli.

Scoppola, P., 1997. *La repubblica dei partiti: evoluzione e crisi di un sistema politico 1945-1996*. Bologna: il Mulino.

Seddone, A., Sandri, G., and Sozzi, F., 2020. Primary elections for party leadership in Italy. A democratic innovation? *In*: A. Alexandre, A. Goujon, and G. Gourgues, eds. *Innovations, reinvented politics and representative democracy*. Abingdon: Routledge, 46–59.

Segatti, P., 2006. Italy, forty years of political disaffection. A longitudinal exploration. *In*: M. Torcal and J.R. Montero, eds. *Political disaffection in contemporary democracies. Social capital, institutions, and politics*. London and New York: Routledge, 244–275.

Segatti, P., 2007. Interesse per la politica: diffusione, origine e cambiamento. *In*: M. Maraffi, ed. *Gli italiani e la politica*. Bologna: il Mulino, 39–71.

Setta, S., 2005. *L'Uomo qualunque. 1944-1948*. [Original edition 1975] Roma-Bari: Laterza.

Shapiro, I., 1999. Enough of deliberation. Politics is about interests and power. *In*: S. Macedo, ed. *Deliberative politics: essays on democracy and disagreement*. New York; Oxford: Oxford University Press, 28–38.

Shomer, Y., 2014. What affects candidate selection processes? A cross-national examination. *Party Politics*, 20 (4), 533–546.

Sikk, A., 2012. Newness as a winning formula for new political parties. *Party Politics*, 18 (4), 465–486.

Snow, D.A., Rochford, E.B., Worden, S.K., and Benford, R.D., 1986. Frame alignment processes, micromobilization, and movement participation. *American Sociological Review*, 51 (4), 464–481.

SPEL - Collectif Sociologie politique des élections, 2016. *Les sens du vote. Une enquête sociologique*. Rennes: Presses universitaires de Rennes.

Stanyer, J., 2013. *Intimate politics: publicity, privacy and the personal lives of politicians in media-saturated democracies*. Cambridge: Polity Press.

Stoker, G., 2010. The rise of political disenchantment. *In*: C. Hay, ed. *New directions in political science: responding to the challenges of an interdependent world*. Basingstoke: Palgrave Macmillan, 43–63.

Stoker, G., 2017. *Why politics matter. Making democracy work*. London: Palgrave.

Stoker, G. and Hay, C., 2017. Understanding and challenging populist negativity towards politics: the perspectives of British citizens. *Political Studies*, 65 (1), 4–23.

Streeck, W., 2014. *Buying time: the delayed crisis of democratic capitalism*. London: Verso.

Street, J., 2004. Celebrity politicians: popular culture and political representation. *The British Journal of Politics & International Relations*, 6 (4), 435–452.

Taggart, P. and Pirro, A.L.P., 2021. European populism before the pandemic: ideology, Euroscepticism, electoral performance, and government participation of 63 parties in 30 countries. *Italian Political Science Review*, (Early view: https://doi.org/10.1017/ipo.2021.13).

Tambini, D., 2001. *Nationalism in Italian politics. The stories of the Northern League, 1980-2000*. London: Routledge.

Tarchi, M., 1998. The Lega Nord. *In*: L. De Winter and H. Türsan, eds. *Regionalist Parties in Western Europe*. London and New York: Routledge, 143–57.

Tarchi, M., 2002. Populism Italian Style. *In*: Y. Mény and Y. Surel, eds. *Democracies and the populist challenge*. Houndmills: Palgrave, 120–138.

Tarchi, M., 2015. *Italia populista. Dal qualunquismo a Beppe Grillo*. Bologna: il Mulino.

Tarli Barbieri, G. and Biondi, F., eds., 2016. *Il finanziamento della politica*. Napoli: Editoriale scientifica.

Teodori, M., Panebianco, A., and Ignazi, P., 1977. *I nuovi radicali: storia e sociologia di un movimento politico*. Milano: Mondadori.

Terracciano, B., 2019. Il sovranismo è servito: la retorica salviniana del buono made in Italy. *E|C. Rivista on-line dell'AISS. Associazione Italiana Studi Semiotici*, (http://www.ec-aiss.it), 1–13.

Thompson, J.B., 2000. *Political scandal: power and visibility in the media age*. Cambridge: Polity Press.

Torcal, M., Gunther, R., and Montero, J.R., 2002. Anti-party sentiments in Southern Europe. *In*: R. Gunther, J.R. Montero, and J.J. Linz, eds. *Political parties: old concepts and new challenges*. Oxford: Oxford University Press, 257–289.

Torcal, M. and Montero, J.R., eds., 2006a. *Political disaffection in contemporary democracies. Social capital, institutions, and politics.* London: Routledge.

Torcal, M. and Montero, J.R., 2006b. Political disaffection in comparative perspective. *In*: *Political disaffection in contemporary democracies. Social capital, institutions, and politics.* London and New York: Routledge, 3–19.

Trigilia, C., ed., 2020. *Capitalismi e democrazie. Si possono conciliare crescita e uguaglianza?* Bologna: il Mulino.

Tronconi, F., ed., 2015. *Beppe Grillo's Five Star Movement : organisation, communication and ideology.* Farnham: Ashgate.

Tronconi, F., 2018. The Italian Five Star Movement during the crisis: towards normalisation? *South European Society and Politics*, 23 (1), 163–180.

Tronconi, F. and Valbruzzi, M., 2020. Populism put to the polarisation test: the 2019-20 election cycle in Italy. *South European Society and Politics*, 25 (3–4), 475–501.

Tronconi, F. and Verzichelli, L., 2019. Il ceto parlamentare al tempo del populismo. *In*: A. Chiaramonte and L. De Sio, eds. *Il voto del cambiamento. Le elezioni politiche del 2018.* Bologna: il Mulino, 209–240.

Truffelli, M., 2003. *La questione partito dal fascismo alla Repubblica: culture politiche nella transizione.* Roma: Studium.

Truffelli, M., 2007. L'antipolitica. *In*: G. Monina, ed. *1945-1946. Le origini della Repubblica. Questione istituzionale e costruzione del sistema politico democratico.* Soveria Mannelli: Rubbettino, 341–371.

Truffelli, M. and Zambernardi, L., 2021. Taking modernity to extremes: on the roots of anti-politics. *Political Studies Review*, 19 (1), 96–110.

Tuorto, D., 2015. Emilia-Romagna, fuori dalle urne. *il Mulino*, (1), 74–79.

Türsan, H., 1998. Introduction. Ethnoregionalist parties as ethnic entrepreneurs. *In*: L. De Winter and H. Türsan, eds. *Regionalist parties in Western Europe.* London and New York: Routledge, 1–16.

Uleri, P.V., 1996. Italy: referendums and initiatives from the origins to the crisis of a democratic regime. *In*: M. Gallagher and P.V. Uleri, eds. *The referendum experience in Europe.* London: Macmillan, 106–125.

Uleri, P.V., 2002. On referendum voting in Italy: YES, NO or non–vote? How Italian parties learned to control referendums. *European Journal of Political Research*, 41 (6), 863–883.

Urbinati, N., 2020. Anti-party-ism as a structrural component of Italian democracy. *In*: P. Blokker and M. Anselmi, eds. *Multiple populisms. Italy as democracy's mirror.* Abingdon: Routledge, 67–85.

Valbruzzi, M., 2020. Technocratic cabinets. *In*: E. Bertsou and D. Caramani, eds. *The technocratic challenge to democracy.* Abingdon: Routledge, 113–130.

Valbruzzi, M., 2021. Choosing party leaders in Italy between personalization and democratization. *In*: G. Sandri and A. Seddone, eds. *New paths for selecting political elites.* Abingdon: Routledge, 20–45.

Vampa, D., 2017. Matteo Salvini's Northern League in 2016: between Stasis and New Opportunities. *Italian Politics*, 32, 32–50.

Van Zoonen, L., 2005. *Entertaining the citizen: when politics and popular culture converge.* Lanham: Rowman & Littlefield.

Vassallo, S. and Passarelli, G., 2016. Centre-left Prime Ministerial Primaries in Italy: the laboratory of the 'open party' model. *Contemporary Italian Politics*, 8 (1), 12–23.

Ventura, S., 2018. The Italian Democratic Party from merger to personalism. *South European Society & Politics*, 23 (1), 181–196.

Venturino, F., 2010. Italy. From partitocracy to personal parties. *In*: J. Blondel and J.-L. Thiébault, eds. *Political leadership, parties and citizens: the personalisation of leadership*. London; New York: Routledge, 172–189.

Venturino, F., 2015. Promoting internal democracy: an analysis of the statute of the Partito Democratico. *In*: A. Seddone and G. Sandri, eds. *The Primary Game: primary elections and the Italian Democratic Party*. Novi Ligure: Epoké, 35–50.

Vercesi, M., 2015. Owner parties and party institutionalisation in Italy: is the Northern League exceptional? *Modern Italy*, 20 (4), 395–410.

Verney, S. and Bosco, A., 2013. Living Parallel Lives: Italy and Greece in an Age of Austerity. *South European Society and Politics*, 18 (4), 397–426.

Vicentini, G., 2015. From 'foreign body' to the party leadership and beyond: explaining Matteo Renzi's path to power through the evolution of his primary election voters. *Contemporary Italian Politics*, 7 (2), 127–143.

Vicentini, G. and Pritoni, A., 2021. Down from the "Ivory Tower"? Not so much... Italian political scientists and the constitutional referendum campaign. *European Political Science*, (Early view: https://doi.org/10.1057/s41304-021-00337-7).

Vignati, R., 2012. The challenge of the Five Star Movement. *Italian Politics*, 28, 78–94.

Vignati, R., 2015. Beppe Grillo and the Movimento 5 Stelle: a brief history of a 'Leaderist' movement with a leaderless ideology. *In*: F. Tronconi, ed. *Beppe Grillo's Five Star Movement: organisation, communication and ideology*. Farnham: Ashgate, 9–28.

Vimercati, D., 1990. *I lombardi alla nuova crociata*. Milano: Mursia.

Vines, E. and Marsh, D., 2018. Anti-politics: beyond supply-side versus demand-side explanations. *British Politics*, 13 (4), 433–453.

Vittori, D., 2020. *Il valore di uno: il Movimento 5 Stelle e l'esperimento della democrazia diretta*. Roma: Luiss University Press.

Vittori, D., 2021. Which organization for which party? An organizational analysis of the Five-star Movement. *Contemporary Italian Politics*, 13 (1), 31–48.

Von Beyme, K., 1993. *Die politische Klasse im Parteienstaat*. Frankfurt am Main: Suhrkamp.

Walzer, M., 1999. Deliberation, and What Else? *In*: S. Macedo, ed. *Deliberative politics: essays on democracy and disagreement*. Oxford; New York: Oxford University Press, 58–69.

Waters, S., 1994. 'Tangentopoli' and the emergence of a new political order in Italy. *West European Politics*, 17 (1), 169–182.

Wheeler, M., 2013. *Celebrity politics*. Cambridge: Polity.

Wodak, R., 2021. *The politics of fear: the shameless normalization of far-right discourse*. London: Sage.

Wood, M., 2021. The political ideas underpinning political distrust: analysing four types of anti-politics. *Representation*, (Early view: https://doi.org/10.1080/00344893.2021.1954076).

Wood, M., Corbett, J., and Flinders, M., 2016. Just like us: everyday celebrity politicians and the pursuit of popularity in an age of anti-politics. *The British Journal of Politics and International Relations*, 18 (3), 581–598.

Zampano, G., 2017. The decline of Rome: the never-ending crisis in the capital. *Italian Politics*, 32, 154–174.

Zanone, V., 2002. La riduzione qualunquista del liberismo. *In*: G. Giannini, ed. *La Folla. Seimila anni di lotta contro la tirannide.* Soveria Mannelli: Rubbettino, 27–38.

Zulianello, M., 2019a. *Anti-system parties: from parliamentary breakthrough to government.* Abingdon: Routledge.

Zulianello, M., 2019b. Varieties of populist parties and party systems in Europe: from state-of-the-art to the application of a novel classification scheme to 66 parties in 33 countries. *Government and Opposition*, 55 (2), 327–347.

Zulianello, M., 2021. The League of Matteo Salvini: fostering and exporting a modern mass-party grounded on "Phygital" activism, *Politics and Governance*, (Early view: https://osf.io/6bvej/).

Zulianello, M. and Larsen, E.G., 2021. Populist parties in European Parliament elections: a new dataset on left, right and valence populism from 1979 to 2019. *Electoral Studies*, 71 (102312), 1–8.

Index